Confederate Incognito

Confederate Incognito

*The Civil War Reports of "Long Grabs,"
a.k.a. Murdoch John McSween,
26th and 35th North Carolina Infantry*

MURDOCH JOHN MCSWEEN
Edited by E. B. Munson

McFarland & Company, Inc., Publishers
Jefferson, North Carolina, and London

LIBRARY OF CONGRESS CATALOGUING-IN-PUBLICATION DATA

McSween, Murdoch John, 1836–1880.
    Confederate incognito : the Civil War reports of "Long Grabs," a.k.a. Murdoch John McSween, 26th and 35th North Carolina Infantry / Murdoch John McSween ; edited by E.B. Munson.
    p.   cm.
    Includes bibliographical references and index.

ISBN 978-0-7864-7210-9
softcover : acid free paper ∞

1. McSween, Murdoch John, 1836–1880.
2. United States — History — Civil War, 1861–1865 — Personal narratives, Confederate. 3. Confederate States of America. Army. North Carolina Infantry Regiment, 26th. 4. Confederate States of America. Army. North Carolina Infantry Regiment, 35th.
5. United States — History — Civil War, 1861–1865 — Journalists. 6. North Carolina — History — Civil War, 1861–1865 — Journalists. 7. War correspondents — North Carolina — Biography. 8. Soldiers — North Carolina — Biography. 9. Fayetteville (N.C.) — Biography. I. Munson, E. B. II. Title.
E573.526th.M 2013
973.7'82 — dc23   2012041476

BRITISH LIBRARY CATALOGUING DATA ARE AVAILABLE

© 2013 E.B. Munson. All rights reserved

No part of this book may be reproduced or transmitted in any form or by any means, electronic or mechanical, including photocopying or recording, or by any information storage and retrieval system, without permission in writing from the publisher.

Front cover images: Background, newspaper, compass, pen and ink, and ledger © 2013 Shutterstock

Manufactured in the United States of America

McFarland & Company, Inc., Publishers
   Box 611, Jefferson, North Carolina 28640
   www.mcfarlandpub.com

To my wife Jane
for 54 great years.
And to our sons and their families:
John and Diana and grandson Samuel Booker;
Paul and Anne-Marie and granddaughters Megan and Sara;
Will and Jessica and granddaughters Alexis, Madison, and Samantha

Table of Contents

Preface and Acknowledgments   1

Introduction   5

1. North Carolina Goes to War   17
2. Camp Mangum, North Carolina, and Richmond, Virginia
   April 10, 1862–June 26, 1962   25
3. Conscription Camps
   August 1, 1862–October 29, 1862   49
4. Reporting from Virginia
   October 31, 1862–March 12, 1863   63
5. War on the North Carolina Home Front
   March 12, 1863–June 1, 1863   110
6. Return to Virginia
   June 9, 1863–July 1, 1863   162
7. Richmond and Petersburg: The Final Year
   July 12, 1864–February 22, 1865   210
8. Fayetteville, North Carolina: Reconstruction Years   231

Chapter Notes   237
Bibliography   255
Index   259

Preface and Acknowledgments

This book is one of those happy accidents or pleasant surprises that occur when your eye is fixed in one direction and something else crosses your line of sight — your curiosity is aroused. I was working in microfilm copies of the *Fayetteville Observer* covering the Civil War period. The *Observer* is North Carolina's oldest still-published newspaper and dates back to 1816. I was looking for advertisements containing interesting information that genealogists could use in searching for particular individuals. At the same time I was giving the other pages a quick scan.

I began to see letters signed by someone calling himself Long Grabs, not at all unusual during the nineteenth century as many letters to newspapers bore descriptive pseudonyms. In this case, however, Long Grabs did not send several letters and then stop, as many did, and fade into history and be forgotten. His began in 1862 and were a regular part of the *Observer*, continuing until March of 1865 although there was a twelve-month silence where nothing appeared. As I continued work on my project, I started collecting these letters, until I had well over eighty.

There have been many collected letters of various individuals who either served during the Civil War or who were there as professional journalists. Some were written to individual family members, who saved them long after the conflict was over, and later donated them to university collections or agreed to their publication. Many were written by these anonymous soldiers and sent to hometown newspapers for their neighbors to read about what was happening on the battleground, who had been injured or killed, what they had to eat, what they needed, and a host of other topics. Some of these have gone into general published collections.

Peter Wellington Alexander (1825–1886) was a professional journalist and was one of the most well-known writers attached to the Army of Northern

Virginia. Using the byline of "P.W.A.," he wrote over 800 letters to the *Savannah Republican* about the war.

Long Grabs is somewhat different. He was not writing to any family member; in fact, through all the letters only an unnamed aunt and his father, also unnamed, are mentioned—no one else. He is anonymous to most of his readers, although he is known to some degree among the regiments serving in North Carolina and Virginia. Unlike Alexander and his writing to the *Savannah Republican*, Long Grabs was not sent by the *Fayetteville Observer* out into the field to cover the war; he chose it and began sending his material to it in 1862. Even the editor of the *Observer* had no idea who he was, but did express his pleasure at receiving the material.

One thing that interested me about Long Grabs, later identified as Murdoch John McSween, and his letters was his variety of subject matter and his polished style in presenting his material. These are the writings of a well-educated individual who had a great interest in what surrounded him, and he obviously delighted in sharing that with his readers. He would write about the soldiers and particular battles in the early years of the war more as the observer/reporter than much later when he was the participant/reporter. He had a tendency to be covering the war then digress into another topic in the following letter. For example, he is in eastern North Carolina in 1863 writing about the fighting at New Bern, Kinston and Washington, but decides to go off to Wilmington and Tarboro just to see what is happening. The reader learns a great deal about what is going on in the civilian backdrop of the war as well as the history of places where he happens to be. He is very specific in writing about the hardships of civilians in Virginia and North Carolina. His writings about eastern North Carolina were especially interesting to me as my home in Winterville is within twenty-five miles or less of places where the armies were fighting—Washington, New Bern, Kinston, and Goldsboro. To have this on-the-spot reporting was a real boon. Long Grabs was no one-dimensional individual. He could be loyal and sympathetic and feel the sufferings of civilians and soldiers, but he was also ambitious and persistent in seeking what he wanted; hot-headed at times and one never to forget a perceived insult. These characteristics would lead him into difficulty with superiors several times. Probably his biggest clash with authority involved General Matt Ransom and Colonel John G. Jones, and ended with him being sentenced to twelve months at hard labor.

He was a survivor, though, and no matter what events befell him, things work out to his satisfaction. He survived the war and returned to Fayetteville, where he began publishing and editing a newspaper, *The Eagle*. As he did during the war, he traveled in and out of Fayetteville, going around the state, and further South into South Carolina, Alabama, and Georgia, gathering news about Reconstruction. Not all of *The Eagle's* copies have survived, but there is enough to give evidence that his eye for details and his opinions are as sharp as ever as he rails against the Republicans' control of state government, scalawags, and carpetbaggers. However, this material is beyond the scope of this book, which deals with his Civil War writings. Some selections are included in the final chapter which deals with his postwar activities and a few in which he is reminiscing about certain war events have been added to the main part where the event occurred.

I acknowledge my grateful thanks to the following individuals: John R. M. Lawrence, department head, North Carolina Collection, Joyner Library, East Carolina University, for answering many questions and providing helpful suggestions; Beth Winstead, East Carolina University copyright officer, for keeping me legal in material selection; Jesse L. Lankford, Jr., state archivist, N.C. Office of Archives and History in Raleigh, for permission to use unpublished material from the *Papers of Zebulon B. Vance*; Donna E. Kelly, Administrator Historical Publications Section, N.C. Office of Archives and History in Raleigh, for permission to use published material from the *Papers of Zebulon B. Vance* and to use information from Louis A. Manarin and Weymouth T. Jordan, Jr., comps., *North Carolina Troops, 1861–1865: A Roster* to verify soldier information in the manuscript; a special "thank you" to Kenrick N. Simpson, Military Collection Archivist, Special Collections Branch, N.C. Office of Archives and History, for transcribing two of the most illegible letters I encountered from the Vance collection; David Pavelich, head of research services, David M. Rubenstein Rare Book & Manuscript Library, Duke University, Durham, North Carolina, for permission to use General Order No. 4; Roy Winkleman, director, Florida Center for Instructional Technology, College of Education, University of South Florida, for permission to use material from the center's Civil War ClipArt file and Civil War Maps; and last, but not least, to my great wife Jane for living through another project with me!

Introduction

In the April 16, 1863, edition of the *Fayetteville Observer*, the editor wrote the following:

> We are reminded by our esteemed correspondent with the euphonious cognomen of "Long Grabs," that it is just a year since he voluntarily offered us the first of those contributions of his pen which have since by turns interested and amused and instructed the readers of the Observer. We have abundant reason to thank him for the selection of this paper as his medium through which to reach the ear of the great public; for the compliments paid him verbally and by letter, and the frequency with which he is quoted by other papers, sufficiently attest the appreciation of his letters. We have had a number of applications for his name, but to these we can only reply that we are not at liberty to give it. Personally he is unknown to us — we have never seen him. But we concur in the general opinion that he has "made his mark."[1]

Who was "Long Grabs"?

Who was this anonymous North Carolinian who cryptically signed the letters he wrote to the *Fayetteville Observer*, in this manner? Could his identity be discovered one hundred and forty-seven years after the Army of Northern Virginia laid down their arms at Appomattox, Virginia, and General Johnston surrendered several weeks later to General Sherman at Bennett Place, near Durham, North Carolina?

This was the task I set myself—find the person behind the name. What I did not know as I began to search for clues was that his name was known to many of his contemporaries; yet for reasons known only to him, he chose not to use it in his correspondence with the *Fayetteville Observer*. Lacking a name as a starting point, I looked for bits and pieces of him that he might reveal through his writings. What follows are my speculations about the kind of person he was based on information in his correspondence and how it was confirmed.

He composed over eighty letters to the *Observer* that reveal him as a highly literate Tar Heel, who was familiar with the imagery of Homer, the eloquence of Cicero, the writing of Thackeray, and intricacies of higher mathematics. He was a keen observer of what surrounded him, and he wrote of what he witnessed in a descriptive style. When he visits Wake Forest, a small college town in Wake County, North Carolina, near Christmas 1862, he finds the college deserted, the professors and students gone to war, and in the building "a silent sadness reigns through the empty halls and even the winds seem reluctant to disturb the sear and fallen leaves" and the only occupant is "a very corpulent rat lounging on the floor and sadly contemplating the literary dearth around him." When he depicts a winter snowball fight between soldiers of the 18th North Carolina Regiment playing the parts of Northern and Southern soldiers, his images are of a real battle planned and fought. He wrote with a sense of immediacy, of putting his readers into the scene of action with strong, vivid words, as in his account of the retreat of the Army from the siege of Washington, North Carolina, towards Greenville, twenty miles distant:

> On we came in the pouring rain, with the murky clouds above, the pitchy darkness around us, and a boundless, bottomless waste of water and mud underneath. The infantry slipped and scrambled and slided and wallowed, swimming, climbing, diving and falling by turns; the wagons pitched and rocked and jolted and cracked, like a vessel in a sea-storm tossed by the waves and occasionally springing a leak; the artillery rattled and slided, often getting out of sight, then rising to the surface; and the various dignitaries on horseback would experience some inconvenience when abruptly dismounted among the vines, brush, &c., or when their steeds, plunging forward into the dark abyss of some unexpected creek or hole, would drown their riders or break their necks. There was one continued scene of geeing, hawing, prizing, lifting, pulling, cursing, grumbling, laughing, quarreling, splashing, crashing, roaring, lightning and thundering. All was darkness, isolation and inundation, except when the dazzling, blinding flashes of lightning would glisten across the endless line of reeling wagons, jammed up artillery and floating infantry.

His words covered nothing up — this is how I saw it — this is how it is. He did not pander, as those who are referred to in this January 15, 1863, article that appeared in the *Fayetteville Observer*. Someone had written to the paper, complaining that "whilst other States have special correspondents who particularize gallant deeds of individuals and magnify insignificant companies into mighty cohorts," North Carolina does not. The remedy offered was that every newspaper should send special correspondents to follow the North Carolina troops wherever they may be. "Not agreed," the newspaper editor replied. "Not only cannot the Press afford the expense, but their correspondents would scarcely be afforded the facilities necessary for the proper performance of their task. We are beginning to think that these hired special correspondents are nuisances, since they lend themselves to a nauseating puffery of favorites (who doubtless feed and drink them,) and depreciation of others who will not condescend to purchase praise."[2] Long Grabs was his own man. He praised those who did their duty, and he criticized those who did not, whether that person was general, doctor, merchant, or politician. He always spoke for the soldier in the ranks.

Long Grabs' first letter to the *Fayetteville Observer* was written from Camp Mangum, a camp for training new recruits in Raleigh, on April 10, 1862. Although he would write a total of seven letters from there, the last being on June 26, 1862, he never identifies himself as a soldier who belongs to a particular company or regiment or what else he might be doing there. Considerable information is related about the camp and the organization of the regiments, but nothing about himself.

Interestingly, Long Grabs left Camp Mangum on June 2, 1862, and arrived in Richmond, Virginia, the next day "to see the great battle and take part in it." He arrived immediately after the Battle of Seven Pines which was fought May 31, 1862–June 1, 1862. Although the battle was tactically inconclusive, a major result was the wounding of the Confederate commander, Joseph E. Johnston. Later this forced President Jefferson Davis to appoint a new commander—General Robert E. Lee.

Long Grabs reports he came to Richmond on a furlough. This could mean he was in the army and got permission to travel, or if not, it could mean he was a journalist moving on to a new area on his own choice to report the news. But if the latter were so, why would he mention traveling on a furlough? While in the city, he stayed at the Ballard Hotel, one of the finer boarding establishments of the period. Lodging cost $1.50 per day, with fuel, soap, and whiskey extra. Meals cost $1.50 for breakfast, $2.00 for dinner, and $1.00 for supper. A Confederate soldier in the ranks received $11.00 a month. Such a place to eat and sleep would probably be beyond the means of a foot soldier. Long Grabs, though, appears to be a person of means, well-educated, and able to pay for train travel, food, and lodging.

Many of the articles and letters published in newspapers about the war or other topics were anonymous. This was true of both Southern and Northern papers, as few of those reporting on the war ever saw their names in print. Some signed their material with initials, as did these writers in the *Spirit of the Age*, a Raleigh paper of the period—T.A.J.F, SWD, and TBM. Others would use fanciful names, as Sylvanus and Nyanius, also from the Raleigh paper. Some left their material completely unsigned. Long Grabs in signing his letters this way follows a long tradition dating from the eighteenth century.

Many, like Long Grabs, wrote to a single newspaper, usually the one that covered their home area. Occasionally one would sign his letters or reports with part of his real name, such as "Nat," who was the correspondent of the *Carolina Watchman* (Salisbury, North Carolina) and the *Iredell Express* (Statesville, North Carolina). Nat was later identified as Jacob Nathaniel Raymer, whose correspondence was later compiled and published.[3] Long Grabs moves about more freely than Nat, who was a private in Company C, 4th Regiment North Carolina Troops. His letters describe life in the ranks of the Army of Northern Virginia and focus on his regiment. Long Grabs, on the other hand, divided his correspondence between North Carolina and Virginia and seems to make his own decisions as to where and when he will go for news. Nor does he appear to have any official sanction to do this.

If Long Grabs is writing to the *Fayetteville Observer* because it is the paper that covers his home area, what evidence was there to support this? In a letter dated March 16, 1863, he writes, "Oh! how I long once more for the good old times of cheapness and plenty on Rockfish, where I used to throw sweet bread at the birds as I rode to church with my old Aunt in a blue-top gig. I love that plain energetic and intelligent people, whose hearts are as pure as the limpid waters of their own Rockfish."[4] Rockfish was a small town in the southwestern part of Cumberland County, and Fayetteville is located in the county. Rockfish no longer exists, having changed its name to Hope Mills when it incorporated in 1891. In a letter written from Fredericksburg on February 9, 1863, Long Grabs is watching two men carrying a barrel suspended from a branch that rests on their shoulders. It reminds him of something from home. "They had the barrel suspended by ropes to a stick which they carried on their shoulders much in the same way we used to carry home a deer on Rockfish in those celebrated 'drives,' when old D. and Dr. McL always brought down an old buck, should he run by the old accustomed 'stand.'"[5] Rockfish Creek rises in nearby Moore County and enters the western side of Cumberland County, flowing across it until it enters the Cape Fear River. Again in the letter of March 16, he writes of his own ancestry:

> It has been many years since I have crossed those ancient thresholds and enjoyed the genuine Scottish hospitality of the land of my birth, and although I have wandered through distant States and seen much that is noble and great, my heart still turns to the simple customs, the manly independent character and the thrilling Scottish legends of "fatherland." If I show some enthusiasm I hope I will not be regarded as sentimental or crazy, for the Tweed had its Sir Walter Scott, the Hudson its Washington Irving and why not Rockfish have its "Long Grabs?" It has been often suggested that the Scotch of the Cape Fear region form a company or regiment to represent more distinctly their nationality and ancient valor. If the war continues much longer perhaps some Scottish Chief (even "Long Grabs") may sound the pibroch, gather the clansmen and unsheathe the claymore and strike as our fathers struck for freedom among the Highlands, and at Culloden, at Bannockburn and at Wagram.[6]

Introduction 9

The Scots were a large part of the population in the Cape Fear Region. Perhaps these sentences from a letter written at Petersburg on June 22, 1863, give the strongest piece of evidence: "When our independence is won the whitest spot on North Carolina's bright page must be left for the people of the Cape Fear. I feel proud, though I hope not in vain, that the ashes of my parents and most of my kindred lie beneath the whispering pines of the Cape Fear region."[7]

When he is at Culpeper Court House, Virginia, in 1862, he stays in camp with the soldiers and endures a November night of cold and snow. There is no indication that he is there as part of a company or regiment. Yet a week later he is back in Richmond, describing the widespread gambling activities and sumptuous rooms where they are held. He is known by officers in high command. Near Culpeper he visits and converses with General Robert E. Lee. Later he is in General J. E. B. Stuart's tent while Stuart is dining on crackers and fat bacon. He knows a number of soldiers in many North Carolina regiments and many regimental commanders, and he travels freely among them gathering news. "As I landed from the cars once more in the Capitol of the Confederacy," he writes on a return to Richmond in June 1863, "a number of voices greeted me with 'How are you, Long Grabs?' It is pleasant to be a great man and to be received with consideration in great cities."[8] Long Grabs travels on a Confederate passport which allows him access to certain areas, but at the same time it is limiting. He sees a great many soldiers in wretched conditions, which he can write about, but he cannot report the goings and coming of the regiments because "by the terms of my passport, I am not allowed to make such facts public unless by consent of the commanding officers of the Army corps."[9]

Near Christmas in 1862, he leaves Virginia and returns to Wake Forest, North Carolina. "I concluded I would enjoy a little of Christmas and let everything take care of itself a while. I have laid aside thoughts of my suffering country for a few days to enter on my duties again with redoubled energy."[10] He does not indicate he has traveled on a furlough from a superior officer, but seems to have left on his own for a bit of rest and recuperation.

His topics are varied, being part about the soldiers and the war and part of what he observes as if he were traveling about as a private citizen and taking in the sights. In Charlottesville, Virginia, he describes and gives his opinion of the University of Virginia, then later visits Monticello, the home of Thomas Jefferson. On his Christmas sojourn in Wake Forest, North Carolina, he describes the college and some of the men who headed it. While at the Virginia Legislature in Richmond, he spends time writing little sketches of some of the members. Later he writes a long letter describing President Jefferson Davis. On his return to North Carolina in March of 1863, he travels about the eastern part of the state describing scenes of Kinston, Washington, Wilmington, and Tarboro. He does all these activities while keeping his eye on the war. His writing around Culpeper Court House and Fredericksburg gives accounts of the soldiers' sufferings and harshness of the Northern army on civilians. In North Carolina he is close to the fighting at Kinston and Washington and is with the soldiers on the retreat towards Greenville.

Soldiers were the largest part of North Carolina's population to move in and out of the state during the Civil War. Merchants and others with means traveled sometimes. For the general population, however, they lived as they had always lived, rarely going but a few miles from their home area. When Long Grabs is writing as though on a tour, he seems to be seeing not only for himself but also for those at home who will never see and experience these sights.

However, what is motivating him to do this is never revealed until the end of his first year of writing. Neither is the source of his funds to meet his expenses made known. Writing on April 10, 1863, exactly one year to the date after he wrote his first letter, he said:

> A man writing as I have done cannot have wide desks and handy inkstands and be surrounded with Webster's Unabridged and long shelves filled with classical volumes. It may not be surprising then under the circumstances that my style has not abounded in studied elegance, classic allusions, chaste eloquence and profound argument, even had I the ability of such production.
>
> But if I have in any way aided our cause in this the hour of our country's severe trial, if I have benefited the soldier, or in any way relieved the unfortunate and the poor or exposed the wrongs and impositions of the strong upon the weak, or if I have strengthened the cause of truth, patriotism and all the manly and virtuous characteristics of civilized man, or afforded instruction or amusement to any class of your readers, I have succeeded in my object. I am not the special friend or foe of any party, clique, man, measure or doctrine. "Long Grabs" stands before the world an odd but independent institution![11]

He is in Virginia when his letters cease in July 1863. Nothing appeared in the *Fayetteville Observer*. Nor could I find that he had been writing to other contemporary newspapers I searched through, such as those in Wilmington, Charlotte, and Raleigh. Did he have an accident? Had he been killed? Or had he lost interest in writing about the war? He kept his silence for a year; then as suddenly as the correspondence had ceased, it began again in July 1864. His explanation for his absence, when given, was very abrupt — "I suppose no apology is necessary for my negligence for some months past. In fact, it is just exactly nobody's business where I have been or what I have been doing."[12]

For the first time he reveals in a letter that he had an interest in raising a company of men at the beginning of the war. He had purchased blankets, pay books, and other material and gone to Elizabethtown, the county seat of Bladen County, to recruit at a meeting of militia and interested citizens. He is unsuccessful and gives up on the idea.

Now back in Virginia in 1864, he spends his time with the soldiers. An editorial in the September 8 edition of the *Observer* indicates the editors have received a letter from him, but for some reason they summarize it instead of publishing it all. It reports "Long Grabs" was in a charge at the battle of Reams' Station, Virginia, going in with the 26th Regiment N. C. T., but with no indication that it was as soldier or civilian. Long Grabs is wounded, a ball striking him between the eyes and passing out just below the left ear. He is with Dr. Manson and doing well.[13]

He does not write again until the last of October 1864. He stated he had returned to his command and had engaged in a fight below Petersburg. Again he is charging the enemy in company with the Pee Dee Wildcats (Company K, 26th Regiment North Carolina Troops) and is knocked down when a ball creases his skull.

These were the first indications in his letters to the *Observer* of a connection with a North Carolina regiment. I started looking through the names of soldiers in the 26th Regiment that were listed in *North Carolina Troops, 1861–1865: A Roster* by Weymouth T. Jordan and Louis H. Manarin. I was searching for someone with the same type of wound. Listed with the sergeants major of the regiment was a man by the name of M. J. McSween. Part of the entry stated that he was shot through the head at Reams' Station, Virginia, August 25, 1864. "[The} ball enter[ed] between [the] eyes and emerge[d] behind [the] left ear impairing vision [in his] left eye."[14] The wording in both the newspaper summary and the roster was very similar, and I felt certain that this was the anonymous "Long Grabs." Still I wanted something more to confirm my suspicion.

In 2007, the North Carolina State Archives had started a project to digitize North Carolina's earliest newspapers. Called the North Carolina Newspaper Digitization Project, it went online in December 2009. I wondered if there could be information in one of the old newspapers that would link "Long Grabs" and McSween. I typed the words "Long Grabs" into the program, and the following short article from the *Carolina Watchman*, published January 29, 1880, came up:

DEATH OF M. J. McSWEEN.— From our exchanges we learn that the above named gentleman, formerly the Editor and Publisher of the *Fayetteville Eagle*, and familiarly known as "Long Grabs," the humorous war correspondent of the *Fayetteville Observer*, died at the residence of his father-in-law, Wm. McSween, Esq., in the State of Tennessee, on the 3d inst. Mr. McSween was born in Blue Spring township, Robeson county, in 1836, was educated at the University, and was peculiarly gifted as a newspaper correspondent. The many friends of Mr. McSween in this section will be greatly pained to learn of his death in the prime of manhood. — *Moore Index.*[15]

The *Moore Index* began publication in Carthage, Moore County, North Carolina in 1879.

With these two confirming pieces of information, I now had the key to search for the man behind "Long Grabs"— Murdoch John McSween.

As he was born in Robeson County, my earlier supposition of his place of birth as being in the Cape Fear region was correct. Further searching revealed that McSween had corresponded with North Carolina's wartime governor, Zebulon Baird Vance. In this material I found a letter in which the Rev. Andrew McMillan, who was McSween's teacher and who prepared him for college, described him as "a poor orphan having lost both his parents as a child."[16] Long Grabs, in one of his letters, had mentioned an aunt he used to ride in a buggy with as they traveled to church, possibly one of the relatives who helped rear him after the passing of his parents. In a letter written after the war on June 5, 1869, and published in *The Eagle,* he revealed the only information I found concerning his parents. He had taken the train down to Morehead City and had gone with some friends to the beach to look out at the ocean. "I have felt attached to the sea, the beauties and its legends. My ancestors from the Highlands of Scotland followed the dangers and the fortunes of the briny deep. A kind father, whose life was not spared through my early infancy, inhabited those surging waves. As a sailor he shared the dangers and pleasures of adventurous seasons for seven years or more. In sentiment and romance, then, I am entitled to 'A life on the ocean wave,' because my father had such a life. But in reality, I would rather not. No, not any, if you please, unless sharks were abolished, and I could swim better. I can lead a more easy life on land, although I like to look at you, Mr. Ocean, at a safe distance."[17]

In 1857, at the age of twenty-one, McSween entered the University of North Carolina at Chapel Hill.[18] That same year he became a member of Sigma Alpha Epsilon fraternity[19] and later of the Philanthropic Society.[20] Among the objectives of the latter organization were improving its members in the skills of debating and in English composition.

An example of his writing ability at this stage in his life is a letter he wrote to Thomas Ruffin in 1858 — a letter that appears rather presumptuous. Thomas Ruffin (1787–1870) was one of North Carolina's most distinguished citizens — CHIEF JUSTICE of the North Carolina Supreme Court from 1833 to 1852, statesman, and one of the state's leading agriculturists.

Introduction

CHAPEL HILL, N.C. Sept. 27th, 1858.

Respected Sir,

I hope you will pardon the liberty I take in addressing you this communication. I am an entire stranger to you, but I assure you that I am induced from the right motives.

I wish you to write in relation to any subject or matter you think proper, and, at such time as you may have leisure and send the manuscript to me, or leave it for me. You are now, I presume, past the three score and ten allotted to man and it is reasonable to suppose that you cannot remain much longer with us. Your intimate connection with public men and things for a considerable portion of your life, enables you to give much valuable information, historical and otherwise, that might never be transmitted to posterity in any other manner; and further, your long and valuable experience and correct observation, entitles your opinions to great weight and enables you to give sound instruction and advice. From these remarks you can form some idea of the character of the work I want. I do not care how large a volume you will make — the more of it the better.

I wish you to prepare it entirely at your own discretion, but I hope it will [be] as plain and simple as possible — no fancy paper nor gaudy covering, but every thing perfectly natural and original — blots, relining and all. I would like to receive, at least a part of it in the course of a year from this time. If it cannot be gotten ready then it would be very desirable to get it in two or three years any how, and if I should leave the University before it could be delivered, it could be left with Gov. Swain directed to me if not otherwise advised. Of course I want to have it entirely at my disposal at least after your death. In consideration of the very worthy manner you have so often performed your duty as a public man and private citizen, I make this request. When these mighty responsibilities will devolve upon the rising generation, it will nerve the energies and brighten their hopes to contemplate the character of the illustrious dead, and particularly, to point to the relics of one whose pure and unpretending life ornamented the society in which he lived and whose name will live in the hearts of his countrymen for many generations to come. Can one, who, though he did not seek emolument, yet never refused his country's call, deny what will be a source of so much pleasure to me and benefit to posterity?

Please write to me upon reception of this.[21]

Yours very respectfully,
M. J. McSWEEN.

Hon. Thomas Ruffin,
Graham, N.C.

I did not find any reply from Ruffin to McSween or whether McSween pursued the subject any further.

While at the university McSween appears to have contact with a person known only as "Dan." During the Civil War, McSween, in several letters, engaged in a playful back-and-forth with "Dan," who was a musician in Iverson's Brigade, over what "Dan" felt were insulting remarks in one of Long

Grabs' letters. In a May 2, 1863, letter, Long Grabs wrote, "Now, 'Dan's' memory is treacherous. Many a night did he bother me from my Greek by blowing and squeaking in the old South Building."[22] Construction on this building at the University of North Carolina at Chapel Hill began in 1798 and was completed in 1814.

McSween matriculated with the class of 1861, but was not a graduate of the university.[23]

It is unknown what occupied him over the next few years from college to the outbreak of war; like many North Carolinians he was probably watching disagreements between the North and South widen the gap between the two sections. There is, however, a tantalizing piece of information found in the *Sumter Watchman* and republished later in *The Charleston Courier, Tri-Weekly,* March 8, 1860, that seems to indicate McSween was in South Carolina and had gone further south into Alabama. The *Watchman* had published an editorial concerning a proposed railroad line from Lancaster to Florence, via Bishopville, and invited Bishopville and Lancaster citizens to comment on it. One had written comments from Montgomery, Alabama. Although McSween's name is not included, the letter writer signed with the name "Long Grabs," suggesting that this was the Long Grabs who wrote to the *Fayetteville Observer.* The editorial said the response was over the significant *nom de plume* of "Long Grabs." Why significant? Perhaps it suggests that other interesting and important letters had been sent to South Carolina papers using this signature.

The editorial and letter follow:

> Bishopville — Rail Road Proposed. — We are gratified to know that the intelligent and public-spirited citizens of Bishopville have not only mooted, but are seriously considering the project of a rail road connection with some point on the Northeastern Road. The people of Bishopville are a host within themselves. If they say the road must be built, with the external assistance they may be able to command, it will be done.
>
> The project is also being agitated of extending the road from Bishopville to Lancasterville. The people of Lancaster have recently spoken in emphatic terms in regard to a rail road for themselves. They, like the people of Bishopville, feel that they are, to a certain extent isolated. A business community which now enjoys not the facilities and advantages afforded by a connexion by rail road with the great commercial world outside, is necessarily restricted and retarded in movement. The man who is now compelled to trudge along even over a score or more of miles in a slow coach, after stepping from the space-annihilating car, drawn by the impetuous and never-tiring iron horse, feels more sensibly then ever the utility of a rail road, and the desire to have it continue to his door.
>
> A road from Lancaster, or the North Carolina line, to Florence, via Bishopville, would command no small amount of freight and travel. Besides the local and intermediate business, pertaining to this State, North Carolina would become a patron to no small extent. It would become the most direct and expe-

ditious route to Charleston for a very large area of the country. What think our Bishopville friends generally, upon this project. We tender them the use of our columns for its discussion. And what think the people of Lancaster of it? A citizen of that place, writing to the Ledger, from Montgomery, Ala., over the significant nom de plume of "Long Grabs," makes the following statement in regard to the project:

"By the way, in Camden I met Mr. James, of Bishopville, a very practical and intelligent gentleman. He informed me that the Northeastern Rail Road Company and the people of Bishopville propose to extend that road from Florence, or Kingstree, to Bishopville. That company has made liberal propositions in the shape of aid. That it was believed by many entirely probable and practical to run the road or continue it from Bishopville to Lancasterville, and ultimately to the North Carolina Road. The distance, by an air line from Bishopville to Lancaster, is about forty miles. The line would certainly pass over a very favorable region of country for the construction of a road. From Kingstree by an air line to Lancasterville is about eighty miles; this will pass by Bishopville. From Kingstree to Charleston by the Northeastern Rail Road is sixty-four miles; this route will make one hundred and forty-four miles from Lancasterville to Charleston. From Camden to Charleston by rail road is one hundred and forty-two miles, and to Lancasterville thirty-eight, making the distance one hundred and eighty miles from Lancasterville to Charleston by way of Camden, Kingsville and Branchville."—Sumter Watchman.[24]

On December 17, 1860, a convention was held in Columbia, South Carolina, to decide on secession. The resolution passed, and on December 20, 1860, South Carolina withdrew from the Union.

For McSween, like many other young men of his era, patriotism coursed through his veins. He was either in South Carolina at the time that state seceded, or went there shortly afterwards to enlist. Two separate dates exist for this. On the Field and Staff Muster Roll for the 26th Regiment North Carolina Troops, dated September and October 1864, the enlistment is dated December 20, 1860, and on the next document for November and December 1864, the date is December 26, 1860. He enlisted at Bennettsville, South Carolina, with Captain Harrington as the enlisting officer, for a term of twelve months. A Captain T. D. Harrington was a company commander in the 9th Regiment South Carolina Volunteers, but a listing for McSween on the roster was not found. No other documentation was found for what he might have done there.

McSween is back in North Carolina in the fall of 1861. He had friends in the 38th Regiment North Carolina Troops, and a controversy soon develops over whether or not he ever joined Company E, captained by Oliver H. Dockery.[25] Captain Duncan G. McRae,[26] Dockery's successor, feels he has and charges McSween with desertion in the spring of 1862. In the meantime McSween has received an appointment at Camp Mangum, a Raleigh military training camp for recruits, as a drill master. Here another controversy erupts when the assistant adjutant general of North Carolina, William B. Gulick, tries to dismiss him because he returned late from a furlough. These two incidents will be discussed in Chapter 2.

Throughout the summer of 1862 and into the spring of 1863, McSween continues his travels as an unofficial, but exceedingly popular, war correspondent of the *Fayetteville Observer*. He eventually joins the 35th Regiment North Carolina Troops on the inducement of Colonel Matt Ransom.[27] Ransom is later promoted to general and Colonel John G. Jones[28] becomes regimental commander. Another bitter controversy develops between McSween and the two men over promises that were made to him and not kept. So cantankerous is it that Ransom has him court-martialed and sentenced to a year in prison at hard labor. This imprisonment is the reason he ceased writing to the *Fayetteville Observer* between the summer of 1863 and 1864.

In 1862, McSween had met Zebulon Baird Vance, governor of North Carolina, and had written him several times seeking an appointment as a war correspondent and at another time seeking permission to return from Virginia to raise a company of men for the war. During 1863–1864, he engages in a lengthy correspondence with Vance, pleading for help in his difficulties with General Ransom.

McSween eventually is released after many months confinement and is given permission to join any regiment of his choice. He picks the 26th Regiment North Carolina Troops and is appointed sergeant major. He writes his last letter from Petersburg, Virginia, on February 22, 1865. It is published March 9; one month later to the day General Robert E. Lee surrendered what is left of the Army of Northern Virginia at Appomattox.

Finding Long Grabs' true identity changed the direction of the book. Originally it was planned as a collection of letters by an anonymous correspondent of the *Fayetteville Observer,* annotated with narratives linking the material. Now his name became the key that opened the door to more information than his letters had revealed up to the time of his wounding at Reams' Station, especially his correspondence with Zebulon Vance. The book became a story within a story — McSween's observations on the war and his struggle for survival against an unjust imprisonment.

McSween's story does not end, however, with the close of the war. He will write again, as revealed in the final chapter, and this time he will have complete control over what he has to say. He will be the editor and publisher of *The Eagle*, a Fayetteville, North Carolina, newspaper.

Chapter 1

North Carolina Goes to War

North Carolinians, being an independent people, differed on whether to go to war. There was an element in the state that pushed for secession, but more of the population preferred remaining in the Union. The economy was a farm-based one. Three-fourths of the population did not own slaves, and those who did owned small numbers of them. In 1860, the white population of North Carolina numbered 629,942, and of that number, 34,648 were slave owners. The slave population was 331,059.[1]

It was the election of Abraham Lincoln in November 1860 that helped to ignite the move toward secession in Southern states. Fearing the consequences of that election and with Union installation Fort Sumter in the harbor at Charleston, South Carolina seceded on December 20, 1860. Six states quickly followed—Mississippi, Florida, Alabama, Georgia, Louisiana, and Texas. Most North Carolinians preferred a wait and see attitude toward what Lincoln's election might mean.

Early in 1861, the question was raised in North Carolina on whether to hold a convention composed of citizens to discuss the issue of secession. After deliberations, the General Assembly of North Carolina issued an act concerning a convention, signed by the governor, after it had been read three times and ratified in the General Assembly on February 1, 1861. The *Raleigh Register* published it on February 6, 1861.[2]

STATE OF NORTH CAROLINA.
A PROCLAMATION,
By JOHN W. ELLIS, *Governor of North Carolina,* to wit:
AN ACT CONCERNING A CONVENTION OF THE PEOPLE.
WHEREAS, The present perilous condition of the country demands, in the judgment of this General Assembly, that the sovereign people of this State should assemble in Convention to effect an honorable adjustment of existing difficulties whereby the Federal Union is endangered, or otherwise to determine

what action will best preserve the honor and promote the interests of North Carolina; and whereas, the General Assembly, on matters of such grave import, involving the relation of North Carolina to her sisters in the confederacy, is reluctant to adopt any settled policy without the sense of the people, in whom, under our government, all sovereignty resides, being first ascertained.

SEC. 1. *Be it therefore enacted by the General Assembly of the State of North Carolina, and it is hereby enacted by the authority of the same, two thirds of all members of each concurring,* That upon the passage of this act the Governor of the State be, and he is hereby required, to issue a proclamation, commanding the Sheriffs of the respective counties in the State to open polls at the several election precincts, in said counties, on the 28th day of February, A. D., 1861, when and where all persons qualified to vote for members of the General Assembly may vote for or against a State Convention; those who wish a convention, voting with a written or printed ticket, "Convention," and those who do not wish a convention, voting in the same way, "No Convention;" also, to open separate polls at the same time and places for the election of delegates to the convention, to be assembled on such times as are hereinafter provided; said polls to be superintended by inspectors, appointed by the sheriffs, with the advice of three justices of the peace, of the respective counties, who shall be sworn according to the provisions of sec. 6, chap. 52, of Revised Code.

Further sections include requiring the sheriffs to make duplicate copies of their polls, one for the county clerks' offices and the other for transmitting to Raleigh; the governor to call or not call a convention depending on the vote count; and a convention of 120 delegates, each county having the same number of delegates as those who represent the county in the House of Commons.

On February 28, 1861, the county sheriffs held the election in the manner prescribed by the act. On March 13, 1861, the *Raleigh Register* published the results. The vote was 47,269 against the convention and 46,672 in favor of it. For the moment North Carolina remained in the Union by a mere 597 votes.[3]

During the following weeks citizens debated what the state should do next, and pressure mounted on the governor to recall the legislature in order to pass a bill that would convene a convention — an attempt that had been defeated earlier.[4] Then, on Friday, April 12, 1861, troops opened fire on Fort Sumter in Charleston harbor.

The following Monday, April 15, President Lincoln issued a proclamation in which he called for an extra session of Congress to be held July 4 and the raising of 75,000 troops to put down the insurrection. It read in part:

Whereas, the laws of the United States have for some time past, and now are, opposed, and the execution thereof obstructed, in the States of South Carolina, Georgia, Alabama, Florida, Mississippi, Louisiana, and Texas, by combinations too powerful to be suppress by the powers vested in the Marshals by law.

Now, therefore, I, Abraham Lincoln, President of the United States, by virtue of the powers in me vested by the Constitution and the laws, have thought fit to call forth, and hereby do call forth, the militia of the several States of the Union, to the aggregate number of 75,000, in order to suppress said combinations, and to cause the laws to be duly executed. The details of this object will be duly communicated to the State authorities through the War Department. I appeal to all loyal citizens to favor, facilitate and aid this effort to maintain the honor, the integrity and the existence of our National Union, and the perpetuity of popular Government and to redress wrongs already long enough endured.[5]

On April 15, 1861, in compliance with the president's proclamation, Simon Cameron, the secretary of war, sent the following message to North Carolina Governor John Ellis and the governors of the other states remaining in the Union:

WAR DEPARTMENT,
Washington, April 15, 1861.

SIR: Under the act of Congress "for calling forth the militia to execute the laws of the Union, suppress insurrection, repel invasions," &c., approved February 28, 1795, I have the honor to request Your Excellency to cause to be immediately detached from the militia of your State the quota designated in the table below, to serve as infantry or riflemen, for the period of three months, unless sooner discharged.

Your Excellency will please communicate to me the time at or about which your quota will be expected at its rendezvous, as it will be met as soon as practicable by an officer or officers to muster it into the services and pay of the United States. At the same time the oath of fidelity to the United States will be administered to every officer and man. The mustering officer will be instructed to receive no man under the rank of commissioned officer who is in years apparently over forty-five or under eighteen, or who is not in physical strength and vigor.[6]

SIMON CAMERON
Secretary of War.

John Willis Ellis, 1820–1862, governor of North Carolina during the period of secession and the first of the three wartime governors of North Carolina. Source: Ashe, Samuel A., ed., *Biographical History of North Carolina from Colonial Times to the Present* (Greensboro, NC: Charles L. Van Noppen, Publisher, 1905–1917), Vol. 7.

The quota specified for North Carolina was two regiments, consisting of almost 1,500 officers and men. Governor Ellis and the other governors received the message by telegraph. He replied quickly and defiantly.

RALEIGH, N.C., *April 15, 1861.*

Hon. SIMON CAMERON,
Secretary of War:

Your dispatch is received, and if genuine, which its extraordinary character leads me to doubt, I have to say in reply that I regard the levy of troops made by the Administration for the purpose of subjugating the States of the South as in violation of the Constitution and a gross usurpation of power. I can be no party to this wicked violation of the laws of the country and to this war upon the liberties of a free people. You can get no troops from North Carolina. I will reply more in detail when your call is received by mail.[7]

JOHN W. ELLIS,
Governor of North Carolina.

Two days later, on April 17, 1861, Governor Ellis issued the following proclamation to the people of North Carolina[8]:

STATE OF NORTH CAROLINA.
A PROCLAMATION,
BY JOHN W. ELLIS,
GOVERNOR OF NORTH CAROLINA.

WHEREAS: By Proclamation of Abraham Lincoln, President of the United States, followed by a requisition of Simon Cameron, Secretary of War, I am informed that the said Abraham Lincoln has made a call for 75,000 men to be employed for the invasion of the peaceful homes of the South, and for the violent subversion of the liberties of a free people, constituting a large part of the whole population of the late United States: And, whereas, this high-handed act of tyrannical outrage is not only in violation of all constitutional law, in utter disregard of every sentiment of humanity and Christian civilization, and conceived in a spirit of aggression unparalleled by any act of recorded history, but it is a direct step toward the subjugation of the whole South, and the conversion of a free Republic, inherited from our fathers, into a military despotism, to be established by worse than foreign enemies on the ruins of our once glorious Constitution of Equal Rights.

Now, therefore, I, John W. Ellis, Governor of the State of North Carolina, for these extraordinary causes, do hereby issue this, my proclamation, notifying and requesting the Senators and Members of the House of Commons of the General Assembly of North Carolina, to meet in Special Session at the Capitol, in the city of Raleigh, on Wednesday, the first day of May next. And I furthermore exhort all good citizens throughout the State to be mindful that their first allegiance is due to the Sovereignty which protects their homes and dearest interests, as their first service is due for the sacred defence of their hearths and of the soil which holds the graves of our glorious dead.

United action in defence of the sovereignty of North Carolina, and of the rights of the South, becomes now the duty of us all.

Given under my hand, and attested by the Great Seal of the State. Done at the City of Raleigh the 17th day of April, A. D., 1861, and in the eighty-fifth year of our Independence.

1. North Carolina Goes to War

John W. Ellis,

By the Governor,
Graham Daves, *Private Secretary.*

Governor Ellis knew that his rejection of the call for troops would eventually lead to North Carolina's secession. He also knew that North Carolina was an agrarian state, not a large manufacturing one. Most manufactured goods came from the North and from England. Out of a population of almost one million, only slightly over 14,000 were employed in any type of manufacturing. Small numbers were involved in making clothes, boots, shoes, and in any type of iron work. Compounding medicine was almost nonexistent. Weapons, both muskets and cannon and ordnance, were limited.[9] Ellis, therefore, moved to do what he could to ensure the state's readiness for war. In a message to the North Carolina General Assembly, published in the *Fayetteville Observer* on May 6, 1861, he said, "Under the advice of the Council of State I have established at the seat of Government a Camp of Instruction, to which I have ordered such troops as are ready for service and are not needed for the protection of the seaboard.... I therefore, in discharge of a plain obligation devolving on me as Governor of the State, and in virtue of the powers invested in me as Governor and Captain General and Commander in Chief of the militia, lost no time in taking possession, in the name of the State, of the Forts, Arsenals, and other property of the Federal Government within the State, and they are now held under my orders by adequate garrisons."[10]

The following General Order was issued concerning the Camp of Instruction. It was published in *The Daily Register,* Raleigh, North Carolina, on April 27, 1861.[11]

State of North Carolina.
Executive Department,
Raleigh, April 24, 1861.

General Orders, No. 4.

The Camp of Instruction for the Volunteer forces ordered to be concentrated in this city, will be the "State Fair Grounds" and buildings.

Col. D. H. Hill, of the Volunteer service, is hereby assigned to the command of the camp and troops until further notice.

By order of the Commander-in-Chief,
R. H. Riddick,[12]
Assistant Adjutant General.

On April 24, 1861, Colonel D. H. Hill issued the following order which was published the following week in *The Weekly Raleigh Register,* of May 1, 1861.[13]

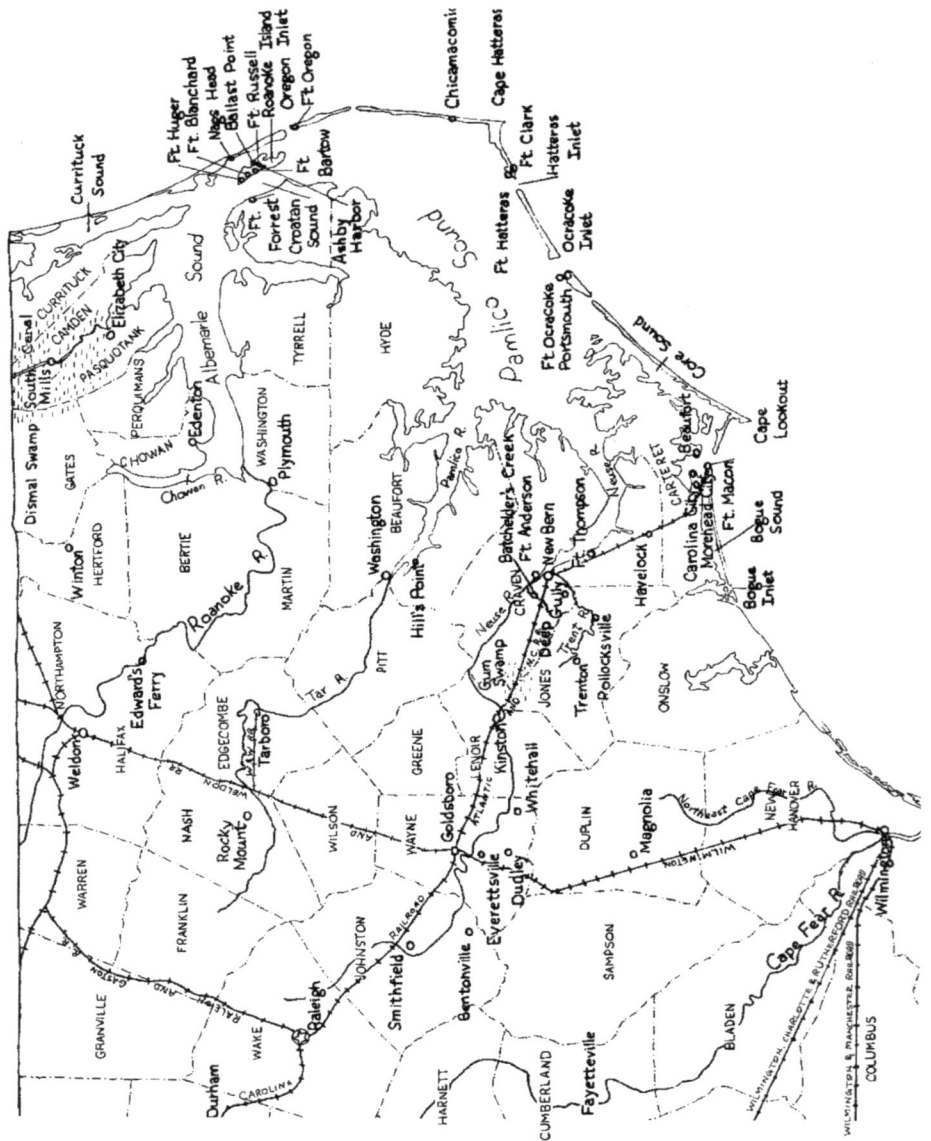

1. North Carolina Goes to War 23

CAMP OF INSTRUCTION,
RALEIGH, N.C., April 24, 1861.

ORDERS, No. 1.

The undersigned being placed by the Governor in charge of the Camp of Instruction and Rendezvous of troops, hereby communicate instructions to the companies to be concentrated at this point. It will be impossible to furnish transportation for trunks, boxes, &c., to any great extent. Hence each soldier should provide himself with a haversack 6 x 4 inches for carrying cooked provisions, a knapsack (even of rough construction) to carry one pair of blankets, an overcoat, flannel shirt and pair of shoes. Every mess of 20 men should be provided with a camp chest to carry cooking utensils, knives, forks and plates.

On arriving at the depot in Raleigh, each Company will march to the Fair Grounds, and the Captain will report himself promptly to the undersigned for duty.

By order,
D. H. HILL, Colonel Commanding.[14]

P. S. The companies which have left home without being supplied as above directed, will be furnished here, if possible.

North Carolina's preparation for war had begun.

In February 1861, North Carolinians had rejected a call for a convention on secession. However, as Governor Ellis concluded his message to the North Carolina General Assembly, reported in the May 6, 1861, issue of the *Fayetteville Observer*, he said, "With the view, therefore, of the secession of North Carolina from the Northern government and her Union with the Confederate States, at as early a period as practicable, I would respectfully recommend that a Convention of the people be called with full and final powers. The powers of the Convention should be full, because the sovereignty of the people

Opposite: Map of Eastern North Carolina, 1861–1865. This map will be referred to throughout the book to trace McSween's movements and the movements of the Confederate and Federal troops. McSween had left North Carolina and his letter to the *Charleston Courier* suggests he was in Alabama in the spring of 1860. By December 1860, he was in Bennettsville, South Carolina, where he enlisted in a company under Captain Harrington. Bennettsville lies in the upper northeast corner of South Carolina on the Great Pee Dee River, about 60 miles southwest of Fayetteville, North Carolina. The following December he returned to Richmond County, 70 miles west of Fayetteville on the border of North and South Carolina. There he joins a company of the 38th Regiment North Carolina Troops, which journeys to Raleigh by way of Wilmington and Goldsboro. In August 1861, Union forces had moved against North Carolina's Outer Banks, capturing Hatteras Island and a number of Confederate soldiers stationed there and taking control of Hatteras and New inlets. Source: Barrett, *The Civil War in North Carolina*. Map by Betsy Johnson, revised by Charles L. Price and John Conner Atkeson, Jr., 1980. Eastern portion of the map provided courtesy of the North Carolina Office of Archives and History, Historical Publication Section, Raleigh.

must be frequently resorted to during the war; and it therefore becomes necessary that it should be temporarily reposed in the Convention. The action of the Convention should be final, because of the importance of a speedy separation from the Northern Government, and the well known fact that upon this point our people are as a unit."[15]

Accordingly, North Carolina withdrew from the Union on May 20, 1861. Although North Carolina would send 125,000 soldiers to war, more than any other state, and suffer more deaths through combat and disease, 40,000, than any other state, as a whole it was ill-prepared for what was coming.

In June, following secession, Governor Ellis fell seriously ill. In an attempt to recover his health, he went to Red Sulphur Springs, Virginia, a popular resort, where the spring waters were reputed to have healing powers. He died on July 7, 1861, and his remains were taken to Davidson County, North Carolina, for burial. Henry Toole Clark, as president of the state Senate, succeeded him as governor.

Colonel D. H. Hill left the Camp of Instruction to lead the First Regiment of North Carolina Volunteers in the Battle of Bethel Church, Virginia, fought on June 10, 1861. The Regiment was known thereafter as the "Bethel Regiment."

Several other commanders were in charge of the Camp of Instruction after D. H. Hill. One, Major H. K. Burgwyn, Jr., moved the camp from the city to the area of Crabtree Creek because it was felt that location would be better for the health of the men.

The Camp was renamed Camp Mangum, in honor of Lt. William Preston Mangum, who was wounded at the Battle of First Manassas, Virginia, July 21, 1861, and died on July 29. The camp of instruction in Raleigh had been in operation for about a year. During that time men and boys had become soldiers, and North Carolina had dispatched many regiments north to help defend the Confederate capital at Richmond. In that time, also, the battles of Bethel and First Manassas had been fought, but after those the conflict seemed to subside, with smaller actions taking place.

One notable event affected the North Carolina coast in the late summer of 1861. On August 27, a joint Federal naval-army expedition arrived off the coast to attack the forts protecting the Oregon, Ocracoke, and Hatteras inlets. Commodore Silas H. Stringham commanded seven ships mounting 149 guns and carrying around 900 troops under the command of General Benjamin Butler. The outnumbered and outgunned Confederates were soon captured. Butler left a strong force to guard the inlets before the expedition withdrew. The approaches to Albemarle and Pamlico sounds now lay open to the enemy.

Chapter 2

Camp Mangum, North Carolina, and Richmond, Virginia
April 10, 1862–June 26, 1862

In October 1861, word was received in North Carolina that a large force under the command of General Ambrose Burnside was preparing for a move south by sea against the state's coastal region. In January 1862, Burnside and his troops sailed with the goal of capturing Roanoke Island, and then penetrating deep into the Coastal Plain. The intent was to open a second route to attack Richmond from the south. Burnside took Roanoke Island in February. (See map, Chapter 1.) Because North Carolina had sent so many regiments to the defense of Richmond, reinforcements for the coastal defenses were insufficient. Requests that had been made to the Confederate government for help to defend this vital section were not heeded. Brigadier General Richard C. Gatlin had sent a letter to the War Department on September 4, 1861, stating that "the only hope for protection to the eastern counties would be to maintain the ascendency upon the sounds and rivers." He recommended "the construction of a number of gunboats to be placed upon the Pamlico Sound."[1] It was not done. Gatlin later stated in a report dated October 1, 1862, that he had sent letters to the War Department on the 1st and 7th of October urging the establishment of the "Department of the Albemarle, and placing it under an experienced officer, but this was not permitted. Had it been acceded to at the time, it is fair to conclude that the island would have been placed in such a state of defense as, with a reasonable force, it might have been successfully defended against General Burnside's attack in February, and thus all our after-misfortunes on the coast avoided."[2] The district was finally established on December 21.

With the Outer Banks and Roanoke Island securely under his control, Burnside could now move further inland, using the Neuse, Tar, and Roanoke rivers. The vital cities of New Bern, Plymouth, Kinston, Goldsboro, and Fort Macon near Beaufort were within his grasp.

While military action was occurring on the Outer Banks and Hatteras Island in late 1861, McSween returned to North Carolina. When he left his company in South Carolina and for what reason is not known; however, a reasonable assumption could be that his enlistment could have been for a period of several months, and his time being up, he came home. Like a number of soldiers who were living in other states at the outbreak of hostilities, he may have preferred to come home and fight with his friends and relatives. There is documentation through a published letter of D. R. McInnis, Manarin and Jordan's Roster, and the Company Muster-In and Descriptive Roll of the 38th Regiment North Carolina Troops, Company E, that he had been enrolled for active service in this regiment on October 30, 1861. McSween would later claim that he was never officially enrolled in Company E and did not belong to the regiment, an assertion that would bring him into conflict with his superior officers.

On December 23, 1861, D. R. McInnis,[3] Orderly Sergeant of Company E, 38th North Carolina Regiment, wrote a letter titled "Richmond Boys" to the *Fayetteville Observer*.[4] It was published December 30, 1861. In the first paragraph he provided a list of the officers and men. Among them is M. J. McSween, who is listed in Manarin and Jordan's Roster as having enlisted in Richmond County on October 30, 1861.

McInnis's letter continues:

> On the 17th, a large concourse of our friends met us at the Mineral Springs, Richmond County, and the Ladies of Richmond presented the Company with a beautiful Flag; on both sides were inscribed, "Fortune favors the Brave." Miss M. E. Dockery made an eloquent and appropriate address on the occasion, which was responded to by Alex. McKay. After several eloquent speeches, the Boys sang "the Richmond Boys," and bid adieu to their friends; and fathers and mothers resigned their sons to the mercies of the God of battles. Though their hearts were sad within, they left with buoyant spirits for the field where glory awaits them, amid the farewell shouts of admiring friends, and the waving of handkerchiefs by the fair ones of the assembly. We took the cars at Trollinger's at 6 o'clock next morning. At Wilmington we met with many old acquaintances; arrived at Goldsborough at 8 o'clock at night, and at Raleigh at 1–2 past 6 in the morning. We then called the roll and marched for Camp Mangum, which is about 4 1-2 west of Raleigh, where we arrived very much exhausted from the want of sleep; many took violent colds on the tour, but all are improving; only two are on the sick list.
>
> Respectfully yours,
> D. R. McInnis, O. S.

On the Company Muster-In and Descriptive Roll, dated Camp Mangum, December 31, 1861, McSween's birthplace is given as Robeson,

North Carolina. He is 24 years old, five feet eleven inches in height, and a lawyer by profession. The document lists him absent without leave on December 31.

On February 3, 1862, the *Fayetteville Observer* published the following news item titled "Another Richmond Company": "Mr. M. J. McSween, of Richmond County, is engaged we learn from the Standard [Raleigh], in making up another Company from that section."[5]

In a letter written on July 4, 1863, from a camp near Richmond, Virginia, he states that at the start of the war he had decided to raise a company of men, just as other individuals who had recruiting papers from the governor were doing. He purchased items such as blankets, pay rolls, and muster rolls and then traveled to Elizabethtown in Bladen County where militias had gathered for a meeting. Although he spent most of the day there, his recruiting efforts were unsuccessful. No one signed up with him, and evidently he gave up on any further efforts to do so.

The Company E Muster Roll for January 31 to March 31, 1862, continues to list him as absent without leave, but with two interesting remarks: One stated that he is "on special duty detailed January 23, 1862," and the other is just a few words — "canceled on the roll." Was he truly AWOL or was his special duty recruitment? The incident seems to be the first of many that will take place during the following years where he just wanders off, visiting many regiments and places, gathering news and writing to the *Fayetteville Observer*, without anyone able to determine what his affiliation is — newspaper or regiment.

McSween's having gone absent without leave caused Captain D. G. McRae[6] of Company E, 38th Regiment to place this advertisement in the *Fayetteville Observer* on May 12, 1862:

> William Clark, Malcom Currie, Murdoch J. McSween and John Wilkes, members of Co. E, 38th Reg't. N. C. V. are hereby commanded to join said Company without delay, or they will be considered deserters.[7]
>
> D. G. McRae, Capt.
>
> Milford's Station, Va., May 8, 1862.

In an advertisement titled "A Card," published in the *Fayetteville Observer* on July 7, 1862,[8] McSween replied to this charge.

> Some time ago I saw an advertisement from D. G. McRae, Capt. Co. E, 38th Reg't. N. C. T., requiring me to go to that company or be regarded as a deserter. I have thought proper to give the facts of this matter in order to remove the impression likely to be formed from such notice.
>
> I was never enlisted in that company, nor sworn or mustered in, nor signed any muster or pay rolls, nor authorized any one to make arrangements for me, although I had taken a very active part, and felt and still feel an interest in the

Company. I had agreed with Capt. Dockery to go with the company independently, tent with him and sustain myself if necessary, and drill the company and aid them in any way, as I had done; and he would assist me in getting an appointment as drill officer or regimental position. Failing in this, I intended to join the company as a private, should further acquaintance justify. Just then there was a great call for troops for the war and I got a recruiting appointment to go home and raise a company. To aid me in securing this I had got the following recommendations as I left:

> "I am acquainted with Mr. M. J. McSween and as he wishes to raise men for the war I take this occasion to recommend him as a very suitable person to entrust with such an enterprise. I regard him as an honorable, accomplished gentleman, and well worthy and competent to fill any company office.
>
> O. H. Dockery,
> Lieut. Col. Com'dg 38th Reg't N. C. T.
> Camp Mangum, N. C., Jan'y 25th, 1862."
>
> "Gen'l. J. G. Martin,— Sir: M. J. McSween, the gentleman spoken of by Col. Dockery, is from the county I have the honor to represent in Convention, and I fully concur in all that is said of him.
>
> Respectfully,
> W. F. Leak.
> Raleigh, Jan'y 25, 1862."
>
> I failed to raise a company, and reported to the Adj't General, and got the appointment of Drill Officer at Camp Mangum, which I have held since. The Adj't General informed me that as I left the Reg't before it was transferred from State authority, and got another appointment before reporting to the Reg't, that this promotion would supersede any supposed enlistment in that company. The authorities have decided that if a man is connected with a company and apparently a member, he can be retained if a statement of facts from the Captain justify. It may be necessary to expose this matter and persons connected with it yet. I am at a loss to conjecture the motives for such a reference to me publicly, in view of the facts of the case. Capt. McRae probably means well generally, but unfortunately, he is regarded as partly insane, and if in that condition at the time, of course I excuse him from enmity and malice.
>
> M. J. McSween.
>
> Raleigh, N. C., June 25, 1862.

This disagreement between McSween and McRae threatened to become a back-and-forth in the newspaper, but the *Fayetteville Observer* quickly put a stop to it in this item published on July 24, 1862.[9]

> We have received from Capt. D. G. McRae, in the Army, a reply to Lieut. M. J. McSween's advertisement, which we decline to insert. Such personalities cannot be admitted, even as advertisements. We admitted Lieut. McSween's, (greatly modified,) because he said he had been unjustly advertised as a deserter. Each of the parties having had one hearing, the controversy in our columns ceases.

McSween is referred to above as a lieutenant. The *Fayetteville Observer* of July 21, 1862[10] carried the following news item: "MILITARY APPOINTMENTS: We learn that the War Department has made the following appointments of Lieutenants in the Confederate Army of this State — J. C. Pierce of Va., Frederick Fetter of Chapel Hill, M. J. McSween, of Richmond County.... Etc." As a drill officer at Camp Mangum, McSween could have held the rank of lieutenant.

His claim of not signing a pay roll can be questioned, however. The Company Muster Roll of January 31 to March 31, 1862, for the 38th Regiment states in the section "Last Paid," that he was paid on February 1, 1862, by A. M. Lewis.

The Company Muster Roll for the 38th for July and August 1862, under the section "Present or Absent," states "Name erased from the roll by order of Col. Hoke, May 1862, being unable to arrest and bring him to the Company."

By this time McSween had wandered off to visit conscription camps in Statesville and other parts of the state. Again, items are being put into his record, but no one seemed to know what to do about him.

Meanwhile, General Burnside had consolidated his forces and moved against the city of New Bern which lies on the Neuse River. (See map, Chapter 1.) The city fell to his forces in mid–March 1862. Moving further south, he next took the town of Beaufort, and from there his soldiers attacked the vital Fort Macon, which protected Bogue Inlet. This was North Carolina's only opening through the Outer Banks which was not under Union control. Burnside could not afford t have the fort in his rear if he chose to move onto Goldsboro and Raleigh. Fort Macon fell in late April 1862.[11]

This was the status of the war in Eastern North Carolina when McSween wrote his first letter to the *Fayetteville Observer,* under the signature "Long Grabs."

> Camp Mangum, N. C., April 10th, 1862.
>
> EDITORS OBSERVER:— Camp Mangum has become an "institution." I have been informed the camp is on land sequestrated or confiscated by the Government — it having belonged to a yankee or resident of the North.

The Sequestration Act,[12] passed by the Confederate Congress, authorized the seizure of all property owned by Northerners which lay within the boundaries of the Southern Confederacy. The *Fayetteville Observer* published a short article about the Act on September 9, 1861.

> Retaliation — The Lincoln Congress having passed an act to confiscate all Southern Property, the Confederate Congress has met this infamous legislation in a proper spirit. They have passed, says the Richmond Examiner, a "Sequestration Act," which makes all Yankee lands, tenements and hereditaments, goods, chattels, rights and credits within these Confederate States, a vast fund, out of which

the losses of our people by Yankee vandalism, are to be paid. It puts the whole machinery of the Confederate Courts into immediate operation for the sequestration of the enemy's property. It sweeps the South of all and every species of Yankee property, places it in the hands of receivers, where it is to be held for the reimbursement of the losses of our citizens. The sequestration act extends to all debts owed by our people to Northern merchants, and exempts only State and Confederate stocks. The act makes it the duty of every good citizen to hunt up and report Yankee property to the proper officials.

Long Grabs continues.

The place has been used for several months as a camp of instruction for Troops. There has been a large number of soldiers here for some months — some 12,000 probably are here now, and still they come at from two to five companies a day from all sections of the State. The 43d, 44th, 45th, 46th, 47th, 48th Regiments are here, and two or three others in process of formation, besides the "Bethel" or 11th Reg't, which is formed. A Reg't or two of Artillery left here some time ago for Richmond. The officers are generally thought to be good selections and much better than selections formerly made.

Col. Leventhorpe[13] of the 34th N. C. T. (12 months,) elected Col. of the 11th Reg't (Bethel,) is a native of England and a physician, received a military education and served in the British army several years. After coming to America he settled in Western North Carolina and married. He is a tall man about 50 years of age and regarded as a splendid officer. Probably there is not a third of the original men of the Bethel Reg't in the present Reg't; still this Reg't is well organized and drilled and its former reputation will hardly degenerate.

At the beginning of the war, North Carolina had a 1st Regiment North Carolina Volunteers who had signed up for six months. There were also regiments of North Carolina Volunteers numbered 1 through 14 who were in service for twelve months. There were regiments of North Carolina State Troops, numbered 1 through 10, coming into service under a law of the May Convention who were in service for three years or however long the war lasted. In November 1861, the Adjutant and Inspector General's office in Richmond, Virginia, ordered that the regiments be renumbered to avoid confusion. The state troops retained their original numbers. The volunteer Regiments were ordered to add 10 to their number, becoming regiments 11 through 24. The 11th Regiment retained the moniker of "Bethel Regiment" because a number of its soldiers had belonged to the original six months' 1st Regiment North Carolina Volunteers and had fought at Big Bethel, Virginia, on June 10, 1861.[14] This was the Regiment McSween referred to in the preceding paragraph.

Craton's[15] Reg't is nearly completed also. I suppose it will be 49th or 50th.

I have never been thrown into a crowd that represents the State so fully and strikingly as the masses of Troops here in camp. Here thousands of the noble sons of the Old North State mingle together — strangers mostly, yet their hearts beat in throbs of sympathetic union. I know they are all North Carolinians —

open-hearted, honest and brave — pledging their "lives, fortunes and sacred honor," to the cause of their country, and especially their own beloved old State — with her to rise, with her to fall!

There is a good deal of sickness in camp now, though not many details.

Volunteers coming here would do well to bring a few cooking utensils with them, as such cannot be had here; and they will find it to their interest not to bring very much clothing — say 2 suits — about as much as can be packed easily in knapsacks. They are required to receive a uniform suit from the Government, but can get money instead of the other clothes, if they have already enough clothing. It is useless for officers to come on in advance of their companies, as all requisitions for supplies have to be made and attended to after the companies get here. It would be well to bring paper and envelopes, as such articles are hard to get here. It is useless for men to bring much money with them — they get their bounty and other money as soon as the doctor examines them and they are sworn in — which is certainly enough for all purposes. Officers' uniforms cost from $40 to $80, swords from $30 to $60, shoes from $5 to $8, boots from $10 to $15, &c. Every mess should have a good servant to cook and wait on the sick, &c. I discover the wires are moving about Governor's election. A great many logs are to be seen about camp — some remarkably large — a fit memento of former logrolling in regimental elections.

Long Grabs.

[We have omitted more than half of our correspondent's article, consisting of an enumeration of some of the recently elected field officers who have already been mentioned in the Observer. We are glad to receive reliable information from correspondents; but also desire that it be conveyed in as few words as possible. — Editors]

[Ed. Munson note: This letter was originally published on April 14, 1862.]

Camp Mangum, April 29.

Messrs. Editors: I was mistaken in giving you an account of the 51st regiment in my last; I meant the 52d. The 51st is Cantwell's[16] regiment, and is formed at Wilmington. Col. Vance will not accept Colonelcy of the 52d, and the Lt. Col. J. K. Marshall,[17] was duly elected Col.; Major Parks[18] Lieut. Col., and John Q. Richardson,[19] a young man from Virginia, Major. He is a graduate of Lexington and has been drill-master here sometime.

The information Long Grabs refers to about confusing the regiments could have been in the part omitted by the editors of the *Fayetteville Observer*.

Interestingly, directly above Long Grab's letter of the 29th was one also from Camp Mangum, dated May 1, 1862, and signed by someone calling himself Left Guide. It is the only letter signed this way in the *Observer* during the four years of war. One could speculate that since the initials are the same, it could have been Long Grabs trying out another name since he was just beginning his correspondence to the Fayetteville paper.

Since it provides more information on the three top officers of the 52nd Regiment, part of it is included here.

Col. James K. Marshall, the Commandant, is a small man — a graduate of the Virginia Military Institute, and commanded a company from Chowan in the Bethel Regiment. He possesses all the elements necessary for the successful soldier. With superior military acquirements he combines strong common sense, a fine discriminating judgment and a heart which prompts him to consult the welfare of the humblest private. Col. M. is what the ladies would pronounce "a very handsome little man." The Lieut. Col. M. A. Parkes, has also seen service, having been in the 2d regiment for eight months past. Maj. John Q. Richardson is also an educated military man — is a superior tactician, and but a glimpse of his eye is sufficient to induce any one to feel that the Major could well be trusted in the hour of battle at the head of a Regiment. The Field Officers are all single men, and therefore have some claims upon the young ladies residing in the different counties which have companies in the 52d.[20]

LEFT GUIDE.

The Long Grabs letter continues:

The 17th regiment (formerly Col. Martin's) is forming here. Martin[21] will be Col. again I suppose. The 17th was captured at Hatteras. Besides the several regiments formed, there are two posts for unattached companies here, — one under the command of Major J. J. Iredell[22] of Raleigh, and the other under Maj. Wimbish[23] of Granville. Maj. Iredell has had charge of a post near Raleigh for several months, and has by this time a good deal of experience in service. Maj. Wimbish is rather an old man, was educated at West Point, and is a high-toned gentleman. They rank as Major and are appointed by the Governor. There are some six or seven companies of the 17th regiment now under Major Wimbish, and there are some eight or nine companies under Major Iredell, which will be in the 53d regiment. Col. Daniel[24] did not accept Colonelcy of the 43d regiment, and Thos. S. Kenan,[25] the Lt. Col. has been elected Col., and Gaston Lewis[26] of Raleigh, recently Major of Avery's (33d) regiment has been elected Lt. Col. Daniel, it is understood, will accept Col. of the 45th. It is thought some of the regiments will leave here soon. I hardly think there is much sickness here now as some week or two ago.

There is rapid improvement in drilling.

A move has been recently made in the Convention to appoint Vance and Singeltary Brigadier Generals in the State service. There was also an effort to elect a Lieut. Governor, or to create such an office. Many members are absent.

Raleigh is crowded. Extortion and speculation are rife.

The superintendent of the hospital here told me that all blankets and articles collected by agents — many of them given gratuitously by the people — were charged against the State at heavy prices.

For Governor, "Long Grabs" unhesitatingly recommends John M. Morehead as the man for the times.

Truly yours,
LONG GRABS.

[May 5, 1862]

John Motley Morehead (1796–1866) had served as governor of North Carolina from 1841 to 1845 and was very knowledgeable of the workings of state government. He was very interested in the state's internal improvements, especially railroad transportation. He was known as the father of the North Carolina Railroad and the company's first president. In 1861, Morehead was selected as one of the members of the North Carolina delegation that represented the state in the peace convention that met in Washington, D.C., on February 14, 1861, to try to avert war between the North and South.[27]

ORGANIZATION OF THE 53D REGIMENT.

This morning's mail beings us the following letter from Raleigh:—

CAMP MANGUM, May 6th, 1862.

Messrs. Editors: The weather has become charming and delightful. The most comfortable thing to camp life is certainly pleasant weather.

The 53d regiment of N. C. Troops organized to-day as follows: Wm. A. Owens[28] of Charlotte, Colonel; James T. Morehead, Jr.,[29] of Guilford, Lt. Colonel; and James J. Iredell[30] of Raleigh, Major.

Col. Owens is 28 or 29 years of age, is a lawyer, has been Mayor of Charlotte, and was captain of the Hornet's Nest Rifles in the 1st Regiment. He graduated a few years ago at Chapel Hill. He was elected Major of the 34th Regiment N. C. Troops last winter, which place he filled for some time and afterwards engaged in raising men for the war, and was recently elected Lieutenant Colonel of the Bethel Regiment, which place he stills holds. Lt. Colonel Morehead is a son of Hon. Jas. T. Morehead, graduated 3 or 4 years ago at the University with first distinction, was in service as a Lieutenant in a company in one of the twelve months Regiments, and is now Captain of a company in the 45th regiment, (Col. Daniel.) Maj. Iredell resides in Raleigh, was also educated at our University, and is a son of the late Gov. Iredell, and has been in command of a camp of Instruction near Raleigh since the early part of last fall.

The companies of the 53d regiment are:

- Co. A, Capt. A. P. McDaniel, of Guilford county[31]
- Co. B, Capt. J. H. White, of Mecklenburg county[32]
- Co. C, Capt. J. S. Leach, of Johnston county[33]
- Co. D, Capt. David Scott, of Guilford county[34]
- Co. E, Capt. James C. Norman, Surry county[35]
- Co. F, Capt. G. M. Albright, Alamance county[36]
- Co. G, Capt. G. W. Clark,[37]
- Co. H, Capt. S. B. Taylor, Stokes county[38]
- Co. I, Capt. E. A. Jerome, Union county[39]
- Co. K, Capt. W. P. Miller, Wilkes county[40]

In the Bethel regiment, there has been some change. Major Eliason[41] was elected Lt. Col. of the 49th regiment, which left the place of Major in the Bethel regiment vacant, and Professor W. J. Martin[42] of Chapel Hill was elected in his place, and has accepted. Maj. Martin is a native of Richmond, Va., was educated at the University of Va., has been Professor of Chemistry at Chapel Hill in place

34   Confederate Incognito

of Dr. Mitchell, and has recently been captain of a company from Orange county, in one of the 12 months' regiments.

Elisha Mitchell (1793–1857) was a distinguished scientist and a professor at the University of North Carolina at Chapel Hill in the mid–nineteenth century. In 1844, he surveyed peaks in North Carolina's Black Mountains and determined that one of them was the highest peak east of the Rocky Mountains. In 1855, his claim was challenged by Thomas Clingman, who said that Mitchell had never been on the highest peak, while he, Clingman, had. In 1857, Mitchell returned to the mountain to prove his claim and during his survey, fell, and was killed. His claim was later proven. The mountain, which rises to over 6,700 feet, was renamed Mt. Mitchell and he was buried atop it[43]

Another regiment will organize in a few days.

The 43d Reg't, Col. Kenan, the 45th, Col. Daniel, the 46th, Col. Hall,[44] the 48th, Col. Hill,[45] the 49th Colonel Ramseur,[46] and the 11th or Bethel Regiment, Colonel Leaventhorpe, have left here in the last few days for places where their services are more needed. The 44th, 47th, 50th and 52d will go before long probably. It has been asked where are the 39th, 40th, 41st, &c. The 39th is Coleman's[47] Battalion at Asheville, soon to be a complete Regiment; the 40th is artillery in unattached companies and batteries; the 41st is unattached cavalry companies; and the 42d is unattached companies of infantry at Salisbury and elsewhere.

Nous verrons,
LONG GRABS.

[May 8, 1862]

Camp Magnum, May 11, 1862.

Messrs. Editors: Again the veritable "Long Grabs" intrudes himself upon your readers. Nature has opened out in all its beauty, and Spring has wrapped up the cold earth in her green mantle. The progress of the revolution keeps pace with the developments of nature, and our heroic troops are driving the foe before them. Great battles and greater events are at hand. And this great camp of instruction evinces an equal spirit of progress, for our motto is, "Forward, guide right, march!"

There is a great deal of sickness here now. Discipline has become more rigid and the affairs of camp have undergone some improvement. "Sperrits" is scarce, and furloughs more so.

An article published in the May 7, 1862 issue of the *Weekly Standard*,[48] a Raleigh, North Carolina newspaper, elaborates on Long Grabs' comment about sickness.

We learn that there is considerable sickness among the soldiers at the camp near this place, and that the accommodations at the camp for the sick are rather below ordinary. The hospital near town is no doubt full, and Dr. E. Burke Haywood,[49] who is at the head of it, is doing his duty; but we repeat, there is a great

2. Camp Mangum, North Carolina, and Richmond, Virginia

want of proper accommodations at the camp. In addition to this we learn that an order has been issued that sick soldiers and soldiers who are recovering, are not to be allowed to go home, where they would receive much better nursing and attention than they do in camp. This order, it seems to us, is both unwise and cruel. If convalescent soldiers were allowed to go home and remain until they were able to take their places again in the ranks, the State would save by it, the service would lose nothing, and many a valuable life would be saved. Every attention and kindness compatible with proper discipline, should be shown to the brave officers and men who are ready to offer up their lives in the common defense.

Long Grabs continues.

That disagreeable companion of camp — the guardhouse — has quite recently excited the disgust of many devoted followers of Mars. Even the proverbial patience and good nature of "Long Grabs" were well nigh disturbed not long ago by the very unceremonious conduct of the sentinel and that remarkable personage, "the corporal of the guard." As the time when the conscription will close down approaches, troops pour in rapidly. Two or three new regiments will probably be formed in a week, and we hear of many companies still behind. The State is making arrangements to transfer this camp and all its fixtures to the Confederate Government.

The blind negro Tom has been performing here to a crowded house. He is certainly a wonder. Though liable to be humbugged sometimes, I think I may speak with certainty about Tom — for he cannot be all humbug. He resembles any ordinary negro boy 13 years old and is perfectly blind and is an idiot in everything but music, language, and imitation, and perhaps memory. He belongs to a Mr. Oliver, of Sumter county, Georgia, who travels with him. He has never been instructed in music or educated in any way. He learned to play the piano from hearing others, learns airs and tunes from hearing them sung, and can play any piece on first trial as well as the most accomplished performer. He can repeat a speech or sermon or tune perfectly and correctly if once heard. He imitated a speech of S. A. Douglas, which was thought correct. His voice is not perfect, but is correct in tone and emphasis. One of his most remarkable feats was the performance of three pieces of music at once. He played Fisher's Hornpipe with one hand and Yankee Doodle with the other and sang Dixie all at once. I could distinctly hear and understand each. He also played a piece with his back to the piano and his hands inverted. He performs many pieces of his own conception — one, his "Battle of Manassas," may be called picturesque and sublime — a true conception of unaided, blind musical genius. The untutored mind, unskilled in the wires and devices derived from the "Tree of knowledge of good and evil," is perhaps the type of man's first estate — "the image of his Maker." This poor blind boy is cursed with but little of human nature; he seems to be an unconscious agent acting as he is acted on, and his mind a vacant receptacle where Nature stores her jewels to recall them at her pleasure.

Truly,
LONG GRABS.

[May 15, 1862]

"Blind Tom" was Thomas Wiggins, 1849–1908, an autistic savant and musical genius on the piano, performing his own compositions and those of others. For readers interested in learning more about this remarkable individual, Overlook Press published a biography of him in 2009—*The Ballad of Blind Tom, Slave Pianist,* by Deirdre O'Connell. "The Battle of Manassas," referred to by Long Grabs, has been recorded and may be heard on an Internet site about "Blind Tom."

CAMP MANGUM, May 19, 1862.

Messrs Editors:—The man who does not want office now is to be pitied. He should be sent immediately to the Lunatic Asylum. There is such a rush and grab for office and place about this already classic camp that the like was never seen before. It is the old game used on life and death occasions, of "Every man for himself, and the _____Conscript take the hindmost." Under the contagious excitement of grabbing for office, "Long Grabs" has been trying to make one good long strong grab, but "unavoidable circumstances" prevented. Oh for the good old halcyon days of Know-Nothingness, when the office was going about after the man, instead of the man after the office.

The 44th Reg't N. C. T., Col. Singeltary,[50] left here today for somewhere. It is one of the best—perhaps the best—drilled regiment here. The Col. will do efficient service and is a man of ability, coolness and energy, but he has a way of disobeying orders of superiors that will always give him trouble. The 47th Reg't, Col. Rogers,[51] leaves here tomorrow.

The 55th Reg't N. C. T. organized today. Maj. John K. Connally[52] of Yadkin Col., Capt. A. B. Calloway[53] of Wilkes Lt. Col. and Capt. James F. Whitehead[54] of Pitt Major.

Col. John Kerr Connally is a young man of 25 or 26 years, was educated at the Naval School at Annapolis, was Capt. of Co. B in 21st Reg't N. C. V., Col. Kirkland, and has been commanding a post here a few days. He is a nephew of Hon. John Kerr. Lt. Col. Calloway was a member of Capt. Brown's company in the 1st Reg't State Troops, Col. Stokes. He recently raised a company in Wilkes and is here now as Capt. He graduated at Chapel Hill about 3 years ago. Maj. Whitehead has been in service before and was, I am informed, taken prisoner on Roanoke Island. He has since raised a company and is Capt. here. The companies are as follows:

A, Capt. W. J. Bullock, Wilson County,[55]
B, Capt. A. S. Calloway, Wilkes County,[56]
C, Capt. Dixon Falls, Cleaveland County,[57]
D, Capt. S. D. Randall, Cleaveland County,[58]
E, James F. Whitehead, Pitt County,[59]
F, P. M. Mull, Catawba County,[60]
G, J. P. Williams, Wayne County,[61]
H, Vandever Teague, Alexander County,[62]
I, W. H. Williams, Franklin County,[63]
K, M. T. Smith, Granville County.[64]

I would again more earnestly call attention to the eminent qualities of Gov. Morehead for our next Governor. I have always been opposed to him in politics, but from his energy, experience, judgment and talents, I think him the man for the place. He is not too old.

LONG GRABS.

[May 22, 1862]

At the beginning of the following letter, McSween makes a very brief reference to Stonewall Jackson's campaign in the Shenandoah Valley conducted between March 23 and June 9, 1862. Jackson's force never totaled more than 17,000, yet he was able to defeat three separate commanders (General Nathaniel P. Banks, General John C. Frémont, and General James Shields) who had three times his total force.[65]

CAMP MANGUM, N. C., May 31st, 1862.

Messrs. Editors:—One more brilliant ray of hope has burst upon the dark Southern sky. The heroic Jackson has swept before him the invader from the rich valley of Virginia and is now beyond the Potomac, carrying the war into Africa. It is probable he may operate in Maryland and about Washington until reinforced. The North is near its climax—if it falls, how great will be the fall thereof! At this hour of our nation's hardest trial it becomes every patriot to lend his aid and encouragement to our cause. Now is the time for our men to become heroes and statesmen, and for our boys to become men. If we keep united and do our duty we are bound to conquer. History records no instances of the subjugation of such a people as we are with one million of armed men fighting for every thing near and dear or worth having. Can any man with self-respect or a love for his section and its people ever again desire a union with such a people as we have just left? Has not this war developed the motives of those people and their aim towards us? I always believed the yankee would act just as he has acted towards us, and that his motives were just what they are now manifested.

The 17th Regiment, Col. Martin, left here yesterday. The 52d, Col. Marshall, and 53d, Col. Owens, leave today. The latter goes to Western Va., the others are not yet ordered out of the State. I am not certain whether the 50th, Col. Craton, is to leave or not. I think it will soon. The 54th, Col. Wimbish, and the 55th, Col. Connally, are here, and seven or eight companies for another. A Regiment is also forming under Col. Radcliff, at Wilmington—one will be the 56th, the other 57th.

LONG GRABS.

[June 5, 1862]

In the following letter McSween says "that he has come to see the grand battle here [Richmond] and take part in it." He mentions that something is going on at Drewry's Bluff, but that "it was not confirmed." His letter does not mention any of the fighting that has taken place since General McClellan had landed his army on the Virginia Peninsula and started his northward march towards Richmond. Battles had been fought at Yorktown, Williamsburg, and Hanover Court House through April to the end of May.

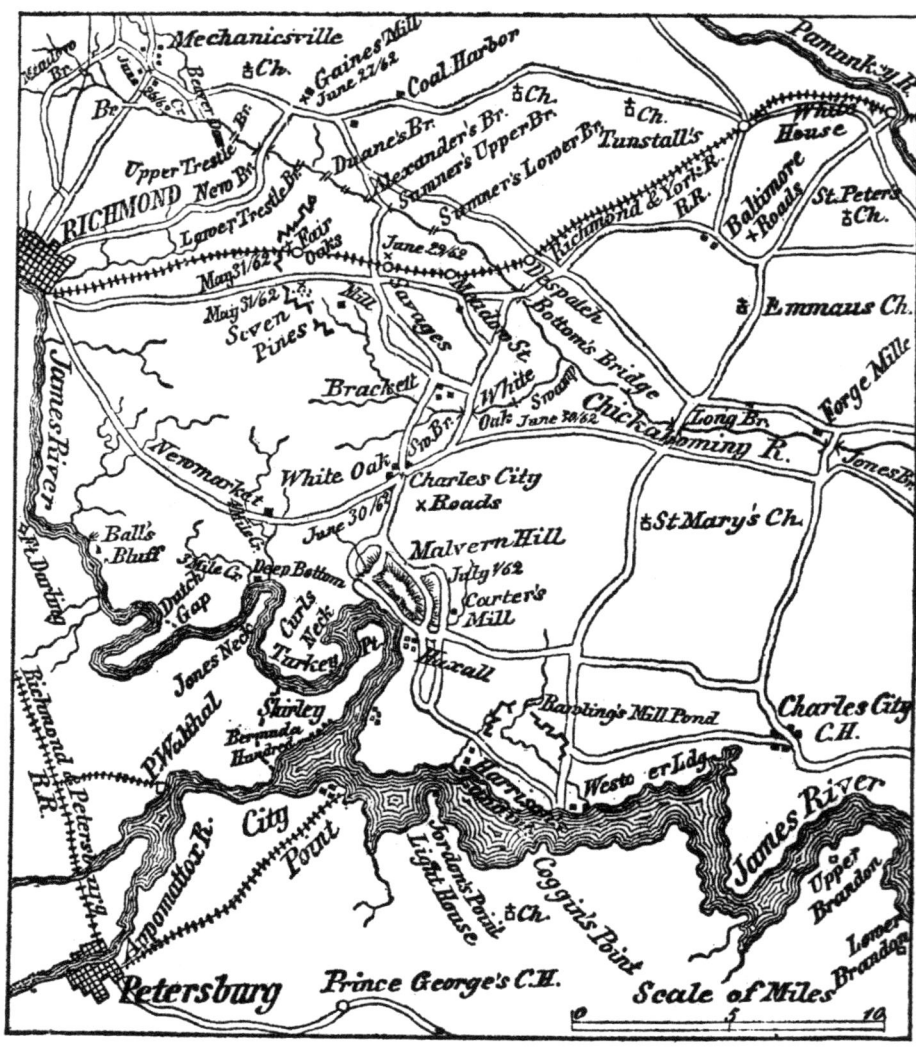

Vicinity of Richmond and Petersburg, 1862. Drewry's Bluff, also called the Battle of Ft. Darling, was fought May 15, 1862, lies about 8 miles south of Richmond, where the James River begins a series of curves. The Battle of Seven Pines was fought about 10 miles east of Richmond. Source: Marcius Wilson, *History of the United States* (New York, New York: Ivison, Blakeman, Taylor, and Co., 1872). Map used by permission of the Florida Center for Instructional Technology, College of Education, University of South Florida.

The "report that the enemy were playing havoc at Drewry's Bluff" was an attempt by a Union force of three ironclads and two wooden gunboats to force their way past the fort atop the 100-foot bluff, sail on to Richmond, and open fire on the city. Heavy cannon fire from the fort turned them back.[66]

While McSween makes no comments on any of these battles, it is possible that he felt that there had been enough newspaper coverage and that the public was generally informed.

The battle of Saturday and Sunday he refers to was the Battle of Seven Pines, called the Battle of Fair Oaks by the North, fought on May 31–June 1, 1862.

McSween's numbers are a bit off. This is understandable since he was writing immediately after the battle when all commanders' reports would not have been received. It is estimated that over 70,000 Northern and Southern soldiers took part, with the Union having 5,031 and the Confederates having 6,134 in killed, wounded, captured and missing.[67]

BALLARD HOUSE, RICHMOND, June 3, 1862.

Messrs. Editors:—I left Camp Mangum yesterday on furlough to see the grand battle here and take a part in it. It is uncertain when it will come off now. I hope it may be to-morrow. There has been nothing doing today so far. It was reported that the enemy were playing havoc with Drewry's Bluff, but that is not confirmed. They are moving in that direction and the next demonstration may be down there. I think their plan now, if it can be carried out, is to occupy Petersburg and take Drury's Bluff and approach Richmond on both sides of the river and try to cut off retreat or reinforcements.

McClellan has in all probability 150,000 men — some think 100,000 — but he probably had more and has no doubt been reinforced lately. The engagements of Saturday and Sunday were brilliant and important, but can hardly be considered more than skirmishes. They were not general. Some upwards of 15,000 of our forces were engaged with 25,000 or upwards of the enemy. The fighting was severe and the loss heavy on both sides. We captured some 500 prisoners. The 4th, 6th, 22d, and 23d N. C. Reg'ts were in the battle on both days. They are said to have fought more gallantly and effectively than any other troops on the field and suffered more.

I shall manage some way to get out among our Reg'ts to-day or to-morrow, though no permits are granted. I have visited several of the hospitals but found few acquaintances. It is difficult to get access to a hospital. There are a great many hospitals and many other buildings are engaged. Some of the wounds are truly hideous to the uninitiated. In the battle a few days ago on the Williamsburg road, some of Branch's Reg'ts were badly cut up — the 18th and 37th suffered mostly. Some 150 more in each regiment were killed or missing, and many dangerously wounded. The 28th and 12th were in the fight. The loss of officers was heavy. I shall visit the 18th and 28th if possible, and as many other reg'ts as I can, and give you a full list of killed and wounded. The 37th N. C. has been transferred to Gen. Anderson. Of our number it may be said that our army is thought to be amply sufficient to meet McClellan's estimated force. The people seem more confident and everything wears a remarkable appearance of indifference. I have heard no cannonading to-day until a short time ago. I can hear it distinctly now occasionally. It was a mistake about one or two divisions of the enemy being water bound on this side of the Chickahominy. The nearest position occupied by the Yankees is about 6 miles from the City — perhaps 5 from the corporate limits. We hold but little beyond the Chickahominy. The Chickahominy heads about 10 miles North of here and runs Southeasterly direction into the James some 25 miles or less from here. The nearest part of the stream is about 7 miles Northeast from here.

About the head, and for miles down, it is cleared up, but where the main body of the two armies is, it is a thick muddy swamp about three-quarters of a mile wide. There are very few streams making into it and it had but few bridges.

I saw to-day a steel pointed ball thrown by the Monitor at the batteries at Drury's Bluff. It is shaped like a pepper box attached to a castor. Both ends are flat, the upper about an inch and a half in diameter, and it widens gradually to the middle, where it is some five inches in diameter, then it comes straight down without any slope till it is some two inches and a half in diameter and continues this size about four inches more in length. It is about one foot long. Gen. Johnston was not wounded seriously. I learn he was seen in the Army yesterday. President Davis was not commanding in person, but intends to so in case of a general engagement. If there is a big battle here before I leave I hope I can give you a full account of it.

RICHMOND, June 5, 1862.

Messrs. Editors:— The big battle is still put off and there has been nothing of importance along our lines. I could not get to camp yesterday on account of the weather. It rained most of the day and every place is so muddy and overflowed that an engagement on the Chickahominy can hardly take place this week. Should it rain no more they may get ready by Sunday. I have been among some of the regiments near the city. In the Richmond papers you can get lists of wounded, though imperfect yet. Among a list of wounded not published yet at the Howard Hospital are C. L. Johnson, 4th Reg't, Co. C, N. C. T.[68]; J. B. Boles, 4th Reg't, from Iredell, badly in the hand[69]; Anderson Green 23d, C, Montgomery, in back by piece of shell.[70] Capt. Ambrose Scarborough, killed Saturday morning in skirmish before battle, also of C, 23d, from Montgomery[71]; and Frank Dumas, in same, killed on Saturday.[72] Maj. E. J. Christian, of Montgomery, 23d, wounded in battle, afterwards died in Hospital.[73] I could not find him. Lt. Nicholson in C, 23d, from Montgomery, wounded in battle and afterwards died in Hospital.[74] In B, 23d, John Holmes wounded in hand.[75] Killed: Jacob Reynolds,[76] Andrew Hyles,[77] Capt. Shuford, (Lincolnton).[78] In Pee Dee Guards, 23d, from Richmond Co., John W. Covington[79] slightly wounded on breast, in Ligon Hospital. Killed in that Co., John C. Ussery,[80] Wm. A. McKethan[81]; and missing, Parks Chappell.[82] Thos. B. Ledbetter[83] slight, shot in foot and hit by piece of shell on back; E. C. Moorman slight[84]; Stephen Webb shot through thigh, flesh wound[85]; Angus Morrison slight[86]; M. Scott slight.[87] 18th Regiment Capt. DeVane's Co.,[88] S. B. Toler, (in Ligon Hospital) from Bladen,

2. Camp Mangum, North Carolina, and Richmond, Virginia   41

wounded at a joint of the elbow.[89] Capt. DeVane was sick and not in the fight of Branch's Brigade: Lt. Wooten[90] commanded the Co. Killed, T. F. Pridgen,[91] W. H. Sykes,[92] John McKethan,[93] Alex Andrews,[94] W. J. Maultsby,[95] Jas. Cromarty[96]; and missing M. V. Sutton.[97] Capt. Sykes[98] of another Bladen Co. also killed. Capt. Norment's[99] Co. from Robeson, 18th, I am informed lost 20 more in killed, wounded and missing. The Scotch Boys from Richmond, I learn, took 60 or more into battle and lost 34 in killed, wounded and missing. These are thought to be killed: Duncan Gibson,[100] Alex Jones,[101] Andrew Clark,[102] Alex McLauchlin,[103] Murdoch McDuffie[104] and Arch'd McRae.[105] Wounded badly, Hugh S. Patterson,[106] Amos Roper,[107] WM. Buchanan, Jr.,[108] Dan'l McKinnon prisoner. 6th N. C. Co. G,[109] Capt. Craige[110] from Rowan — Killed: Sergt. John Barringer,[111] Sergt Rufus R. Owens,[112] Andrew Gullet,[113] WM. Porter.[114] Capt. Freeland,[115] Orange, badly wounded and taken prisoner. The wounded of these do not appear in the lists published. At Spotswood Hospital, W. J. Lacock,[116] Co. C, 6th N. C., flesh wound, leg; J. G. Cockerman[117] Co. I, 16th, in thigh; W. P. Rees[118] Co. G, 16th, concussion, left arm; M. L. Hurly I, 16th fracture of the forearm[119]; N. J. Edney, C, 16th, wound in back[120]; Lt. L. A. Ward[121] Co. I, 16th, hip; Sergt. J. P. Johnson[122] do., right shoulder; J. L. Hitcher[123] do., left breast; also, Thos. Y. Whitlock[124] of Davie, 4th, foot — amputated. Killed in that Co: Jas. Cook,[125] J. Barlow.[126] Also. Lieut. White[127] of Iredell, C, 4th; Capt. Simonton[128] of Iredell, A. 4th, and Lt. Redding[129] E, 4th, killed. E. A. Morrison[130] A, 4th; wounded in side slight.

Also, in 23d Reg't, Lieut. Hill,[131] H, from Gaston, in Ligon Hospital, arm shattered. Capt. Hill,[132] of same, mortally wounded — shoulder and thigh. 16 wounded in all in the Co., among them Jas. C. Robinson[133] mortally, and several badly. Capt. Miller,[134] Catawba, died in Hospital. Here is a list of wounded North Carolinians in Banner Hospital never yet published. Not more than half the Hospitals have had their lists published.

From the appearance of the weather this morning I think I can get out to camp to-day. I may be able to give you more particulars soon. I think I will leave this evening or to-morrow morning if there seems no prospect of immediate engagement. The city is very much crowded, and still large numbers of soldiers flock about the streets and any number of finely dressed officers may be seen any time.

Truly,
Long Grabs.

[June 9, 1862]

Camp Mangum, N. C., June 15, 1862.

Messrs. Editors:— The 54th Reg't, Col. Wimbish, and the 55th, Col. Connally, are here yet, all the others having left, though most of them are still in the State. There are eight unattached companies here which will be organized into a regiment soon, and another company or two are expected here in a few days. Only 3 or 4 of the companies here are full. The camp of Instruction is now under Col. H. B. Watson of Johnston county. He served awhile in the old U. S. Army in the Marine corps, and had command of the detailed or drafted Militia at Weldon some months ago. The companies at this post are: Capt. Luke from

Camden Co., Capt. Lockhart from Northampton (combined with Lieut. Lutterloh and some 20 men from Cumberland,) Capt. Graham from Orange, Capt. Lane from Henderson, Capt. Schenck from Cleaveland, Capt. Roberts[135] from Cumberland, Capt. Halyburton[136] from Alexander, and Capt. Lyons from Pasquotank. According to the Law, before this time every thing in the military line would have been managed under the Conscription bill, but the men in charge of affairs prefer to have no clash of authority or at least they wish to encourage volunteering instead of enforcing the Conscription. So these and other companies can have a reasonable time to organize and recruit and they can fill up with conscripts any how. Another regiment is forming under Col. Radcliff at Wilmington. I learn it is about ready to organize. I presume Vance's Legion will be filled out and organized pretty soon. The rendezvous for the new companies of his Legion is now at Kittrell's Springs. There is a cavalry company there from Anson, Capt. Johnson, and three or four infantry companies, and the others are expected soon. No conscripts have arrived here yet, though the enrolling has been going on in the Eastern part of the State for some time.

All the troops in this State now have prayer at Dress Parades. This was commenced a week or two ago. There has been doubt whether it would effect any good. I think it will have a beneficial effect. Man's patriotism and bravery is based mostly on his moral nature, and the conscience — the seat of the moral qualities, should be educated and developed. Nothing can better tend to this than habitually associating together and reverently exercising the moral powers of the soul in the holy attitude of prayer. It reminds us afresh too of the dangers around us and of our entire dependence on the great God of battles. It elevates and refines the man and counteracts that brutish, selfish disposition so generally evinced in some portions of the army. An infidel will not pray anyhow, and every moral man possessing a belief in Christianity can endorse most of the prayers used, and none are compelled to pray though present.

LONG GRABS.

[June 19, 1862]

On his return to Raleigh, McSween learned that he was in trouble with the higher authorities because he had overstayed the time allowed on his furlough to Richmond. The following exchange of cards and letters was published in the June 25, 1862, edition of the *Raleigh Standard*:

A CARD.

MR. EDITOR:—I regret to appear publicly in a card of this sort; but I am compelled to do so to vindicate more fully my honor, and to relieve myself of an awkward position. On Sunday night, the 1st inst., I got a furlough from Capt. Luke, commanding the camp in Col. Watson's absence, for four days, beginning 2d inst., to go to Richmond, to see and participate in the big fight expected about that time. On Monday morning early, 2d inst., Mr. Gurlick approved the furlough and that night I got to Richmond. I was unwell and did not return till two or three days after my furlough had expired. The physicians attending me advised that it would be prudent to remain and take good care of myself for some days. I got to Raleigh Sunday, and reported early Monday morning at

2. Camp Mangum, North Carolina, and Richmond, Virginia 43

camp, though still unwell. Col. Watson told me he was requested to tell me to report to Adjt. General's Office on my return. I reported there that evening and Capt. Gulick told me my services as Drill Officer were no longer required. I had no right to demand why, but simply asked the reason for this. He replied, because I overstaid my furlough. I said I could get certificates from Doctors in Richmond accounting for my delay from sickness — a privilege always allowed officers and soldiers. He said I might then consider it without any reason. I replied, if he wanted to discharge me, why not do it openly and at once, without pretext or subterfuge? and that I was at a lost to understand the matter. He said I might think just what I "damned please" about it, or take it just as I "damn please." I then said he was acting officially, and in such position that I could not resent insult as I could under other circumstances. He further said, I had urged him to continue me through June. I told him he was certainly mistaken, for I had thought all Drill Officers were to be discontinued on 1st June, and the whole matter transferred to Confederate authority, and that I intended to apply to Confederate Department to be continued, and not to him. I had only recently heard that Drill Masters would still remain with regiments till transferred from State authority. He said he would take oath that I did so urge him, and I said I would take oath that I did not, when he said I would take an oath on what was not so. I remarked that he had generally treated me gentlemanly till that evening, and left the office. This is about the substance of the interview. Early next morning I sent the following:

RALEIGH, N. C., June 19th, 1862.

Sir: Our interview yesterday evening terminated unexpectedly to me, and some remarks were used by you, that probably deserve further attention from me. In reply to a question of mine as to what you meant, or on my saying that you were in your office in official capacity, you said I "might just think what I damn please about it," or "take it just as I damn please." You also said you would take an oath that I requested you to continue me Drill Master during June, and when I said I would take an oath that I made no such request, you said, I would then take an oath on what was not true. I am not aware that my conduct and language was other than gentlemanly and respectful throughout the interview. I wish to know if I can communicate with you on equality, that is, if you will discard your official position, and thus put yourself on an equal footing with me, and correspond with me on the subject, with a view to better distinction of the issue between us, and more definite settlement. My friend Capt. Lockhart will hand you this note.

Your ob't serv't.
M. J. MCSWEEN.

W. B. GULICK, A. A. G.

Having received no answer, I sent another note by Capt. Satterthwaite, to know if I could get a reply, and when. On the 13th inst., at night, I received at the Post Office the following anonymous letter, marked on outside envelope "Adjutant General's Office, official business." It is evidently Mr. Gulick's reply to my notes, though at first I doubted whether it could be considered any reply at all:

"Captain Gulick acknowledges the receipt of Mr. McSween's two notes. In causing his discontinuance as Drill Master, he performed merely an act of official duty. If Mr. McSween feels aggrieved, he can appeal to the Governor. When Mr. McSween applied to Capt. Gulick at his residence on Sunday, the 1st inst., for a furlough, he certainly made the impression that he desired to be continued in service, notwithstanding the order dismissing the Drill Masters, otherwise, there would have been no necessity for such application. Upon subsequent consultation with Col. Watson, it was thought proper to enforce against Mr. McSween the order discontinuing Drill Masters. If, on account of his importunities, he was subjected to harsh language when he complained of this action of the office, he has no one to blame but himself. This reply is made in compliance with promises to Capt. Lockhart and Capt. Satterthwaite. No further communication with Mr. McSween on the subject is necessary.

Adjutant General's Office,
Raleigh, June 13, 1862.

This is no answer to my first note, and is, altogether, an evasive, indefinite document. It goes far enough to reiterate the insult, which was the only matter referred to in my correspondence. I had made no complaint as to my discontinuance, but thought it unjustifiable on the reasons alleged, especially since I was superseded by another, when my services had been generally acceptable. Mr. Gulick said further, that Col. Watson went to see him after my furlough was out, and said I had not returned, and had not been attentive to my duties before. Col. Watson says he said no such thing, and the he called on Mr. Gulick a day or two after I left, when the conversation occurred about me. I have Watson's statement in writing. He said Gulick told him I had annoyed him a great deal about a furlough, and that if dismissed, I would probably not be much loss to Watson. I have never asked for furloughs but twice in my life — once when a private in a S. C. regiment some 18 months ago, and this time with Gulick. He tries to find excuse for asserting that I asked to be continued, on the implied ground that I got a furlough after 1st June. I did not know whether the Drill Masters would quit on the 1st June or not, as I had seen no such order, nor heard any read. I asked Col. Watson if he requested me dismissed and his son put in my place. He declined to answer. Notwithstanding Gulick's repetition of the insult in his note, he apologized for it to Captain Lockhart and Satterthwaite and said he was sorry for it, and used it through passion, and no doubt if we could talk it over, we would understand each other. The officers in Watson's command gave me a recommendation, which I produce, only to show what they think of me. They may have, for aught I know, a high estimation for the other parties above alluded to.

Camp Mangum, June 1862.

We, officers and members of the unattached companies at this camp, are acquainted with Mr. M. J. McSween, who has been Drill Officer among us for some time, and so far as we know, we regard him as a very suitable person for that place. We can say that we are well pleased with the manner in which he has discharged his duties, and we think he discharged those duties punctually, faith-

2. Camp Mangum, North Carolina, and Richmond, Virginia 45

fully, and efficiently. We regard him a gentleman and a worthy man, and would recommend his continuance as Drill Officer; and we have no doubt of his competency for a much higher position.

J. B. Lutterloh, 1st Lt.[137]	O. P. Wills, 1st Lt.[145]
W. S. Moody, 2d Lt.[138]	J. W. Graham, Capt.[146]
H. T. Schenck, Capt.[139]	H. E. Lane, Capt.[147]
T. J. Palmer, 2d Lt.[140]	J. G. Lockhart, Capt.[148]
J. R. Williams, 2d Lt.[141]	G. B. Barnes, 2d Lt.[149]
A. R. Grigg, 2d Lt.[142]	B. D. Lane, 2d Lt.[150]
G. G. Luke, Capt.[143]	Jno. B. Lyon, 1st Lt.[151]
R. D. Graham, 2d Lt.[144]	Thos. Snavelly, 2d Lt.[152]

Besides this I have others of the same purport, signed by over forty officers in several regiments organized near here within a few months past. Among these names are Col. Kenan, of the 43d Reg; Lt. Col. Parks and Maj. Richardson, of 52d Reg; and Capt. Little and his Lieutenants and Sergeants, (from my own county,) of 52d Reg. Some of them have but slight acquaintance with me, and others have known me many years. It therefore appears that Mr. Gulick has shown much inconstancy and evasiveness, uttered many falsehoods, acted ungentlemanly and unofficer like, and has taken advantage of his position to insult an inferior in rank, and when approached to give satisfaction for it, places himself still higher on his official dignity and repeats the insult, and that too, after he had cringed and apologized to a friend verbally.

This person, (Gulick,) I am informed, is a native Yankee,— a mere adventurer,— once an editor of a little paper in one of our villages, and, unfortunately, now in power here to lord it over true Southerners, and outrage their feelings with impunity. I do not intend the least reflection on those noble men of Northern birth, who have not hung around the precincts of power, and who have given their means, blood and lives in our cause. Mr. Gulick must admit that he has acted the unprincipled petty despot and coward, and that he merits a place below the contempt of respectable gentlemen. An impartial public will draw their own conclusions from this statement, and if Mr. Gulick "feels aggrieved, he has no one to blame but himself."

This appeared to end the matter as far as the newspaper was concerned as no further statements from either party appeared in 1862 publications. What might have gone on in other comments and encounters and whether the bitter feelings between the two men continued is not known. McSween appears a man quick to respond to a perceived insult and a challenge to his honor.

CAMP MANGUM, N. C., June 26, 1862.

Messrs. Editors:— Very few soldiers at Camp — gone home to save their wheat and oats. There has been a recent arrangement to let all men go home who have wheat crops and harvest their wheat. Electioneering in the new regiment has become monotonous and has by general consent been discontinued. All the logs about camp have been rolled long since and most of the brush gathered. But little is left to do except "digging stumps," for which there is not much fondness.

It has been suggested that the ladies spare all fans they can for hospitals. Towels and clean rags (of any color,) are of very great use about hospitals. This seems to be a good fruit year and great quantities of all kinds of fruit should be dried. A good deal of cider should be made from which to make vinegar. Now that the season for taking honey from bees is at hand, and as it is still time for swarms to come out, all should endeavor to get as much gums and bees as possible. In this way and from Chinese sugar cane we must expect to get our sweetening for some time.

Everything that can be cultivated and saved with little work and waste that is well adapted to raising stock, should be grown largely this year. It would be well to plant large crops of potatoes and turnips, clover and the grasses, ground peas (very valuable for oil,) pumpkins, peas and grain generally. In stock, our attention should be given mostly to cows and hogs. The country will need these faster than they can be raised. Large quantities of poultry should be raised for home use, which will require but little salt. I think it would be a good plan for parties to go to the sea-shore as soon as they finish their crops to make salt. It will probably be harder to get salt next winter than it was last, and while we have yet the opportunity we had better use it.

I hope there will be no canvass for Governor. All ought to feel generous and patriotic enough, while such dangers surround us, to unite in a common cause, forget self and party and bury party issues and prejudices, and partisans. I think Z. B. Vance will be elected Governor. He was not my first choice, but will do very well no doubt. We ought to have either an old experienced man of energy, prudence and talents, or a brave, dashing young man of genius, wisdom and popularity.

LONG GRABS.

[July 3, 1862]

In August 1868, McSween came to Fayetteville from Richmond County to become the publisher and editor of a local newspaper, *The Eagle*. As part of his duties he traveled about North Carolina to gather news on how the state was recovering from the war. On October 10, 1868, he was in Raleigh. Memories of his time as a drill master at Camp Mangum and Camp Holmes came back to him; he wrote a long column, sometimes humorous, about them, especially the dress inspections, and as always he signed his work "Long Grabs."

Before the war, during the war and since the war, I have "Loafed" about here muchly. Near here I served an apprentice-ship at Camp Mangum and also at Camp Holmes. To think of Raleigh is to me like some long, mysterious and terrible dream. Notwithstanding all the humbug, hypocrisy, corruption and oppression calculated to shock the feelings of a conscientious man here during the war, I have enjoyed much of the happiness of my life about Raleigh. I have not visited Camp Mangum this time. I learn the place is only a skeleton of its former greatness. Thousands of tar-heels assembled there — and such "pomp and circumstance of glorious war" had never been seen in this old fogy country before. There was the great J. G. Martin, the one armed hero of the Tarboro raid against

Foster.— Martin wore an awful and terrible military hat like those we have seen represented in the pictures of Gen. Taylor. He is said to have lost his arm in Mexico and for that reason he demanded the biggest kind of bomb-proof place and got in it. Anyhow, he was Captain of the regular army, Brigadier-General of the volunteer army; or volunteer militia, (as a fellow by the name of Randolph at one time Confederate Secretary of War called Lee's veterans); and Adjutant-General of N. C. with the rank of Major-General. He was also ex-officio Inspector-General, Commissary General, Quarter Master General and the great Mogul, the Ajax, Telamon and the Jupiter Tonans of all Tar-Heeldom in a military way. Powerful man this Martin. He may have been named Martin from his martial genius. But when Vance came in power in 1863 he claimed to have some control of the military affairs of the State as Governor. Martin became indignant at such disobedience of his orders. Vance decided that it was due himself as Governor to be boss and he ordered Martin away and revoked his commission as Adjutant-General of the State.

But Martin was as tenacious as the cunning opossum, when you pull all his feet away from the limb and he still holds on by his tail. Martin lost the place as Adjutant General for the State, but still held the office of Brigadier-General, in command of the Department of North Carolina. But I have left my subject. J. G. Martin drew all the pay, forage, room rent, rations, stationery, commutations, &c., due the various offices he held. But his great and grand duty, and about his only duty, was to have an inspection twice a day, in all the dazzling splendor of martial army.

I remember as well as if it were yesterday,

How we all marched through that large field at Camp Mangum, with old flint and steel muskets, and awaited the approach of the royal caravan. Very often we had no guns. Gideon Fulford, a low squatty Dutchman, from Cabarrus, marched at the head of the column, with a bass drum some 5 feet in diameter. The tap of Gideon's drum sounded like distant thunder as he beat the measured step of the left foot. About every fourth lick he would double his beats to suit the step of both feet and then the measured left step again four times, and then the double lick again, and so on. Enoch Misenheimer, of Rowan, with that melodious instrument, the fife, and Nathan Braxton, from Lenoir, with his kettledrum roaring like two saw-mills, walked up on the right oblique, marked time, left-dressed and joined Gideon's band.

Suddenly we would be commanded to halt and hold our breath. The officer of the day who is posted on the lookout bawls out something to our field officer. We then file-right by left flank, turn heels over head and fall into double column at half distance. As soon as we recover our senses from this movement, we turn our eyes toward the distant hills in the direction of Raleigh. We can just distinguish in the distance, the hero of the Gen. Taylor hat, the one armed martyr of Buena Vista and his host of staff officers and attendants.

They fly over hill and dale at lightning speed, one after the other like so many Comanche chiefs on the prairies of Texas. Soon the royal J. G. Martin, in dazzling uniform and rattling armor, gallops on his foaming steed through our widened columns from one end of the field to the other. About 50 yards behind him came A. Gordon, A. A. A. General. At the same interval came Shepard another A. A. A. Gen'l., and then in succession Gulick, Hogg, Moore, and a dozen others in buff gauntlets and sky-blue pants.

And lastly came little Snow, on a bushy-tailed Mexican pony, as cornier and hostler. The sage of the old Guion Building and the hero of the Tarboro raid, having thus secured a stand near an old persimmon tree, in the farther end of the old field, we then left wheel, right dress and march in review. At this critical moment Capt. Lyons, of Granville, displayed that military genius and courage for which he has become so famous. Capt. Lyons halloed as much to his men as Robards of Granville did to his conscripts. Robards was a drill master of conscripts and from the moment he went to roll call in the morning till dress parade was over in the evening, you could hear him all over the camp as follows: "Steady men, steady! right dress! front! two inches forward on the left! an eighth of an inch back on the centre! steady! front! forward! guide left, steady boys! step off firmly with the left foot, touch to the right and dress to the left! front, steady my boys, MARCH! Hep — hep — hep! mark time! steady men! HALT!"

But Capt. Lyons did the thing in a style somewhat different from Robards. I think he first attempted this drill at Gen. Martin's request. Dickerson was an important character in his company. Lyons did not talk much but when he did it was in this style: "I will have you right shoulder shift ARMS left DRESS! Back there Dickerson about two inches in the centre. (Pay attention now and quit chawin' tobacco there Fullenwider, and keep your hands out of your pockets Thompson.) FORWARD! guide left! (Hold up your head there Dickerson, you d__n fool and quit looking for snakes.) MARCH!

When review was over the royal procession would take its flight back to Raleigh in the same order as it came, only faster. Thus they came and went from day to day and this was called inspection. Back we went to our quarters and thought we had done something bully. We felt like we could whip the world, for we made a great show; and we did a good deal towards it afterwards, but Martin and his caravan were not with us. I had intended to make this letter much longer, but must stop here for the present.[153]

LONG GRABS

[October 22, 1868]

Chapter 3

Conscription Camps
August 1, 1862 – October 29, 1962

As North Carolina's participation in the first year of the war drew to a close, many of those who had volunteered for six and twelve months' enlistments looked forward to returning to their homes, families, and jobs. In April 1862, enlistments for one year would be up; many of the soldiers were farmers and there were fields waiting for the cut of the plow and plantings to follow. This was true of other Confederate states as well. Enthusiastic about the war in 1861 and the formation of their own country, tens of thousands of men and boys had joined the army across the Southern states, but by early 1862, this volunteer spirit was waning. However, in the North General McClellan had an army of 100,000 men, and he was preparing for his move against Richmond.

Faced with depletion in manpower at this critical juncture, the Confederate Congress passed on April 16, 1862, what has been called the first American military draft, or the Conscription Act. In the months ahead 81,993 men would be conscripted into the Confederate Army. Of those, one-fourth would be North Carolinians — 21,384. North Carolina's contribution was also seven thousand more than any other state.[1]

Compulsory military service, while not a new concept, bothered some state citizens and the soldiers. Some felt that Southern men had enough patriotism to keep the regimental ranks filled without resorting to forced service. There would be grumblings and some resistance, but in the end people in North Carolina and the other states accepted the law as necessary to the war effort.

W. W. Holden, editor and publisher of the *North Carolina Standard* in Raleigh, expressed the feelings of a number of citizens when he wrote in the April 23, 1862, issue of his paper:

> This act breaks the faith of both the State and Confederate Governments with the twelve months men, by compelling them to remain two years longer in the war. We regard it as inexpedient, unnecessary, oppressive, and unconstitutional.

It places the rights of the States and the liberties of the people at the feet of the President....We can only hope that this measure will not seriously injure the Southern cause, and that good results, and not calamitous ones, may flow from it. But we enter our protest against it; and if evil comes of it, it shall not be said that we were the advocate of, or the apologist for, so monstrous and dangerous a measure. Again we admonish the people who are fighting against despotism from without, to look well to the encroachments of power within. The price of liberty is not only treasure and blood, but sleepless vigilance.[2]

Henry Toole Clark, who became governor after the death of John Ellis in 1861, expressed a more conciliatory tone toward the law in a letter he wrote to George W. Randolph, the secretary of war, on April 24, 1862: "Sir: I desire to carry out the conscription act fairly and to the fullest extent to the wants of the country; and presume, as a guide, that you will publish some regulations and instructions in detail to aid in understanding the method in carrying it out."

Yet he had questions, such as: Did North Carolina have the required quota of soldiers in the field? Would volunteering cease when conscription became law? Would the Conscription Act take in the militia officers as well as the privates? Would bounty payments continue to volunteers?[3]

Randolph replied with a letter explaining some of the provisions of the Conscription Law. The letter was published in the *Fayetteville Observer*, May 8, 1862.

> Confederate States of America
> War Department, Richmond
> April 30, 1862

His Excellency Gov. Henry T. Clark, Raleigh, N. C.:

Sir: Your letter of the 24th inst. was received on yesterday. In reply, I have the honor to say, that the effect of the Conscription Act is to suspend calls on the States for quotas. The number of men between the ages of 18 and 35 is assumed to be precisely in the ratio of population.

The first effect of the Act is to retain in the service all soldiers who were there on 16th April. The next, to fill up the regiments and companies with men liable to military duty under the act, by replacing those men on service who will be exempt from age, with those not now on service, not so exempt, and thus to fill and keep full the existing corps to the maximum allowed by law. If any States have not enough regiments in the service, or heretofore authorized by the Department to be raised, to absorb the material between the ages of 18 and 35, the excess will be collected in Camps of Instruction, disciplined, and brought into service, pursuant to Section 9 of the Act.

I will accept the State Troops in their present organization, to be received on the same footing with other regiments already in the Confederate service, the men over 35 and under 18 to be discharged within 90 days from the 16th April, and their place supplied by the enrolled Conscripts. The right of reorganization, by election, belongs only to 12 month men. Those whose enlistment is for a longer or a shorter period, remain in the service on their existing organizations. These general remarks are supposed to answer several of your specific inquiries. The enrolment of Conscripts will be made as soon as the requisite regulations can be prepared, in order to relieve the men now in service who are over 35 years of age.

2. The State Troops will be received as stated above

3. Men over 35 years of age now in service will be discharged within 90 days. They or others not now in service will be at liberty to serve voluntary enlistments, but not in lieu of Conscripts, except as substitutes.

4. Volunteering is not stopped by the Conscription Bill. By section 13, persons liable as Conscripts may volunteer in any company now in service. You are referred specially to Regulations 8 and 1* inclusive. The Act approved December 11, 1861, providing for the payment of bounty to volunteers for the war continues in force.

5. Militia officers between 18 and 35 are embraced by the Conscription Act.

The quota of each State, under existing laws, will be liable to military duty under the Act of April 16th.

I enclose a copy of the Act and Regulations established for carrying it into effect. Very respectfully, your obedient servant,[4]

GEO. W. RANDOLPH, Sec'y. of War.

After the Act was passed, the secretary of war sent out an order to the states with instructions on how the conscripts would be mustered in, how they would be transported to the training centers, basic training, and what would be done with them at the end of their instruction. Each state would have two camps of instruction. An officer with the rank of major or above would have charge of the camps.[5] States could have more than two camps but not "not without authority from the [War] Department."[6]

Major-General Theophilus Hunter Holmes, a career military man and commander of Confederate forces in North Carolina, chose Captain Peter Mallett to take charge of the camps. Holmes promoted him to the rank of major.

The Conscription Act required all the volunteer training camps to be closed by May 17, 1862. Mallett selected land in Raleigh near the capitol for the first conscription camp and named it Camp Holmes in honor of his friend and mentor, General T. H. Holmes. Camp Hill, the second camp, was at Statesville, in Iredell County and was named for General D. H. Hill.[7]

McSween is still in and around Raleigh. For the next two months he will travel to Camp Holmes and Camp Hill and send his observations to the *Fayetteville Observer*.

RALEIGH, August 1, 1862.

Messrs Editors:—"Long Grabs" is still alive and a kicking. Those who thought he had departed for the land of "sperrits" are mistaken.

There have been some 8000 conscripts at the camp near here, and they are still coming in. 2000 probably have been sent to Richmond. I think Maj. Mallett sends them to the Department as fast as they are ready, and from there they are sent as far as practicable to the regiments they wish to go to. They have plenty of room now and good fare at the camp, and are generally enjoying themselves very well. Some 250 in all have left without proper permission, but many of them are returning. One man came back as soon as he plowed his corn over. Most of those that left did so through ignorance of their duty and misapprehension. Every thing was in such confusion at first, and the place so overcrowded, that they could hardly get accommodations. Some had left their crops in such condition that they would be lost, and their families were suffering. Their course in leaving was no doubt from honest motives, and under some circumstances may be excusable, but many had no reasonable excuse and have shown themselves cowardly deserters — the basest character pertaining to any one claiming the rights of citizenship. There is but little sickness in the camp. The business is conducted rather hurriedly and confusedly and the few men transacting it have been so busy that they cannot give proper attention to what they do. They have no time for any thing out of their regular course, and have to refuse hundreds of special private applications.

The 56th Reg't organized at Camp Mangum yesterday; Paul F. Faison[8] of Northampton, Colonel, G. Gratiot Luke of Camden, Lieut. Colonel, and H. F. Schenck of Cleaveland, Major. Col. Faison is a young man; graduated at West Point 2 or 3 years ago, and was Major in 14th Reg't, Col. Daniel. Lt. Col. Luke was Capt. of Co. H in 32d Reg't., and is Capt. here now. Major Schenck is also Capt. now. All will no doubt make good officers. This is one of the finest, if not the best Reg'ts formed here. The companies are

Co. A, Capt. Luke,[9] Camden County,
Co. B, Capt. F. N. Roberts,[10] Cumberland,
Co. C, Capt. White,[11] Pasquotank,
Co. D, Capt. Jno. W. Graham,[12] Orange,
Co. E, Capt. J. G. Lockhart,[13] Northampton
Co. F, H. F. Schenck,[14] Cleaveland,
Co. G, Capt. H. E. Lane,[15] Henderson,
Co. H, Capt. Halyburton,[16] Alexander,
Co. I, Capt. Harrill,[17] Cleveland,
Co. K, Capt. Alexander,[18] Mecklenburg.

LONG GRABS.

[August 4, 1862]

The Captain McRae referred to in the next letter was James Cameron McRae, who like Major Mallett, was from a prominent Cumberland County family. Mallett named him commandant of Camp Hill[19] in Statesville, which is about 150 miles from Raleigh.

McSween mentions a victory that Stonewall Jackson achieved over "the arch-fiend Pope." It was the Battle of Cedar Mountain, also called Slaughter's Mountain, which was fought August 9, 1862.[20]

FROM THE CAMP AT STATESVILLE.

CAMP HILL, N. C., Aug. 14, 1862.

Messrs. Editors:—There are about 800 conscripts here now and none have been yet sent off. The men here are mostly married, healthy and stout, and seem to be well satisfied. I see no difference in this and a Camp of volunteers. So far they have excellent and abundant accommodations and are well pleased with their officers. The greatest inconvenience is the want of a variety of cooking vessels and other similar articles of camp furniture.

Orders have been extended to all counties for the men to come to camp immediately and I suppose they will continue to come rapidly from now on. There are but a few behind in counties that have sent any at all. I have heard of but very little practical direct opposition to the carrying out of the Conscript Law. The mountain people will yield promptly to the necessity of the case and come forward with enthusiasm.

Capt. McRae had adopted a calm, firm course, and a well regarded system of business, and this, with the energy, promptness and spirit of accommodation so plainly manifest, will no doubt ensure the operation of the camp and its officers to be successful and satisfactory. The plan adopted here was to allow men to select their own companies as far as possible though it cannot be put into effect now fully; but any how all men from this camp can go to regiments that have companies from their respective counties.

This is certainly a very liberal, enterprising and patriotic community. Fruit is very abundant and crops are generally good, though it has been too dry for the last two or three weeks, which will shorten the corn crop. The Western N. C. R. R. is completed to within 6 miles of Morganton, and the Atlantic, Tenn. & Ohio R. R. (a big name for a little road) is done from Charlotte to within 6½ miles of Statesville. Our camp (named after D. H. Hill) is between the terminus of the latter and the town.

North Carolina should feel more than a general interest in "Stonewall" Jackson who has just gained another victory over the arch-fiend Pope. He married a Miss [Mary Anna] Morrison of Lincolnton, a sister of Mrs. Gen. D. H. Hill and cousin of Gov. Graham. Long live old "Stonewall" and may his shadow never grow less!

LONG GRABS.

[August 18, 1862]

CAMP HILL, N. C., (NEAR STATESVILLE,) Aug. 25.

Messrs. Editors:—There are some 500 conscripts here now. About 1000 have been sent off—some 400 of whom went this morning. Among those this morning were about 100 men from Rutherfordton for the 18th Reg't. They were very much opposed to going to that Reg't, as they had no acquaintances or friends there. The 18th is a very fine Regiment, formed from counties entirely around Wilmington, and it seems hard to send Rutherford men there; but they submitted like soldiers and gentlemen, and it is to be hoped that the officers of that and other Regiments can effect an agreeable exchange. It is a common but erroneous opinion that the conscript law itself guarantees men the right of choosing their companies. The law only says they shall be assigned to Regiments from the same State. But the Secretary of War advises those appointed to carry out the conscription law to allow men to select the commands they prefer, as far as practicable.

The 57th Reg't organized some time ago at Salisbury and have since left. The Col., A. C. Godwin,[21] is a native of Va., and has been in the service since the war began. He resided in California for several years in the capacity of Agent of Indian affairs under the U. S. Government, and it is thought he will make a fine officer. His regiment is made from the vicinity of Salisbury. Hamilton C. Jones, Jr.[22] is Lt. Col. He resides in Rowan, and has been Captain in the 5th Reg't, Col. McRae, and graduated at Chapel Hill 3 or 4 years ago. Maj. Craige,[23] son of Hon. Burton Craige of Salisbury has been Captain of a company also since the war began.

The yankee prisoners have all been sent away from Salisbury.

I learn the 8th Reg't N. C. T. will be reformed in a few days. It was captured at Roanoke Island. Col. H. M. Shaw[24] of this Reg't is I have heard a classmate of Gen. Burnside and native of New Hampshire, though for the last 20 or 30 years a citizen of this State.

But very few have deserted this camp yet; good order is preserved and the health of the men very good. We have quite a religious camp, if praying, singing and preaching be any evidence.

Gov. Vance passed up a few days ago. A good many are speaking of attending the grand inauguration to take place the 8th of next month. I believe Vance is the youngest Governor ever elected by the people. He left Chapel Hill I think in 1852, where he had been a year or two an irregular student. I understand Gov. Swain assisted him in procuring an education, as his means were moderate. In personnel he is about six feet high and would weigh probably 175 lbs. His face is rather round and full, his head indicative of intellect, his hair dark brown and about one third grey. He has florid complexion, small grey eyes, a shrewd comprehensive glance and an honest, social countenance. He is very free and easy in his manners, inclined to drollery and fun, careless about his dress and appearance, and meets his friends in a free, knowing and how-d'ye-do manner. He is some 32 years of age. Mr. Johnston, his opponent, is a man of very dignified and refined appearance, dark hair and eyes and very intellectual countenance, medium size and height, and 40 years of age or over.

The Concord Female College is a flourishing Presbyterian institution in Statesville under Rev. S. C. Miller, now numbering 60 to 75 pupils.

P. S. I said the A. T. & O. R. R. was done to within 1½ miles of Statesville; you mistook me in stating it 6½.

LONG GRABS.

[September 1, 1862]

CAMP HOLMES, (near Raleigh,) Sept. 15, 1862.

Messrs. Editors: We have "changed our base" again. It must be regarded as "a great strategic movement," though it is still undecided whether it was a retreat or advance. While the victorious veterans of Jackson and Lee were on the march across the Potomac to yankee-land, we, too, took up the line of march from

Statesville to this inhospitable clime and braved the dangers of that impassable defile the North Carolina Railroad, with our provisions safely locked up in the depot, "nary red" in our pockets, no "kiver" but the blue sky, and nothing whereon to rest but the rickety open cars beneath. But few incidents occurred on our journey to interrupt the dull monotony of cinders and smoke. However, Jim and Poss had provided a bottle of medical stuff that helped very much keep my spirits up. Many of our conscript friends were leaving their native regions for the first time, and of course were much amazed and interested. One fellow of huge dimensions and ancient looking clothes carried on his head an immense load of wheat straw in the shape of a hat. While deeply absorbed in the wonderful scenes about him, his hat blew off. With a convulsive effort that seemed to shake the train, he leaped over [his seat], the huge bulk resembling a man suspended in a balloon. He looked long and dolefully after his departed treasure as the train sped its way, heedless of the jeers and shouts of his comrades. It was suggested he use a tray that he swung to his knapsack, as a hat, to which he agreed.

We have now here some 700 conscripts, over 600 of whom are in guard companies for the camp. Why it takes 600 men to guard a small camp and two or three dozen conscripts I am unable to explain, but I suppose the companies are intended to be sent after conscripts who will not come till forced. It would have been well to have been at this place all the time as much as possible. I learn that over 4000 men have reported to this camp, and the entire number at Statesville was over 2400, making about 7000 in all — about half of what is supposed to be the whole number.

The 8th and 31st Regiments are at Camp Mangum, and will be ready for service again in a few days. They are large, fine regiments.

There are many institutions about Raleigh, accounts of which would be interesting, and I shall speak of them again. The paper mills near here are worthy of extended notice. The Forestville Mills, some miles north of Raleigh, and the Neuse River Manufacturing Company, several miles east, are said to be the largest and most complete establishments of the kind in America. The paper made here is superior to any made in the South, and equal to any at the North, and much cheaper and in larger quantities. It is a remarkable fact that the New York Tribune, Times and Express, and all the Charleston papers, and others North and South, were for years supplied with paper from these mills. The mills are kept going night and day now, and the owners are coining money. There was another paper mill near this camp that made wrapping and stiff paper, but it is now discontinued and will be occupied as a powder mill. I see a great many establishments for making guns on private enterprise in different sections of the State

Truly,
Long Grabs.

[September 18, 1862]

    Long Grabs refers to two deaths in the following letter: General Lawrence O'Brien Branch, a native of Halifax County, and Henry Watkins Miller, a native of Goochland County, Virginia, who moved to Raleigh when he was twelve years old.

General Branch was educated in Princeton, New Jersey, and later moved to Florida where he had a law practice. He returned to Raleigh in 1849, and in a few years the directors of the Raleigh and Gaston Railroad Company elected him president. He was elected to the House of Representatives in 1855, 1857, and 1859. He was going to run again in 1861, but after President Lincoln's proclamation, he stepped down. When the war broke out, he joined the Raleigh Rifles as a private. His rise was rapid, being appointed Quartermaster-General of North Carolina, Colonel of the 33rd Regiment North Carolina State Troops, and finally Brigadier-General.

He was killed at the Battle of Sharpsburg, Maryland, September 17, 1862. He died shortly after being struck in the head by a ball.[25]

Henry Watkins Miller graduated from the University of North Carolina in 1834 and entered into the practice of law. He was well-respected as a lawyer, orator and statesman. He was a candidate for election in 1861, with Branch, but both withdrew together after the Lincoln proclamation. He was forty-eight years old at the time of his death.[26]

CAMP HOLMES NEAR RALEIGH, Sept. 26, 1862.

Messrs. Editors:— Gen. Branch was buried at Raleigh to-day with military honors. He was in many respects a noble man and was rapidly becoming an excellent officer. His death has cast a deep shadow of gloom over this community. Thus with the loss of the lamented Miller have two of our best citizens gone down to the grave and two of Carolina's brightest lights have ceased to exist. The fatality among our best and greatest men at present is unprecedented. Truly we may say:

> The great are falling from us, one by one,
> Like patriarchs of the forest trees;
> The winds shall seek them vainly, and the sun
> Gaze on each vacant spot for centuries.

In the account of the killed in the last battles I regret to see the name of Robert Walker Anderson[27] of Wilmington. He was a gentleman, a scholar and a christian. Possessed of manly virtues and rare talents, he died as he had lived, noble and honorable. I cannot leave this melancholy subject without paying a slight tribute to the memory of Lieut. Lawrence Stewart[28] of the 18th Reg't, from Richmond county. He fell while gallantly leading his company in one of the most desperate engagements of the war. High-toned, modest and courageous, he was the model of Southern character and Southern chivalry. In him were combined the qualities of the genuine man and patriot. He was kind, generous, sincere in his attachments, and true as the needle to the pole. He was no ordinary young man and he gave undoubted promise of great usefulness and distinction. Although unknown to fortune and to fame, his memory will be revered among his own circle of friends, and they will ever cherish the fond consolation that among all our honored dead, none lived a purer life or died a nobler death than Lawrence Stewart of Richmond.

Conscripts are now coming in pretty rapidly. Capt. McRae is rendering very efficient service in the Western counties in gathering up the conscripts by his mild, firm and gentlemanly course.

LONG GRABS.
[October 2, 1862]

CAMP HOLMES, near Raleigh, Oct. 3.

Messrs. Editors: Lincoln has played his last card in a desperate game. He believes he will win, but we must and will prevent him. We cannot and will not be subject to such a people.

The theatre of war now presents a noble opportunity for example of heroic and patriotic devotion. Never was there a wider field for talent or deeper soil for genius than is now presented in the cause and destiny of our native South. Every good citizen and friend of liberty should lend his best energies to the work, and by word, thought and act, whether in the field or at home, should give aid and encouragement.

Conscripts are arriving rapidly under the energetic and efficient management of Gov. Vance. They generally are more easily disciplined and are men of more tender feelings (those that have come in) than any class of military men we have. They are mostly good citizens in modest circumstances, with good and dependent families. They are not able to get substitutes or to leave home till actually compelled. They come here to do their duty and submit to orders because there is necessity, and not for frolic and excitement.

Zebulon Baird Vance (1830–1894) was the 37th and the 43rd governor of North Carolina. During the early part of the war, he commanded the 26th Regiment North Carolina Troops at the Battle of New Bern, North Carolina, in the spring of 1862, and that summer in the battles around Richmond. Later in the year he was elected governor. After the war he was again elected governor and later was a popular United States senator. This meeting between Vance and McSween would have important consequences, as McSween would write to him in 1863 asking for appointment as a war correspondent, then permission to go home and raise soldiers for the war. When his troubles with General Matt Ransom and Colonel John G. Jones arose, he wrote almost a score of letters to Vance pleading for help. Source: *The Life of Zebulon B. Vance*, Clement Dowd (Charlotte, NC: Observer Printing and Publishing House, 1897).

The Lunatic Asylum near Raleigh always attracts the attention of travellers. The building is very large and conspicuous. It cost the State $250,000 and has been in operation about seven years, during which time there have been over 500 patients under treatment — some 200 hundred of whom are there now. An ordinary case of insanity, Dr. [Edward C.] Fisher, who has charge of the Institution, says requires about six months' treatment. Not one-fifth are restored. Most of the patients are sustained by the State, for which there is an annual appropriation of $25,000. $200 is charged a year for board and treatment of a patient. The celebrated Miss [Dorothea Lynde] Dix, a northern lady who has devoted her time to charitable institutions and is now attending hospitals at the North, was instrumental in founding this Institution. A library is much needed, and there should be gardens, fields, woods, mechanical shops, and every practicable variety to suit different tastes. This would no doubt tend to palliate and remove mental derangements, which I think must be increased by idleness and solitary confinement.

Your correspondent hopes he can soon address you from the army in the field — from his post "by the flashing of the guns."

LONG GRABS.

[October 6, 1862]

Raleigh.

Messrs Editors: — The stock of goods on hand in this place is remarkably large under the circumstances, and I learn the same is the case in most other Southern towns. I understand there is more goods in Richmond than ever before. A man can buy almost any thing he wants here for money enough, which shows that the desired articles exist but are held at enormous rates. Immense quantities of goods have been smuggled in from the North under a system of connivance from both sides.

The 8th and 31st Reg'ts are still at Camp Mangum, the latter re-organized recently. Of the 8th is Col. H. M. Shaw of Currituck, Lieut. Col. W. J. Price[29] of Wilmington, and Maj. George Williamson[30] of Caswell. The companies are:

A, Capt. Hinton,[31] Perquimans,
B, Capt. Whitson,[32] Currituck,
C, Capt. McRae,[33] N. Hanover, Edgecombe and Franklin,
D, Capt. Rogers,[34] Granville and Warren,
E, Capt. Murchison,[35] Cumberland,
F, Capt. Jones,[36] Warren,
G, Capt. Yellowly,[37] Pitt,
H, Capt. Barrier,[38] Cabarrus,
I, Capt. Cobb,[39] Alamance,
K, Capt. Kennerly,[40] Rowan.

Capt. Shaw and Capt. Whitson's company are still detained in the yankee lines.

Of the 31st is Col. J. V. Jordan[41] of Newbern, Lt. Col. E. R. Liles[42] of Anson (formerly Fowle of Raleigh,) and Maj. Jesse J. Yeates[43] of Hertford. The companies:

A, Capt. Godwin,⁴⁴ Roberson,
B, Capt. Lindsay,⁴⁵ (Liles) Anson
C, Capt. Long,⁴⁶ Wake,
D, Capt. Bryan,⁴⁷ Wake,
E, Capt. Allison,⁴⁸ Orange
F, Capt. Knight,⁴⁹ Martin,
G, Capt. Pipkin,⁵⁰ Hertford,
H, Capt. Todd,⁵¹ Wake,
I, Capt. McKay,⁵² Harnett,
K, Capt. Whitley,⁵³ Craven.

The Hospital at the Peace Institute is admirably managed. I cannot speak of the scientific and professional ability of the Physicians, as I am not a competent judge, but the outward management, discipline and system is superior to what I have seen in many other hospitals. It is in a new building not completed and intended for a Presbyterian Female College and named after a gentleman who exerted himself for the enterprise and gave a liberal donation. It is under charge of Dr. Hill of New Hanover, and Dr. Joe McConnaughy of Salisbury, and another whose name I do not know.

There is nothing new in the 'Spatch, 'Spress or 'Zaminer and but little of interest any way.

      Truly Yours,
      LONG GRABS.

[October 9, 1862]

      RALEIGH, Oct 11.

Messrs Editors: I believe the "Observer" is the only secular newspaper in the State that has not at any time appeared on a half sheet. I think every paper in the State ought to maintain its size and circulation if possible. Now while we are in revolution and surrounded and beset with danger on every hand, the popular mind excited and the whole body politic agitated, it is vey essential that the Press of the State be managed with greater ability and exert an increased and beneficial influence. Newspapers make public opinion. The Press is now the most direct, speedy and powerful way to reach the populace. Editors should feel it a duty not to lie themselves nor circulate lies knowingly. It would be a great convenience if all the papers in our country could unite in some proper way, after the manner of the "Associated Press," to collect and disseminate the greatest amount of useful information. Why can't we have our soldiers duly supplied with papers and the fullest and latest news? There are plenty of wounded men who could act as couriers and carry papers and letters to every regiment and company. There should be more of energy and enterprise on the part of editors and publishers. All necessary information concerning killed, wounded, dead, missing, &c. could be readily furnished by Adjutants, officers, and others in all parts of the army, if they had any means of sending it or any body to collect it. One Adjutant cannot leave his post to visit another brigade or division, and he has not even time to write or go with his letters to the office, which may be several miles away. Much of this might be obviated by energetic and united action on the part of editors.

If newspapers could get news direct from the scene of action through their agents or associates, it would be more reliable and come quicker. The papers at the North have a system of this kind, but they cannot get correct intelligence because they all lie, from their Generals down. Our papers should discuss all questions of national policy. The people should know what they are doing. The masses should be kept intelligent and moral else the foundations of government and liberty are weakened. This responsibility rests more heavily on the conductors of the press than any other class. The people duly appreciate the duties and influence of the Press. Congress recognizes these high responsibilities, and has exempted Editors from the toils and dangers of military service, that they may encourage, enlighten and rally the people. They are sentinels on the watchtower of Liberty, to warn of danger without and expose vice and error within. The country expects these duties at their hands. Shall we be disappointed?

It has been suggested that the plow be adopted as our national coat of arms. I cannot think of a more appropriate emblem. We are the nation of the Plow. Agriculture in all its branches is represented by the plow. The plow is significant of honesty, peace, literature and christianity. The followers of the plow have in every age been distinguished in learning and the arts and famous in war. Cincinnatus quit his plow to save Rome after statesmen and heroes had failed. Washington said "if you want a great man, take him from the plow handle." This great man revered the plow. Then let us adopt the plow, which is emblematic of every thing the great Washington loved and lived for, and show by a returning sense of reason that we honor his name and appreciate his lessons of wisdom, though we did not realize them before.

The State is having a great number of guns repaired and fitted up. I see several hundred old rifles, muskets and shot guns, bought all over the State, now remodeled and turned into fine looking valuable arms. It is to be hoped that there will be a practicable outlet from the Deep River coal mines for transportation. Our country can very soon manufacture any amount of munitions for war. It would surprise many to know the number of iron foundries, smelting and rolling mills, in Lincoln, Cleveland and Gaston counties, and that section.

St. Mary's Institute, the well known Episcopal school here, is in a very flourishing condition. The number of pupils is large, and many of the most lovely and beautiful imaginable. Even the uncouth and savage nature of "Long Grabs" melts away in their charmed and angelic presence. The ladies visit the camps frequently and seem to be very fond of coming. They seem to understand camp etiquette better than formerly. At the first of the war the ladies hardly knew what to do with themselves in camp — whether to act as if they were at Church or at a party.

       Truly yours,
       Long Grabs.

[October 13, 1862]

       Raleigh, Oct. 23.

Messrs. Editors: The best and finest building in the South, that is finished, is said to be the Capitol here. It is built of granite taken from quarries in the edge of town. It was begun on the 4th July 1833 and finished 20th July 1840, the same day the completion of the Raleigh & Gaston Rail Road was celebrated. The building cost $540,000 and the furniture some $60,000 more. It is exactly where the old Capitol stood. It combines, taste, convenience and comfort, in its appearance and arrangement, and is certainly a State-ly edifice. There is a State Library containing many thousand volumes. Many of the works are more valuable from their age and scarcity than from variety of subjects and ability of contents. The Law Library in the Supreme Court room is large and very valuable, containing many important Reports and works not to be found elsewhere. In brief it is a huge vade mecum, belonging to every North Carolinian in fee-simple.

The bronze statue of Washington, from Houdon's in Richmond, adds a pleasing contrast to the carelessly arranged grounds in the beautiful enclosures. It cost $10,000 and the pedestal, railing, &c. some $3,000 more, and was erected 4th July 1857. It represents Washington as delivering his "Farewell Address," and is therefore a speaking likeness.

It is the approved opinion that commissioned officers of the army elected to the Legislature are ineligible, as the State Constitution says, persons holding places of honor, profit or trust under the Confederate Government cannot be members of the General Assembly at the same time; but it is hardly probable the issue will be made on this disqualification till the end of the first session, if then.

It is thought that all persons who furnished substitutes under 45, and residing in this State, will have to go into the service now themselves. It may be that a different construction will be adopted by the War Department, as I think should be the case. It was discretionary with the Department before to make all necessary regulations about substitutes, and a rule could have been made to exempt one furnishing a substitute for three years or until all men fit for duty had been called into service, and then it would be the duty of everybody to go. Paying a substitute to go is equivalent to going once, and no one ought to go again till all have had their turn. It is hard for a man to pay all the money he can raise for a man to go in his place and have to go himself in a week, when there are others subject to duty who are not required to go themselves nor hire others.

The impression prevails that Gov. Graham will be elected Senator in place of Mr. Davis.

Mr. Whitaker has recently bought 6,000 bushels of Salt at the Salt Works in Virginia as agent for this County. He paid $1 50 a bushel, and it will cost perhaps a dollar more per bushel to get it here. This is a good arrangement. The rail roads will bring it for him a good part of the way. It is very fine white salt and hardly as strong as Liverpool salt. It is said that Sound salt if it is bitter, will not cure meat well.

There should be two or three more stages between here and Fayetteville to accommodate increased travel.

The "Southern Illustrated News" is a fine large paper recently started in Richmond. It seems to be as well managed and is beginning to gain public confidence and favor. Such a work properly conducted is much needed just now. Most of the writers of the South are engaged to contribute to it, but what do you think? Not a word has been said to "Long Grabs" to correspond! (By the way, the Petersburg Express must give due credit when it uses articles from "Long Grabs.")

I fear there is much suffering among the poor classes. A very old and feeble woman met me on the road and begged me to help her get something to eat. I run my hand in my long and almost empty pocket and after diligent search could find only a small shinplaster, which I gave her with a most sympathetic flow of "pheelinks." (Of course them agents of Ladies' Societies will not call on L. G.) It seems that matters are coming to a focus and if times get much harder a good many of us must do like Red Hugh—hunt out a hollow tree to live in.

LONG GRABS.

[October 27, 1862]

RALEIGH, Oct. 29, 1862.

Messrs. Editors: A few days ago I took a stroll in the department of the Southern Tract Society here, which is under charge of Rev. W. J. W. Crowder. He is devoted to the work and evidently manages the affairs of the Society with great energy and efficiency. Thousands of tracts containing moral and other valuable instruction are daily sent from here to all sections of our country, and especially to the army. The influence thus exerted on our troops has undoubtedly effected much in the way of discipline and moral courage, and patience and fortitude when exposed to danger and hardships. This way of being exposed to all manner of disease and continually liable to be shot at, has a great tendency to make one think solemnly and seriously about matters, unless he has been raised to such business and never knew any thing else. Consequently people are apt to give more sincere attention to religion under such circumstances. All the Tracts issued here are prepared under the joint supervision and consent of four Ministers — the pastors of the Methodist, Baptist, Presbyterian and Episcopal Churches of Raleigh. The New Testament is published here too, but the printing is done at Atlanta. The entire Bible has not yet been published South, but soon will be by this Society. All this work is paid for and kept up by voluntary donations and contributions throughout the country. The works are distributed gratis. Mr. Crowder charges nothing for his labor. He belongs to the Methodist denomination and was raised in Wake county.

Messrs. Thiem & Frapps have a manufactory here to make saddle frames and wooden bottom shoes. They are Germans, are practical mechanics and have been in this country several years. They employ some 125 hands (mostly citizens of Raleigh) and have large contracts of Government work. They are engaged now on saddle-trees, and make over 100 a day. They make large quantities of glue, much of which is used by themselves, and they supply the Ordnance Department at Richmond also. Wooden bottom shoes will answer very well for plantation use when nothing better can be had. The bottom should fit the foot well and the upper may be of leather or strong cloth sewed or nailed to the bottom.

Copperas, I learn, is made in Cleveland and Johnston counties, and alum is found in McDowell county and elsewhere. People everywhere would do well to gather such herbs and roots as are in great demand for their medicinal properties, and forward them to the Doctors appointed by the Government to get these things and manufacture medicine for the army. They will pay high prices for the articles for which they have advertised.

LONG GRABS.

[November 13, 1862]

Chapter 4

Reporting from Virginia
October 31, 1862 – March 12, 1863

After his travels to the conscription camps and looking around Raleigh, Long Grabs left for Virginia, where, as he wrote earlier, he hoped he can soon write to his readers from the army in the field — from his post "by the flashing of the guns." McSween probably took a train from Raleigh to Weldon on the Raleigh & Gaston Railroad. He could take the Weldon Railroad, also known as the Petersburg Railroad, to Petersburg, and then take the Richmond & Petersburg Railroad into the city.

He will spend about five and a half months there, with a short break around Christmas, when he returns to North Carolina for some rest and relaxation. There is still no indication that he belongs to any military unit. His last assignment was as drill master at Camp Mangum and Gulick had dismissed him from that after he was late reporting back from his first trip to Virginia. So, as he did on his trips to the camps and sightseeing in Raleigh, he wanders from place to place, visiting the regiments and talking with the soldiers and commanders, gathering news, without anyone seeming to have the slightest idea where he belongs or what he is doing. It would be interesting to know how he passed himself off to the people he met on his wanderings and whether he was in military uniform or in civilian clothes, but there is no information on this point. Whatever his condition he was always well-met and accepted for whatever he was doing.

He stops in Richmond and Charlottesville, then visits camps in Culpepper. In Charlottesville he visits the campus of the University of Virginia, and as he attended the University of North Carolina at Chapel Hill, he makes comparisons, indicating what he likes about the Virginia school and what he does not. He does feel, though, that the University of Virginia has a more handsome president than Chapel Hill's.

During his travels to Statesville and other western areas, Long Grabs had become acquainted with the newly elected governor of North Carolina,

64 Confederate Incognito

Zebulon Baird Vance, the former commander of the 26th North Carolina Regiment. He wrote to him in late November describing the plight of the North Carolina soldiers, especially after the Maryland campaign. It would be the first of many letters he would write to Vance. In December the Battle of Fredericksburg took place and Long Grabs makes attempts to get there, but the Confederate authorities were preventing newspaper reporters from going there. There is the threat of being locked up in Castle Thunder, a Confederate prison, for those who disobeyed the orders. He does go later and discusses the battle with General Stuart.

He spends considerable time in Richmond, visiting various places of entertainment, describing the goings and comings of the citizens, and visiting the Confederate Congress with Generals A. P. Hill and Stuart and writing sketches of some of the members. All of these activities he faithfully reports to the *Fayetteville Observer*. He writes a final letter describing President Jefferson Davis before his return to North Carolina.

EXCHANGE HOTEL, RICHMOND, Oct. 31, 1862.

Messrs. Editors:— It is much easier to get into Richmond than to get out. Old Job could not have been the man he was if he had visited Richmond. By the time the old man would have gotten through with all the officers and departments necessary about his furlough or passport, I think he would have indulged a few oaths if he did not become belligerent. But I must say that all the officials in the several departments are disposed to accommodate and will do the best they can for every one if approached intelligently and respectfully, so far as my experience goes.

The C. S. Surgeon General, I am informed, dislikes the action of Congress in classifying the Hospitals according to States. It is very desirable that the sick and wounded of each State be kept separate as far as possible. All the States sent abundant supplies to their sick and showed great attention to them last year, but since then I learn that North Carolina and Georgia alone have kept up these duties. Our noble old State provided for her troops in the way of clothing, pay, bounty and other things, better than any other. There may be some 3,000 sick and wounded about the city now and in quarters near the city. The sick here in many places need potatoes (Irish are best) and all kinds of vegetables and fresh meats and clothing. Any thing that will not be damaged by a few days delay will be forwarded by Dr. Warren at Raleigh, if left to his care — or it would be better to send direct by some one coming through — Dr. Warren would furnish transportation. Clothing had better be sent in bundles and other articles in bags, as much as possible. The person bringing them must hire them carried from one train to another at Weldon, Petersburg and here again from Railroad to Hospital or wherever they are to go. The Railroad authorities are very careless and no one should leave to them the entire management of transportation, but attend to it himself at all times.

Gen Bragg is here. An officer of a Tennessee Reg't, a native of N. C., who was at the battle of Perryville, says our victory there was decisive. The yankees were driven clear off the field and we fell back the next day to save our immense stores that might be endangered and to unite with Smith who had gone to another place where the battle was expected instead of Perryville.

The cost of living and all necessaries here is enormous. For instance, hotel charges are, breakfast $1 50, dinner $2, supper $1, lodging $1 50, with fuel, soap and whiskey extra. There are cheaper hotels but it is not prudent, unless they are properly recommended, as crime and robbery are very common.

I leave to-morrow for the army of the Potomac.

LONG GRABS.

[November 6, 1862]

Long Grabs described a cemetery which lies on the grounds of the University of Virginia. At the time of his visit there were 600 Confederate graves. As the war intensified, more bodies were brought there for burial, and by the end of the conflict, 1,097 Confederate soldiers were interred there.[1]

CHARLOTTESVILLE, Va., Nov'r 2, 1862.

Messrs Editors: This is rather a hard place, but a darkey got very mad when I said it was a one-horse town. There is one very bad custom here which will injure the reputation of the town abroad. The barkeeper pours out your drink himself (a very small one too) for which half a dollar is charged. Every good citizen must feel indignant that the ancient privilege of every freeman to measure his own drink has been violated.

I did find the hospitals here in better condition and the sick are better attended to that I have seen yet. The number of sick and wounded soldiers here is not now so large as formerly. Many of them are North Carolinians, but they need nothing except perhaps clothing. They get furloughs to home generally as soon as they are able to travel, and they can get clothes then more conveniently at home. The ladies of the town have formed an Association and take it by turns to attend the cooking and superintend the hospitals. They do a great deal for the sick and send them nourishments. Many a poor soldier will remember the kindness of the ladies of Charlottesville with heart-felt gratitude. The hospitals are comfortable and well ventilated. The Surgeon in charge is Dr. Cabell of the University, an excellent, kind and accommodating man, I think. Dr. Warren sent a lot of medicines and hospital stores with me, which I left in Richmond, where there is certainly great need for them.

I visited the University burying ground yesterday, where there are some 600 soldiers' graves. I saw the names of many North Carolinians. Friends, brothers and strangers, from every part of the Confederacy, they stood shoulder to shoulder in a common cause while living, and now lie side by side in death, an everlasting monument to their devotion to each other and to their country! Let the invader know as he advances, that we are united for weal or woe, and will share together one destiny — a glorious victory or die a glorious death.

The University of Virginia is near this place. There are only some 40 students this session. There have been over 600 in times past. The buildings, I think, are badly constructed and arranged. The dormitories are all one story and have a

Burial markers were usually of wood, with a name and regiment carved on. Often, after the battle parents, relatives, or friends would come to claim the remains and take them home for burial. Sometimes bodies were shipped home in wooden caskets or were buried without a headstone but near a particular landmark like a tree or rocky outcropping. In the illustration here, friends or fellow company soldiers are burying the soldier, and in some cases the body was retrieved after the war and brought home. Depending where the soldier was and the location of the battlefield, his comrades would wrap his body in his blanket and place him in the ground. Source: "Soldiers' graveyard, in the camp near Falmouth, Va."— Frank Leslie, *Famous Leaders and Battle Scenes of the Civil War* (New York: Mrs. Frank Leslie, 1896) p. 455. Used by permission of the Florida Center for Instructional Technology, College of Education, University of South Florida.

useless display of round-top windows and prison-like apartments. Huge pillars and almost endless lines of colonnade encircle the campus, which must have originated from a very imperfect conception of beauty, convenience and economy in architecture. There is a very large building which is a centre for the others. (Headquarters, a la Militaire,) containing the College Library, Commencement Hall, &c. which resembles a large depot and engine house combined, if I can compare it to any structure. View it from any side you please, it seems to set backwards. There are a great many buildings scattered irregularly around the hills and valleys. The University was established by the Legislature of Virginia in 1819, and went into operation in 1825. Mr. Jefferson did more than any one else in establishing and sustaining the College. Students take such studies as they choose here. It would require six or seven years to graduate in all the Departments, with a good preparation at the start. Very few students remain longer than two or three years. Out of 600 students a year there are not 20 graduates. Certificates of completing particular Departments area given, but no regular Diploma for graduation unless all is completed. I do not think the students study as hard here as at Chapel Hill, and there is not so much attention given to the Societies. The College Library has some 30,000 volumes and the Societies have no libraries, I believe. Not more than half the students belong to the Societies. There is no regular Chaplain or system of religious instruction. The students and faculty employ some Minister for a term of two years, and take them alternately from four orthodox denominations. There is not that sociability, intermixing and competition that exist at Chapel Hill. This has a large and abler Faculty than any other Southern College and is better supplied with all the Departments, necessaries, appliances, &c. A young man can find no better opportunities of a thorough education than is afforded here, if he chooses to use them; but there is very little constraint to study. The college and all its fixtures up to this time have cost, (Dr. Maupin says) about $600,000. The University at Chapel Hill is better arranged and in a much prettier place, but has not so handsome a President as the University of Virginia.

I visited Monticello to-day, the former residence of President Jefferson. It is about three miles off, on the top of a high hill, and commands a beautiful view. It is a plain brick structure with two or three porticos and wings, and it seems that Mr. Jefferson intended everything about there for use as well as ornament. The estate once embracing thousands of acres now number only 200, and belonged to Capt. U. K. Levy of the U. S. Army, but will now go to the Confederacy under the Sequestration Act, as Levy left us and took the oath of allegiance to the Northern Government. He died in New York last April. The place and buildings are in a very dilapidated condition. An old miserly looking individual occupies the house and shows people around with as much indifference as a large hog would eat an ear of corn. He charges half a dollar for this interesting proceeding. The family burial ground is some 300 yards from the house, and a plain granite block marks the last resting place of the great Jefferson. The magnificent edifice, once the centre of splendor and greatness, is now tumbling to ruins, a mournful emblem of the disruption of that Government the "sage of Monticello" had labored so long to establish.

The crop in this vicinity I learn is not an average one, and it is thought there will not be much to spare from home consumption.

It is evident that the army is falling back from Winchester, and I will be more apt to meet most of the N. C. Regiments by changing my route by Culpeper C. H. I could tell you of some important movements soon to be effected by our troops, but by the terms of my passport I am not allowed to make such facts public unless by consent of the commanding officers of Army Corps.

LONG GRABS.

[November 10, 1862]

Long Grabs refers to a battle fought on August 9, 1862, at Cedar Mountain, also known as Slaughter's Mountain or Cedar Run. There Union forces under the command of General John Pope clashed with the Confederates under Stonewall Jackson. Victory and possession of the battlefield was won by the Southerners, but with a price. Losses on the Confederate side were 1,314 in killed and wounded, while Northern losses were 2,381 in killed, wounded and captured.[2]

He also refers to the "celebrated orders" issued by General Pope and their effect on civilians. Among them were General Order No. 5, which directed his soldiers to live off the land and pay only loyal citizens for anything taken from them; General Order No. 6 ordered his men to travel with only two days' rations and take anything else they needed from civilians; General Order No. 7 made the civilian population responsible for stopping any destruction to Union property and guerrilla activity. Anything destroyed, like a food depot or telegraph line, had to be replaced by the citizens where the event happened. Anyone caught in an act of destruction was to be shot. Still, despite the harshness of these and other orders, many Federal units continued to act toward the civilian population with restraint.[3]

CULPEPER C. H., VA., Nov. 5, 1862.

Messrs. Editors: This was once the flourishing, enterprising centre of a wealthy, intelligent county, but it is distressing to see the devastation and ruin committed by Pope and his devils during their six weeks' stay. The fertile fields of Culpeper are now one desert waste. There may not be 100 negroes in the county, and there were many thousands before. There is hardly a wagon, horse, hog or creeping thing left in the whole country; and smoke houses, cribs, barns and gardens have been completely robbed and nearly every stick of fence is burnt. Families however and their houses and furniture here at the time were not interfered with otherwise seriously except in a few instances. The yankees would often come to houses and demand something to eat and would sometimes require clothing and supplies for their sick and wounded. The battle of Cedar Run took place six miles south of here, which ended their career in this section. Pope had his headquarter here when he issued those celebrated orders authorizing his men to do as they pleased. These citizens still remaining are trying to live, but starvation and misery seem inevitable. Yet they bear their calamities with heroic fortitude and are doing all they can to accommodate the soldiers and supply the sick, of whom there is a great number now in the hospitals here. Longstreet's Army corps is here and others are expected to pass along this way, and they are leaving the sick and worn out mostly here, as this is the first station they could reach on the Railroad.

The ladies have formed an Association for the purpose of supplying delicacies and necessaries to the Hospitals, and some one or two of them are at the place of deposit every day to deal out to the different wards as they need. But few articles can be had, as there is no poultry, vegetables, and little bed clothing in the country. The sick are certainly suffering for such necessaries. There are no servants nor

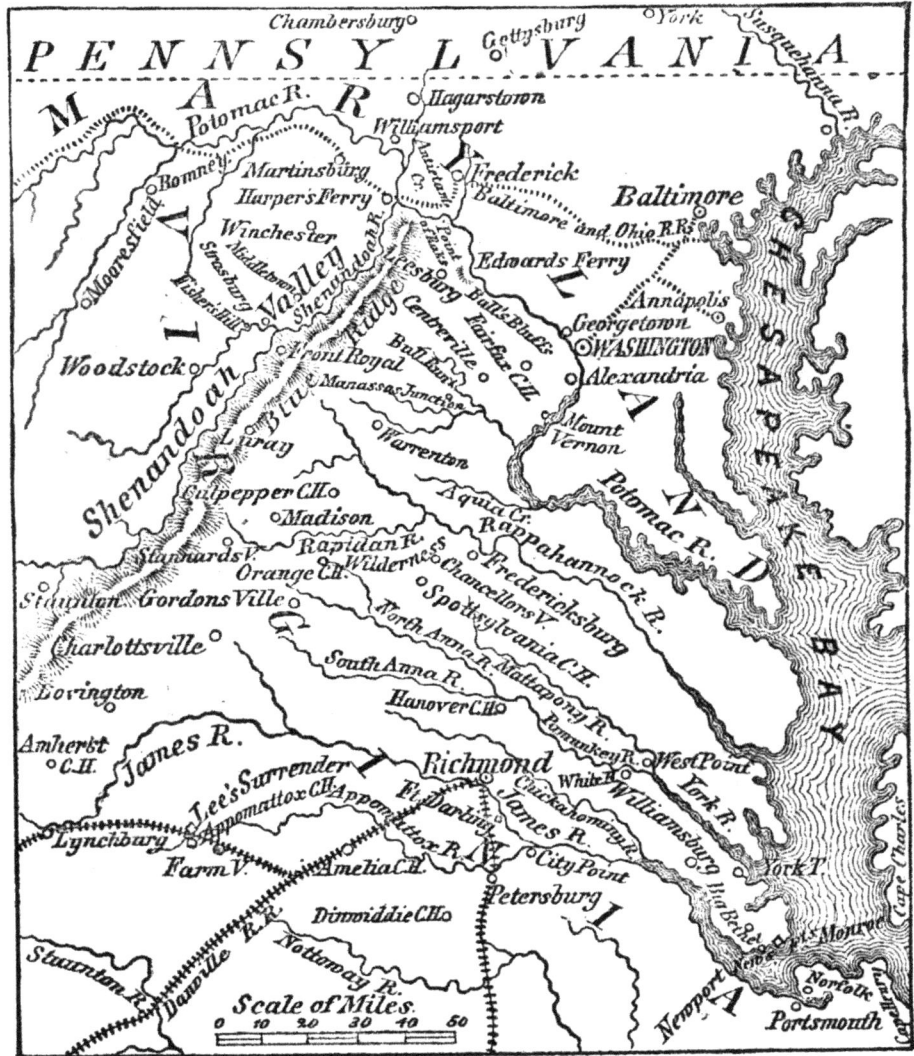

Seat of War in the East. McSween travels west to Charlottesville, a distance of about 70 miles. From there he will head north to Culpepper [*sic*] Court House, about 45 miles away. In November he returns to Richmond. In December he will try to get to Fredericksburg, almost 60 miles north of Richmond, to gather information on the battle, but the authorities are keeping most reporters away. After taking time off for Christmas and a visit to Wake Forest College just north of Raleigh, he visits Fredericksburg, spending almost a month there before returning to Richmond. Source: Marcius Wilson, *History of the United States* (New York, New York: Ivison, Blakeman, Taylor, and Co.,) 1872. Map used by permission of the Florida Center for Instructional Technology, College of Education, University of South Florida.

"Culpepper [*sic*] Courthouse, capital of Culpepper [*sic*] County, Va. This pretty little place, more frequently called Fairfax, in honor of Lord Fairfax, the old proprietor of the land hereabouts, is a post village on the Orange and Alexandria railroad. It is surrounded by a finely diversified and fertile country, and has many fine old-fashioned planters' seats scattered about. In 1862 it contained four churches, two newspaper offices and a Masonic Hall. Its population was about eight thousand two hundred. It was established in 1759 and incorporated in 1834. It is named Culpepper [*sic*] after Lord Culpepper [*sic*], the English Governor of Virginia from 1703 to 1708. It is thirty miles from Fredericksburg, nearly ninety from Richmond, and twenty-six from Gordonsville. Fairfax or Culpepper [*sic*] was distinguished early in the war of the revolution for the services of her gallant 'minute men.'" Source: Frank Leslie, *Famous Leaders and Battle Scenes of the Civil War* (New York: Mrs. Frank Leslie, 1896) p. 371. According to the 1860 Census, the total population of Culpeper County was 12,063, and half of them were slaves. Used by permission of the Florida Center for Instructional Technology, College of Education, University of South Florida.

hospital furniture enough. Hundreds of patients are coming in every day but there is little accommodating for them. Those who are able are sent away to Orange C. H., Gordonsville and Richmond. Many of those here are very sick. The most fatal disease I believe is pneumonia. Our army in marching four days continuously from Winchester has been badly used up. A good many too are barefooted and they have but few blankets and tents and not much clothing and that in bad condition. A few regiments have recently drawn clothing and shoes. The decrease in numbers by death, mostly from disease, is almost incredible. These men have evidently seen service, but they are still ready for the enemy and as determined as the first day they left home. The army of the Potomac justly deserves the title of the "noble army of Martyrs." My observation teaches me that he that belongeth to Lee's army is of few days and short rations. He striketh his teeth against much hard bread and is satisfied. He goeth away that he may get food, but lo! the long roll beateth and he cometh away empty. He layeth himself down in the wilderness and straightway giveth up the ghost and no man knoweth of his sepulcher.

I regret very much to see that gambling is carried on so extensively in the army. The old games of faro and chuckaluck much practiced at the Scotch Fair for many years are most common. Soldiers bet away their pay, bounty, clothes and every thing they can get. I have seen little of this however among North and South Carolinians. The discipline here is not rigid except perhaps Ransom's Brigade. There is a universal condemnation of straggling; it is the most serious evil under which our Army labors. Gen. A. P. Hill was raised in this place and is a native of the county. Mr. Wallack's family, Editor of the Washington "Star," reside here. Their premises were hardly molested by the yankees, but I believe our troops are helping themselves, and I regret to say that our troops take from the citizens nearly as bad as the yankees did. Tuesday I was talking with Mr. George, a Baptist Minister near town, and he was pointing out the destruction done by the yankees on his plantation, when we discovered a soldier from some artillery company riding off Mr. George's only horse. A party had been there a few minutes before and carried off his grindstone and a load of cabbage.

There are a great many reports of skirmishes, battles, &c. above here and towards Loudoun and Manassas. There certainly has been fighting, but how, when or what, I cannot say. I heard heavy cannonading that way to-day. There may be a general fight somewhere in this section before the winter sets in fully. McClellan's army has fallen back no doubt on Washington, and may try to come through to Richmond this way immediately. He may try to cut our army off in detail, but if he does he will be very apt to be devoured by piece-meal. The soldiers are unable to get news from home or to see any papers. It is almost a state of exile to them. Can't the people at home send them papers containing news about home? They can hear all accounts of battles, &c. and often see Richmond papers — foreign matter to our soldiers. Let the old copies of papers in the State be sent continually.

LONG GRABS.

[November 14, 1862]

CULPEPER COURT HOUSE, VA., Nov. 7, 1862.

Messrs. Editors: We now have snow and very cold weather which certainly places our brave troops in a very distressing situation. Most of them have no tents, no blankets, and some are bare-footed. Just think of the poor soldier who is sleeping among brush near a cold smoking fire, with nothing to protect him from the snow and cold. I stayed in camp last night, and it is certainly an exposure which the most robust constitution cannot undergo long. Let the people send a pair of socks, a blanket, quilt or coat, or something of the kind, and send it too so as the soldier may get it. Much of the loss of baggage and clothing results from the mismanagement and want of vigilance on the part of Quartermasters. Much of the baggage left by the army on the march is plundered and stolen by other troops. Yesterday I heard a Captain speaking of the good clothes and useful articles he and his friends secured from the baggage of the 14th N. C. Troops, if I am not mistaken, stored at Gordonsville. He was a Virginia officer and had been sent there with a detail of men to take care of the baggage of his division. The hospitals here are filled and more arrive continually in large numbers. All the sick are being removed to Gordonsville, which is to be a distributing hospital, and these are to be discontinued. Some of the troops here are moving about, but probably none have entirely left yet. The balance of the army is still in the Valley up towards Winchester. Cavalry skirmish from Harper's Ferry to Warrenton. It seems that our authorities anticipate no serious engagements along the Potomac this winter, but it is generally expected that we are to have desperate work on the coast. Gen. Lee stays in a small tent, notwithstanding the weather. Like Napoleon, he refuses quarters in lordly palaces and prefers to share the life of his soldiers. He has the universal respect and admiration of the army as far as my observation extends. I was at his headquarters and had a good opportunity to see and converse with the man who wields in his hand the destiny of the Confederacy. He seems to be some 60 years of age, about 6 feet high, and weighs probably 175 lbs. He has a noble countenance, mild, generous and manly; a quick, soft dark eye and a firm intellectual brow. His beard is full and long and nearly white, covering a rather dark face of fine shape and well formed features. His manners are those of a high-toned gentleman, with whom refined society, the business of the world and the character of men are alike familiar. He speaks in a pleasant tone, distinct, slow and careless, but to the point, and with an easy, but not useless, flow of language. His dress, furniture and equipments are simple, neat and necessary, and he is entirely approachable by the meanest private, without any salute, form or distinction of rank. His staff officers mingle with him and act in his presence as they would with an aged and esteemed friend. There is an irresistible something about him that commands respect, and you go away from him satisfied that he is a man of genius, talent and greatness, but why you cannot explain. His family now resides in Raleigh and he has a daughter at St. Mary's School. He is of Episcopalian persuasion. I saw on the Comptroller's book that he has taken $8000 N. C. State Bonds at one time, and perhaps more again.

Some portions of the medical department in Virginia are certainly very badly conducted. The neglect and mismanagement of some physicians have no doubt done much to bring many of our brave boys to an untimely grave, till the decrease of our army is truly appalling. I must give you an order from one of the hospitals on the Quartermaster for a coffin, which is decidedly significant though not intended to express its full meaning:

    Hospital No. _____, Nov. _____, 1862.
Capt. _____, A. Q. Mm, Post _____:
 Furnish coffins for three patients who died in Ward No. 10 this morning.
       By order of
    _____ _____, Surgeon in charge.

Where are the Chaplains and what are they doing? I have seen but one Chaplain at his post. I think all our N. C. regiments had Chaplains who are probably getting pay, but the troops, it seems, have no one to cheer them and comfort them in danger and calm their dying moments with the consolations of our holy religion.

       Long Grabs.

P. S. I have just learned that there is probability of an immediate battle about here. There have been so many exaggerated reports of the kind recently that I attach but little importance to them. This, however, seems to have the shadow of authenticity. It is stated that the enemy are advancing in force from Warrenton, 25 miles distant. Cavalry are scouting, supported by heavy forces of infantry and artillery. I saw a Lieutenant of the 19th N. C., (cavalry,) who had been with a detachment of some 800 cavalry in occupation of Warrenton for the last two weeks. They were driven away day before yesterday by a superior force and narrowly escaped capture. Stuart and his cavalry fell in with them on their retreat and came on with them, and they are all encamped six miles North of this place. I hardly think the whole army of McClellan is coming over. Longstreet's army corps is here and Stuart with some 1200 cavalry. All the artillery and forces are held ready to move and the hospitals are being moved.

L. G.

[November 14, 1862]

RICHMOND, Nov. 14

Messrs. Editors: The Army about Culpepper has undergone but little change in any respect since I last wrote you. The enemy is in strong force near there, but there has been no general engagement and it seems that both sides are not disposed to have a great battle. It is generally conjectured that Gen. Lee wishes to draw Gen. McClellan away from the Potomac. If the yankees fight at Culpepper or between there and Gordonsville, our forces will have the advantage in ground, transportation and supplies. In case of defeat McClellan would have a long and difficult retreat through a country incapable of affording him sustenance; while in a similar event our forces could fall back by railroad and otherwise towards Richmond and collect supplies and reinforcements abundantly and rapidly. Gen. Lee can combine his forces very easily if he considers it necessary.

There must be great difficulty in battle to distinguish the Northern and Southern soldiers, as a great many of our soldiers wear yankee clothing. It will certainly result in confusion and injury to our cause if continued. Our troops are so scantily furnished with clothing now that they are compelled to wear whatever they can get, but the coats should be dyed another color. Some of the good people of Fauquier were frightened very badly at what they thought was a regiment of "blue coats," but really our own men with yankee uniforms.

I heard this morning that the yankee army near Culpepper has fallen back. It is supposed that there were some 50,000 or more of them on a sort of reconnaissance, and that they have made a feint of retiring and intend to advance in full force. I have confidence in our ability to sustain and repulse an attack in the vicinity of Gordonsville and Culpepper.

Developments from Lord Lyons, who has just arrived in New York, are awaited in anxious suspense. We may expect something, but it will no doubt consist of indefinite propositions, or at least such as are not practical or pertinent at immediate action. Simple recognition at this time by the European powers would be as much value to us as anything they are likely to do, but this is not expected by those whose opinions command most respect.

I visited Drury's Bluff yesterday. The fortifications there are very formidable

"Drury's Bluff, a Confederate position on the James River, near Richmond, Va. The principal Confederate defense of Richmond was Fort Darling, a heavy work on a high bank called Drury's Bluff, eight miles below Richmond. Here the river was closed with heavy piling and vessels loaded with stone sunk in the channel. The work was casemated and mounted with heavy guns. It will be remembered that the Federal ironclads, the *Galena* and the *Monitor*, were repulsed here during the progress of the Peninsular campaign. The *Monitor* was unable to elevate her guns sufficiently to reach the works, and the sides of the *Galena* were not thick enough to resist the plunging shot from the fort, which struck its sides at right angles. The *Naugatuck*, the only other vessel engaged in the assault, burst her single gun on the second discharge." Source: Frank Leslie, *Famous Leaders and Battle Scenes of the Civil War* (New York: Mrs. Frank Leslie, 1896) p. 362. Used by permission of the Florida Center for Instructional Technology, College of Education, University of South Florida.

and are sufficient to resist any attack from the river. The iron clad Merrimac No. 2 is now about completed and there are two or three other gunboats building here also, and the steamer Patrick Henry and three or four other smaller vessels, all well armed, occupy the river above Drury's Bluff.

I learn the Government here will be unable to supply shoes and blankets to all the troops and cannot furnish the necessary clothing and must rely on the States and patriotism of the people for these things, or the soldiers must suffer. I believe enough material can be procured for shoes and clothing, but the articles cannot be furnished from Government sources till late in the winter, if at all. The people should act in this matter at once and with more system and less extravagance than before.

LONG GRABS.

[November 17, 1862]

On November 17, McSween wrote a moving letter to the governor of North Carolina, Zebulon Baird Vance:

4. Reporting from Virginia

It may be proper to give you a brief statement of the condition of the N. C. Troops in Virginia whom I have recently seen — Our troops about Petersburg & Richmond are not in absolute need of many articles. Our soldiers in the Army of the Potomac need shoes, blankets & clothes very badly — The companies there average probably 30 effective men each. About one third are barefooted or the same as barefooted — I saw many men marching in the snow entirely without shoes or any substitute — There are perhaps 10 men in a company well shod — Very few men are amply supplied with blankets, many have none and others have only one thin blanket apiece. Our soldiers in the Army of the Potomac have been generally several weeks without changing their clothes having left or lost their baggage before their trip to Maryland. They are of course ragged and dirty, and itch vermin and disease are very prevalent — Much of the baggage they left when starting on their march has been damaged, stolen or misplaced since they left — Nearly every soldier in the Regiments that have been through the battles in Northern Virginia and Maryland are without sufficient clothing, and a great majority of them are in very great need of all articles of clothing. The articles I think most necessary are shoes, blankets, pants and coats & should be supplied first — Many of the Quarter Masters are endeavoring to get supplies for the men, but they have to await the action of the Quarter Masters Department at Richmond — Col. Myers the Quarter Master General told me that the Government proposes to furnish the troops, but that it would be late before it could be done — He says he will be very seriously embarrassed in this arrangement if he cannot have control of the resources & manufacturers of North Carolina — From what I could ascertain I am satisfied the authorities at Richmond will be unable to supply all the troops properly — It will certainly be impossible for them to get shoes and blankets enough in time — Gen. Lee says he does not wish the troops to have two or more supplies and hopes that economy and system will be practiced — He regards an over abundant supply as a useless waste of our scanty resources & a serious impediment to his movements & plans. I do not think overcoats strictly necessary, and they are certain to be lost if the army has to fight & march much — There is but little use for them on the march or in winter quarters — A good common suit with plenty of under clothing and a good large blanket is amply sufficient and as much as the soldier can possibly carry & save — The soldier can generally buy socks & underclothing or get them from home, but outside clothing & blankets cannot be got by the privates generally.

Any sort of a hat or cap will do and they manage to make substitutes for gloves & socks from old clothing — It matters but little what is the color of the clothing — so it is not blue — It is very unfortunate so many of our men wear Yankee clothing and blue uniforms — It would be well if the coats were dyed another color — It would be to the interest of North Carolina & her soldiers if the state would retain control of her own manufacturers & resources till her own troops are supplied, for I have noticed that other States have furnished less & their troops in greater need than ours and thus her resources might be exhausted on others while her own sons are suffering — The hospitals are generally needy of supplies — I think it highly proper to have the hospital furnished with underclothing for the patients — These articles should remain at the hospitals & only be used by the soldiers while there — This change & cleanliness would no doubt have a very desirable effect — Many a sick soldier lies for weeks in rags and filth and actually rots away with disease — When such is the case the citizens have been entirely robbed by the enemy or have exhausted their supply heretofore by furnishing the hospitals. The Government does not furnish these articles — The proper vegetables & nourishment for the sick are needed especially in Richmond, Gordonsville & Culpepper & and there is no way to get them. The State should assist in the manufacture & purchase of medicine.4

RICHMOND, VA., Dec. 9, 1862.

  Messrs. Editors: Again would the veritable "Long Grabs" drop a few lines for the consideration of the good people and bad, pretty people and ugly, in divers places, who read the Observer. Richmond, I suppose, is now the greatest place in the Confederacy. It is still the same old Richmond that used to be a dull monotonous country town, regarded by travellers as a country borough and rail station, but now aroused into all the activity, enterprise and energy of the Metropolis of a Great Republic. The city is taxed beyond its capacity in almost every respect, but an enterprising people moved by necessity and other influences will soon remedy this deficiency. There are many objections to making Richmond the permanent Capital of the Confederacy, though its prosperity as a city need not depend on that. With all its recent growth and improvement the city has greatly increased in those vicious elements of society more common in Northern cities. Hundreds of desperadoes and all sorts of evil doers who have for years infested Baltimore, Washington and other cities, now cluster here like birds of prey and find a rich and open field for their operations. The authorities make great efforts to suppress and eradicate them, but it is like separating the "tares from the wheat" — the one cannot be destroyed without the other. These pests of the community often meet with deserved punishment, but like bad boys at school who remember the rules only while they feel the lash, they respect the law only when they feel its penalties. It has been a noticeable fact that since our separation from the North we have been clear of pick-pockets, but we meet with a more unwelcome character in the person of the garroter. The pick-pocket had great respect for your feelings and glided his slippery fingers about your pocket book or watch without disturbing or offending the most delicate sensibilities; but the savage garroter throws a rope around you and jerks you into a dark passage, knocks you down, puts out your eyes, chokes you, takes all your valuables and even your clothing, and leaves you very much like him of olden time who "fell among thieves," except that you may wait in vain for the "good Samaritan." It is extremely dangerous to go about the city much at night. When I have occasion to be out, if it is very dark I walk the middle of the street and keep a constant look out above, below and all around me, with my hand on my repeater. There are a great many gambling places, notwithstanding the law against it; and they enjoy a bounteous patronage from officers and other moneyed men. Faro is mostly practiced, from which the proprietors soon amass great fortunes — often clearing thousands of dollars a day, and a day's operations hardly ever foots up any loss to them. Some of these establishments, especially one or two on Main street, are fitted up and furnished in the most extravagant style. The halls, dining rooms, carpeting and furniture are really magnificent; superb paintings grace the wall; the table is furnished with all that the heart can wish; the daintiest dishes and the richest meats served in the most elegant china, are strewn over the snow white cloth, interspersed with flowered napkins, silver spoons, castors, and plate, and glittering goblets filled with mellow sparkling wine,—all free of charge to every comer and goer who can give "the countersign" and pass the "inner gate." You feel as if you were feasting with the gods instead of eating forbidden fruit within the tempting realms of Satan. Day after day, and night after night, officers, government clerks and "high officials" resort here expecting some new "streak of luck" or turn of "tide in the affairs of men," with that blind infatuation so characteristic of the victims of ruin and vice. The misfortunes of the country have been an inducement to many a young man to yield his honor and integrity under the powerful influence of these and similar allurements of vice, till many a pure heart and noble soul have sunk first to recklessness and vice and finally to crime and disgrace. Many finely dressed young men, government clerks and refugees I suppose, can be seen every night at these faro banks, and are always full of money. Where or how they get it is a mystery. One of these worthies draws out from $1000 to $5000 of new money and very probably loses it all, and in a night or two he comes up again with the same or a larger amount. He gets only a few hundred dollars a year as a clerk, and perhaps the yankees destroyed or confiscated his property if he had any. Then how is this money produced? There is something — much — wrong hereabouts — something "rotten in Denmark." One of these establishments is owned by a wealthy man who has already acquired a princely fortune at the business. He entrusts the management of the business now entirely to clerks and employees, while he lies back in royal luxury, surrounded by every comfort and object that can gratify human desire and passion.

"All quiet along the Rappahannock to-night."

Truly yours,

LONG GRABS.

[December 11, 1862]

RICHMOND, Dec. 12, 1862.

Messrs. Editors:—North Carolina needs an agency here for her soldiers and for receiving and transporting supplies, baggage and private donations, papers, &c., for the army. There has been a depot here for N. C. Troops, but the plan on which it is established and its mode of operation have not been such as to secure that success and benefit intended. There should be a wayside home for every North Carolina soldier—a place of intelligence, where the soldier could get information about any thing pertaining to his duty or interest. Gov. Vance has endeavored to establish such an institution, but the depot organized here before by Gov. Clark or Ellis remains the same and is not adequate to the present exigencies. As to what he wished the agency to be, Gov. Vance said in a letter to the gentleman who was to carry out the object: "I desire it to be a general Headquarters for every North Carolina soldier, where he can feel at home and always find a ready welcome. Let the soldier know that he is among friends and furnish him with all necessary comfort and accommodation. If he be hungry, feed him, if he be naked, clothe him, if he be sick and distressed, minister to his wants. Assist him to the hospital or in getting his pay or passport, furlough or discharge if necessary; if he cannot find his regiment, direct him where it is; see that he gets on the cars properly and tell him where he must change his route and how and who he must see. Make it your duty to relieve the wants of our brave soldiers, to instruct and encourage them as to their duties, interests, &c., and to send them on their way rejoicing. Employ every means and afford every facility to them and their friends to the attainment of these objects, and spare neither pains nor expense to their accomplishment."

It would be proper that such an agent be empowered also to collect all claims of widows and orphans of deceased soldiers. The greatest difficulty heretofore in collecting arrears due deceased soldiers is to prove that the soldier is actually dead. In many cases it is impossible for the widow or daughter to produce any evidence except hearsay or some private letter from some unknown or irresponsible person, which cannot admitted as evidence before the Auditor of government accounts. But a genuine application and statements of facts could be made by the claimant to this agent, whose duty it would be to ascertain the fact of the soldier's death from the officers of the company or regiment or hospital register.

Too much praise cannot be awarded to the noble ladies of Richmond. Ever since the first regiments from other States passed here 18 months ago they have worked with untiring zeal and unexampled liberality. They have made uniforms for thousands of Troops, often contributing the materials as well as the making.

The ladies of Richmond will assemble at their Churches to sew for the soldiers and they still visit the sick, and one or two of the hospitals are entirely managed

by them. They constantly supply the hospitals with delicacies, clothing and furniture. This zeal and benevolence is confined to no particular circle. The wealthy and accomplished, the poor and ignorant, work alike and put forth their hands together to lift up the helpless soldier in his sick bed, to close his eyes, or smooth his brow in death.

The small pox is alarmingly on the increase here. It is in many private families and nearly all the hospitals. One hospital has 80 or 100 cases, and it supposed there are near 1000 cases in the city and vicinity. It prevails to some extent among the troops and hospitals in the country. The people of Richmond and the soldiers are generally pretty thoroughly vaccinated and it is thought it cannot become epidemic or very fatal. One thing is certain, "Long Grabs" will leave these "diggings" as soon as practicable.

The Richmond correspondent of the London Times is here. His name is Lawley,[5] and he was once member of Parliament and has also been Private Secretary

Opposite: "Bombardment of Fredericksburg, Va., by the army of the Potomac, commanded by General Burnside, Thursday, December 11th, 1862. Our correspondent's report of this event: 'At ten o'clock General Burnside gives the order, "Concentrate the fire of all your guns on the city and batter it down!" You may believe they were not loath to obey. The artillery of the right — eight batteries — was commanded by Colonel Hays; Colonel Tompkins, right centre, eleven batteries; Colonel Tyler, left centre, seven batteries; Captain De Russy, left, nine batteries. In a few moments these thirty-five batteries forming a total of one hundred and seventy-nine guns, ranging from 10-pounder Parrotts to 4½-inch siege guns, posted along the convex side of the arc of the circle formed by the bend of the river and land opposite Fredericksburg, opened on the doomed city. The effect was, of course, terrific, and, regarded merely as a phenomenon, was among the most awfully grand conceivable. Perhaps what will give you the liveliest idea of its effect is a succession, absolutely without intermission, of the very loudest thunder peals. It lasted thus for upward of an hour, fifty rounds being fired from each gun, and I know not how many hundred tons of iron were thrown into the town. The congregate generals were transfixed; mingled satisfaction and awe was upon every face. But what was tantalizing was, that though a great deal could be heard, nothing could be seen, the city being still enveloped in fog and mist. Only a denser pillar of smoke defining itself on the background of the fog indicated where the town had been fired by our shells. Another and another column showed itself, and we presently saw that at least a dozen houses must be on fire. Toward noon the curtain rolled up, and we saw that it was indeed so. Fredericksburg was in conflagration. Tremendous though this firing had been, and terrific though its effect obviously was on the town, it had not accomplished the object intended. It was found by our gunners almost impossible to obtain a sufficient depression of their pieces to shell the front part of the city, and the Confederate sharpshooters were still comparatively safe behind the thick stone walls of the houses.'"— Frank Leslie, 1896. Source: Frank Leslie, *Famous Leaders and Battle Scenes of the Civil War* (New York: Mrs. Frank Leslie, 1896) pp. 296–297. Down on the river the pillars of a destroyed railroad bridge can be seen as well as pontoon bridges under construction. Used by permission of the Florida Center for Instructional Technology, College of Education, University of South Florida.

to Mr. Gladstone, but had some difference with him. I believe he intends writing regularly for the Times.

LONG GRABS.

[December 15, 1862]

RICHMOND, VA., Dec. 13, 1862.

Messrs, Editors: I have tried all manner of means to get up to Fredericksburg yesterday and to-day, but [to no] purpose. I had decided to go out of the city by private conveyance, and get to the first station above the city and then take the cars, but accidentally learned that some individuals who had tried that plan brought up Castle Thunder. "P. W. A."[6] of the Savannah Republican also made great efforts to get off but failed. Lee can outgeneral Burnside or any body else on the American Continent in massing troops and grand tactics. Burnside may move where he will, but when least expected he will meet old Lee before him looking straight at him through those old silver spectacles.

No amount of military talent and no grand strategy and manoeuvring, howerer, can balance off with overwhelming numbers and odds. Burnside has a larger army than Lee, but he is not capable of managing and much of his army is of very indifferent material. Lee has an army of veterans and patriots sufficiently large for the occasion and although he can handle his own army with ease he will show in these engagements he can handle Burnside's army equally as well. What are the yankee's facilities for reinforcing is another consideration. It will be unfortunate for our wounded to be sent here among so much small pox.

Last summer I had a conversation with Maj. Vodges while a prisoner at Salisbury[7], and was struck with some remarks he made. He said the plan of operation against the South contemplated by the best heads in the North was to gain possession of New Orleans, Nashville and Richmond, which with the coast would give them such advantages that we would be compelled to yield sooner or later. He said Richmond would be finally taken after much fighting and perhaps several campaigns, by gradually weakening our great army which would finally wear away and be disorganized and overwhelmed by superior numbers, and then we might adapt ourselves at our leisure to the consequences of defeat. These are plausible views and show some good judgment, but Lord North reasoned equally as plausibly against the Colonies in '76. Whose army has been disorganized and wasted away, two or three times? Whose army is now stronger, better appointed, and more determined to defend their hearths and shrines than ever before? Ah! Maj. Vodges, your arguments show only what are your vain hopes and wishes. This "gradual operation" is the most fatal mistake you have made, you could not have selected a policy more advantageous to us or more damaging to yourselves. Had you struck a universal death blow before we became strong, united and ready, you might have accomplished your vile ends, but now in vain may your hirelings be hurled against us. Never can you conquer a million of freemen, hold their vast territory in bondage, blot out their righteous cause from the scrolls of heaven. Meanwhile take care of the fate of your own reckless, unfortunate Republic.

Should the enemy destroy the bridge at Weldon, the bridge at Gaston would serve us every purpose, as it is equally as good as the other. We would have to keep a strong force on the river between the two places, which are some ten miles apart in a straight line. Gunboats can come near enough to shell the bridge at Weldon but no further. Freight trains generally cross on the Gaston bridge. Connection from Goldsboro' to Petersburg would still be open by Raleigh and Gaston should we lose the Weldon bridge. I think I will make a trip to Weldon and Gaston should times become more active there, as I cannot get to Fredericksburg well.

Truly yours,
LONG GRABS.

[December 22, 1862]

After he wrote this letter, Long Grabs took a little time off to enjoy Christmas and returned to the village of Wake Forest, located in Wake County near Raleigh. He returned to Virginia in January 1863, and this time was able to get nearer to Fredericksburg. Had he been able to earlier, he would have witnessed the results of the events described in the following letter by a young lady who endured the bombardment and Yankee attack. The *Fayetteville Observer* published it on January 12, 1863.

HORRORS OF A BOMBARDMENT.[8]

The following are some extracts from a private letter from a young lady who remained in Fredericksburg during the late bombardment, to a neighbor, at

Castle Thunder, Richmond, Virginia, one of the Confederate prisons known for its abominable conditions. Source: John Gilmary Shea, *The Story of a Great Nation* (New York: Gay Brothers & Company, 1886) p. 903. Used by permission of the Florida Center for Instructional Technology, College of Education, University of South Florida.

present sojourning as a refugee in Lynchburg. They possess deep interest for our readers.

On Thursday, December 11th, we were awakened by two cannon. At 5 o'clock we arose and dressed. About six the firing began in earnest. We packed our trunks amid it all, made a fire in the cellar, and thither repaired. We had not been there an hour when a shell went through our attic room, breaking bedsteads, etc. One shot went through the parlor; five in all through the house. As they passed, the crash they made seemed to threaten instant death to all; it sounded as though the house were tumbling in, and would bury us all in its ruins. We knew the danger, but our trust was in God, and we were calm. Aunt Clara (the colored woman who lives opposite) was with us. Darkness came on, and the cannonading ceased. B. went to the gate and returned with the news that there was fire in different parts of the

"A Street in Fredericksburg, Va., showing the result of the bombardment — federal soldiers grouped about. Our correspondent wrote: 'Considering the terrible nature of the bombardment, it is wonderful that not a single inhabitant was killed by it, although many families refused to avail themselves of the opportunity to leave before the firing commenced. These found shelter in the cellars of the houses, and thus escaped. The rest of the building, in many cases, was so shattered as to be perfectly uninhabitable. A fine old mansion in Main Street presented a melancholy spectacle, no less than thirty round shot having gone right through it, leaving the appearance of so many portholes. In the street the Federals bivouacked the night before the battle and the night after.'"— Frank Leslie, 1896. Source: Frank Leslie, *Famous Leaders and Battle Scenes of the Civil War* (New York: Mrs. Frank Leslie, 1896) p. 363. Used by permission of the Florida Center for Instructional Technology, College of Education, University of South Florida.

town, and that a company of our men were at the corner firing on the pontoon bridge. Though the bombardment had ceased, the musketry sounded to my ears yet more awful, for I knew they were fighting in the streets. My ears are suddenly shocked by a shout of demonical glee—"Here are the rebels! here are the d__d rebels! fire, boys, fire!" Two dreadful cries rend the air—our gallant Capt. Cook is killed at our corner. To hear the fiendish cry of the enemy unnerved me more than the explosion of thousands of shells that burst around us.

All being now quiet for a time, we lie down, but not to sleep; for, hark! They are breaking into houses like so many demons. With terrible force they throw themselves against our doors, back and front, but an officer (Yankee though he was,) saved us. We hear them break into your house, but we dare not utter a word, lest they slay us. Oh! who can tell the horrors of that night? [undecipherable] They order my father out, declare that he has wine in his cellar, &c. He assures them he has only his unoffending wife and eight children there.

Thus passes the night, the fire still raging. About 8 o'clock the flames burst forth in our vicinity, and we expect every moment to find our own roof on fire. In the midst of the excitement a soldier rushed in with his bayonet, which he pointed at my father's breast and ordered him to follow him. My father asked why? but the manner in which he repeated the order convinced him that he must follow or die. This occurred in the back porch; I was at that time in the front porch watching the sparks and expecting our house every moment to take fire. They carried father to headquarters, and after accusing him of firing on them from his house, he was released, the officer before whom he was arraigned reading a lie in the face of the accuser, and innocence in that of the accused. While he was gone, soldiers came to me at the front door, and to mother behind, and assured us that the house was on fire; but such was not the case. The trick did not succeed, nor did the story afford them the opportunity they sought, to rob the house.

The next day every unoccupied house was plundered and every piece of furniture destroyed. In order to save your furniture we told aunt Clara to move into your house, which she did. You would have had nothing left but for this. The first night they took a crock of lard, and ate up your preserves and pickles. Your candles, also, they made way with, but we do not know of anything else. They pulled everything out of your drawers and trucks, burst open closets, etc. No shell went through your house, and if you saw the sufferings of most of the people you would think you had indeed fared well. Mr. A. lost everything—his store, furniture, etc.; his house is riddled with shell and his wife and child with northing to wear but what they have on. Hundreds are in the same situation. As shells were being thrown by our men on Friday, Saturday, Sunday, and Monday, we spent each of these days chiefly in the cellar, as well as Thursday; thus five days in all.

Mary Price, a black woman, was killed by a shell—cut quite in two. She had gotten for protection, under a bed in a room, through which a shell passed. I saw her on Wednesday. She had been killed the previous Thursday, but there was no one to bury her....

Every house not inhabited has been sacked and ruined inside. They committed every species of outrage.

[January 12, 1863]

WAKE FOREST — THE COLLEGE
WAKE FOREST, N. C., Dec. 30, 1862.

Messrs. Editors: I concluded I would enjoy a little of Christmas and let every thing take care of itself for a while. I have laid aside thoughts of my suffering country for a few days to enter on my duties again with redoubled energy.

This is a refined and enterprising community and I meet everywhere with that old-fashioned North Carolina hospitality, that sincere cordial greeting and constant effort to please and make happy, which makes man think better of his kind and feel more attached to this wicked world.

The Forestville Paper Mill is near here on Neuse river. The mill was built some 8 or 10 years ago and was owned recently by G. W. Mordecai, W. R. Pool and Lawrence Hinton, all of this county, and sold by them a few days ago to Tyler, Wise & Allegre of the Richmond Enquirer for some $50,000 cash. The original cost of the mill and location was about $80,000. The premises consist of the paper mill, a saw and grist mill, shop, office, warehouse and 300 acres of land. Just at present it is thought to be the best paying property in the Confederacy. It is almost impossible to get some machinery and articles necessary to the operation of the mill, among which are felts, wire sieves, acids and other chemicals for sizing, bleaching and coloring. There are some 12 hands engaged in the mill and perhaps a half dozen more on outside work, and they often work 18 out of the 24 hours. About an average of 100 lbs. of paper is turned off per hour. Paper of the size and quality of the Observer weighs about 35 lbs. to the ream. The machinery is propelled by water power, but steam is used to dry the paper, boil rags, &c. The building is of rock and the machinery, neither complicated nor extensive, and with the floors, engines, pumps, &c. is getting out of repair. No writing paper is made here except an inferior kind for envelopes. I will endeavor to describe the process of making paper at some future time.

The paper mill burned on March 15, 1871. The *Raleigh Sentinel* reported, "The paper mill of the Forest Manufacturing Company near Forestville was totally destroyed by fire Sunday night. We have not ascertained the amount of loss, but understand it to be covered by $15,000 insurance. Two previous attempts were made to fire this property but were fortunately frustrated. On this occasion the flames gained such headway before being discovered that nothing could be done to extinguish them."[9]

Long Grabs continues:

The College has not been in operation for several months and will remain closed I learn during the war. The institution is under the direction of the Baptist Church of N. C. and was established in 1834 under the title of "Wake Forest Manual Labor School," with a farm of a few hundred acres of land attached. It was an old heathen notion of those days that young men at College ought to work in the field. Little was done, however, as sickness prevailed to an alarming extent among the students except at meal times. The custom was soon abolished as it had such a bad effect on the young men's health, followed by the crop becoming grassy and finally lost, and five or six years after the organization of the School the present building was erected and the old one removed. There is only one large three story brick building, beautifully located and capable of accommodating a hundred students or more. It afforded a fine prospect from the Raleigh & Gaston Railroad which runs near the College grove. A silent sadness reigns through the empty halls and even the winds seem reluctant to disturb the sear and fallen leaves, for Professors, students and all "have hung their harps on the willow and are off to the wars again," and their Alma Mater is draped in mourning for the loss of many a noble son in the cause of liberty. I stepped into the room where the beautiful imagery and smooth numbers of Homer and thrilling eloquence of Cicero used to be recited, and the only occupant was a very corpulent rat lounging on the floor and sadly contemplating the literary dearth around him. In another place devoted to sines, co-sines, angles, hypotenuse, logarithms and infinitesimals, I found a large pile of pea-hulls. It seems that the old negro who has charge of the premises either intended to carry out the original labor system of the institution or having lost his vocation of boot blacking, turned things to account by raising a pea crop in the Campus, which accounts for the chamber of Euclid being converted into a forage house. Rev. Dr. Wait was the first teacher and president. He is a native of Vermont, was connected with the College a great many years, is over 70 years old and now resides here. Dr. Hooper, formerly Professor of Latin at Chapel Hill, was President of the College also for a time, since which the Rev. Mr. Wingate has filled the place. Prof. Wingate is a native of Darlington District, S. C., was educated here several years ago and has been connected with the College ever since. He is a very pleasant gentleman, of middle age, and possesses energy and talent. His labors have been useful and successful and he is highly respected and admired. The cost of the present building and fixtures was about $14,000. The course of instruction is pretty thorough, embracing modern languages, but the opportunities for teaching the arts and practical sciences are not very extensive. There were once 140 students here at one time, but the number for some years has not exceeded 80 or 90. Many eminent Baptist Ministers have been educated here, and not a few distinguished men in other walks of life. The Trustees were originally appointed by the Legislature, but have since selected their successors. Among the trustees now are Hon. Calvin Graves, John Kerr and Gen. A. Dockery. The College has no library and but little if any fund, but two literary Societies have libraries of a few thousand volumes.

    The old year is closing and will soon be numbered among the things that were, but the events it has added to the page of history will leave an impression on the world that can never be erased. We enter another year under remarkable circumstances, and as time rolls by in measured periods we must meet the future, for we cannot escape it, and work out our manifest destiny. Our boys and girls should make good use of their time at school, for in times like these we are more fully convinced of the value of education. Amid the misfortunes and revolutions that now surround us, a good education, with energy and integrity, is worth more than land, negroes, family, or money. It is very essential also for every body in these times to know how to travel at night by the stars, how to use a gun, and ride horseback, swim, and climb trees.

LONG GRABS.

[January 8, 1863]

RICHMOND, VA., Jan'y 15, 1863.

Messrs Editors:—Within the last few days I have seen a number of ladies and gentlemen immediately from Norfolk, Edenton and Elizabeth City, and learned from them much of interest from that section. Lincoln's proclamation was fully and practically enforced down there. Gen. Viele is represented as being a very equivocal, deceitful man. The 99th N. Y. Reg't, stationed at Norfolk, is spoken of in terms of commendation. Its officers and men have befriended the citizens and afforded them many advantages and favors. But the 19th Wisconsin, also there, is represented as a band of villains and devils incarnate. Many persons get back their negroes through the 99th N. Y. by paying the yankees a trifling bribe. Any one can get his negroes in this way if that regiment be on duty at the time, and it is believed that many persons have gone down there and got negroes that did not belong to them. About $25 apiece is the principal evidence to be produced that the negro is your property. Any number of letters pass out and in by paying a bribe of $5 or $10 on each letter. But the cute yankee very often exercises his natural love for the "filthy lucre" so far that he butters his bread on both sides. The citizen outside sends a letter to Norfolk and when it is delivered beyond our lines to a yankee officer, he promises to forward it to the other party, for which you must pay him $10, but the post master in Norfolk must have $10 again when the letter is delivered to the person addressed. Thus the amount allowed by the authorities must be paid to get the letter into yankee hands and the same again to get it out, whether sent to or from the city. If you mark "paid" on the envelope they tear it off and put on another, so there may be no evidence of postage prepaid. A great many valuable articles and goods are got through by smuggling and bribery.

LONG GRABS.

[January 29, 1863]

CAMP 2D REG'T N. C. T. NEAR FREDERICKSBURG,
January 20, 1863.

Messrs. Editors:—Once more doth "Long Grabs" resort to ye quill as ye army correspondent. I have seen many of the North Carolina Regiments but have not yet had sufficient opportunity to learn fully much of interest. It so happens that I find several acquaintances in every N. C. Regiment and many regiments from other States and several of them are "big officers," so that I ramble about and see and find out much more than officers belonging permanently to different Brigades and Divisions, for no one knows much out of his command. But we are all profoundly ignorant of the secrets and the plans of Old Stonewall, Lee and Longstreet.

I find the Army in excellent condition. It is well clothed and shod, though more shoes, blankets and underclothing could be disposed of to advantage. There is better system and discipline now in the army than I have ever known before, and this I am informed results directly in a great degree from the able management and untiring exertions of Gen. Lee. It is very evident that our army organization is approaching perfection much resembling the armies of the great warriors of Europe in durability and efficiency, without that harshness and cruelty of detail common to them. I am led to this conclusion because there exists an increased confidence and disposition to obey and respect authority on the part of the soldiery and a greater willingness to perform duty faithfully and promptly on the part of officers. The military courts are more efficient and decisive; the system of dropping delinquent officers has a wholesome effect; and examinations of incompetent officers by boards have been managed with better judgment and results. And generally, the privileges of inferior officers are properly limited and better defined and the rights and interests of the soldier better defined and preserved. The rations are rather short now, but from necessity I presume.

The health of the army is remarkably good. There are but few tents, but the army is beginning to regard tents as a nuisance. Much soldiering has made the men very sharp and gives them a full knowledge of the law of self-preservation, and they seem to have the same instinct as the beaver, for their operations very much resemble the habits of that animal. Brigades move about near thick woods to get supplies of fuel and for benefit to health. When the troops stop to camp you see them scatter about and become very busy and in the course of an hour or two the whole Brigade has disappeared. You can hear voices and noises and see moving things, and you almost think it is a vision or a haunted place, but after some painful suspense you are enabled to understand this sudden and strange "transmogrification." The drum-beat summons the men to duty or inspection, and all at once from holes, clay-roots and hollow trees all around, you can see hundreds of heads protruding and then the shoulders and finally the whole body and the entire Brigade appears before you as it was a few hours ago. The soldiers had dug out holes, caves and cellars, over which is a roof of close brush covered with a thick coating of dirt to turn rain and weather while the tenement below is warmed by a snug and well filled fire place cut in the solid earth on the side; and such are the winter quarters of Lee's army.

I was at Gen. Stuart's headquarters to-day and saw him eating some hard crackers and fat bacon. Gen. Stuart is a flashy, dashy, fancy fast man, though by no means foppish, harum-scarum or reckless. He is very free, sociable, agreeable and lively, and is a gentleman of high toned accomplishment and rare genius. He is of more than ordinary size, some 30 years old, very handsome, fair complexion, with bright beaming eyes of quick perception and deep expression. His dress and appearance correspond well with the rest of his character. He is brother-in-law of N. Boyden, Jr., of Salisbury, and his wife is daughter of Philip St. George Cooke of Missouri and sister of Gen. J. R. Cooke in Ransom's command and formerly Colonel of 27th Reg't N. C. T. He has several odd and fantastic characters with him and on his staff. His cook is a Frenchman from one of the café houses in Paris, a ventriloquist and comical genius; the principal business man in his office is a Prussian, a man of education, distinction and wit; and in the musical department he has Sweeny, Jr. son of Old Joe — and were he to add the Siamese twins, Tom Thumb, and "Long Grabs" to his list, his cabinet of curiosities would be complete. I intended to give you some reflections and observations on the battle of Fredericksburg, relative to the location, the merits and results of the battle, but must defer till my next.

LONG GRABS.

[January 29, 1863]

CAMP NEAR FREDERICKSBURG, Jan. 25.

Messrs. Editors: Yesterday we exchanged some papers with a yankee picket across the river, but Jonathan practiced his cheating propensities by giving us N. Y. Ledgers nearly a month old. The pickets have quit firing at each other and they are so close (the narrow Rappahannock intervening) that they can converse easily. Some of our men frequently go over the river make purchases and exchange articles. One party went over a few days ago and were received by the yankee officer of the guard and treated to fine liquors and an elegant dinner and brought back with them several late Northern papers and other valuable things. Yankee officers have been on our side and got tobacco and were treated with the same courtesy. This visiting and exchanging is positively against orders on our side, and theirs also I suppose, and is kept from the knowledge of our Generals. It depends entirely on the honor of the respective officers on post whether persons crossing over in this way be retained as prisoners or allowed to go back. Two of our men went over some days ago with tobacco to exchange for coffee and sugar but when they reached the other bank the yankees marched them off and they have not been seen since.

From all information I can obtain the main bulk of the yankee army is a few miles over the river yet and the opinion seems to prevail that they meditate the principal attack here while making diversions at other points. But let them come and go or move as they please, the country need not hesitate to repose implicit confidence in this army and its Generals. I have often entertained doubts as to certain probabilities and circumstances pertaining to the war in Virginia, but I can now without any mental reservation express entire confidence in the progress and management of our cause here. Events have sometimes occurred calculated to mar the effect of success; and occasionally unexpected disaster has blighted our reasonable hopes; but such things are always within the range of human probability and beyond human control and foresight. I now believe that the yankees have just about done their do in Virginia and are much weaker here than at first, while we are much stronger than we have ever been. I had feared that the impulsive, independent nature, so characteristic of the Southern people, could not easily adapt itself to patience and effective discipline, but the sequel has not justified the apprehension. Our army has hardly a parallel in history for unanimous devotion to duty, voluntary self-sacrifice and constant endurance of hardship.

There has been much rain and disagreeable weather for several days and the roads are almost impassable.

Gen'l. D. H. Hill has tendered his resignation and has gone home to improve his health I am informed. It is said he will not resume command in this army even should his health justify his returning to the service. Brig. Gen. Rhodes of Ala. is in command of Hill's Division and will probably be appointed Maj. General. Col. Rob't. F. Hoke of 21st Reg't N. C. T. from Lincoln has been appointed Brig. Gen'l. and will have a Brigade of N. C. Reg'ts, embracing the 6th, 54th and 57th, which will be in Jackson's Corps. There are many other changes and promotions, some of which I will mention again.

The damage done the town of Fredericksburg has been greatly exaggerated. A few houses have been burnt and several have been damaged and a few ruined by shot and shell. The yankees have destroyed furniture in vacant houses, fences and other property, as they have done everywhere. They no doubt intended greater destruction to the town than was accomplished. The city is somewhat larger and more compact than Fayetteville, but did not have as large a wagon trade nor business with as large a section of country. The society has always been very superior. The place is very old and has a prominent place in the romantic annals of the Old Dominion, and under the quiet shades of this ancient borough lie the remains of Mary Washington, Gen. Washington's mother. A line from Alexandria by Richmond and down the James including this place, Williamsburg and that portion of the State east and southeast of this, constitutes the Old Dominion proper. Here we find the incidents and scenery of Thackeray's "Virginians" among these old mansions and magnificent patriarchal estates. That pure elevated old English society ripened into mature patriotism and attachment to liberty in these old homesteads now deserted and desolated like the Parthenon and Coliseum, and like them not only monuments of ancient purity and greatness but modern outrage, folly and wickedness.

The battle of Fredericksburg has been denominated a barren victory and a golden opportunity lost. Very severe criticism is indulged by many because the yankee army was not annihilated. I was disposed to attach some plausibility and importance to these disparaging reflections on the results of the battle and the judgment of our commanders, but after a careful consideration of the circumstances and a full examination of the ground I regard these criticisms totally unjust and improper — and so must any one who will inform himself fully on the matter. I think it clearly appears that the battle was as well fought as it could be and that it was impossible for us to have made it more decisive, in which opinion Gen. Stuart entirely coincided in a conversation I had with him a few days ago.

On the Southern side of the Rappahannock at Fredericksburg is an extensive plateau for several miles up and down and of irregular width. The plain is a continuation of elevated table lands intersected by deep ravines or little streams, ditches and roads, and is generally termed with us river low-grounds, though the river never overflows this land. The entire plain is cleared and has been in a high state of cultivation from times "whereof the memory of man runneth not to the contrary." Splendid mansions of every color surrounded by magnificent groves, like so many flowers among rich shrubbery, dot the surface as far as the eye can reach, lending additional charms to the lovely, inspiring and almost endless prospect. This plain is occasionally interrupted by gradual elevations and declivities, the most extensive of which forms a range of bluffs immediately on the Southern border of the town, nearly surrounding and partially covering it from view on that side. The River in the vicinity and the streams that make into it are bordered by steep bluffs, the bed through which the channel flows resembling a deep cut. Down the margin of the river between the bluffs which form the banks is a strip of dry land mostly on the South side, and when the river is very low this margin is from ten to one hundred yards wide. The plateau of table lands before mentioned is some over a mile in width just at Fredericksburg and for some distance above, and widens out southward to near Hamilton's crossing, the head of Railroad communication from Richmond, which is some five miles from

Fredericksburg, until the distance across the plain to the river is over three miles, as the river turns a little North below Fredericksburg. From the head of the Railroad, which runs somewhat parallel with the river, this plain gets narrower down the river, till it gets to the width of a mile or over again. All along on the Southern border of this table land is a range of steep hills and bluffs of considerable heights in places which command the town and every part of the plain to the river. This range of hills formed our line of battle, on which our artillery was posted and where our infantry lay in security. The roads through this plain are marked by continuous rows of small cedars and by deep ditches on each side, the dirt from the ditches being thrown next to the farm, forming a steep bank on top of which are posts intertwined with plaited brush or else green hedge which serves as fencing. Behind one of these enclosure on a line from Hamilton's station, the head of the Railroad straight to the river across the widest part of the plain, was Gen. Stuart and his cavalry and horse artillery, forming a boundary to the battlefield on the Southeast. On the Northern bank are continuous ranges of hills rising abruptly from the river in many places and much higher generally than the hills occupied by our troops, and they extended up and down the river with but little level plain between them and the river. These hills, called "Stafford Heights," completely command the town and plain across the river and the river itself, and were literally covered with the enemy's artillery. One pontoon bridge was near the upper end of town, another at the lower end, (a mile from the first) and the other at the mouth of one of the little streams forming a deep ravine through the plain, through which a body of the enemy made their way safety to a short distance of our batteries. When the two divisions in town united and became unmasked by the elevated ground forming the second range of bluffs on the suburbs of town, and as the others emerged from the ravine, all making a charge forward, they were exposed to Stuart's fire on their left flank and to fire from the hills on their right nearer Fredericksburg, besides the fire in front. Several charges were made, but that they were failures is no wonder. Portions of our infantry were frequently used with advantage on the retreating columns of the enemy. The numerous ravines utterly prevented any effective pursuit by cavalry. Our batteries could have battered down the town, and when the enemy fell back on the town if our artillery had opened on them indiscriminately the enemy could in a few minutes have withdrawn his whole force a few yards down on the margin of the river under the bluff which is thirty or forty feet high, nearly perpendicular, and rested perfectly safe. If our infantry had rushed over this plain in pursuit, the batteries of the enemy on Stafford Heights could have cut them to pieces, and might have confused and disorganized them and given the enemy a chance to rally. It would have been useless to destroy the town.

Long Grabs.

[February 2, 1863]

Camp Near Fredericksburg, Jan. 30.

Messrs. Editors: We have had one continued spell of rain, cold and snow. The snow is now a foot deep in many places and would have been much deeper if the ground had been dry. This is about the worst kind of weather in camp and the sharp north wind off these bare hills soon places the "uninitiated" hors du combat, while the old soldier frolics about, stands on his head, or wallows his comrade in the snow with as much hilarity of spirits as if it was May.

I have not as yet been able to appreciate the manner of felling trees in camp, though a man will be considered eccentric here if he does not fully endorse all camp customs which experience has established. The other day some men took a fancy to a large tree near the tent I was in and proceeded immediately to cut it down. The tree being surrounded by tents for some distance, and there being no certainty as to which way it would fall, it was thought useless to notify any one till the tree started, when we informed of the danger just in time to scramble out like a parcel of rats and escape a general smash up. I felt surprised, serious, mad and indignant by turns, while everybody else regarded it as a good joke. The Lt. Col. of the 1st Reg't Rifles, (S. C.) was badly hurt a day or two ago by a tree being cut on him. He is not expected to recover. It is quite dangerous to have large timber standing near a camp while it is so stormy and the ground so soft. Night before last several trees blew down in our camp, smashing three or four tents, but no one was hurt. I was awake nearly all night, expecting every moment to be my last, and about midnight while a violent snow storm was raging, down came a big pine — kersmash, right across the tent next to ours, throwing snow and mud in my face. A short time afterwards I heard another crashing sound as though the universe were falling to pieces. I learned next morning that it was caused by the falling of a very large tree which brought down several smaller ones. The top of the tree fell on a tent where a captain and two or three other officers were sleeping, mashing the tent to the ground and tearing it badly, but the occupants were not hurt and never moved or allowed themselves to feel disturbed by the accident.

The army is rapidly consuming the last remains of the sustenance this country affords. The timbered tracts have long been more highly valued and carefully preserved then the open land, but very soon not a vestige of the regional forests will remain, and those majestic old oaks, that witnessed the sports and vows of the red man, and afforded comfort and protection to the banished and persecuted of our own race, can never again shelter either exile or invader.

Snow-balling is the great amusement just now in the army. Two regiments went at it yesterday led by their Colonels on horseback, and representing yankees and Confederates a la Manassas and a la Fredericksburg. They charged, flanked and shelled and went through the "changes of base" and "strategic movements" and finally came out without losing a man but badly worsted on both sides. A more scientific engagement or "skirmish" took place in the 18th Reg't last night. Dr. M. and his infirmary corps, the non-commissioned staff and several teamsters, representing our forces, while Capt. T., Capt. P., Lieut's L., A., and J., and Maj. B., represented the enemy. A small branch separated the quarters of the combatants, representing the Rappahannock. It was proposed to lam out Dr. M. and his crowd and take possession of their camp, and Maj. B. was to act the part of Halleck and direct all the grand movements at a safe distance, while Capt. T. was to be Burnside and take post a little nearer the field of carnage; the others undertook respectively the parts of Hooker, Siegel, &c. At last Capt. T. orders an advance, "Onward to Richmond." They arrive at the branch and find no

The snowball battle near Dalton, Georgia, between several regiments of Confederate soldiers, a pencil drawing by Alfred Rudolph Waud, 1828–1891. There are a number of snowball fights among regiments; one of the largest took place on the Rappahannock in 1863, and involved 10,000 Confederate soldiers. This illustration is used to give an idea of what was taking place in the snowball fight the 18th Regiment engaged in. Source: The Confederate Veteran (Nashville, TN.: S. A. Cunningham) Vol. 21, May, 1913, p. 218.

pontoons, but after a serious and vexatious delay they cross. They find things different from expectations and a council of war is held. Maj. B. advises that the heights commanding Dr. M's tent be occupied so as to drive him from his stronghold. This is accordingly done and they throw over a few shells and send out skirmishers, but there is no response from the enemy. They conclude that the enemy is either surprised or retreating, and they rush forward with a rapid charge and terrible fire, when all at once the Confederate batteries open like a clap of thunder and the columns of the invader are stunned and confused, but they rally again and rush recklessly forward till they are overwhelmed by an avalanche of snow from one end of the lines to the other. Now the Confederates dash out, bayonets are crossed, and a hand-to-hand fight ensues. First one side then the other gives way amid the roar and yell of battle. Two hostiles single out each other and pitch in pell mell, mixed up and rolling over and over into brush heaps and mud holes till there is but little left of either. Siegel's corps of reinforcements comes up, but the action is rapidly being decided, and Burnside, after all manoeuvres and strategic movements, is forced to withdraw his forces. Flags of truce pass and the wounded are cared for, the dead decently buried, and the yankee general tries to take advantage of this intermission to renew the conflict. In vain he attempts to rally his demoralized forces and finds that his only safety is in precipitate flight, regardless of pontoons, while the Confederates furiously shell his unprotected rear. Then appear explanations and discussions, and Capt. T. assumes all responsibility, acknowledges his incompetency and asks pardon, but Maj. B. demands his removal — Capt. T. tenders his resignation — investigation, &c.; but Burnside is fully restored and it turns out that everybody did just the thing that was right, and it all happened just as was expected and finally every body becomes perfectly satisfied.

It will probably be many weeks before there can be any movements towards battle, though had the weather permitted, I believe there would have been a fight before now. A considerable portion of the enemy had moved with apparent intention of crossing some 10 miles above Fredericksburg, while I am credibly informed their pontoons were nearly the same distance below. Gen. Lee keeps an eye on the pontoons as the "main chance." He is fully informed from various sources.

The 1st and 3d N. C. Reg'ts have been transferred from Dole's Brigade, D. H. Hill's Division, to Taliaferro's Brigade, Trimble's Division (Stonewall Jackson's old Division.) Gen. Ramseur, formerly of the 49th Reg't, has been assigned to the command of the Brigade commanded by the late Geo. B. Anderson. Gen. R. F. Hoke, recently Col. of the 21st Reg't, has a Brigade of the 6th, 21st, 54th and 57th Reg'ts in Ewell's Division. All these troops are in Jackson's corps, and there are very few North Carolinians in Longstreet's corps, perhaps not more than two regiments.

Truly,
LONG GRABS.

[February 5, 1863]

CAMP NEAR FREDERICKSBURG, Feb. 2, 1863.

Messrs. Editors: — The weather is fair and warm, with a strong wind, and in a few days the snow will be gone and the roads in traveling condition. Then will come the yanks, like ticks, scorpions and other pestilential insects and vile things from their cells of winter torpidity. But the omens are against them, and the yankee General, like his predecessors, has started to Richmond on the wrong time of the moon. I learn also that he forgot something and had to turn back, and shortly afterwards a rabbit ran across the road before him.

It has been almost impossible to get sufficient supplies over the wretched roads to the different camps. It would probably be an improvement to use sleighs. In this way a good team could drag heavier loads over the mud, snow and ice, like reindeer, a la Lapland. I believe I will suggest it to the Quartermaster General. The improvement might be applied to artillery also, and then wouldn't we slide around the yankees while they are stuck in the mud?

The first idea that occurs to a man of sense on beholding a great army in the exercise of all its operations in active service is its enormous expense. Thousands of officer and hundreds of thousands of soldiers must be fed and clothed and provided with medical aid; tents, cooking utensils, axes, spades, desks, paper, pens, arms, equipments, ammunition, drums, flags, wagons, horses, mules, forage, saddles, halters, harness, cannon, caissons and ambulances, all must be paid for by the gov't at high prices. Then all property destroyed or appropriated by the army; freight on stores and supplies; transportation for troops, and for the sick and discharged; rent for buildings for hospitals, ranging in Richmond from $1500 to $3000 a year, for each warehouse or building needed; bounties, hospital attendants, stores, medicines and liquors; together with exorbitant prices, swindling, forging, speculating and extravagance, foot up an amount truly astounding. It makes one think that the gov't pocket is full of holes through which the money is going out, and only one where it comes in, so that at a period not very remote there might be "nary red" in the till! It is to be hoped that a rigid economy may be practiced in our affairs, although efficiency be somewhat impaired thereby.

I have not seen any late yankee papers and we have no late definite news of importance from the Northern army on the other side of the river. It is generally conceded that they are determined on an advance from their present position as soon as the condition of the roads and weather will allow. It is not probable that they will rely solely on an attempt at Fredericksburg again, but will make the principal effort some miles above or below, on the assumption that, if such a flank movement succeeds in securing to them our strong position, they will beat us on equal ground. The river, however, for miles up and down presents nearly everywhere positions equally advantageous as at Fredericksburg, and as it requires but small immediate force at such places, our army is capable of indefinite extension, while we can rapidly concentrate as they. And should they flank our positions and even gain them partially, they would fight to great disadvantage, in addition to the demoralization which they cannot remedy; for the deep Rappahannock would separate them from supplies and probably from reinforcements or retreat. In the present condition of the two armies I would have but little apprehension of the result on a fair open field, and the surrounding country is better adapted to defence than to attack.

Among the many allusions to individual gallantry, I see but little mention of North Carolinians, who deserve such compliments to the full extent enjoyed by the troops of any other State, as the following incident will show. I have not yet heard of any feat of individual bravery and coolness more worthy of admiration or indicative of true gallantry and chivalry. During the battle of Fredericksburg, Serg't. Covington, of the "Pee Dee Guards," 23d N. C. T., and son of Dr. C. C. Covington of Rockingham, became separated from the Regiment and the rest of our army, when, being unarmed, he met with two armed yankees, one of whom immediately leveled his gun at Covington, who ordered them to surrender and called out, "Come on, boys, here's two more prisoners." At the same instant he seized one yankee's gun, who surrendered without firing, and then pointing the gun at the other yankee, he laid down his arms and surrendered also. Covington quickly marched them off to the regiment, first loading them with valuables and provisions, the yankees in the meantime being very inquisitive as to where were the "other boys." They had gone some distance before they understood the matter, when they manifested very bitter remorse and self-reproach at their own stupidity and cowardice. Serg't. Covington was highly complimented for his gallantry.

Truly,
LONG GRABS.

[February 9, 1863]

4. Reporting from Virginia

CAMP NEAR FREDERICKSBURG, Feb. 6.

Messrs. Editors: Everything remains quiet as when I last wrote you. The weather is now colder than any I have experienced this winter, and the sky is clear and the ground frozen stiff.

I have just been taking a view of the yankee camps through a glass from a very high position used by our signal-corps. Judging from the direction, noise, smoke, &c., I saw about one-third of their camp. Their encampments seem to be as regularly laid off and kept as clean as used to be the case at our camps of Instruction. There appeared to be an abundance of new commodious tents. I think the greater portion of their camp is in one connected body. There is no necessity for them to scatter their forces up and down the river as they have no expectation of our crossing — their pickets only being in front of ours at every point. I did not see as much activity as I observed several days ago by the same instrument. From the ground and number of tents I saw, I suppose there were quarters for twenty-five or thirty thousand men.

Maj. Wharton of Salem, formerly Capt. in the 1st Reg. N. C. T., but now commanding the 1st N. C. Battalion in Gen. Hoke's Brigade, was unfortunately captured by the yankees a few days ago. I have the facts from Gen. R. F. Hoke, who speaks in the highest terms of Maj. Wharton. It seems that Maj. Wharton and Serg't. Adams of Lincoln county were in a canoe in a small creek near where it runs into the river, probably in search of ducks. The river was very high which caused more water than usual about the mouth of the creek, and as they had to go some further down to get out, a very strong wind blew them into the channel of the river and with the current and finally threw them on the other side, when the yankee pickets immediately took them prisoners and they are still retained.

There is much complaint from North Carolina soldiers that they do not get their N. C. papers. The chief difficulty I think is the postage. The Postmasters at offices near the army will not deliver the papers at the office unless the postage be paid in advance for at least three months. The messenger for each division cannot pay it and risk the collection from the different subscribers who cannot well attend to it in person, and when the army moves to a new office the postage must be paid there again, and so every time there is a move. The better plan at present is to prepay the postage at the office of publication and to have each package marked "paid" distinctly and directed simply to the subscriber with his company, reg't, brigade and division, Richmond, Va., (if in the army.)

Immense quantities of apples, ginger cakes, goobers, &c., are disposed of here at the most extravagant prices. Many soldiers make hundreds of dollars in the year in the cake and apple business. Yesterday I saw two men carrying a barrel of ginger cakes from the Railroad to their Brigade several miles off. They had the barrel suspended by ropes to a stick which they carried on their shoulders much in the same way we used to carry home a deer on Rockfish in those celebrated "drives," when old D. and Dr. McL always brought down an old buck, should he run by the old accustomed "stand." Proceeding in this manner with the barrel packed full of ginger cakes and one head out that they might readily accommodate any way customer, they came to a creek which the recent snow and rains had swollen. There was no alternative but to walk through in the manner of cousin Sally Dillard[10]. They managed to keep their freight above board until the

Soldiers gathering wood for their camp stoves. To the left is a row of chimneys that Long Grabs described. Source: John Gilmary Shea, *The Story of a Great Nation* (New York: Gay Brothers & Company, 1886). Used by permission of the Florida Center for Instructional Technology, College of Education, University of South Florida.

foremost one stepped in a hole and falling precipitated the open barrel of cakes into the stream. Before they could recover the barrel every crumb of bread "had been cast upon the waters' but not to be "gathered many days hence."

Tents are now more numerous and to each one is a stick and dirt chimney, making it really comfortable. The only way known or practiced at the first of the war to have fire in a tent was by means of a stove, but the chimney is an infinite improvement. I hardly think it necessary to supply infantry with over coats; a thick stout blanket is much more valuable. On the march one soldier cannot carry his over coat and other necessary equipments, and has often to throw his over coat away. In battle he can seldom use his over coat and consequently it gets lost. While in camp and by good fires he does not need it, and if on picket or on other duty he can easily tie his blanket around him, if it is practicable to wear over garments, so that his blanket which he is required to carry will do in all occasions in place of an overcoat as well as to sleep on. I think both from experience and observation, that thick woolen cravats are an injury rather than a benefit to the soldier. The ordinary clothing can generally be so arranged as to afford sufficient protection to the neck, while a thick woolen wrapping causes the pores of the neck and throat to become open, rendering that sensitive and vital part of the body more liable to disease from exposure. It would be better to use the material for gloves, socks, and under clothing, which with blankets and gloves are always most needed.

Truly,
Long Grabs.

[February 9, 1862]

4. Reporting from Virginia

RICHMOND, VA., Feb. 12, 1863.

Messrs. Editors: Everybody still succeeds in the great object of life — that is in getting enough to eat. Although every thing is so high, yet every hotel here is as well supplied as it has ever been. Hotel keepers you know always complain of the high prices and scarcity of butter, eggs, fish, milk &c., but hardly ever furnish these articles whether high or low. When I hear my landlord complaining about these things it reminds me of old Ike's indignation at the increased taxes, when it is affirmed that he has never paid one cent of tax within the memory of the oldest inhabitant.

Richmond is more crowded now than usual, and it is almost impossible to get accommodations. A great many persons, mostly women and children are constantly arriving from Washington and beyond our lines. Congress seems to be paralyzed and hardly displays action and spirit equal to the emergency. I have witnessed their proceedings and listened to their discussions frequently, but have observed nothing of special interest. The matter of finance seems to present the greatest difficulty, and well may the wisest heads maturely consider all measures pertaining to this subject before they adopt them. Provisions for the defence of the country and keeping up of the army have generally received prompt and efficient legislation. The evils of extortion and speculation, it seems cannot or have not been remedied. The matter of retaliation on the enemy for crimes and outrages, upon which the country has anxiously awaited and expected legislation, has not yet been voted on. It is a subject of vast importance. Congress hesitates at the mention of retaliation, and shows timidity, doubt and want of confidence, like a bashful young man when about to "pop the question" to the adored object of his affections. This indecision weakens us and strengthens the enemy the longer we indulge in it. It has been one of our most serious faults to be too slow to appreciate the true character and motives of the enemy and to counteract his designs. That it is our imperative duty to adopt rigid and prompt retaliation is to me perfectly plain. Individuals may do well as good members of society to forgive insults and injuries, and in conformity to divine injunction may submit to all manner of outrage; but nations are governed by very different obligations. The honor, interest and welfare of a whole people are under the control and protection of the government and the authorities must "take care that the Republic suffer no harm." When an enemy persists in departing from the customs of civilized war in depriving our citizens and soldiers of life, liberty and property, we should not hesitate to inflict like punishments on their people. It is urged that they would again inflict similar penalty on those of us they might capture. This they do anyhow, and they would have shown no quarter from the start had they not feared retaliation, and just as soon as they find retaliation abandoned then they will carry into effect their original programme. Their government is committed to this policy and their laws require that all rebels be put to death, or at least lose their property and citizenship. This is their judgment and they only need power and expediency to carry into effect. So what can we lose by taking the life of a yankee soldier for every Southern citizen or soldier executed by the abolition forces and authorities?

Our people will endure such measures much longer than they, as the past history of the war proves. The more considerate of them will take due notice of the fact, and see it in a new light, that the Yankees have necessarily to come here and force us away from our homes to murder us, while we only execute them on our own soil — a fate they may easily avoid by staying home.

Such a game would soon have a more decisive check on the advance of the enemy than the delay of pontoons. Hundreds of our citizens have been murdered or are dragging out a weary existence in loathsome dungeons. How long must this be so? Are we afraid to assert and maintain our rights? By hard blows, bold strides and daring achievements we are what we are. Our future policy must be like our past in this respect, and when we see our duty we should not hesitate to perform it. We are able to retaliate on the enemy and make him respect us far enough to compel an observance of the rules of civilized warfare. He has never yet failed to yield when the test was properly put. We have heard the mighty lion roar, we have met him and bearded him in his den, and with all his rage and fury we have dealt him blow after blow and sent him reeling back to his couch till his fierce fiery eyes begin to look drooping and languid and the thunder of his roaring is mingled with pitiful wailings. We have jostled whole yankeedom from centre to circumference, and they have long since found out this is no "artificial revolution," but a terrible illustration of the "irrepressible conflict." The mere indecision and discussion of the subject betrays weakness and want of confidence on our part, while they are encouraged to greater effrontery and injustice. Let it be at once agreed to have a life for a life, punishment for punishment, always decided and prompt, and we may secure the desired object; but if not we cannot be worsted. Those of the enemy in league with armed slaves should suffer whatever penalties the laws impose for such offences, but in a more expeditious way than by common trial. If it be irregular to transfer these cases to the civil authorities of the States, let Confederate tribunals — military or civil — dispose of them.

The excuse that the yankees troops are only agents of their government in this kidnapping and insurrection and not therefore personally and maliciously criminal, is entitled to all but little consideration. Were we at war with a foreign nation, such right might be derived from a state of war as a proper war measure to damage the adversary, but the United States under the Constitution cannot adopt this course. But they have authorized the freeing and arming of Slaves, the reduction of States and other acts completely violating and nullifying the Constitution, pledged faith and all civil and republican law. If we admit this usurpation and evil legislation, and report them as legal acts of a proper government, we must admit also that we all should be hung, our posterity forever disenfranchised and our property be owned by any body strong enough to take it. No. We are sure, the Constitution and laws of the United States, and of the respective States, and of our own Confederacy, forbid such acts, and it is sufficient for us to know that some person or persons from the U. S. have violated these laws and not from any necessity in war, and it is then our plain duty to inflict the penalty.

Truly,

LONG GRABS

[February 23, 1863]

RICHMOND, Feb'y 15, 1863.

Messrs. Editors — I forgot to tell you that an incident occurred as I was leaving camp the other day that came near being the last of "Long Grabs." I was riding a wild horse to the Railroad, and while going through a plantation I discovered a negro on horseback coming towards me as fast as his animal could bring him. He had two immense bundles of straw tied together and swung across the horse's shoulders presenting the appearance of two or three haystacks revolving in a whirlwind. Horses, like people, prefer company when danger is about, and being terribly frightened, I suppose his horse was trying to get up with mine, that he might receive some sympathy in his troubles. I was hardly able to control my animal till I could comprehend the approaching object, when he darted away with me, dashing over fences, ditches and woods. On we went through valleys and over hills, the old negro's horse mending his speed and gaining, and whickering with all his might, while the old negro implored me to stop or invent some plan for his safety. The dogs chased us as we passed houses, the people shouted and got on top of gates and fences, while the little negroes, pigs and geese opened a wide way somewhat as the water of the Red Sea did for the children of Israel. At one moment I was dodging a limb or sapling and at the next glancing back to ascertain the condition of my sable follower, but was unable to distinguish horse, negro or straw in the rolling mass, only that they seemed to go by turns from bottom to top. Finally one of the bundles became untied and scattered out and the weight of the other turned the saddle over, breaking the girth and dropping saddle, negro and all on the ground. The horse soon stopped and I found the negro unhurt but very serious. He manifested extreme disgust at that method of carrying straw, and affirmed that another negro in his regiment, "who never had no sense no how," had invented the plan.

The new Theatre here has been in operation for the last week or two and is a splendid structure. The inside presents a magnificent appearance; the frescoing is beautiful and displays superior taste; and the curtains, paintings and scenery are appropriate and elegant. A few of the actors and many of the plays are equal to the surroundings, but most of the performances are quite inferior. The house is crowded every night with the various grades of the best and worst of society in Richmond. The house will seat some 1500 persons, and counting those who stand on your toes and "scrounge" in, I suppose it will hold 2500. From the moment the doors open it is one universal "irrepressible conflict" till the house is crammed and jammed, and Niblo's Garden, Barnum's or Laura Keene's might well envy the crowds that flock here. It takes a person of superior talent and much study to perform well on the stage, but the players here seem unable or unwilling to present thorough and correct representations, and if they should, their labors would not be appreciated by the audience nor would so much interest and amusement be manifested.

The City Battalion, raised in the city and on local duty, has dress parade every evening in the most public part of the Capitol Square. It is worth the trouble occasionally to see the crowd there assembled and read man's diversified character there so indelibly written. First you notice the dazzling gaudy officer with much brass on his coat and little brains in his head, strutting pompously to the beat of the drum, a la turkey gobbler, with white kid gloves, red sash and sabre salute a la Francaise. Then you are attracted by the exquisite profile of the Baltimore Plug detective, standing vis-à-vis and cigar-a-cigar with the sleek, well fed, well dressed faro dealer, and next to the bewitching figure in rustling silk and broad crinoline flirting with half a dozen smitten and youthful members of the Legislature and juvenile officers. Then you meet a couple of fast young refugees — rares aves — who perhaps have lost all but airs and affectation, love novels and nonsense and now find happiness and plenty therein.

Then there is the mother, growing in years, with her frolicking little chaps whose father has "gone to the wars." She tells the little folks that this is the way papa's regiment does — the swords are all like papa's sword, &c. The lovely bride recently "wooed, wed and won," by the "nice gentleman" in "one of the Departments" strolls leisurely along, hanging on the arm of her husband, happy alike in the sweets of the honeymoon and in the knowledge that he is not compelled to go to the war. Next is a group of prattling, boisterous young ladies and young gentlemen — all delighted with each other — so many "oh my's" and "so glad's" and "so sorry's" and "right mad, indeed." The next chapter of gossip is read to last till next coming evening — consisting of all the "good jokes," "secrets," "stories," "fibs" and "messages" about each other and their acquaintances. Then there is the non-descript — the "man-about town," the officer, government agent, or whatever he can be called, who lives fast, but has no visible means of support. He is from parts unknown, hires fine carriages, has fine clothes, knows all the "big fish," boards at the Ballard Hotel, Spottswood at $6 per day, but never pays his bills. He shapes the fashions and also public opinion in all great sensational matters and is par excellence the critic of men, things and measures. Then we see the dignified, self-important member of Congress, balancing his gold headed cane in his hand with his opera glass dangling from his side and imaging to himself that every body is beholding the eloquent and able member that bored his house with such a windy speech a few days ago. Next is the long, lank knock-kneed, drop-to-pieces individual who reports for the Examiner, his face resembling a circular saw, and his nose and chin nearly meeting, as though he were intended to be an honorary member of the hook and ladder company. Then there is the ragged, saucy news-boy, bawling out, "Here's yer Whig, 'Spatch, 'Zaminer and Enquirer," and the sly colored nurse telegraphing mysterious signs by nods and winks to her sable admirer as he passes on errands. Sic transit glories mundi

Truly,
Long Grabs.

[February 23, 1863]

Richmond, Feb'y. 18.

Messrs. Editors:— Yesterday Gens. A. P. Hill and Stuart visited the Virginia Legislature, which body received them with due respect and took a recess for a few minutes. (Long Grabs was in the party too, but by some strange blunder the Speaker omitted any allusion to him!) Gen. Hill is a small but good looking man, and is about 35 years of age, and graduated No. 15 in a class with Burnside, who was No. 18. He has a keen eye, well formed forehead and full long whiskers like most other military men. He is very pleasant and affable, though apparently silent and reserved, and shows in every movement courtesy and sincerity. Strange to say he and old "Stonewall" do not agree very well. This has probably resulted from some accidental difference or prejudice, and each has a spirit too independent to condescend voluntarily to remove the misunderstanding. Of Gen. Stuart I have already given you some account.

In the lower house of the Confederate Congress the man who makes the most fuss and show, next to the Speaker and reading Clerk, is Henry S. Foote of Tenn. Although he has "played out" several times, he has again turned up anew and is one of the most fluent talkers I have ever heard, not even excepting Venable and his Western rival. There is an old "legend" that once upon a time a bet was made in Washington that Venable was the greatest talker in Congress. It was immediately taken up by the friends of a celebrated Western campaigner, and arrangements were made for the "match," and whichever battery would be silenced first should lose and not be considered "game." They "set to" after dinner and at bed time neither had much advantage of the other, when the spectators all retired leaving the combatants alone. Next day after breakfast the judges went in to note the stages of the race, when they found the western man exhausted and swooned away, his head on the back of his chair and his arms hanging by his side, while Venable had closed in upon his antagonist with his mouth close to the unfortunate man's ear, stating argument after argument and illustration on illustration, while his right forefinger vibrated up and down upon his open left palm, keeping time with the ceaseless roll of his tongue. But I believe Foote could have worn both out in detail. Mr. Foote is a remarkable man and was once described in the old Congress as a "great humbug, perfect gentleman, entire horse, and part alligator." He was born in 1800, in Fauquier Co. Va., educated at Washington College, a Presbyterian Institution at Lexington, Va., studied Law, and settled in Alabama in 1824 and in Mississippi in 1826. He was elected Governor of Mississippi in 1845 over Jefferson Davis, was Senator from Mississippi, 1847 to 1858, and was chairman of the committee on Foreign Relations. He afterwards lived in California and subsequently settled in Memphis to practice Law and is now Representative from the 5th Congressional District of Tenn. He is very formal, sensitive, quick-tempered, of inferior talent and of little influence and consideration among other members. Among the most leading and prepossessing members of the House are Speaker Bobcock of Va., W. P. Miles of S. C., Chilton of Ala., Barksdale of Miss., Smith of N. C., Jones of Tenn., and Perkins of La. Thos. S. Bobcock, Speaker of the House, and who would in certain contingencies have to perform the duties of President, was born in Buckingham county, Va., and is some 40 or 45 years of age. He was a poor boy, and educated by friends and is a self-made man. Mr. Bobcock is a man of superior talent, pleasant manner, and dispatches business with great energy, promptness and ability. He served a few terms in Congress at Washington and was once nominated and supported for Speaker on some of the balloting previous to the election of Pennington of N. J. William Porcher Miles is also a self-made man and was raised in Charleston, educated at Charleston College, and was for some years Professor at that Institution. He was elected to some city office and immediately afterwards elected to the U. S. Congress in place of Mr. Aiken. He is rather under medium size, some 35 years of age or more, with mild but solid and profound expression of countenance, dark complexion and long brown beard. He has kind of acquired foreign accent, speaks well and pleasantly, is very neat and is one of the most courteous and accomplished gentlemen I ever saw. Mr. Miles is a man of talent, great energy and industry, has many warm admirers and will make his mark in the future of our Confederacy. He never assails the motives of his fellow members, and cheerfully yields his measures when there are more available. Although he has his faults, as all others, it affords confidence and satisfaction to know that we have such men in our councils while we have a Lee and Jackson in the field.

In the Senate one's attention is first attracted to Hon. R. M. T. Hunter, Senator from Va., and at present performing the duties of President of the Senate in Mr. Stephen's absence. Mr. Hunter (or Run-Mad-Tom as he was called by his confreres at Washington) is 45 to 50 years of age, was born in Essex county, Va., and educated at the University of Virginia. He became a lawyer and was several times member of the Va. Legislature and was elected to Congress in 1837 and once or twice afterwards, and officiated as Speaker one term. In 1847 he was sent to the U. S. Senate and continued here until Virginia seceded. He is a large, indolent looking man, weighs over 200, and makes an efficient presiding officer. When he rises to put a question or decide a point of parliamentary usage, he talks very loud and fast, seeming in a great hurry to get through so that he can sit down again. He is a man of good order of talent, sound judgment and strong intellect, but not thought to possess superior original powers of mind or versatile genius. Prominent in the Senate are Hill of Ga., Yancey and Clay of Ala., Phelan of Miss., Johnson of Ga., Semmes of La., Davis of N. C. and Burnett, of Ky.

"Yourn till deth,"
LONG GRABS.

[February 26, 1863]

RICHMOND, Feb'y 20th.

Messrs. Editors: Yesterday I thought I would avoid poor fare and high charges and take dinner at a restaurant, one of the "crack" places. After a long time I succeeded in getting one of the servants to notice me and I ordered some steak, sausage, eggs and a cup of coffee. I could have eaten twice as much as was brought, but my purse admonished forbearance. I asked the consequential individual behind the counter what was my bill. "Three dollars and seventy-five cents," replied my hospitable friend. I came, I forked over, I left. City regulations control charges of hack drivers and draymen and should be enforced against other petty extortioners.

The army is on the move or rather on the scatter some way, but nobody knows anything about it. President Davis and Gen. Lee, when questioned on the matter, always express entire ignorance of the whole affair. Gen. Lee keeps a secret well, but I cannot say as to old Jeff.

There are more romantic and historical reminiscences connected with Richmond than a man could study in a year; and it would be impossible to relate many of them only when appropriate to the subject matter. The old building — St. John's church — in which Patrick Henry delivered his celebrated speech of "give me liberty or give me death," to the Virginia Legislature, still stands in the lower part of the city. There are some old tomb stones pointing away back to the time of John Smith and Pocahontas, and many old buildings reared by the hands of the old colonial fathers. But Richmond has not much extraordinary history —

that is reserved for the future. What the present bloody page, that is being added to the annals of the world, may relate of Richmond, cannot now be known; but it has already awarded it a fame co-extensive with that history of Troy.

I regret that the N. C. Legislature made no provision to raise a reserve force for the defence of the State. Any direct or intentional conflict with the general government in the proper exercise of its duties, would of course, be deprecated, and should not be encouraged; but proper and satisfactory arrangements for such a force could have been made without leading necessarily to such consequences.

There should always be, if possible, a force near the enemy when there is a large wealthy district exposed, in order to save as much property and provisions as we could, to protect our people and to keep the enemy within his limits. The condition of North Carolina and Louisiana have been very different from any other States after large portions of their most valuable territory had been occupied, and the Confederate forces were concentrated at other points where more good could be done in the same time. Virginia, Kentucky, Missouri, Tennessee, Mississippi and Arkansas were more overrun than any other sections, but all that could be done any how was done by Confederate forces in their vicinity, and there could not be much use for the State forces if they had raised them. But Eastern Carolina and Central Louisiana have been left at the mercy of squads of yankees and bands of negroes and buffalos[11]. Is it not perfectly plain that a few thousand armed men stationed at the crossings among the swamps and rivers of those sections would effectually check these bands of marauders and murderers? What would be the paltry expense of maintaining this organization in comparison to the loss of millions and millions worth of property, negroes, horses and provisions, that might have been removed and saved by the aid of this force? Louisiana was hardly able to bring out this force after the heart of the State was laid open to the enemy, but North Carolina is able and is still abundantly able and there is time enough yet to do much good, though the lost opportunities can never be recovered nor remedied.

I have recently mingled with the officers and men in nearly all the N. C. regiments in Va. and I find the almost universal sentiment against the Ten Regiment Bill recently under consideration in the Legislature. Many however have not been properly informed of the real merits and provisions of the Bill. I am satisfied this is the sentiment generally entertained in the army, for I made it an object on every occasion to ascertain the feeling on the subject and had every opportunity to do so.

The Opening Address, a poem by Henry Timrod of Charleston, was delivered in the New Theatre last night for the third time. I regard it as an ordinary production, really evincing no very high poetic conception. It is void of inspiration or rapturous thought. Performance last night rather badly rendered.

Truly,
LONG GRABS.

[February 26, 1863]

RICHMOND, Feb'y 22.

Messrs. Editors:—While we repose confidence in our eastern defences, our affairs in the West are not in so hopeful condition. The enemy still struggles to gain control of the Mississippi River, and once fully in possession of it, he cannot be driven from it till forced to make peace and recognize us, and the possession of that river will be a powerful advantage to the enemy in making a treaty of peace. To get full and immediate control of that river and its tributaries would, I believe, ensure an increase of the yankee army of 500,000 men. Vicksburg has been termed the key of the Mississippi, though I regard Port Hudson of much greater importance. If Vicksburg be the key, Port Hudson is the lock of the Mississippi. Port Hudson is a very strong position among gigantic bluffs on the east side of the Mississippi river in Louisiana, a considerable distance below the mouth of the Red river and 10 or 15 miles above Baton Rouge. It is connected by a short railroad (probably not completed) with Clinton, La., some 30 miles Northeast, and Clinton is probably 40 or 50 miles from the nearest point on the N. O. & Jackson R. R. The space between Port Hudson and Vicksburg, some 200 or 300 miles, is the portion of the river we now hold. The Red river, which flanks the state of Arkansas on the South and South-west, flows in between these points, and the Wachita, which penetrates the heart of Arkansas from the South, joins the Red river some 50 miles or more above the mouth of that river. It is said that Port Hudson is the only place in our possession where gunboats can be prevented from passing, and should that place fall it would necessitate the abandonment of the whole State of Arkansas and North-western Louisiana and a falling back on Texas as a base, and Vicksburg would then be of little importance to us.

There being no railroads in that country, and the dirt roads being often impassable, there can be no effectual transportation except by the rivers. If we should throw troops across near Vicksburg the enemy would soon send forces on their front from the Wachita, on both flanks from the Red and Arkansas rivers, and in their rear from the Mississippi. By the fall of Arkansas Post the enemy has Arkansas river, which traverses the State diagonally and gives him free communication to the capital and heart of the state at high water; and the White and St. Francis rivers have been for some time under his control. Should Vicksburg fall or be of no avail, other points below, capable of formidable defence, such as Grand Gulf, Natchez, Fort Adams, and many bluffs and places not named on the maps. The river makes a large bend eastward at Vicksburg, somewhat like a horse shoe though not of that form exactly, and the town and fortifications are on the outside of this bend. The yankees are now cutting a new channel on the river, entirely leaving off this bend and thus straightening the river. Several beds in the river have been cut off in this way and I do not see any reason to doubt their success in this attempt. They succeeded at Island No. 10, and indeed the river often makes these "cuts-off" itself, Sunflower, Tensas, Atchafalaya and Bayou Teche are really "cut-offs." Whether they succeed in changing the bed of the river or not they can convey transports and gunboats. We could still hold Red river and a portion of the Mississippi if we have proper fortifications below Vicksburg, while if Port Hudson falls we lose the river on the other side and all the advantages that our possession of Vicksburg now affords.

It is remarkable that the yankees let two of the noblest opportunities presented during the war, pass unimproved. Just after the destruction of the Merrimac the gunboats could have easily passed Drewry's Bluff and got to Richmond; and Port

Hudson was not fortified till some time after the fall of New Orleans. Let us hope that both places will prove equally successful barriers against the attacks of the invader.

The next Governor's election is attracting some attention in this State. It comes off in May I believe. The present incumbent will not be a candidate I suppose — probably on account of ineligibility. Gov. Letcher has acted a more prominent part in this revolution than any State officer, though Gov. Pickens was perhaps more conspicuous at the commencement. John Letcher was born in Lexington, Rockbridge Co., Va., March 29th, 1813. He entered Washington College but graduated at Randolph Macon; studied law and commenced practice and publishing the "Valley Star" in Lexington in 1839. He was a member of Congress for many years, where his candor, zeal and faithful discharge of duty secured for him the title of "Honest John." In May 1859 he was elected Governor of Virginia for four years over Wm. L. Goggin, a man of great ability and reputation. Gov. Letcher has always been a Democrat and an able advocate of State Rights and has displayed much skill and statesmanship in managing the affairs of the State. In personnel he is of medium size, with blue eyes, florid complexion, lower jaw longer than the upper, nearly bald, and 50 years of age. He wears spectacles, smokes a big clay pipe with reed stem, dresses plainly and is careless, independent and somewhat abrupt in his manners, but has a turn for popularity. It is said that he was an emancipationist early in life; and also, that he is intemperate in his habits.

There has been a great rush for clerkships and positions in the Department here, and it is said that in the Treasury Department alone there are 300 applications and only one vacancy and that is prospective. Judging from the Confederate Almanac and other sources there are but few North Carolinians in office here. I am informed of only two — Mr. Page of Randolph, Doorkeeper of the Senate, and Mr. Fuller of Fayetteville, a clerk in one of the bureaus — I hope these gentlemen will stand up for the rights of our State, for in all measures of National policy and in treaties with other nations the Old North State must look to them as her representatives to exert a due share as her representatives among the Executive heads of the nation.

Of what may be termed the President's staff is Adjutant and Inspector General Cooper, Quartermaster General Myers, Commissary General Northrop, and Surgeon General Moore, all with rank of Colonel, as provided by Act of Congress — President Davis, however, assigned Gen. Cooper, who was a full General, to the duties of Adj't and Inspt'r Gen'l and as a superior officer always retains his higher rank with its pay when performing the duties of an inferior, Gen. Cooper ranks as General though in the office of a Colonel.

Gen. Samuel Cooper is a native of New Jersey, graduated at West Point, was in the Mexican war, and is author of a revised edition of Macomb's tactics. He is some 70 years old, is hard of hearing, has a way of squinting and holding his head to one side and is very quiet and unpretending. He is very assiduous, systematic and energetic in the duties of his office, and is thought to be an efficient officer.

A. C. Myers is of Jewish descent though not a Jew himself. He was raised near Georgetown, S. C., was in the Quartermaster department of the U. S. Army and married a daughter of General Twiggs of the old Army and more recently of N. Orleans. He is some 40 years old, of good education and business qualifications, and deserves more credit than he has received for the management of the Quartermaster department.

L. B. Northrop is also a native of S. C. near Charleston, and was in the old army. His father was a Northern man and his mother was a Bellinger — a family of distinction in S. C. He belongs to the Roman Catholic Church, as did his mother's family.

S. P. Moore is a South Carolinian and an old army surgeon. He is a sour looking individual, some 50 yrs. old, a harsh, profane man, not possessing in my judgment qualifications and disposition requisite for that position.

Truly.
Long Grabs.

[March 2, 1863]

President Jefffeson Davis.

Messrs. Editors: Perhaps it may be interesting to some to review again the history of our Chief Magistrate.

Jefferson Davis was born in Christian county, Ky., in 1805, and while an infant moved to Mississippi with his father, Samuel Davis, who had been a revolutionary soldier. He entered Transylvania University at Lexington, Ky., but left without finishing the course and went to West Point in 1824, where he graduated in 1828, No. 23 in a class of 38 members. He remained in the U. S. Army till 1835 — being seven years required to serve after leaving West Point, — when he resigned and engaged in planting. He was 2d Lieutenant in Infantry from 1828 to 1833; 1st Lieutenant in Dragoons from 1833 to 1835; was Adjutant of the Dragoons and served in the Quartermaster Department at different times. He served in some of the Indian Wars and is said to have captured the celebrated Black Hawk. In 1844 he was Presidential Elector on the Democratic ticket in Mississippi; in 1845 he was a member of the U. S. Congress, and about the same time was defeated for Governor; in 1846 he was made Colonel of the 1st Regiment Miss. VO. (Rifles) in which capacity he served in the Mexican War. He displayed much gallantry, and was severely wounded on one occasion. While in Mexico in 1847 he was tendered the appointment of Brigadier General, but declined it, and in the same year he was appointed U. S. Senator to fill an unexpired term, till 1851, when he was re-elected for six years. He was Secretary of War under Pierce from 1853 to 1857, from which time he was U. S. Senator from Mississippi until that State seceded. During a great portion of his Senatorial career he was Chairman of the Committee on Military Affairs; and while at the head of the War Department he managed its affairs with more ability and success than any of his predecessors. His rule was to encourage merit and sterling worth wherever found, and many of the present officers in the U. S. Army owe their prominence and promotion to him. Feeling a warm interest in McClellan, he sent him and two others to take observations of the siege of Sevastopol, and gain from the Eastern World any information of value to military science.

In 1835 he married a daughter of Gen. Taylor, and some years after her death he married his present wife, Verina Howell, an amiable and excellent lady, daughter of a wealthy commission merchant of New Orleans, and granddaughter of Gov. Howell, of New Jersey, of Revolutionary memory.

President Davis is about 5 feet 10 inches high, and weighs some 140 lbs. He has a well formed and intellectual head, with forehead bulging out considerably, aquiline nose and compressed lip. The cheek bones are prominent, causing the cheeks to appear hollow; his hair is of dark color, mixed probably with gray; and his face is of sallow paleness, but with his keen, steady, dark eye, shows much more color, boldness and animation, than is usually represented in the pictures we see. He wears no whiskers except under his chin and around his throat; and one of his eyes is said to be defective in sight, but this would escape observation.

From his manners and appearance one would naturally, at first, regard him as dignified, morose, and even repulsive; but further acquaintance removes much of this impression, and Mr. Davis appears an agreeable, earnest, candid, accomplished and interesting gentleman. His voice is on an elevated key, distinct and full, and although a little rough is not unpleasant.

As a public speaker, he is practical and impressive, inspiring solemnity and inducing conviction. He neither drives the imagination to the giddy heights of eloquence and intellectual splendor, nor stoops below honor to tickle popular fancy and popular applause; but appealing more to the moral then the sensual attributes of the soul, he speaks what he feels and seems what he is, with that peculiar eloquence with truth, directed to the conscience, always imparts.

He is of the Episcopalian persuasion and was confirmed two or three months ago I learn, and with his family attends St. Paul's Church regularly. On his withdrawal from the U. S. Senate, after the session of Mississippi, he showed, by a very able and powerful

"Jefferson Davis, president of the Confederate States of America." Source: E. Benjamin Andrews, *History of the United States from the Earliest Discovery of America to the Present Day, Volume III* (New York: Charles Scribner's Sons, 1895) p. 320. Used by permission of the Florida Center for Instructional Technology, College of Education, University of South Florida.

speech which did honor to his head and heart, that he fully realized the awful responsibility of the issue forced upon us. It was with deep and unfeigned regret that he felt it his duty to relinquish that government which he had served so long and so faithfully, and for which he had cherished such filial attachment. On that occasion Mr. Davis rose calm and collected, and although the blood of the nation was hot and the popular heart throbbed with agitation, his magnanimity and sincerity extorted admiration and sympathy even from his enemies. With eyes downcast and body motionless, and in a calm, manly, emphatic tone, he said, in substance: "I now leave you for other and different duties, and will never again mingle with you as I have done for so many years. If I have done any one of you injustice, I now ask forgiveness. If in debate or otherwise, I have wounded any Senator's feelings, given insult, or violated courtesy or confidence, I now retract it all. I have been devoted to our once noble government; and I have tried faithfully in the various distinguished positions I have been honored with, to promote its prosperity, purity and durability. I have given the best season of my manhood to the sustaining of the Constitution and the Laws, even when violated and trampled on by others. I have borne aloft that once proud flag amid the roar of battle, and freely poured out my blood in my country's cause. We of the South have offered you compromise;—we have yielded every thing save honor and liberty, that the government inherited from our fathers might not be disrupted and devastated, and in vain. But, gentlemen, appealing to a just God for the rectitude of our intentions, we do solemnly vow that to such outrageous violation of the Constitution, such insane fanaticism, such usurpation, such sectional, tyrannical, constant and dangerous legislation, we will never, never, NEVER submit."

I have had from the first an unwavering confidence in President Davis. This is however my own opinion. I know there are some whose judgment is entitled to respect that do not entertain favorable sentiments towards our chief Executive; and when I find my opinion erroneous than I will change it, but not before.

Although Mr. Davis may have occasionally displayed an unyielding, unaccommodating spirit, we have found in him that tenacity of purpose and those sterling reliable qualities so requisite for a leader in such a crisis. It would be invidious exaggeration to say that all our successes and achievements result from his efforts. But he has shaped the means to the end, fitted the cause to the effect, and so directed the details of our national progress and maintained such a constant firmness amid all the ebbs and flows of popular opinion and prejudice, that the people find a soothing consolation in confidently relying on the wisdom, the ability and the patriotism of their President. He has given caste, character, prestige, to our government at home and abroad, and proved to an unwilling world that he and the government he represents are not the creature of circumstance nor the slaves of expediency. With a sagacity superior to that of most of our public men, he has formed a more correct conception of the character of our enemies and the Revolution which has drenched our unfortunate country in fraternal blood. He insisted that our army be raised for five years, but his recommendation was overruled. He predicted the first serious difficulty of our enemy,—that of finance, and time has verified the prophecy. King Cotton has not yet driven the kings of the east into a supplicating attitude; foreign recognition has been an empty shadow, nor have political divisions yet weakened the hopes of the North; but their debt and financial system is the yawning abyss that threatens to engulf them. He has pursued the same course, unmoved by praise, unmindful of slander, with the success of our cause and the welfare of our country as his highest objects. While the country was enshrouded in gloom and when despondency hung like a pall over the land, with the courage of a hero and the heart of a patriot he lifted his eyes heavenward and rising with the emergency he led the ship of State over the waves of adversity. As has been said by one of the noblest and ablest men of the nation, "President Davis, unlike most leaders of revolutions and with the doom of the chief of traitors full before him in case of failure, has not found it necessary to trespass on the rights of the humblest citizen." Deriving his youthful impressions among the Northern people, having long associated with their best and worst men in the field and in the cabinet, in the National council and in private life; with a pure and proud record behind him; and with the confidence and admiration of a powerful people around him,— a soldier, a statesman, a christian, I know of no one more competent for the position,— no one so well suited to the emergency. Posterity will venerate his memory, and long will his parting words to the U. S. Senate ring in the ears of his Northern associates, and like the last agonizing cry of murdered innocents will haunt their fiendish spirits to perdition. I am not one of those who applaud from sinister motives, but have awarded this tribute to truth and justice. I have never sought any office or favor within the Executive patronage nor do I expect to. Mr. Davis has four or five small children, the oldest — little Jeff— is certainly a "bird," if not a "spoiled chicken." He is a rare specimen of Young America, Jr., is at home in a row among other little boys, often "curses out" the crowd, and generally sets the nursery and whole juveniledom in an uproar. He can use more profanity, turn over more furniture, torment more cats, and invent more scenes of devilment, than all the little boys within his father's jurisdiction. Inheriting the military qualities of his ancestors he is skilled in all manner of infantry; and if they are correct who say old Jeff is the embodiment of self-will and obstinacy, little Jeff is certainly a "chip off the old block."

Truly yours,
LONG GRABS.

[March 12, 1863]

Chapter 5

War on the North Carolina Home Front
March 12, 1863–June 1, 1863

Long Grabs returns to North Carolina and visits the cities of Raleigh, Kinston, Goldsboro. Wilmington, Tarboro, Washington, Greenville, and Hookerton. He reports on the fighting at Washington and at Kinston in 1863. Strangely, he makes no mention of the great battle fought at Chancellorsville, Virginia, in early May; nor does he make any comments on the Federal operations in Eastern North Carolina during the fall of 1862 when he was in Virginia.

General Burnside had taken complete control of New Bern and territory as far south as Fort Macon at Beaufort. Secure now from any attack from the coast in his rear, he prepared to move on the vital railroad center at Goldsboro. However, his plans were interrupted when he was recalled to Virginia to aid in the fighting around Richmond. Later, in December, he would command the Union army at Fredericksburg.

General John G. Foster[1] succeeded him. He strengthened the defenses at New Bern, but he was not a commander to sit behind them awaiting the enemy. He planned a series of raids in the east to keep the Confederates off balance. He ordered the two salt works at Currituck and Bogue inlets destroyed, and he led 5,000 soldiers on a raid toward Tarboro in early November.[2]

The Confederate forces in North Carolina were small, but they were not inactive. Captain S. D. Pool led a small group of soldiers in a surprise attack against the Federal garrison at Little Washington on September 6, 1862. Concealed by morning fog, the force of about 800 men got by the pickets and charged the town, throwing the Union soldiers into confusion. As the fog lifted, two Union gunboats, the *Louisiana* and the *Picket*, opened fire on the

5. War on the North Carolina Home Front 111

Confederates; *Picket's* magazine exploded, sinking the ship and killing the captain and nineteen others. The two forces fought hard for almost three hours; then Pool and his men withdrew, taking with them three field guns and ample ammunition. Later, in December, Confederates staged a raid on Plymouth.[3] While these raids annoyed General Foster and his men, they did not stop their offensive movements.

Reinforcements were sent to New Bern, and in December, Foster took a strong force of about eleven thousand soldiers and headed west toward the vital railroad bridge at Goldsboro. (See map, Chapter 1, for route of Foster's march.) He was pretty much unopposed until he reached the bridge over Southwest Creek below Kinston. It had been burned, and the Confederates were waiting for him on the opposite shore. In time Foster crossed the creek and pushed the Confederate force under General N. G. Evans[4] back to the Neuse River. Here they fought again near the Kinston Bridge, and again Foster drove them across the river.

"General John Gray Foster, born in Whitefield, N. H., May 27th, 1823, died in Nashua, H. H., September 2nd, 1874, was graduated at the United States Military Academy in 1846, assigned to the Engineer Corps, and served in the Mexican War under General Scott. He received the brevets of first lieutenant and captain for gallantry. At the beginning of the Civil War he was stationed at Charleston, S. C., and safely removed the garrison of Fort Moultrie to Fort Sumter during the night, December 26th–27th, 1860. He was made brigadier general of volunteers October 23rd, 1861, commanded a brigade in Burnside's North Carolina expedition, and received the brevet of lieutenant colonel for his services at Roanoke Island. While in command of the Department of North Carolina, in 1862-'3, he conducted several important expeditions. In 1865 he was brevetted brigadier general in the regular army for gallant services in the capture of Savannah, Ga., and major general for services in the field during the rebellion."— Frank Leslie, 1896. Source: Frank Leslie, *Famous Leaders and Battle Scenes of the Civil War* (New York: Mrs. Frank Leslie, 1896) p. 278. Used by permission of the Florida Center for Instructional Technology, College of Education, University of South Florida.

The retreating Confederates set the bridge aflame, but Foster and his men were coming up fast, and the flames were put out. Evans moved a few miles beyond Kinston and prepared a new line of battle, but with darkness approaching the fighting ceased. The Confederates later withdrew. By December 16, Foster reached Whitehall; again he found the bridge burned, and the Confederates waiting on the other side. He was eighteen miles from his objective.

He had learned that Burnside had been defeated at Fredericksburg a few days earlier, and that reinforcements were heading to North Carolina. With time becoming an issue, he left a small force at Whitehall to deal with the Confederates and pushed his main body hard toward the Goldsboro bridge. He arrived on the morning of the seventeenth where a strong force awaited him. Heavy fighting raged for two hours, but Federal soldiers got close enough to fire the bridge. With the Wilmington and Weldon Railroad line now severed, Foster and his men headed back to New Bern.

However, in the next two weeks, Confederate engineers repaired the torn up rails, built a new bridge, and reopened the line to carry vital supplies to the north. When Long Grabs returned, Union forces still controlled a large portion of Eastern North Carolina.

There is no indication of Long Grabs' location when he wrote the sketch of Jefferson Davis; however, on the date the *Fayetteville Observer* published it, he was back in Raleigh, writing a letter to Governor Zebulon Vance on that day requesting an army position in order to further a writing project he had in mind.

Raleigh, N. C.
March 12th, 1863

Dear Sir:

I am informed that you will now appoint an Adjutant General. I would like to get the position of one of the Assistants Adjutant General. It would materially assist me in facilities for preparing some historical sketches of the North Carolina Regiments during the war that I have in contemplation. From a pretty long and varied experience my services might be satisfactory and creditable if not as valuable as those of some others.[5]

Very Respectfully,
Gov. Vance   M. J. McSween

On the back of the letter this was written: "The Gov. has already selected officers for the positions addressed to.— ZBV."

Word of his project began to circulate and on May 18, 1863, the *Fayetteville Observer* published an article which the editors had taken from the *Raleigh Standard*. It was titled "History of the War."

We learn that Lieut. M. J. McSween has been collecting material for a history of all the North Carolina troops in this war. Officers, chaplains, and all others who can do so, would do well to furnish him with any items, sketches or

5. War on the North Carolina Home Front 113

descriptions of battles, marches, acts of individual merit, &c., with a full, connected and impartial history of regiments, companies and detachments. He designs especially, as far as he can, to award to North Carolina her just deserts. Any thing pertaining to a fair and faithful record of the part performed by North Carolina and her people in this great struggle, will appropriately belong to this work. Any information of the kind referred to will be duly forwarded, if left to our care. Lieut. McSween has been connected with the army since the formation of the first regiments in South Carolina when that State seceded; and besides his experience in service, he has had extensive opportunities for seeing the different portions of our army. It will of course require much time and labor to prepare such matter as this, but North Carolina will never get justice except at the hands of her own sons.[6]

It was an ambitious project; however, it is unknown what, if anything, was sent to him about regimental activities or even if he made a start on it. We have hints of what it might have been from his soldier descriptions while in Virginia and his short narratives of individual participants in the war. Had it been written, it would have provided an eyewitness, on-the-spot view of the war as it happened and not a look-back through the mists of time when memories may have faded.

Eastern North Carolina was a rich farming area, producing crops much needed by Lee's army, but with Union troops controlling a large section of the area, harvesting and shipping them would be difficult. They would have to be held in check in tidewater Virginia and in North Carolina's coastal plain for supplies to move northward. To do this, General James Longstreet would move against Suffolk, Virginia. He also dispatched Major-General Daniel Harvey Hill, a native North Carolinian and the brother-in-law of Stonewall Jackson, to create diversions at New Bern and Washington. Hill took command of the troops on February 25, 1863.[7] An unidentified letter writer to the *Observer* confirmed knowledge of this diversionary movement in a letter written from Kinston on March 17 and published in the *Observer* on March 26, 1863:

> Messrs Editors: Having accompanied the main column in the recent advance upon Newbern, I can give you some particulars which you may not find elsewhere.
> It is generally understood that it was only a strategic movement to cover an attack elsewhere, and yet I suppose, if all the parts of the plan so well conceived had been carried out successfully, Newbern would have been entered.[8]

Around the same time, Long Grabs set a missive.

> RALEIGH, March 13.
>
> Messrs. Editors:—We have rumors of something awful about to happen down about Newbern, but what, how, or when, has not yet been made known to vulgar ears. Just a year ago Newbern fell, and its recapture at this time would be

very gratifying. If anything very serious takes place down there, "Long Grabs" will be on hand, and in the language of Phil "will either get killed or distinguish himself." Everything remains in status quo in Raleigh, though not entirely in status quo ante bellum. You see pretty much the same old faces — some handsome, some hideous — the same signs, the same stores, the same sharp looking man with the same sharp pen behind his ear at Yarborough's, the same omnibuses, the same little boy with a bunch of Daily Progresses, and the very same bar rooms on "grog alley" with the same glasses and decanters, and you run against the very same lamp post as you leave there.

A day or two ago I visited the Confederate Hospital at the Fair Grounds. I find there is great improvement in this establishment and that it is admirably managed now, with very few deaths and not many serious cases. My opportunities for observing the management of hospitals have been very good, especially those about Raleigh, and I have not seen more attention to patients and better management of all hospital affairs than is the case at the Fair Ground Hospital, though the hospitals in Charlottesville, Va. are perhaps equally as well conducted. The hospital is in charge of Dr. E. Burke Haywood[9] of this place, assisted by Drs. Little of Raleigh and Gilliam of Bertie, who are very kind and attentive. Dr. Haywood is one of the most eminent physicians in the State, and is one of those liberal, energetic, unselfish and conscientious men of high honorable principle, kind and obliging disposition, whom we so much need and so rarely find in these degenerate times. He confines himself most assiduously to his duties, visiting the whole establishment twice every day and often visits patients during the night if they are seriously ill. He requires prompt and faithful discharge of duty of all the employees in the hospital, and sees that everything is accounted for and properly appropriated. He is a man of fine judgment and business qualifications and enjoys in a great degree the confidence and respect of those under his charge. There are some 75 or 80 patients there now. The old hospital buildings at Camp Mangum are used for small pox, and there are some 25 or 30 cases I learn and in charge of Dr. Page of this county and Dr. Anderson of Stanly.

I find it my duty to "tell" on some of the officers and soldiers in Virginia. I know I promised to say nothing about it, but I have too high a respect for the wives and sweethearts of the soldiers and it must "out." The whole matter is that some of our soldiers who have wives and children at home have married again among the Virginia girls. The sweet lovely damsels of the Valley and Fredericksburg little think as they take these gay young gentlemen "for better or for worse" that they have left other devoted wives and prattling chaps behind. An instance of this sort "leaked out" a short time ago. A "nice young Lieutenant" of a Louisiana Regiment wrote a very long endearing letter to his newly married bride who was staying a few miles away from camp, and accidentally, but unfortunately for him, he sent the wrong letter to each, so that his lovely bride got the letter intended for the wife of his "buzum" and she the other. I guess that made a "fuss in the family," if not in both families.

LONG GRABS.

[March 16, 1863]

General Hill began his move against New Bern on March 13. Four roads, which Long Grabs will discuss in a later letter, lead from Kinston to New Bern and beyond. Brigadier-General Junius Daniel took his brigade down the lower Trent Road; he soon encountered pickets and drove them back to their entrenchments at Deep Gully. With four companies, Daniel changed them and drove them out, but darkness halted further action. Reinforced, the Yankees tried to retake Deep Gully the next morning, but failed, and retreated back to New Bern. Brigadier-General B. H. Robertson, who commanded the cavalry, was moving on the south side of the Trent River with orders to tear up the railroad tracks. Brigadier-General James Johnston Pettigrew, along with artillery, headed for Barrington's Ferry with orders to bombard Fort Anderson and the gunboats in the river. (See map, Chapter 1.)

A soldier in Pettigrew's Brigade, signing his name "Percy," described their part of the action at Fort Anderson, in a letter of April 8, later published by the *Fayetteville Observer* on April 16, 1863:

> Gen. Pettigrew's Brigade left the vicinity of Goldsboro' the 9th of March. We left our baggage and knapsacks at Kinston and continued our march down on the north bank of the Neuse. After two or three days' hard marching through the mud and swamps of Eastern Carolina, and very often wading water over knee deep, on the 14th of March, the anniversary of the fall of Newbern, we drove in the enemy's pickets at Barrington's Ferry, opposite and in full view of Newbern. In a few minutes our Artillery was in position and thundering away upon a small fort on the north bank of the river. The enemy were completely surprised, and utterly astonished at the audacity of the rebels appearing in force with artillery, where for twelve months a single scout had scarcely dared to show himself. The town was soon in a great bustle and signal guns were fired from batteries and gunboats in every direction. After shelling the fort a few minutes, Gen. Pettigrew sent a flag of truce and demanded a surrender of the fort, (and I expect he wanted to find out whether or not the place could be charged by infantry.) After twenty or thirty minutes deliberation the commander refused to surrender, and our batteries again shelled the fort for half an hour or more, nearly every shell bursting over it. Our rifled pieces hit the gunboats a number of times as they came up, but our light artillery had to retire when the boats got in good range with their heavy guns, after bursting one of our best guns and wounding three men severely, one of whom has since died. The 26th Reg't remained in sight of the fort and exposed to the shells of the enemy four or five hours; we had two killed and about twenty wounded during the shelling; two of our men have since died. We waited till evening to see if the enemy would come out of the fort. But he did not venture out to see where we were.[10]

"Percy"

RALEIGH, March 16.

Messrs. Editors:— There has been fighting at Kinston, but the result is not fully known here yet. The action so far as I have learned appears to have been skirmishing. It seems that an onward movement and a general attack by our forces is designed, but it is rumored that Gen. Hill has fallen back to within 15 miles of Kinston. We have many large, fine N. C. Reg't's down there though but few of them have ever been in battle. The enemy can reinforce very promptly I presume, unless we should get possession of the river below Newbern, and then, controlling the river below, we would be able probably to capture the town and all in it.

Board is increasing here every week and provisions seem to be getting higher and scarcer. Five dollars a day for transient custom is charged at the principal hotels. I cannot think however that the prices of provisions justify these charges. I heard a gentleman say to-day that he has some six or eight in family, mostly grown persons, and that it cost him $10 apiece a week to feed them. He lives as well as the market affords but has to buy every thing he uses, and besides he is a refugee and had to commence house keeping anew entirely some months ago — $10 a week is about $40 a month, and $5 a day is about $150 a month and even $3 a day is $90 a month. This difference with scanty fare will give an idea of the profits of hotel keepers.

Oh! how I long once more for the good old times of cheapness and plenty on Rockfish, where I used to throw sweet bread at the birds as I rode to church with my old Aunt in a blue-top gig, and where the honey was thrown away because there was no place to put it and butter given to the hogs! While memory lasts (especially when hungry,) I shall cherish a fond recollection for those hallowed places. I love that plain energetic and intelligent people, whose hearts are as pure as the limpid waters of their own Rockfish. There the latch string hangs outside and happy faces and warm hands greet you within. It has been many years since I have crossed those ancient thresholds and enjoyed the genuine Scottish hospitality of the land of my birth, and although I have wandered through distant States and seen much that is noble and great, my heart still turns to the simple customs, the manly independent character and the thrilling Scottish legends of "fatherland." If I show some enthusiasm I hope I will not be regarded as sentimental or crazy, for the Tweed had its Sir Walter Scott, the Hudson its Washington Irving and why not Rockfish have its "Long Grabs?" It has been often suggested that the Scotch of the Cape Fear region form a company or regiment to represent more distinctly their nationality and ancient valor. If the war continues much longer perhaps some Scottish Chief (even "Long Grabs") may sound the pibroch, gather the clansmen and unsheathe the claymore and strike as our fathers struck for freedom among the Highlands, and at Culloden, at Bannockburn and at Wagram.

It would be highly proper to modify the conscript law so as to allow the men to form new companies and regiments and elect their own officers. This suggestion is offered with reluctance, as I have studiously avoided any kind of partisan or political discussion, and cannot sympathize with any movement solely for party purposes or needless opposition to our cause during the war, even though it proceed from pure motives. Having had ample opportunity to see the operation of the conscript law in its present form, I am satisfied that some improvement of the kind is necessary to its efficiency. I have found that where men have been sent in small squads, and even in larger numbers, to regiments, and especially regiments not of their choice, that they are unhappy and discouraged. They are ridiculed and scoffed at till they feel mean; and, cowed and despairing; many desert and are disgraced, or become demoralized. In new organizations of their own they fight with equal if not superior bravery to any other troops. They feel like a persecuted band of brothers against whom the world's scorn and suspicion is directed, and they make greater effort to retrieve a reputation thus assailed. As an instance of the 57th Reg't composed largely of conscripts has covered itself with glory. Old regiments could be consolidated and satisfactorily, and all being veterans would experience little difference. A conscript is as good as any body else, but the old volunteers won't treat them so. Recruits become drilled nearly as quick in a new as in an old company now. I fully believe the best way to recruit the army in numbers and efficiency is by new regiments.

LONG GRABS.

P. S. It was in 1851 and not 1845 that Mr. Foote defeated President Davis for Governor of Miss; the data from which I collected my sketch being erroneous. In speaking of W. P. Miles, I intended to say "a full brown beard mixed with gray."

L. G.

[March 19, 1863]

Long Grabs' comment in the previous letter that "General Hill has fallen back to within 15 miles of Kinston," was correct. Since neither Pettigrew nor Robertson had achieved their objectives, Hill had to withdraw from New Bern. At Goldsboro, where he now had his headquarters, Long Grabs would have some contact with the general, who turned his attention now toward Little Washington. His orders from Lee and Longstreet were to avoid an all-out attack on the city, but to take it by siege. By March 30, he had achieved this. It also gave him time to send some of his soldiers out into the surrounding counties to collect bacon and corn for shipping north to Lee's army.

CAMP NEAR KINSTON, N. C., March 22.

Messrs. Editors: A few more "long grabs" and I have pulled up here. I left Raleigh in company with my affectionate friend, "Lemons," expecting to write my next from Newbern, but I learned on the way that the movement of our troops was a feint both on the yankees and all other outsiders. I confess I was as badly sold as the yanks. At Goldsboro' I met up with Gen. Hill and staff and sundry other dignitaries and was honored with a drink of "old Apple" from the "____ Jug." This jug is a huge structure, capable of holding three or four gallons and travels round occasionally free of rail road freight, for sick and wounded soldiers. It had no doubt dispensed its blessings freely as I found not exceeding a quart in it.

Kinston is a pretty place and is the centre of what was once a wealthy, thriving and intelligent country. I once heard when a boy how the place got its present name. It was first called Kingston or Kingstown, in honor of George the Third. During the last war with Great Britain, the citizens determined not to retain a memento of a ruler who had inflicted on them such wrongs. As the most pointed way of showing their hatred for King George and his country, they changed the name to Kinston.

The Neuse flows along the southern border of the town, and has furnished us large quantities of shad until the recent rain. I have been luxuriating in shad (making way with two or more each meal) until I no longer sigh with the poet:

> Oh! for some vast wilderness
> Some boundless contiguity of shad,
> Where rumor of hunger and want of sleep
> Might never reach me more.!"

I find that certain degraded specimens of humanity have been speaking in very disrespectful terms of my good looks and personal appearance. Now I would politely request these individuals to attend to their own business. A man should not be blamed because he happens to have big feet, or big hands and ears, or looks ugly.

Gen. Hill's headquarters are now at Goldsboro. He believes in active operations and intends giving the yanks a lively time. He makes many pointed remarks and issues many pointed orders that cut deep and wide. The shrewd officer or cute old soldier who tries to come the "dodge" over him generally gets out second best. The guilty and innocent sometimes share alike his surplus satire and wrath; and pious, simple-minded officials on petty courts-martial are not unfrequently shocked at the summary manner in which he knocks all their carefully arranged proceedings into a cocked hat. Just before Gen. Hill left the army in Virginia, Dan _____, chief musician in Iverson's Brigade, sent up a furlough for approval. The aforesaid Dan had devoted his time almost exclusively to music at Chapel Hill along with _____ _____, and carried on an organized Band for several sessions, so that when Dan went into the army his appropriate sphere was music. Well, Dan thought as he had been so long inspiring his countrymen with the lays of martial music that he might claim a furlough with the rest, although he had killed no yanks. Imagine his chagrin when his furlough was returned, endorsed: "Respectfully disapproved. Shooters before tooters. D. H. Hill, Maj. Gen. Com'dg."

Daniel's Brigade is here at present and others are not far off. All the troops move about so much that when you see a regiment you can't tell when or where you will meet it again.

From Kinston to Newbern is 34 to 36 miles by different roads, of which there are four proper, all running between the Neuse and Trent rivers. The one next to the Neuse is called the "Neuse river road," the next "Dover road," the next the "Lower Trent road," and the other the "Upper Trent road." The Neuse heads in Caswell county and runs generally South-east near Wake Forest and some six miles East of Raleigh, by Smithfield, Goldsboro,' Kinston, to Newbern, where it widens out into a bay and continues in the same direction for 26 miles, getting wider, and then turn North-east and uniting with the Pamlico river (another name for Tar river near its mouth,) it forms Pamlico Sound, a large inland body of water separated from the main ocean by a long narrow strip of sand bank.

The Trent River heads in Duplin county and flows East through Jones county

5. War on the North Carolina Home Front

by Trenton and Pollocksville, and into the Neuse just below Newbern. The Trent is said to be navigable for small steamboats to Pollocksville, some 15 miles, and is distant from the Neuse opposite Kinston some 20 miles, South. The Neuse is navigable at high water to Goldsboro,' and is now very effectually blockaded a few miles below Kinston. Core creek runs into the Neuse on the South side, and some 20 miles perhaps above Newbern. Deep Gully is a small stream some 8 or 10 miles from Newbern and runs South into the Trent. This stream is a deep ravine on the road where Daniel's Brigade made their recent advance. Swift Creek is on the North-east side of, and somewhat parallel with, the Neuse, and runs into it a few miles above Newbern. The road from Newbern to Washington runs from Newbern South of the Neuse and crosses it above the mouth of Swift creek bridge.

It is said that Newbern is very strongly fortified and that there is a semi-circle of breast-works some mile or two west of the town, extending from the Neuse to the Trent. In front of this, dirt and timber embankment it is said there is a wide deep ditch mostly filled with water, and at each end is stationed a gunboat, one in the Neuse and the other in the Trent. There are said to be fortifications on the East side of the river opposite Newbern, and also down the Railroad towards Morehead City; and some other gunboats anchored in the river near town. In the recent movement a portion of Daniel's command advanced between the Neuse and the Trent, and Robertson took some cavalry and went South of the Trent and tore up the Railroad below Newbern, while Pettigrew went down East of the Neuse with some troops, all converging in the vicinity of Newbern. Gen. Pettigrew found a fort on the East side of the river near Newbern, but occupied by a small force of infantry. None of the guns had been mounted though several were there. The permanent occupation of this place would have afforded ample opportunity to shell Newbern, but it was impossible to shelter his men from the gunboats nearby. He fired for sometime however on the fort and at the gunboats, but found it necessary to retire. It is reported that the enemy in the fort asked half an hour to consider whether to surrender, during which time the gunboats moved up to a better position, which forced our men to retire. Our troops displayed the gallantry of veterans at Deep Gully, where they encountered some artillery, 4 infantry companies and some outposts in a strong position. As the enemy saw our men about to charge, they fled in the greatest confusion, carrying their cannon muzzle foremost, and scattering knapsacks, blankets, &c., as usual, which our boys gathered up eagerly. Some of our advance guard displayed great coolness and daring. The 43d Reg't, which is one of the finest regiments in service, attracted special attention.

Marching in this country among the swamps and mud is worse and destroys health sooner than the tramp in Virginia. But there are two great luxuries the soldier finds here that he seldom gets in Virginia, lightwood knot fires and potatoes. In Virginia he has to nurse and blow his fire a long time to get it to burn, but here he can pile up a few knots, strike a match and in a few minutes it illuminates the surrounding woods. This was once literally the land of "milk and honey," and the goddess of plenty shed her sweetest smiles on its inhabitants. But now desolation and ruin, starvation and misery, pervade the hills, the waters and the very atmosphere. Scarcely do we see

> One rose of the wilderness left on its stalk,
> To mark where a garden has been.

The finest plantations of our own Carolina have been almost blotted out of existence, and nothing remains of these old happy and hospitable homesteads but a pile of cinders and ashes, and naught disturbs the sad serenity of the scene but the hooting of the owl:

> For there the voice of mirth resounds no more,
> A silent sadness through the place prevails;
> The distant main alone is heard to roar,
> The hollow chimneys hum with sudden gales.
> Vain was the widow's, vain was the orphan's cry,
> To touch their feelings or to soothe their rage —
> Vain the fair drop that roll'd from beauty's eye,
> Vain the dumb grief of supplicating age.

Truly yours,
LONG GRABS.

[March 26, 1863]

CAMP NEAR KINSTON, March 24.

Messrs. Editors: The country is infested with four plagues — the small-pox, the yankees, the conscript, and starvation, — and some one of them is almost certain to get a fellow. If the conscript gets him, and the yankees afterward take him, and he then have small-pox and starve to death, it would indeed be a quadruple misery.

There is an old negro barber here — Mose — who once belonged to Edward Stanly's[11] father, but was emancipated many years ago by his old master. Mose nursed the bogus Governor while an infant and has been very anxious to visit him at Newbern and get him to quit his foolishness and not take sides against his old master's friends. Mose entertains extreme disgust for the yankees. (They broke into his shop while at Kinston and took all his razors and some hundred dollars or more of specie.)

Yesterday I visited Gov. Caswell's grave, two miles above Kinston, and was no less surprised than humiliated to find not even a sign of a grave to mark the last resting place of Richard Caswell, the first Governor of the State and the first field-officer of N. C. Troops in the war of '76, and one of North Carolina's greatest and best men. Gov. Caswell was twice married, and a small oak on the north bank of the Neuse, between the graves of his two wives, marks the spot where rest his ashes. Nearby are several graves of the Caswell family and others, which can be seen from the Railroad, which runs within two hundred yds. on the north. A short distance from the grave stood the house where Caswell lived, but there are but few visible signs of the old signs of the old residence now. The surrounding fields, now a part of Mr. Desmond's plantation, have been cultivated over a century. The most expressive monument I ever saw was a plain granite slab in a church-yard in Charleston, marked simply "Calhoun," and a small square stone or obelisk placed on this grave, with the word "Caswell," would convey a volume of sentiment, and its simplicity and significance would leave an impression on the memory never to be erased. It is a disgrace to the State and a mockery on our pretended veneration for the departed great, that the grave of Richard Caswell has been forgotten and dishonored by the neglect of ungrateful posterity. What is the Historical Society doing? Where is "old Bunk?" Caswell's ancestors came from Maryland I think, and Gen. Gatlin's mother and Mrs. White of Raleigh (mother of Governor Swain's wife and also the wife of Dan'l L. Barringer, former member of Congress from the Wake District and more recently of Tennessee) were his daughters.

The citizens of this section express the highest opinion of Gen. Evans as an officer and as a man, and so do the troops who have acted with him.

Yesterday private D. B. Thompson, from Guilford county, in Co. D, 53d N. C. T., received 39 lashes on his bare back in the presence of the brigade for desertion. He is also to be confined 2 hours in the stocks and the same time in the pillory each day for 15 days. It seems that while at Goldsboro' some time ago he left his company and with malice aforethought and without the fear of the Army Regulations before his eyes, he did feloniously take, seize, steal, possess, appropriate and borrow a certain horse while the owner was absent, and with several days' rations he did maliciously, covertly, in his right mind and of his own free will, attempt to bribe the pickets and escape to his affectionate friends the yankees at Newbern. He is a small man of some 25 years, and stupid, hang-dog countenance, and seems devoid of self-respect or pride of character, and probably ate as much dinner after the whipping as any one who witnessed the scene, though he bellowed out while receiving it. He will never survive the disgrace, and with his descendants is an object of pity.

Perhaps some of the most striking and interesting classes of men in the army are the teamsters, pioneer corps, couriers and scouts. They constitute the feet, the eyes and the ears of the army, and are usually from that most useful and energetic branch of society — the middle class. They are generally shrewd, hardy men, of fair education and moderate means. The teamsters and forage masters are mostly cunning horse traders, experienced horse-doctors and good riders, and understand well how to shift off heavy duties and responsibilities on their unsuspecting associates. The pioneers and working parties are skilled in carpentering, mill-wrighting, and blacksmithing, and have long been the centre channel for all neighborhood gossip while working at their trade through the country or in their public smithy at the forks of the road near some Church. The couriers and scouts are generally mail-riders, stage-drivers, deputy sheriffs, hunters and surveyors, who have been through all sorts of places in all sorts of weather, and met all kinds of men at all times of night or day. They are all well posted in strange hearsay history, traditions, ghost stories, and "old wives fables," and are familiar with the stars, and the changes and times of the moon. They know the best time to kill meat, to fish, and to bait turkeys. They can make poultices, teas and salve, cure sprains, coughs and rheumatism, and invariably love a dram and know how to make themselves comfortable. Can such a people be whipped, when all the elements and essence of society are combined with the vast resources of the country into such a powerful, determined army. All the characters I have mentioned are as useful and as honorable in their spheres in the army as heretofore in their respective callings, though too often abused and insulted by snobs and upstarts accidentally and unworthily their superiors in rank.

I am satisfied that the disloyalty which has been charged to this section by some whose motives I shall not discuss, is confined almost entirely to worthless characters or persons of Northern or foreign extractions. The citizens of responsibility, character and respectability have almost unanimously stood up boldly for our government and its interest, and still maintain their integrity and proudly defy the savage invader, though their property and families have been ruined and they themselves subjected to every species of outrage and degradation. But there is a class, consisting of the depraved and unprincipled as well as simple and ignorant, which seek refuge in the bosom of their country's enemies and aid in thrusting the dagger at the heart of those who once protected them and made them what they were. This class however is comparatively small and is controlled and sustained by desperadoes, northern adventurers, horse-thieves and men who have escaped the gallows or suffered punishment for crime. Of this place, was a man named Watson, a native and passingly respectable, but always unreliable, forward and deceitful. He offered himself as guide to Gen. Evans and was accepted as he knew the country and possessed intelligence. He discharged his duties faithfully for Gen. Evans and then deserted to the enemy and acted as faithfully for them, by which they got all necessary information and he is now with them in Newbern.

The lands in this portion of the State are very fine and farming is much more profitable than in the upper portions of the State. The range, especially for hogs, is superior to any I have ever seen. Cotton yields better here than in the Pee Dee section of either North or South Carolina, and has been cultivated since the country was first settled, but not extensively till fifteen or twenty years ago. Corn grows as finely as in Alabama or Mississippi, and the crop is much more certain as drought affects the land but little and it is sufficiently sandy and elevated not to be much injured by wet. Fig, grapes, apples, peaches and such fruits, grow with little attention. Timber is abundant and pastures can be extended at pleasure. Turpentine and timber added a small increase to business ten or fifteen years ago, but corn, pork, beef-cattle and cotton have been invariably the products of this whole country from the earliest settlements. From a period of about 30 to 15 years ago eastern and central Carolina was nearly depopulated by emigration to the South and West, but since that time emigration has measurably stopped, farming has improved, internal improvements commenced, and the resources of the country have been slowly developing, and consequently a tide of permanent solid prosperity has set in till temporarily interrupted by the war.

The troops here are in good health and spirits and there are some changes and movements on hand, but of what character or importance remains among the impenetrable secrets of our Generals.

Truly yours,

LONG GRABS.

[March 30, 1863]

KINSTON, N. C., March 26.

Messrs. Editors: While this war so far has developed but few great heroes and generals, there are many who have written their names so high and carved them so deep on the Temple of Fame that Time's effacing finger can never blot them out. Among those who have earned enviable distinction is Maj. Nethercutt of Nethercutt's Battalion. The Yankees call the Battalion "bush whackers," and the common people in the low country call it "Nethercutt's Folks." Maj. J. H. Nethercutt is a citizen of Jones county, was Sheriff of that county for some time, is a man of great energy, and admirably qualified for partisan warfare. It is said that the Yankees have offered or pretended to offer a reward for him and some of his men. They frequently promise rewards for persons, but refuse payment when they get the prisoner, a small but just requital due such a miserable scamp as would betray his fellow countrymen. Maj. Nethercutt was 1st Lieut. in the 27th Reg't N. C. T. under Col. G. B. Singeltary, and was detached on scout or outpost duty and commenced operations with only six men. He afterwards raised his command to a company, and more recently a battalion of four companies. His home and property have been destroyed by the Yankees, and his men, who are chiefly from Jones and adjoining counties, are generally in the same condition. They have pledged hostility and destruction to the invader. They know every path, slip through swamps, woods and ravines unperceived, and "at such an hour that the yanks think not, Nethercutt and his men come." They go on foot, and have only a few mounted scouts; indeed cavalry is not of much service in swampy countries, unless to make sudden raids or traverse an extensive region. Nethercutt's troops have taken a large number of prisoners, killed many of the enemy, and have been a terror to yanks, buffaloes, and runaway negroes. It is said that Nethercutt will not travel on a public road any where if he can find a hog path. He has paid but little attention to the minutiae of drilling, and his men know but little about "column, on right by file into line," present arms — one, two," and that classic term, "hep." When Nethercutt brought his men up to be mustered, Col. Kenan said, "just break your battalion into columns, Major." The Major looked at his men and they looked at him, and then turning to Col. Kenan with a vacant smile, he said, "Do what, Colonel?" The Col. repeated, when Maj. N. replied, "you must do that yourself, for we nothing about it."

An intimate friend, who is an officer in a battery from Macon, Geo., that accompanied Gen. Pettigrew on his recent move against Newbern, has given me some additional information of that expedition. The Brigade, with two batteries, moved in splendid order and very cautiously, marching day and night, and halted a while before daylight some two or three miles from Newbern, east of the river. About daylight, on the day after the Deep Gully skirmish, they moved up within two or three hundred yards of the fortifications on the east bank of the Neuse, and parked their artillery — 13 guns — in a semi-circle around the enemy's works having driven in their pickets a few minutes previously, completely surprising the whole force. The river is about a mile wide at this place, which is directly opposite Newbern, and two gunboats were visible on the side next to town. Gen. Pettigrew demanded surrender of the work and force in front of him, which after 20 or 30 minutes' consultation was refused. His artillery then opened on the place (about sun-rise) and although our forces were so close (the infantry being just behind the artillery) not a shot was fired by the men in the fortification, through they were armed with muskets and rifles but did not have any cannon mounted. The batteries on the other side of the river and the gunboats replied to our artillery, and finally got the range pretty exactly. The action continued thus for some time, and the number of gunboats increased to a dozen or more, when our forces retired, having disabled one or two gunboats and damaged others. The number in the fort was variously estimated at from 250 to a full regiment. The gun which my friend had charge of burst during the action, knocking him down, killing one man and wounding several, some of whom died afterwards. Many of the enemy were killed and wounded, and we lost one killed and a few wounded. Some surprise has been expressed why our infantry was not ordered to charge the fortifications and take the garrison prisoners; but I presume satisfactory reasons existed for not doing so. The place itself could not have been defended against gunboats, though it might have been taken. Our batteries could have easily shelled the whole town from their position, and some shells were thrown into it. Our forces then retreated rapidly, but in tolerable order, and double-quicking much of the way for 20 miles or more, many became exhausted and broke down. The enemy had thrown a large force up Swift Creek in our rear, and there were but one or two roads, through interminable swamps, for our retreat.

A soldier in Pettigrew's Brigade, signing his name "Percy," described their part of the action at Fort Anderson, in a letter of April 8, later published by the *Fayetteville Observer* on April 16, 1863. He also took issue with Long Grabs about his comment that their soldiers double-quicking in their retreat: "I see that one of your correspondents heard that we retreated in tolerable order, double quicking nearly twenty miles. That was a great mistake; we retreated in as good an order as could have been desired. Our main force rested and slept half the night afterward in five miles of the fort, and were only twelve miles distant next day at 12 o'clock. We did double quick part of five or six miles the next day to get a position at Swift Creek Village, which we heard the Yankees were trying to occupy to cut us off, but there was no disorder at all, except that a few sick and weak men could not keep up."[12]

Long Grabs continues.

Conspicuous in the northern suburbs of Kinston is the magnificent residence of Mr. Washington, a prominent citizen of this section. The house is a substantial brick structure, surrounded by a beautiful grove on a wide hill overlooking the town. The yard is adorned with rich evergreens, shrubbery and mounds, intersected by clean pebbled walks. The fragrant flower garden, with its ornamental arches and arbors, and elegant family burial-ground, displays at once the beauties of nature and art combined. The fruiteries, vineyards and orchards show much taste and skill in their collection and arrangement. Mr. Washington is a brother of Gov. Graham's wife and of the wife of Mr. Bryan, a lawyer of reputation formerly of Newbern and now of this place. He has lost considerably by the Yankees, but they did not stay long enough to damage his place materially. A number of his negroes had packed up some wagons and started, "bag and baggage," to their northern brethren, but our forces came up in the meantime and Gen. Evans would not let them pass our lines, and being just "a leetle too late," they returned home and were much mortified when their master did not want to receive them.

Daniel's brigade has been relieved here by Kemper's brigade and gone to "parts unknown." Of North Carolinians here are Nethercutt's battalion, Cummings' and Bunting's artillery companies from Wilmington, and Cameron's battery from Hillsboro.' Robertson's cavalry brigade is "all about," and it is said we have batteries, squadrons and detachments all along the roads and rivers and at tollbridges (to collect the toll from the yanks when they cross I suppose.) It is rumored that the enemy has reinforced Newbern and strengthened and advanced his pickets all around. The pickets have not become civilized yet, like those in Virginia, but fire on each other when they can. They are usually from 5 to 15 miles apart below here. There are rumors of occasional skirmishes down east between detachments of the enemy and advanced posts of troops.

Gen. Kemper's brigade is a fine body of troops and are veterans in the service. The General is a relative of the celebrated Kemper of Kemper's battery, and is prominently mentioned as a candidate for next Governor of Virginia.

The skies are again clear and mild sunshine and gentle breezes indicate the approach of Spring.

Truly yours,

LONG GRABS.

[March 30, 1863].

GOLDSBORO, N. C., March 28.

Messrs. Editors: Ransom's Brigade is here now, except the 24th Reg't, which is somewhere below here on the Railroad towards Wilmington. The Brigade consists of the 24th, 25th, 35th, 49th and 56th N. C. Reg'ts. It is thought they will not remain stationary long.

The government has had 20 or 25 workmen engaged in constructing pontoons here since sometime in Dec. There are some 19 or 20 pontoon wagons that were captured near Fredericksburg, and 15 or more pontoon boats and accoutrements made here, now ready for service. The pontoon is of good pine lumber, 12 or 14 feet long, 4 feet wide and some 3 feet deep. It is shaped like an ordinary ferry boat, left open on top and made as light as possible. The wagon is a very strong frame work on heavy wheels, and the pontoon is placed on it like a wagon bed, and may be piled with baggage, lumber or forage, like a wagon. Six horses or more are attached. The pontoon is placed lengthwise in the stream and held steady by a small anchor and chain, and the sleepers and flooring, which are also carried on the wagon, are then laid across the boats from one to another till the bridge is complete. Trestle work is carried along also and surplus timbers. Lt. Col. Stephen D. Pool of the 10th Reg't, (Artillery) is organizing this pontoon train and has with him now 3 companies of the 10th Reg. formerly at Ft. Macon — to be hereafter of the Engineer Corps I suppose. He has moved the pontoons to a place for drill. The government has not horses yet to supply the train.

Farmers in this vicinity are preparing for planting as usual at this season. Very little cotton will be planted.

LONG GRABS.

[April 2, 1863]

"The Pontoon Bridge 'On The March' — the pontoon wagons on their way from Aquia Creek to the Rappahannock. Our correspondent wrote, under date of December 6th, 1862: 'Affairs in Virginia are assuming a portentous significance. General Burnside's army is concentrated on the north bank of the Rappahannock, opposite Fredericksburg, and the railway connecting his camps with his base of supplies at Aquia Creek, on the Potomac, is completed. A number of gunboats have ascended the Rappahannock to within fifteen miles of Fredericksburg, and will probably ascend the river quite to that point. Pontoon bridges and other appliances for crossing the river have also reached the Federal army, and the conditions for a speedy advance are nearly complete. Meanwhile, and in consequence of the delay of the Federal forces, itself the result of a rapid change of base without adequate advance provision, the Confederates have succeeded in concentrating their army in front of General Burnside, where they have been and still are busy in erecting fortifications to oppose his passage of the river.'" — This could be an illustration of the wagons Long Grabs mentioned as being captured at Fredericksburg. Source: Frank Leslie, *Famous Leaders and Battle Scenes of the Civil War (New York: Mrs. Frank Leslie, 1896)* p. 343. Used by permission of the Florida Center for Instructional Technology, College of Education, University of South Florida.

Long Grabs now leaves General Hill's forces for trips to Wilmington and Tarborough and returns to join them at a camp below Little Washington in early April.

WILMINGTON, N. C., March 30, 1863.

Messrs. Editors:—Wilmington has heretofore resembled a city in din and bustle of business more than any place in the State. The war, the blockade and the recent epidemic have almost suspended business and very much blighted the appearance of the place. Still Wilmington moves and breathes, crowds are seen on the streets and foreign ships are at her wharves. Some of her business men are now swelling their coffers faster than they ever did before. Among them may be mentioned the firm of Kidder & Martin, who own several vessels and have made, it is said, over half a million on goods and merchandize run through the blockade to and from the West Indies.

The town is said to be strongly fortified and there are a good many troops in the vicinity.

There were several important manufacturing establishments discontinued on account of the yellow fever that have not yet resumed operations.

There are no schools of much note here, nor literary or scientific institutions. The building which contains the Town Hall, Mayor's office, Theatre, &c., is very large and imposing edifice. It is one of the largest separate buildings I ever saw.

There are two or three elegant churches, and a great many magnificent private residences, and some beautiful yards and gardens. There are also a due proportion of old shabby houses, dirty shops and irregular streets, and although there are many fine locations splendidly improved, the general appearance of the town is any thing but pleasing and beautiful.

Wilmington, though, will see a bright future if she be true to herself and make a proper use of surrounding circumstances. After the war, the Confederate States will be a separate, independent nation—which will be some time. Trade will not be carried on entirely from North to South as before, but our exports and imports will be more direct to Europe and the West Indies. There is a very large and prosperous section which will have Wilmington as its most available shipping point. It is true that very large vessels cannot come to Wilmington; but you may observe the shipping of New York or any port, and where you find one large vessel you will find three small ones, so that while your large vessel is going into Norfolk or Beaufort three small ones may come to Wilmington and bring as many or more goods. Wilmington has no competition in foreign trade from Norfolk to Charleston—a larger space of coast than any other Atlantic city; and no direct competition in coast and inland trade, especially as a shipping point, from the Neuse on North, to the Pee Dee on the South, and as far west and northwest as Charlotte and Greensboro'—a region much larger and richer than that which formed the basis of prosperity for many of our largest cities. Wilmington can get merchandize to and from all parts of this region cheaper and quicker than can be regularly done from any other point. She can and ought to be secure and control the whole cotton trade North of the Pee-Dee and must still retain the monopoly of the turpentine and lumber trade as formerly, and the corn and produce trade of the east. She should open an iron trade with Lincoln, Gaston and the coal region and start extensive iron manufactories and ship building, and her greatness will shine as the sun.

LONG GRABS.

[April 2, 1863]

WILMINGTON, N. C., March 30, 1863.

Messrs. Editors:—Yesterday I visited the forts and batteries below here, and I regard these fortifications efficient to defend the approaches to Wilmington against whatever attacks are likely to be made by the enemy. A very large fleet of powerful ironclads and mortar boats might perhaps, after a long and desperate siege, take Forts Caswell and Fisher, but then the taking of Wilmington would involve new and greater difficulties. Experience has demonstrated that thorough obstructions, with formidable batteries well manned, to protect them, are the most effective defences of our rivers. The obstructions in the Cape Fear are said to be ample and are being made more substantial. The batteries that protect them are well located on high bluffs, where we could also use large land forces, if necessary. Fort St. Phillip is on a very commanding position on the west side of the river, at what was once Old Brunswick, some 15 miles below Wilmington by the river. Old Brunswick was an important place in old Colonial times and once carried on some trade and was a sort of center of royalty and aristocracy of the first rulers and proprietors of the Cape Far region. The walls of what must have once been a large and splendid church still stand, and nearby are several ancient tomb-stones some of them with inscriptions completely erased. I noticed a slab on the grave of one who died in 1762. Fort Caswell is on the west side of the river, about 30 miles by water from Wilmington, and Smithfield, the county seat of Brunswick, is two miles nearer, and it is about 10 miles from Fort Caswell to Fort Fisher, which is on the east side of the river and about 15 miles from Wilmington by land. Camp Wyatt (named after Wyatt of Edgecombe who was killed at Bethel) a mile or two from Fort Fisher towards Wilmington. The river widens regularly till opposite Fort Fisher, where I suppose it is nearly two miles wide.

The map in Chapter 1, shows the location of North Carolina's Outer Banks and some of the Inlets Long Grabs describes in the following paragraph.

There is a narrow sand bank around the whole coast of North Carolina, forming several regular curves or arcs of nearly equal dimension, with the concave side next to the ocean. The first curve extends from the mouth of the Pee Dee to Cape Fear at the mouth of the Cape Fear river; the next from there to Cape Lookout near Beaufort, and the next from there to Cape Hatteras, from here this bank, which has continued Northeast, thus far, runs due North to Cape Henry, east of Norfolk. This bank or bar is cut in several places by inlets which connect the ocean with the sounds and bays stretching along the inside of the sand bank and separating it from the main land. The largest of these is Old Topsail Inlet near Beaufort, and the most important and second in capacity is the mouth of the Cape Fear river. Then there are New Inlet, an outlet from the Cape Fear river on the east at Confederate Point, Ocracoke Inlet, about midway Pamlico Sound on the south and opposite Hyde C. H., New Inlet between Cape Hatteras and Roanoke Island, Bogue Inlet, near Swansboro,' Onslow county, New River Inlet, mouth of that river on State line, the inlets near Masonboro,' some 10 miles east of Wilmington, and Shallotte inlet, Brunswick Co. Fort Caswell is on what is called Oak Island; but more properly a long strip of the main land in Brunswick county bending round from the west in the shape of a hook which points up the river. On the extremity of this point is the Fort, and the channel for a mile or two above the mouth of the river makes a curve southwestward to fit the bend in the hook of land, enabling the guns of the fort to command the channel not only in front, but for a long distance on each side. Elizabeth river heads in Brunswick county and runs north-east into the Cape Fear between Smithville and Fort Caswell and in the rear of the Fort. Smithville is on the west bank of the Cape Fear above Fort Caswell, and Fort Johnson was just in front of the town on the river's bank, and is not garrisoned or fortified now. There are some earthworks and batteries about Smithville, and forces are stationed there. The communication from Fort Caswell to Smithville — 2 miles — is by water, as the distance is 15 miles or more round by land. Across Cape Fear river — which is two miles wide — from Fort Caswell, is Smith's Island, better known as Baldhead, which is some 10 miles long and 3 or 4 miles wide at the southern end. This island is of a triangular form, with one angle — a right angle — opposite Fort Caswell, another opposite Fort Fisher up north, and the other terminates in the south-eastern point of the island called Cape Fear. Just north of Smith's Island is New Inlet, a mile wide or more, and beyond it is Fort Fisher on Confederate point (formerly Federal,) the extreme southern point of land between the ocean and the Cape Fear river on the east. It commands New Inlet and also the river immediately west of it. Zeke's island is a small island of land between Forts Caswell and Fisher within two or three miles of the latter and north-west of Smith's or Baldhead. Battery Island is still smaller and between Caswell and Smithville. Fishermen and wreckers live on these islands and cultivate vegetables. Vines, bushes and weeds grow also and wells of fresh water are obtained. The water at the Forts is supplied from cisterns. The main current of the tide as it rises flows through New Inlet as that is the most direct way from the middle of the ocean, but when returning it flows more freely down the river to its mouth. Fort Caswell is a five-sided structure with the longest side next to the ocean and facing the bar. There are two circles of fortifications containing sand and casemated batteries. The garrison and armament are thought amply sufficient, if not beyond the capacity of the Fort, which has undergone much improvement and remodeling. Lt. Col. Gwathmey, formerly of the U. S. Navy and more recently in Confederate service at New Orleans up to the fall of that place, is in command at Caswell. He is some 50 years old, a native of Va., and I believe graduated at West Point. He preserves good order and discipline and enjoys the respect of those under him. Fort Fisher was named in honor of Col. Chas. F. Fisher of the 6th N. C. Reg't who fell at the First battle of Manassas. It has been made very strong and is well garrisoned. Col. Lamb of the 36th Reg't is in command I believe. He is a native of Norfolk, and some 26 or 28 years old, received a military education I think, makes an efficient officer and is highly esteemed as a man. There is usually one vessel blockading New Inlet and two over the bar at the mouth of the river. It is about 4 miles from Caswell to the bar and about 6 to the blockading vessels, which are plainly visible.

Those who run the blockade say the best time to come in is in the day time when there is a fog, or a clear night. They go from here to Nassau in four days, and frequently have to run the blockade there again, as yankee war vessels are often seen within a few miles of Nassau. Some of these vessels charge $150 in gold for passage and none of them desire many passengers. Nearly all the goods brought from Nassau are yankee goods, and it is said the place is full of yankee speculators who buy cotton, tobacco, sugar, &c.

Long Grabs.

[April 9, 1863]

In October 1868, McSween, now editor and publisher of *The Eagle,* returns to Wilmington on a fact-finding trip to learn how Wilmington is recovering from the war. As happened in Raleigh, it brings back a particular memory.

[I am reminded] of one time in 1863 when Phil. S.-------and myself were here. It happened to be the day when all the provost guards, bridge guards, home guards, train guards, &c., were sent suddenly all over town to catch conscripts. The merchant going from his store to dinner was taken to the calaboose and kept till he could send for his papers. The man going post haste after the doctor for his sick family was snatched up "like a brand from burning." The panic spread and the streets became deserted as if yellow fever had broken out. I saw the press-gang grab Phil. He was taken by surprise, rather in medias res, but he explained and illustrated to them earnestly and ably. I was not near enough to hear him. He finally succeeded in convincing them I think that he was one of their own force, who had just come from another post of duty for the same purpose as themselves. They let him off; I was stopped several times, and sometimes was released very reluctantly. No two squads had the same orders and very often none of them could read.

On one occasion I found no one of the crowd could read, and I showed them an old receipt of the Express Company, which they took for a passport and released me.

During the day I came to our room, and Phil was there quiet and demoralized with the door locked. He said he had been waiting patiently there for the last three hours. On separating again, he said particularly: "Now, if you don't find me at supper, you may know where I am, and you must be sure and see me before you leave if the officer of the guard will let you in." The contest raged thick and heavy till near sundown and produced utter confusion in the domestic affairs of this good old town. My own papers and showing were not much as to rely safely on against new and rigid orders. So Phil. and myself left by the next train. Some wounded soldiers, still on furlough, were hustled off to the conscript camp in Raleigh — one of them John F. McNair, of Richmond County. But the wide awake Provost never caught the blockade-runners of Wilmington napping again. Blockade running was all the go, after that, and became useful in domestic affairs as well as foreign.[4]

TARBORO', April 6.

Messrs. Editors: This place is on the south bank of the Tar River and at the head of navigation. The population before the war was near 1000, and it has been for many years noted for its enterprise, wealth, and refinement. The surrounding country has long excelled other portions of the State in farming, especially in raising cotton.

A railroad, 16 miles long, connects Tarborough with Rocky Mount, on the Wilmington and Weldon Railroad. This road is entirely south of the Tar river, and is merely a branch of the other road. The coaches are light and small, very much like a goodly sized omnibus, and make a rattling, roaring noise, like empty barrels rolling down steps. I believe it was intended to continue this road across the river down east. There is now but one train a day, and it leaves Tarboro' at 2 in the evening and arrives at Rocky Mount by 4, and then leaves Rocky Mount about 7 P.M. and gets here about 9. Bully travelling.

Tarboro' is beautifully located and has some elegant residences, among the finest of which is the house of Mr. William Battle.

In the Court House square is a handsome granite monument erected to the memory of Col. Louis D. Wilson. He was a citizen of this place and for many years represented Edgecombe county in the Legislature. He went off as a captain to the Mexican war and President Polk afterwards appointed him Colonel of the 12 Reg't in the U. S. Army, but on his way to take command he died at Vera Cruz, Aug.12, 1847. He was a bachelor and left by his will some forty or fifty thousand dollars to the poor of Edgecombe county. The county of Wilson was named after him. Gen. Pender lives here. There have been two papers here — the Southerner and the Mercury. The Southerner has only been published to the present time, but will now probably be discontinued, as its editor, Mr. Howard, (Judge Howard's father,) died about a week ago. A gunboat has been in the process of building here for some time, but the work is now stopped, and will probably be resumed.

I learn from what seems to be authentic sources, that our forces are investing Washington. The enemy's force is estimated to be 1500. Daniel, Pettigrew and others are south of the river and Garnett and others north of it. Our lines are said to surround the town on every side within two or three hundred yards. Our forces are getting heavy siege guns in position, and it is expected to make a general attack in two or three days. Our batteries command the river at Hill's Point (formerly Fort Hill,) 4 miles below Washington. The river is said to be about a quarter of a mile wide at Washington, and not over a mile at Fort Hill, where the channel runs within 300 yards of our heavy guns. Some gunboats have been disabled and one or two (reported) sunk at this point, but later information says two have passed the batteries at night. These boats are not iron-clad or very imperfectly so if ironed at all. The strong heavy iron-clads cannot get up that far. If this be so, our siege guns can soon sink and disable the gunboats near town, while our batteries can prevent transports going up, and even gunboats in day time. It is said the yanks carried away most of the stores when they first heard of our movement, several days ago. There has not been much fighting of importance down there yet. Washington is in Beaufort county, on the north side of Tar river, some 25 miles below Greenville, which is 25 miles from here on the south side of the same river.

LONG GRABS.

[April 9, 1863]

CAMP SIX MILES BELOW WASHINGTON, N. C., April 8.

Messrs. Editors:—There are five large rivers in N. C. which run southeast and somewhat parallel and enter the ocean within a space of 400 miles—the Pee Dee, the Cape Fear, the Neuse, the Tar, and the Roanoke. The Pee Dee and Roanoke are the largest, and heading in the same section at the foot of the Blue Ridge they encircle the others, the first running nearly south and the other nearly east. The space between all these rivers averages from 50 to 100 miles, widening towards the ocean, forming peninsulas. North Carolina extends 250 miles farther east into the Atlantic than South Carolina, and as far if not farther than Virginia. The Roanoke runs along near the line between N. C. and Va., occasionally crossing it till it gets below Weldon, where it bends considerably south for 40 or 50 miles, and then turning east it unites with the Chowan river just west of Edenton and forms Albemarle Sound, which extends some 50 miles eastward to the sand-bank at the ocean. The sound is from 5 to 12 miles wide and resembles very much the root of a cotton plant with the stalk towards the ocean, the bays and rivers making into it on each side representing the smaller roots and fibres of the cotton stalk. Danville, Clarksville, Gaston, Weldon, Halifax, Williamston and Plymouth are on the south bank of the Roanoke (the first two on the Dan river.) Tar river heads in Person county and runs southeast, near Henderson, Louisburg, Rocky Mount, Tarboro', Greenville and Washington, and from there it widens out and is called Pamlico river for 30 or 40 miles till it unites with the Neuse to form Pamlico Sound, a body of water 80 miles long and 25 or 30 wide, somewhat in the shape of a huge crawfish with one claw up the Neuse and the other up the Tar river. These two sounds, from 50 to 75 miles apart, bend toward each other at their eastern extremities, uniting at Roanoke Island by Croatan sound on the west side of the Island and Roanoke sound on the east of it. These sounds (Pamlico and Albemarle) enclose a peninsula embracing Hyde, Tyrell, Washington, and a part of Beaufort counties, the richest corn district in the Confederacy, and almost entirely at the mercy of the enemy. There are about 12 counties in eastern Carolina open to and under control of the enemy. The Nottoway and Blackwater heads in Va., run together near the State line, and a few miles farther south unite with the Meherrin between Murfreesboro' and Winton to form the Chowan, which runs nearly south for some 50 miles to the head of the Albemarle sound. The Yankees have control east of the Chowan river—five counties. Plymouth is opposite some islands near the mouth of the Roanoke river where Cushie creek, which runs by Windsor, enters Roanoke on the northside. It is said to be strongly fortified, and like Washington and a few other places is used as a depot by the Yankees, while Newbern is their main headquarters. Tranter's creek on the north and Bear swamp on the south are on the line between Pitt and Beaufort counties and both run into Tar river just above Washington.

The most direct communication from the vicinity of Washington to the State farther west at present is by Railroad from Rocky Mount to Tarboro', from where a boat goes occasionally to Greenville and places below there near our army. Wagons, &c., run continually from Greenville to our camps and sometimes from Tarboro' to Kinston. The hire for horse and conveyance is enormous. The most certain way is to go on foot, which is tolerably pleasant considering the water is not more than waist deep in some places. The boat comes down to Boyd's Ferry, 8 miles above Washington, from which place you get off to the regiments 10 or 15 miles away as you can. Gen. Hill's headquarters at present are at the cross roads called Bellevue, 3 miles southwest of Washington on the Newbern road.

We have two places fortified on this side of the river — Hill's Point, six miles by water below Washington, and Rodman's farm (Wm. B. Rodman's residence) opposite or a little below the town. From Rodman's the town can be shelled at any time, and Gen. Hill has directed the commander there not to spare the Yankees. We have ascertained the portion of the town chiefly occupied by the Yankees and our batteries give them frequent and effective shots. The enemy's batteries around the town reply occasionally. A demand was made through Gen. Garnett a few days ago for the removal of the women and children or the surrender of the place, but the officer in command refused either, plainly showing, though not in so many words, that he retains the women and children to protect the place from violent attack.

I visited Hill's Point yesterday evening. There was considerable shelling there all day yesterday and some dozen gunboats participated, of which four were visible when I was there — all having retired down the river. These boats are ordinary steamboats and light schooners and steamers with no iron protection and bearing two or more heavy guns apiece. Hill's Point is near the bend of the river to the eastward, just above a little branch or swamp that makes into the river on the south side. Two short ravines heading near together make into the river, one above the other below, leaving a tongue or peninsula of high bluff is the shape of a T. The ridge representing the body of the letter runs off level with the main land nearly perpendicular to the river and is about 200 yards long, while the cross or top of the letter forms the river bank for 150 yards — the whole elevated 30 or 40 feet above the water. Several guns are located on this high bluff between the two gullies. All the space around these works and for several hundred yards back is cleared land, including a small farm with buildings. Just above the upper ravine in the edge of thick woods is another battery on another bluff which has a swamp or valley immediately in the rear. The place is naturally very strong, for if a shot from the boats hit the hillside no damage is done, and if they go over the top they fall away back in the ravines and valleys and hurt nobody. So that they must hit the gun or gunners directly to have any effect, and this is very difficult as they are almost entirely protected by the high thick banks in front of them — a narrow trench only being cut down to point the muzzle of the cannon through. The channel is very difficult and torturous and all the buoys have been destroyed. The river is a little over a mile wide and the whole channel is within 350 yards of our guns, and the bend below gives us a double chance at it besides the part in front. The river about here is mostly lined with thick timber and marshes covered with water. The yankees have been in the habit of going up in canoes at night along the other side, but our troops over the river now have a battery of small pieces opposite those on this side to prevent any more running of the blockade.

Some of the gunboats have been hit and probably disabled, but there has been no hard fighting nor much attempt to attack but everything is quiet, and arrangements are progressing to completion, and I think Washington will be taken and we are to have some heavy fighting. The enemy has not shown more than a force of 3000 by transports and boats down the river. We heard yesterday morning of a heavy force advancing from Swift Creek in our rear, but from later information it seems to have been only a feint, and a small guard engaged Capt. Whitford's artillery. Boats came up Swift Creek 8 or 10 miles — some 18 or 20 miles from here. There are 2500 negroes in Washington, and the 27th and part of the 44th Mass. reg'ts, two Buffalo companies and one cavalry company. Col. Lee is in command now, but heretofore Col. Lyman of Mass. was. It is thought there is not much ammunition nor provision in the place. The fortifications are not very strong but the guns are formidable. I think Gen. Hill wants to draw them out from Newbern and fight between here and Swift Creek.

      Truly,
      LONG GRABS.

[April 16, 1863]

    CAMP NEAR WASHINGTON, N. C., April 10.

Messrs. Editors:— One year ago to-day "Long Grabs" wrote you his first letter. My communications, though not worthy of much consideration, have occupied a portion of your columns pretty regularly for one whole year — a year of sunshine and of shade, big with events which have shaped the destiny of a new nation. They have been written under various circumstances. Sometimes I have jotted down a few hasty lines with a lead pencil by the "struggling moonbeam's misty light," and again when shivering with cold and blinded with the smoke of hundreds of camp fires; and, not infrequently have I collected a few scattering ideas "solitary and alone," in a small, crowded and leaking tent, after waiting till the "wee small hours of morn" for the noise and bustle to subside.

A man writing as I have done cannot have wide desks and handy inkstands and be surrounded with Webster's Unabridged and long shelves filled with classical volumes. It may not be surprising then under the circumstances that my style has not abounded in studied elegance, classic allusions, chaste eloquence and profound argument, even had I the ability of such production.

But if I have in any way aided our cause in this the hour of our country's severe trial, if I have benefited the soldier, or in any way relieved the unfortunate and the poor or exposed the wrongs and impositions of the strong upon the weak, or if I have strengthened the cause of truth, patriotism and all the manly and virtuous characteristics of civilized man, or afforded instruction of amusement to any class of your readers, I have succeeded in my object. I am not the special friend or foe of any party, clique, man, measure or doctrine. "Long Grabs" stands before the world an odd but independent institution! He has his own eccentric notions on politics, science and religion, but he regards the present agitated state of the country an extremely inopportune time for any bitter, excited discussion of the peculiar tenets and abstractions of either. If he had his way he would confound the language of those ill-fated partisans who disturb the harmony and divide the strength of the country in this time of peril. In days of yore this had to be done, and this suicidal abuse would soon stop, if when one politician would exhaust the Dutch vocabulary of slander, the other could only reply in hideous accents of the Feejee Islanders.

We have been expecting battle for several days and yesterday and to-day there has been every reason to look for fighting to commence every hour. For over two weeks our forces have been investing Washington but in the whole time there has not been half a dozen men killed nor fifty wounded accidentally or otherwise. Four gunboats lie at Washington and a dozen or more are seen below our fortifications occasionally. There is shelling between our batteries and the gunboats every day. I see the shelling and am occasionally exposed to it. There is no communication between the town and the enemy outside. A road extends from Greenville all the way down the south side of the Tar river to the head of Pamlico Sound. The lower end terminates at several points and landings below here. From Washington and some of these landings below, roads cross this road and extend towards Newbern. Blount's creek 10 or 12 miles below Washington and running into the Pamlico river is crossed by this road at a mill a mile or two above its mouth. At this place there was a considerable skirmish between the outposts of the 11th, 26th and 29th Reg'ts and the advance guard of the enemy. The engagement lasted several hours and ceased at night. Our scouts found this morning that the enemy had retreated 8 or 10 miles, obstructing the road behind them. It has not been ascertained whether this force landed from boats below or came across the Peninsula from Newbern by some lower roads before mentioned, but more probably the latter. It is reported and seems reliable that there were 19 regiments and 18 pieces of artillery with some cavalry making a force of 10,000 or more. Pettigrew's and Daniel's Brigades, two of the finest bodies of men in service, were there to receive them with other troops in supporting distance. A few of our men were wounded — one or two seriously, who will probably die if not already dead. Our scouts bring intelligence of 17 of the enemy wounded, including a Colonel who has died. No doubt others were carried away of whom we have no account. The troops are in good spirits and health.

There are two great objects in a soldier's life, one to get a furlough, the other to get his share of the rations.

The weather is beautiful and the roads have become good. If I never get back any more give my last and most sincere regard to the ladies.

LONG GRABS.

[April 16, 1863]

The siege of Washington had lasted from March 30, 1863, until April 19, 1863. The Washington garrison was composed of six regiments and artillery, and was opposed by General Hill's one division. The battle, for the most part, was an artillery duel; on the river, Union ships and gunboats bringing supplies and reinforcements from New Bern were under almost constant fire. Some made it unscathed; others did not. Casualties amounted to forty for the Union and sixty for the Confederates.

Hill's supplies were dwindling, and the arrival of Union men and supplies at Washington made the siege unlikely to succeed. However, he had accomplished to a certain degree what he had been asked to do — create a diversion and to gather food from Eastern North Carolina and ship it to Lee and not to make a frontal assault on the city. Hill had also received a message from Longstreet asking for reinforcements for the battle at Suffolk, and Lee was withdrawing other units from North Carolina for the invasion of Pennsylvania.

General Hill broke off the siege and began withdrawing his troops on April 15.

General Foster in his official report on the battle wrote:

April 16 — At daylight five deserters from the enemy (conscripts of the Eighth Virginia) arrived in Washington and reported that the enemy had retired from our front and were retreating on Greenville.

In the meantime I returned to New Berne and proceeded to organize operations so as to effectually raise the siege. To distract the enemy I directed General Prince to march up the railroad as fast as he could toward Kinston and make a vigorous attack, continuing it for several days. At the same time I crossed the Neuse with all my available force and marched directly towards Blount's Creek. The movement toward Kinston with this latter movement, together with the enemy's information of the accession strength Heckman's Brigade and the fact that after fourteen days of close siege of Washington General Hill had failed to obtain a single advantage or to advance one step nearer his objective, in all probability caused him to retreat."[13]

CAMP BELOW WASHINGTON, April 15.

****************** I learn on good authority that the enemy has not laid waste much of Hyde and that there are Guerilla companies there which check the plundering squads so common in the eastern part of the State.

McSween sent a missive just before the siege ended, prompting the editors of the *Observer* to write, "The following letter only reached us this morning. Besides what we publish, our correspondent favored us with views and speculations as to movements and results which it is needless to publish since the raising of the siege of Washington. We therefore omit these portions of the letter."

The editors refer to the lifting of the siege of Washington, and Long Grabs had probably written something of it; since it was a deed accomplished, they felt it was unnecessary to cover the same details once more.

***********************We are ample in numbers and no doubt will soon be equally so in means and appliances. Take a survey over the whole extend of our lines, east, west, north and south, and it will be seen that there is nowhere a more available, practicable field of aggressive operations on our part than here. Should we succeed only in part, it will then require fewer troops here than now, besides limiting the domain of the enemy. At present we have about as many N.

C. regiments in this State as in Va. and the reg'ts here have generally twice as many men. There is also considerable force in the State from Va. and S. C. and the some artillery from Ga. and Ala.

We have heavy rains now and any amount of water and swamp mud. It is very difficult to get supplies in this section as most of the prominent citizens left long ago and the substance of the country has been carried away or destroyed by the enemy. There is not town or central point, or base where men and officers can purchase extra provisions and necessary articles.

I have conversed with prominent reliable citizens of Washington who left there a few weeks ago and with much pleasure and satisfaction I have learned that the great body of the people, rich and poor, are as true as steel to our cause. It is to be regretted, however, that several persons in town and through the surrounding country have steeped their souls in the indelible dye of treason and cowardice. But the same remarks I made of a similar class below Kinston are equally applied here. I have observed but little evidence of disloyalty, treachery or sympathy with the enemy among the citizens of this community, and I have mingled with them pretty freely and employed various means as to ascertain their sentiments. Many of them have traded with the yankees but from necessity. Some allowed yankee officers to stay and live at their houses and treated them respectfully and even with apparent cheerfulness, but from a sense of fear and necessity. A few took the oath of allegiance and many the oath of neutrality under a panic and for temporary security of life and property. But many of these same men yearn from the bottom of their hearts for the success of the Confederacy and have no corn or meat to spare to sell to the enemy, but are anxious to get out all their bacon at 20 cts a pound and all their corn at five dolls. a barrel.

It is impossible to assault Washington from this side of the river, for besides the river, there is a thick miry swamp a mile wide on the south bank of the river. The entire swamp bordering the river on this side is a mile and a half wide opposite Washington. The road from Newbern by Swift Creek runs nearly straight through an embankment of timber and sand. It first passes over a half mile of swamp and then about 300 yards across an open sandy island which extends two or three miles up and down, parallel with the river down to the river bank below. Beyond this island, which contains Rodman's farm and negro quarters, is the thick swamp a mile wide, before mentioned. Near where this island approaches the river bank, about a mile below the town, is some heavy artillery, but the timber on the eastern point of the swamp does not allow a full view of the town. About a quarter mile further down at the eastern end of the island is some more artillery. The lower end of the island (or it may be a peninsula) is level and much elevated above the river, and the river banks are steep bluffs. There is, though, near the water's edge, some low ground covered with cypress, black gum and other growth, which partially obstruct a view of the river. Our heavy batteries here, however, have full view and range of the eastern portion of the town and the suburbs on that side where fortifications and blockhouses are visible. A block-house is a small strong fort of strong heavy timbers. Our guns at Rodman's play on these positions continually. I am not familiar with the fortifications on the other side.

MORNING OF 16TH APRIL— Since I commenced this letter we have fallen back

10 miles. Our front is on Chockowinity Creek — the same creek alluded to already as forming a bay in the river just below Rodman's Point. Our fortifications on Hill's Point, Mouth of Blount's Creek, &c., are all abandoned and the guns brought out. The Cross Roads at Bellevue, mentioned by me before, where the river road south from Greenville crosses the Washington and Newbern road 3 miles fom Washington — a half mile north of the creek here which forms our southeastern line — is at present our centre of operations. The yankees are reported to be advancing from Newbern by the Swift Creek road on our southwest, and also on the road from Barrington's Ferry, running here from towards the Sound on the southwest. Their force is said to be heavy. We still hold Rodman's Point and all west of the Chocowinity. The road from Bellevue Cross Roads to Washington is our communication with Rodman's island. Should the yanks attack us immediately the battle ground will be on a dry level plain partly cleared and settled, of a few miles extent, near these cross roads, in Beaufort county.

I believe there is no change in affairs on Rodman's island and over the river. Ransom is in supporting distance from Kinston or Greene county. We retreated last night in heavy rain over almost impassable roads and through much water. The flank movement of the enemy on our north would have the effect of separating us more completely from our force over the river and of cutting off our retreat, while gunboats and other forces could advance up the river in our front.

The troops, either carelessly or designedly, allow their camp fires to set the woods on fire. Smoke and flames can be seen some times for miles. This is very wrong and should be prevented. The valuable pine forests of turpentine orchards, fences and even houses and other property are wantonly destroyed.

The citizens seem much discouraged and despondent at their situation, and this feeling is increasing now that the decisive moment has been delayed and a general retreat indicated. "Hope deferred maketh the heart sick," and now they have every reason to believe that if they are again exposed to the inhuman foes they must suffer increased injury, degradation and terror. But I cannot think a general retrograde movement is in process of execution. We have a fair field, splendid troops, and gallant officers. Our artillery is extensive and well organized and our entire force in numbers and efficiency is calculated to inspire the liveliest hope and confidence. A decided land victory over the heavy columns of the enemy, would be the most opportune event that could precede the final siege and investment of the positions on which we have advanced. The day opens mildly and the heavens smile auspiciously; but if there be a battle, circumstances are calculated to delay it yet a day or two more.

Truly yours,

LONG GRABS.

P. S. Afternoon, April 16. — It appears that the yankees have only made a feint and are now expected to make a general attack on us here. It is probable also that a retreat and falling back on Kinston or Greenville is now contemplated — I am informed that our guns on Rodman's farm have been removed preparatory to evacuation. I learn also that the Yankees have burned some houses on the farm (by shell I suppose.) The enemy has kept up a terrific shelling on our works down the river. I hope they wasted much ammunition. Thus the present indications induce the supposition that all the system and magnitude I have attributed to what might have been a brilliant illustration of grand strategy and bold energetic achievement suddenly collapses. I of course confess my inability to see what we have been driving at. There has probably been some successful accomplishment, but I hardly think people generally will be able to appreciate it, especially those in the eastern section of the State. But it was not my business to advise and suggest the movement, nor is it my peculiar duty to indulge useless criticism. It will all come right before the expiration of the next 200 years.

L. G.

[April 23, 1863]

Long Grabs made reference to the sufferings of the Washington people at the hands of the Yankee soldiers under the occupation and from treacherous individuals who supported them. Two letters, one from a woman who was unable to leave because she lacked any funds to support her large family if she did and another from a person who had escaped and was living as a refugee in neighboring Pitt County, reveal the harshness of life under the Union troops.

The April 30, 1863, edition of the *Fayetteville Observer* carried a letter from a woman living in Little Washington.

> We have seen a letter from a lady in this ill-fated town, giving a sad picture of their distressing conditions. She enclosed a printed order from the Yankee Brig. Gen. Potter, stating that many of the residents had openly displayed their sympathy with the rebel besieging forces and had communicated with them by signals, and therefore ordering that "all persons" shall take the oath of allegiance to the U. S. or leave the place within five days. The lady writes that she and others are nearly crazy. They cannot leave, for they have no place to go but the wild woods, and no means to live upon if they go, for they are forbidden to carry any thing with them but their clothes. At first the order allowed them to take their effects, but afterwards it was changed to allow only clothing. She says that they make no complaint against our own forces, for they failed to take the place only out of sympathy for the women and children, but the Yankees are now wreaking their vengeance on the poor innocent people. The conduct of the Buffalos and negroes is perfectly outrageous, and she cites instances of their insulting behavior. "Everybody is perfectly crazy (says she;) they do not know what to do. God help us ! Pray for us — tell all the people to pray for us, and for Heaven's sake don't call us traitors, for we are driven to it. Our whole hearts are with the South, and the thought of _____ taking that oath is killing to me, but we have such a large family and no money that it is impossible for us to go."
>
> She relates a Yankee raid on a farm down the river, where they stole everything, provisions, clothing, &c., one of them holding a bayonet at the breast of the only white person present, a boy of 14 years, daring him to open his mouth, for they would kill him on the spot. "We are ruined, ruined; and now I want the Confederates to come and burn the town; if we cannot enjoy it, I don't want the Yankees to do so."[14]

Citizens forced to leave their homes carrying what they could — while the location is not mentioned, it is representative of events in Eastern North Carolina. Source: John Gilmary Shea, *The Story of a Great Nation* (New York: Gay Brothers & Company, 1886) p. 908. Used by permission of the Florida Center for Instructional Technology, College of Education, University of South Florida.

On May 11, 1863, the *Observer* published an excerpt from a letter of an individual who escaped the Union occupation:

> The failure to take Washington was most unfortunate for all who resided or owned estates in the lower part of Pitt and Beaufort counties. Since Gen. Hill has returned from that section with his forces, the Yankees have been making dreadful havoc upon all the plantations around and adjacent to Washington. Many fine residences have been burnt down; mules, horses, and all kinds of stock stolen and destroyed; and many of the citizens have been arrested and sent off to Newbern. The slaves are going off in large numbers, and all of the principal farms in that section have been abandoned by their owners. We were getting along tolerably well and had our crops all planted when Gen. Hill came down with his large force and began the siege of Washington. A general state of intense feeling took possession of the whole people; all believed that Washington would certainly be taken. You can better imagine than I can describe our state of feeling, when we saw the forces all leaving us at the mercy of an excited set of abolitionist marauders. Our worst fears have been and are now being daily realized. All who can are fleeing from their homes, leaving the enemy to take possession. An awful responsibility rests somewhere for the sacrifice of this part of the State.[15]

FOR THE OBSERVER.
CAMP NEAR FREDERICKSBURG, April 16, 1863.

Editors Observer: In glancing over a copy of your paper some time since, I found a paragraph in a letter from your correspondent "Long Grabs," devoted to "Dan_____, Chief Musician in Iverson's Brigade," and I here beg leave to make a trifling correction, which perhaps, "Long Grabs," in his effort to be funny, overlooked. As the article first appeared in your journal, since copied in others, I thought it proper that the slight mistake should be corrected in the same; thereby disabusing the minds of the public in relation to "Dan _____."

And first: as he regards me "la psus pennae," in question, "Dan _____" has never "sent up" an application for furlough to Gen. D. H. Hill as stated by "Long Grabs" (only a trifling discrepancy.)

Again: on only three occasions at College — Senior speaking, — together with the time employed preparatory therefore, has "Dan devoted himself almost entirely to music." Mr. "Long Grabs" was certainly misinformed in the premises.

Lastly: As regards Gen. Hill's "endorsement on my application," I merely remark that he has never had the opportunity of making fun at my expense. I will mention, however, for the benefit of "L. G.,' that Gen. Lee has approved furloughs for all the bands in this Corps, ours among the rest.

I am not prepared to deny that Long Grabs may have sufficient grounds for his remarks, but he is entirely mistaken in the man. I will add by way of advice, that "L. G." in an undertaking of this kind should fully ascertain the facts.[16]

"Dan _____."

[April 27, 1863]

Publication of most of the following letters was on May 4, 1863. They were written from Greenville (April 18), Hookerton (April 20), and Kinston

(April 22 and 26). The letter following these, which was written from Kinston on April 28, was published on April 30, and is placed afterwards to keep the writing dates in sequence. The *Observer'* editors noted that the letters "have been a long time in reaching us, but they are of sufficient interest to claim insertion even at this late date."

Greenville, N. C., April 18.

Messrs. Editors: Our forces have fallen back to this place after a tiresome retreat, which has somewhat demoralized "Long Grabs." A man always finds difficulty in getting baggage carried on a march, especially in retreat; but after various "strategic movements," I am indebted to the transportation of the Confederate army for conveying mine, (though but few besides myself know anything of it.) I had stowed myself and baggage nicely away in the ordnance wagon of the 52d Reg't. The ordnance train has always been expressly prohibited from carrying baggage. Pretty soon Gen. Pettigrew rode up, and stooping down, looked into the wagon, and in a loud, angry tone, said (in substance,) "Come out of that wagon! It's no use to say you ain't in there; I see your luggage sticking out." "Long Grabs" evaporated, and baggage ditto. I then got the aforesaid baggage in the ordnance wagon of the 44th, but very soon I learned that one of the ordnance officers came around to see if all was right, and he very unceremoniously placed the "contraband" luggage in the road, for the general use of the public. I accidentally came along, however, in time to save it and procure safer passage elsewhere,

Our retreat is to be put down as a thing to be remembered and expatiated upon. "It was night," (nox erat,) and the blackness of darkness shone round about the Confederate hosts. The watery elements had almost drowned the earth, presenting to our astonished views very impressive illustration of the floods common in Noah's time. Under such circumstances as these the order to fall back rapidly, 10 miles, was extended to the different troops about dark, and many of them packed up during a heavy rain and started. On we came in the pouring rain, with the murky clouds above, the pitchy darkness around us, and a boundless, bottomless waste of water and mud underneath. The infantry slipped and scrambled and slided and wallowed, swimming, climbing, diving and falling by turns; the wagons pitched and rocked and jolted and cracked, like a vessel in a sea-storm tossed by the waves and occasionally springing a leak; the artillery rattled and slided, often getting out of sight, then rising to the surface; and the various dignitaries on horseback would experience some inconvenience when abruptly dismounted among the vines, brush, &c., or when their steeds, plunging g forward into the dark abyss of some unexpected creek or hole, would drown their riders or break their necks. There was one continued scene of geeing, hawing, prizing, lifting, pulling, cursing, grumbling, laughing, quarreling, splashing, crashing, roaring, lightning and thundering. All was darkness, isolation and inundation, except when the dazzling, blinding flashes of lightning would glisten across the endless line of reeling wagons, jammed up artillery and floating infantry. The sudden flashes of lightning were of such brilliant brightness as to strike you with blindness for a minute of two, as if at mid-day you were suddenly plunged into Egyptian darkness (and at the same time plunged into a hole of water over your head.)

Federal baggage train on its way to the army. The immense labor and fatigue attendant on operations of the Federal and Confederate armies such as carrying the troops' baggage, commissary supplies, and ammunition may be conceived by this sketch. The rough, rutted roads, the storms that would sweep over them in any season, the constant fear of surprise by the enemy, where escape and defense are alike impossible, give to the life of the army train all the perils one can imagine. Source: Frank Leslie, *Famous Leaders and Battle Scenes of the Civil War* (New York: Mrs. Frank Leslie, 1896) p. 272. Used by permission of the Florida Center for Instructional Technology, College of Education, University of South Florida.

Thus for most of the night we were getting over some of the worst roads I have ever seen, not even excepting the prairies of Alabama. There was one continuous flood of water, with occasional trees across the road which the fires had burnt down, and heaps of poles and brush to keep from breaking through the top crust of earth into the "unfathomable depths" below. In short, the roads were navigable, and it was affirmed that gunboats would follow up our rear.

We were not hurried away by the yanks, nor were we forced to leave, but it was entirely a voluntary panic or "bust," gotten up on our own hook and for our own enjoyment.

The apparent cause of the failure in this whole movement on Washington is the fact that we had not sufficient guns in position to command the river below Washington. The town could have been taken any time during the siege, but could not have been held without control of the river below. Both the Whitworth guns burst in the early part of the siege — a fact which I did not mention before, as one of Gen. Hill's staff told me that it was desirable that such information be not published at that time. There should have been several heavy guns at Hill's Point, but there were only some light field pieces which could do but little damage farther off than a mile. But one 32-pounder was on our works at Rodman's and on our retreat the yankees captured the carriage of that. The whole fleet in the river could have passed three or four days before it was attempted, had they known defences and the guns we relied on. On the night of the 11th inst. three of our men deserted from Wyatt's Va. Battery, and after that on the same night two of the enemy's boats went up to Washington, and next morning after daylight a large transport, supposed to convey Gen. Foster and staff, went down the river by all our batteries. There was very little if any firing at this boat from Rodman's, but the four or five small field pieces at Hill's Point fired as hard as they could while it was in reach, amounting to some 50 shots in all, some of which took effect. I saw this boat distinctly myself on the evening of that day we were ordered to fall back from all our works below to the Chocowinity.

It is humiliating and deeply affecting to abandon these noble and devoted people under such circumstances. They have been experiencing adversity in its broadest meaning. They have been plundered, assaulted and oppressed by a savage enemy, and slandered, suspected, and scoffed at by their own countrymen. They have met with coldness, extortion and reproach as refugees, and yet their spirits are as unconquerable as ever, and their hearts are devoted to the cause of their native South.

This is a pretty hard place and had a population of five or six hundred before the passage of the conscript law. There is a fine large Court House here and some neat cottages. Pitt is a wealthy, large county and has yet considerable provisions. Cotton has been extensively raised and there are many splendid farms through the county. "New Dip" also abounds, which is a very peculiar thing these times. In former times this was probably a rough and tumble place during court weeks, elections, musters, &c., not unfrequently on the "knock-down and drag-out" system. The place looks that way. I have not been favored with ocular demonstrations on the subject.

General Foster recorded the incident Long Grabs referred to of running the blockade in his official report on the battle:

April 13.—That night the steam-transport Escort with hay bales placed on her guards and decks as a protection, ran the batteries. There also arrived two small schooners with ammunition and commissary stores.

April 14.—Regarding everything as safe in the town, and the reinforcements and men, with the supplies of ammunition and provisions, as ample until I could raise the siege, I determined to run the blockade and place myself at the head of the relieving force in order to insure more efficiency in its conduct. I therefore embarked on board the Escort for the purpose of running the batteries at night, but the pilot could not distinguish the necessary marks to proceed by and therefore waited till daylight.

April 15.—At daylight the Escort started and ran the batteries. She was fired at one hundred times by the Rodman's and Hill's Point batteries and was struck forty times, but with no material injury. The pilot, Captain Padrick, a brave and skillful man, was killed by a rifle-shot.[17]

HOOKERTON, April 20.

This place was named after a very prominent and estimable citizen of the name of Hooker, who lived here. The place is in Green County, 24 miles southwest of Greenville and 12 from Kinston, rather between the two places. It is a quiet, pleasant and beautifully located village, in a fine, rich farming country, and on the south bank of the Contentnea Creek or Mockasin River, a large stream heading in Franklin County and running south-east into the Neuse some 15 or 20 miles below Kinston. Pettigrew's Brigade has gone into camp here permanently, as a reserve corps.

KINSTON, April 22.

Ransom's Brigade is near here, and the 17th Reg't, Nethercutt's Battalion. &c. It is a beautiful country from here to Greenville, and many magnificent farms spread out around you at every turn. "New Dip" has a wonderful effect on my friend "Lemons," causing him to become oblivious to the weather.

LONG GRABS.

CAMP BELOW KINSTON, April 26, 1863.

Messrs. Editors:—Our pickets extend to Core creek towards Newbern and within 4 miles of Trenton. All of Ransom's Brigade are in this vicinity on both sides of the river, with the 17th Regiment, Nethercutt's Battalion, and several artillery companies. There is some cavalry force about here also, but I do not know what forces or how much. Most of the citizens in this section who left because of the advance of the yankees have returned and are becoming fixed up again and making preparations for farming.

The lie of permanent defences south of the river will probably be on southwest creek, which runs into the Neuse about 4 miles below Kinston. All the four roads to Newbern cross this creek, and the Dover road—the main route to Newbern—crosses at South-west mills, formerly Cobb's mills. This is a pretty large stream with a good deal of swamp. The whole surrounding country is level and affords no commanding positions for defence. Innumerable paths intersect the flat piney woods and marshes in every direction, furnishing approaches for either force. Both armies too are familiar with the country. The yanks are said to be reinforcing or contemplating some movement below, and we expect to see or hear something of them at any time.

There is a remarkable squad connected with the 52d Reg't, generally under charge of Maj. R. I could not learn whether they belonged to the signal corps or were detailed on some other special duty, but certain it is that their way of defending their country is a peculiar one, not fully appreciated by Maj. R. They are Quakers and conscientiously opposed to war and every thing pertaining to war. There are four of them, all quite good looking healthy men, and three of them quite young. They were brought out by the conscript law and have persistently refused to receive bounty, pay, clothing or arms. They will not wait on the sick nor take any non-combat position, and will not even load wagons nor clear out roads. They would not receive rations at first, and I believe provisions were brought and cooked for them awhile. Afterwards they were told to go after their rations or do without. They resolved to do without. Things went on in status quo, till the fourth day, when their appetites overcame their consciences and they came up promptly to the commissary and have been very punctual every draw-day since. They were ordered to help load a wagon with fodder, but would not "budge a peg." As they would not assist they were sentenced to be punished by being tied so as to walk behind the wagon for several miles. The road led through larger swamps covered in many places with water nearly waist deep. And thus they "brought up the rear" a very cold morning, after having been promised a ride back on their wagon should they assist in loading. They are dressed in brown home-made jeans, coat and pants; double breasted vest of "turkey red" and blue filling buttoning up to the neck; and broad country-made wool hats. They carry an incredible amount of "budgets" and "wallets." Their habitual manner is silence and solemnity, but if you come about them or mix much with them they lecture or sermonize over the state of the country. One of them lectured "Long Grabs" about the error of his ways till nearly a whole regiment of listeners were attracted around, when being less interested than my pious friend I perpetrated an impoliteness by leaving him abruptly.

While I maintain a high admiration for the honest, unpretending, industrious and moral Quaker character, I cannot but indulge in common with others, a feeling of impatience and disgust at the absurd squeamishness manifested by some of the sect. It is a misapprehension of the real tenets of their own faith,— an extreme narrow-minded fatalism, or an unwholesome conscientious fanaticism, leading to palpably false notions of moral obligations. The Bible nowhere enjoins on man to be untrue to his country, but exhorts all to obey "the powers that be." It is admitted to be a well established principle, that if a man from cause beyond his control be compelled to participate in an act or business, public or private, he does not criminate himself, and by acquiescence in such necessity does not render himself culpable. There can be no such thing as absolute neutrality in this war by any citizen, South or North. The laws already allow much favor to those sects who entertain conscientious scruples against War and its consequences. This squad of "brotherly love" no doubt experiences for the "faith" many troubles, trials, tribulations, vaccinations and starvations to tell their posterity.

Truly,

LONG GRABS.

[May 5, 1863]

CAMP NEAR KINSTON, April 28.

Messrs. Editors:—A heavy skirmish took place this evening at Gum Swamp [see map, Chapter 1], 8 or 9 miles below Kinston on the Dover Road. Three Companies of the 56th Reg't—an excellent Reg't—were on picket at this point, and engaged the enemy, who advanced in heavy force, 8000 or more.

Our troops, after fighting gallantly for two hours, were compelled to fall back, when the enemy pressed and flanked them with great odds. Col. Faison was in command and acted with great coolness and courage, often bringing down a yankee with a musket himself.

Some 4 or 5 of our men were killed and a dozen or more wounded—some of them very badly. The killed and many of the wounded were left behind.

Lt. J. B. Lutterloh of Fayetteville was severely wounded in the breast by a musket or minnie ball. His recovery is doubtful. The Companies engaged were Capt. Lockhart's from Northampton, Cumberland and elsewhere., Lt. Lutterloh commanding; Capt. Lane's Co. from Henderson, Lt. Lane commanding, and Capt. Harrel from Cleaveland and Rutherford.

Those killed in Capt. Lockhart's Co. are Neill T. McNeill[18] of Harnett, and Washington M. Vickers[19] of Orange; wounded: Malcom McNeill[20], in foot, and J. B. Parrish[21] of Harnett, in hip, and Wm. T. Brewer[22], right arm, of Northampton.

Lt. Gross[23] of Harril's Co. with 25 men was off at a different post and may be cut off, as he has not been heard from.

The men and officers engaged displayed much bravery and deserve high praise for their gallant conduct. I went with Capt. White's company which had been held at camp as a reserve and we met the others a half mile from their field on the retreat. There was no artillery on either side. As we approached the endless rattle of musketry and shouts of the Yankees became plainer till the smoke and lines of battle were just before us. It is thought they are advancing in heavy force for battle; in which case the giving up of Gum Swamp necessitates our falling back on Smith Creek.

LONG GRABS.

[May 4, 1863]

KINSTON, April 30.

Messrs. Editors.—The enemy seems to have fallen back to Newbern after the brilliant little fight at Gum Swamp. Our cavalry occupied the battle ground early next day and from appearances the yankees loss must have been considerable.

At the first of the war this would have been called a great battle and it was really about as much of a battle as it could be. A more minute sketch of the place and engagement may interest some of the friends of those who fought. About 9 miles below Kinston, Gum Swamp—a small stream running towards the Neuse — crosses the Railroad and the Dover road about the same place. The Dover road runs in a zigzag course along with the Railroad, crossing it several times, and just after it crosses Gum Swamp on the South side of the Railroad it runs nearly perpendicular across the Railroad a few steps from the creek. Just on both sides of the creek the Railroad is on embankment 3 or 4 feet high, otherwise the road is level with the ground and straight for long distances running a South-east direction from Kinston to Newbern. On the Railroad just below where it was crossed by the other road was a small earth work, behind which two of our companies were posted. The other company (Capt. Lane's) was placed in the edge of the woods or swamp east of the Railroad and creek and on the left of the Dover road, which turned to the right after crossing the Railroad. Both sides then lead through a farm — the Railroad through a field to the right of a house and the other through a lane on the left of the house. Some three-quarters of a mile down both roads were our out-posts of infantry, but on the approach of the enemy they fell back and formed in the position stated.

The enemy advanced by both roads and had, it is believed, a force of at least six regiments. The portion that came round by the Dover road pressed back Lane's company, who defended the road as well as the left flank of the other companies on the Railroad, so that this company was finally forced to the Railroad in rear of the others, and then across it. The enemy then having the Railroad in front and rear protected by Railroad embankment, the other two companies had to give way. They then fell behind another small and badly constructed breastwork just this side of the crossing on the creek, the work commanding the ford.

This work was in the edge of a little old field, and ran parallel with the Creek, which can be crossed by infantry above and below without much difficulty. Even in our new position the enemy had previously gained a position from which he could soon control our left flank, and by crossing above, our men would be exposed to an enfilade fire on both flanks without any protection. Before the enemy fully effected this, however, our men retreated about a mile by the Dover road to where it crosses to the east of the railroad again. Had the yankees gone up the railroad immediately — the shortest route — they could have cut our force, but they were content with occupying our works and did not even follow. The rest of the 56th regiment was divided up in squads and on picket at other points, except Capt. White's company, which was at camp up the road, some five miles from Kinston. This company was moved down promptly when the fighting was heard of and I went down with it, but just as we were reaching the scene of action we met the others falling back. We were about half a mile from the battle ground, and I could see the yankees down the railroad and hear them cheering. They seemed to be advancing, and we formed about this last crossing place of the two roads, but they did not follow. We remained here some half hour or more, ascertained something of the wounded and missing, got breath so as to be ready for them as they came up again, and then moved back some half mile farther to where the Dover road crosses back to the West side, and stayed there till late in the night, when orders came to fall back towards Kinston.

The retreat was slow and entirely in good order. The men fought like heroes, and the officers acted with remarkable coolness and bravery. Capt. Harrell was in command until Col. Faison arrived, about half an hour after the fight commenced. Both these officers displayed coolness and courage. Col. Faison fired several times with muskets of wounded men. The men and officers have great confidence in him. The fighting lasted from about 3 o'clock to 5½ in the evening (Tuesday 28th.)

For some two hours the fighting was severe — almost one incessant volley. Many of our men shot away nearly all their 40 rounds of cartridges. The yankees were often within 40 or 50 yards. Our men had to lie down and act with caution in rising to shoot. Our loss is not so heavy as first supposed — being now about 10 killed, wounded and missing; all the others have come or are accounted for.

LONG GRABS.

[May 4, 1863]

KINSTON, May 2.

Messrs. Editors:— Allow me to digress from the usual topics to place one flower in the wreath of affection that encircles the memory of another noble spirit this cruel war has torn from us. It is a mournful task to record the death of such a man as Lt. Jarvis B. Lutterloh. He was an intimate friend, and I had known him long and well. We can hardly realize that he is surely dead and passed forever from our sight. But yesterday his manly, familiar voice rang through the camp, and his loud, happy laugh drove away sad thought and dull care from every mind, and to-day that manly brow lies pallid in death. A musket ball penetrated his breast on the right side and lodged within the skin on the left side, at the skirmish on Gum Swamp, 9 miles below here, on Tuesday the 28th ult. He grew gradually weaker till early next morning, when he died at the hotel in Kinston. He retained his senses to the last, seeming fully aware of his condition, and breathed his last quietly and peacefully. His last words were that "he had tried to do his duty and would do the same again were his course to go over," and of affectionate messages to his father and mother. Lt. Lutterloh was about 22 years old, and graduated at Chapel Hill in 1860. He was a private in the 1st or Bethel regiment, and afterwards recruited men enough to get the appointment of 1st Lieutenant and was attached to Capt. Lockhart's company from Northampton, then not full, which was assigned to the 56th Reg't N. C. T. He has been regularly at his post of duty and fell gallantly in his country's cause. He was beloved by his men and was a general favorite in the regiment.

He was one of those men whom you would find the same under all circumstances. His manners were free and unpretending, and the same towards all. Though of apparent harshness and roughness, there were few men of more tender sensibilities or more refined nature. Of strong purpose, great force of character, even tempered, of comprehensive liberal views, faithful in all relations, of extensive and correct knowledge of human nature, sincere, candid and devoted in his associations, and naturally witty and jovial, he presented such an attractive combination of character as is seldom found in this selfish deceptive world. His large circle of friends and admirers will cherish his memory and sigh long and heavily ere they find his like again.

With feelings of equal sadness it is my melancholy duty to pen a line of grief over the grave of Serg't Duncan J. McLeod of Capt. Culbreth's Co., 54th Reg't N. C. T., who died of fever in the hospital at Richmond a few days ago. Serg't McLeod was a native of Moore, but resided in Cumberland when he entered the army. He was a young man of piety, spotless integrity, rare and sterling worth. With a few friends and slender fortune, he had just entered the world on his own resources; and, from his own native energy of character and inherent merit, he had already won for himself high consideration and a host of friends. He was a literal exemplification of that modest, enterprising, conservative and consistent Scotch Presbyterian character which is everywhere such an ornament to the church, society and State. True, the crowd did not know him — the nation will not miss him, for no deafening cannon roar nor muffled drum announced his death but there are a few hearts that are saddened and a few tears have flowed from the pure fountains of affection. At least one little family altar is draped in mourning — one little circle is grieving. I would not give these unknown and heartfelt tokens of pure filial devotion for all the popular cant, display and mourning for the "hero of a hundred battles." The common soldier is the hero of the war — the life and the stay of the country, and when he is stricken down in death, then falls one of the strongest props upon which the existence and destiny of the nation depend. Serg't McLeod possessed an amiable disposition, fine talents and accomplishments and a sacred regard for truth. He sealed his devotion to his country with his life. It was all he could do. He had manfully and gallantly performed every duty, and his ashes now lie "unhonored and unsung" in a stranger's land, under a stranger's sky; but not without friendly tears to weep his fall and fond hearts to cherish a lasting remembrance of his many excellencies of character.

There are no indications of any important movement of the enemy in this vicinity. A skirmish took place a day or two ago near Core Creek, between some pickets of the 25th Reg't N. C. T. and the outposts of the enemy. The recent demonstrations of the enemy below here I am disposed to regard as feints to divert from operations at Fredericksburg.

All citizens in Washington and Newbern are required to take the oath of allegiance or come within our lines. They are not allowed to bring any property with them. Several citizens of Newbern have arrived here in consequence. They say there are some 15,000 troops in Newbern and vicinity. Things are growing worse and worse there. Many who formerly took the oath to save their property, now being plundered as badly as others. Some of the Buffaloes have been used as tools by the yankees as long as they chose to use them, but are now dismissed and treated as others. They are thus between the wrath of both governments and must enjoy peculiar misery, a fit reward for their diabolical conduct.

There is some charge in the disposition of our forces going on, but all such facts and information I can never give specifically without violating the confidence and courtesy of commanding officers. It is frequently very injudicious to make public certain information that the enemy might use to advantage, and I always endeavor to refrain from it. What I may know myself and what should be published, are two things. Many however do not restrain themselves in this way. Nor can it be my province or privilege to send you daily such items and dispatches as you are better able to get otherwise. My communications are necessarily different.

LONG GRABS

[May 7, 1863]

In June 1869, six years after he recorded the death of Lt. Jarvis B. Lutterloh, McSween was the editor of *The Eagle*, a newspaper published in Fayetteville. He had taken the train down to Wilmington to see how the city was recovering after the war. As he journeyed there, he passed near the spot where his friend had died, and the memories came back. He later wrote of them for *The Eagle*.

I saw the place a few miles below Kinston on the R. R. where that noble young man, Jarvis B. Lutterloh was mortally wounded. His regiment, the 56th N. C. T., was doing picket duty in Dover Swamp in May, 1863, when the yankees advanced on them in heavy force, and there was a severe skirmish with a small detachment of the 56th. One or two of our men were killed and 6 or 8 wounded before our troops retreated. Our reinforcements at once moved forward and all got to their positions in a few hours. I met with the foremost, and we met the retreating squad some half mile from the place of battle. Two or three men had carried Lt. Lutterloh on a blanket, running part of the way through briers and [undecipherable]. [He was] sinking very fast, a [minie ball] having entered the lower part of his breast. He was perfectly conscious, but seemed to regard his wound as severe and fatal.

The whole party stopped here a while, and we could see the yankees distinctly, although it was near night. They did not follow us, but fell back to Newbern. I was more at liberty than the other men there, and as the time was thought rather a critical one, every man had to be at his post. We all went back a mile or two towards Kinston that night and we managed to convey Lt. Lutterloh to a vacant house further on by the road-side. Here we laid him on a pile of straw, bathed his wound and gave him a little coffee and corn bread, all the rude comforts we had. He grew weaker and paler. At that stage of the war, more feeling was manifested for the dead or wounded, than afterwards. It troubled him to think he must die away from home. It was late in the night and raining.

He caught my hand, for I had remained with him much of the time, and told me to go at once to Kinston, and telegraph to his parents in Fayetteville, and to Mr. Freeman in Goldsboro, that he was "severely wounded." There was no way to go but to walk; I at once set out through the pitch darkness and heavy rain to Kinston, 6 miles off. It was a dismal night, stumbling through the monotony of pouring rain, the ponded water along the road, and the occasional meeting of couriers. One courier had got his horse killed in trying to cross a bridge, and was afloat carrying his saddle. I reached Kinston after midnight and luckily found the telegraph office open, as the military authorities were sending and receiving dispatches. I sent a dispatch to Raleigh to be sent to Fayetteville, but the rain storm was such that we had to repeat it two or three times to get it through. Before sunrise in the morning, I was about to start back to the camp and see about Lutterloh. I learned that he had been brought in town about daylight or before. I immediately went to see him, but he had just died a few minutes before I entered the room. His face was not yet entirely cold, and the half closed eye seemed still to reflect his bright generous smile. There were but two or three of us — his own servant one of the number — to appreciate the spirit that had gone. We were wet, tired, sleepy and hungry, but a thrill of sincere grief moved every bosom. He knew his wound was fatal, but did not expect to die so soon, nor did I expect it.

There lay the silent manly form on a straw mattress with a knapsack for a pillow, in an unoccupied room of Stephenson's Hotel, far away from the loved ones he had been speaking of so tenderly in his last moments. There was no cup to give him water, except the rude canteen and no soothing comforts to relieve his pain and prolong the young soldier's life. He had been my friend ever since schoolboy days. We had entered the war almost side by side, and there so early and unexpectedly, lay his dead form, his manly brow growing cooler and deadlier as his warm young life faded away. We did for him all we could. I telegraphed at once of his death, and we sent his remains forward the same day.

Yet a lady of Fayetteville, whose acquaintance I have never formed, yet have respected her highly, would say, as I hear, that the *EAGLE* descends to low things and disgraces himself.— Yes, the *EAGLE* goes high or low to do his conscientious duty. Not even midnight storms, nor the threatening terrors of radical wrath, can prevent him from attempting what is right. Yes, the *EAGLE* descended low to help carry your wounded son on his bloody blanket to a place of safety, and to answer his dying requests, and comfort him in his [last moments]. [The remainder of this paragraph and those following are smeared by large ink blots that prevented their reading.][24]

LONG GRABS

[June 7, 1869]

KINSTON, May 4, 1863.

Messrs. Editors: A friend has shown me a late No. of the Observer (I do not see the Observer regularly when moving about) in which is a card from "Dan _____" that requires notice.

I do not remember the exact words in the case of "Dan," but I know that no insulting or disrespectful remark was used, and certainly but a joke was intended. I have always had high respect for "Dan," and would not do him injustice intentionally, and regret that he misconstrues my motives. The facts of the case, however, as far as I know, justify my statement. I spent some time in Iverson's Brigade last winter and heard several officers say that "Dan's furlough was returned from Gen. Hill endorsed: Respectfully disapproved — Shooters before tooters," or words of the same meaning. Indeed this incident was a subject of remark, and was regarded by all, except "Dan," as a good joke. Although "Dan" is mad with Gen Hill he should not pour out his wrath upon "Long Grabs," who only made "an effort to be funny" by playfully alluding to an occurrence already public. "Dan" says he was only with the band two or three times at Senior Speaking. Now, "Dan's" memory is treacherous. Many a night did he bother me from my Greek by blowing and squeaking in the old South Building. Of course "Dan" attended to other things too, though music is certainly honorable and desirable. Many would not have noticed the matter, and some would have merely requested explanation. But "Dan" gets angry and uses harsh words at an imaginary wrong. The public must overlook the sudden lapsus irae of "Dan," owing to his extreme youthfulness. He is a very clever fellow, and although unfortunate in this display of weakness, he means no harm by it. If "Dan" is willing, we will take a drink precisely at 12 M. on the 20th of this month (each one wherever he may then be) and "drap" the thing; or we will fight with 10 inch Columblade — distance, 3 feet. If "Dan" don't do one or the other and "dry up," and quit his big dictionary words and Latin, I will make a "long grab" that way — reaching from "Dan to Be-ersheeba"— and destroy him.

The enemy has rebuilt the Rail Road over halfway to Kinston, and it is said they have a Rail Road Monitor — an iron-clad concern that is run out occasionally to shell the woods with. Profitable experiment. Our picket lines are the same as heretofore. It is a common thing for the enemy to dash up in force and attack our pickets. Their only object in this seems to be cutting off or capture of detachments of our force. The only tactics they seem capable of is to sneak round, strike slyly and cowardly, and then run for dear life till out of harm's way.

Some gentlemen are here from Newbern to negotiate arrangements with our officials for the removal of all families and citizens from Newbern who will not take the oath. The Provost Marshal in Newbern told them he wanted transportation for seventy families. This will take nearly all the balance of the population of the town. I suppose three-fourths of the people have left long before this. Here is conclusive evidence of the heroic devotion of the Eastern people to our cause. These are mostly mechanics and working people in limited circumstances. I hope these outraged and unfortunate people may find a ready welcome. In the name of humanity I hope they will not be treated with such indifference and contempt as has in some cases been shown toward other "highfalutin refugees." I have been reliably informed that Caldwell and Wilkes counties afford superior advantages to refugees at this time. That section is not crowded with an exiled population, and produce, provisions, farms, and other accommodations, are said to exist in good abundance and on good terms. Besides, more farm labor is very much desired there now. Cannot subscriptions of money or provisions be raised for the benefit of such of these people as may need aid till they can get located and employed? They have lost all, but must live. Who says and how much?

LONG GRABS.

[May 7, 1863]

KINSTON, May 22d.

Messrs. Editors:— The enemy advanced to-day on our outposts on the Dover road at Gum swamp. The 56th Reg't was stationed here, Colonel Faison commanding, supported by 6 or 8 companies of the 25th. Fully half of the 56th have been captured, perhaps more. Col. Rutledge of the 25th got all his men away safe. Only three companies of the 56th got out, Lane's, Harrill's and Grigg's, but large squads from all the others escaped, and many still come in. There was not much fighting and not many killed or wounded of our men or the enemy. Lt. Ray of Orange, of Capt. Graham's Co., was killed. The 56th escaped through swamps, and many have been most of the day coming through the swamps and mud. Several lost their accoutrements in their retreat.

The enemy were five regiments, with some cavalry, and perhaps artillery, all under command of Gen. Jones of Pa., a bold, skilful and competent officer. We were informed of their advance last night, as our cavalry pickets 4 or 5 miles below had been driven in, and the enemy was expected to advance in force early this morning. Our entrenchments have been somewhat enlarged since the skirmish there with the 56th some two or three weeks ago. Most of the men were just over Gum Swamp and on both sides of the Dover Road on the left of the railroad, a few yards in advance of where they were in the previous fight. About day-light the enemy showed himself in front, but not in very large force, and scattered around in sight from the railroad away to the Swamp on our left. The enemy did but little if anything in our front, but kept up a fire from the Swamp on our left. Our men fired occasionally, more, because they could do nothing else and remain behind their breastworks. About 10 o'clock everybody was startled by volley after volley poured right into our men by two or three regiments of yankees drawn up directly in our rear, commanding every avenue of retreat. There was no alternative but a retreat and each man to take care of himself. Most of the firing was done at this time by both sides, and most damage done. The 25th being farther to the rear were not so entirely flanked and surrounded, and by skillful management all escaped. One gun of Starr's battery was at the breastworks and was captured with 6 splendid horses. Lt. Whitmore and 12 men (among them John Dobbin of your town) were with the gun and probably captured. It is said they stood manfully at the gun till the last. Adj't Hale of the 56th had a ball pass through his coat sleeve, grazing his arm; after a long and tiresome retreat, he came out safe with 22 men. The 56th lost its ordnance wagon, medical wagon and ambulances, with their teams and contents. Baggage &c. saved.

The enemy then advanced up some two miles and fell back, pursued by our reinforcements, and Gen. Hill is still following them, shelling them. He intends to pursue them below Core Creek.

Citizens say they saw 175 of our prisoners going on with the yankees, but they probably took more than that. It is thought the enemy got round in position in our rear during the night. It has occasioned surprise why the enemy should be able to so completely surround our picket post with such a force without their knowing it. It was certainly a very unfortunate thing, and it is to be hoped it will not occur again. Definite information cannot be had now, and when the facts all appear, you can get a more satisfactory account.

They got in our rear by flanking our right and coming through the creek. They came very near capturing Gen. Ransom and staff, reconnoitering.

Truly,
LONG GRABS.

[May 25, 1863]

KINSTON, May 25.

Messrs. Editors: The number of prisoners captured by the enemy a few days ago at Gum Swamp will be less than I estimated before. Squads have been coming in constantly from the swamps and hopes are entertained that nearly all will yet come up. The number of prisoners taken may not exceed 100, and some think it will be less. Our reinforcements came up in a few hours and Gen. Hill with his forces here followed them up by the different routes. The enemy immediately made a rapid retreat towards Newbern. Our troops are still down that way and it has been reported that they were in 6 or 8 miles of Newbern and that we had troops in rear of a position of the yankees, who were scattered and demoralized. A large portion of the yankee force in this department will go out of service soon.

Dover Swamp is some 10 or 15 miles in extent, embraces Gum Swamp and Core Creek, and lies directly between here and Newbern on the Dover road and Rail Road. This swamp has much timber and thick undergrowth. It has ridges, points and islands all over it in places. The balance is under water and mud in the winter and nearly dry in the summer. There are but few farms or openings, which are usually small. It is almost impossible to fight a big open battle by several thousand men in this swamp. There is no way for either side to capture or damage the other materially without being exposed to equal damage himself. I think we might open new roads in every direction in our lines so that we could retreat more safely and rapidly or to be able to throw forward force in time to cut off the yankees when on these bold advances. Our positions are more traps as they are.

LONG GRABS.

[June 1, 1863]

In the June 1, 1863, issue of the *Fayetteville Observer*, the editors also reprinted parts of two letters from the *Raleigh Journal* that had been sent from Kinston that give some information on General Ransom and the capture of the gun from Starr's Battery.

The first, dated May 23, says, "Gen. Ransom was fired upon by the yankees in his rear before it was known that the enemy was flanking our works. Gen. R. made his escape good but it was with great difficulty he succeeded in doing so."

The second, dated May 26, says,

A friend has handed to us a letter from his son, a member of Starr's Battery, dated May 25th. He states the Lieut. Whitmore with 12 men and a howitzer went down to Gum Swamp on the morning of the fight, agreeable to orders. When the enemy appeared, the detachment begged for leave to fire, but Col. Rutledge[25] refused, as there was danger of killing more of our men than of the enemy. The artillerymen refused to leave their gun and were all captured with it, together with 8 fine horses. The Artillerists were Lt. Whitmore,[26] Serg't Sedberry,[27] Corp'l Dobbin,[28] privates T. W. Carroll,[29] T. J. Campbell,[30] W. L. Duke,[31] H. Cloninger,[32] S. Waller,[33] John A. Brown,[34] B. Plummer,[35] R. B. Braswell,[36] John McLean,[37] Irving Jones.[38]

Gen. Hill pursued the enemy to within 9 miles of Newbern on Saturday evening, when they had a very brisk skirmish, between Cooper's, parts of Branch's, Bunting's and Starr Batteries, and the 54th Pennsylvania Reg't. commanded by Col Jones. We lost 2 killed and 3 or 4 wounded. 2 yankees were found dead.

KINSTON, May 25.

Perhaps a glance at the history of these "classic scenes" may not be uninteresting to your readers.

In 1707–1709 Palatines, French and Germans came to North Carolina. Palatines are the people of a palatinate, a sort of country or district under the jurisdiction of a Count Palatine, a kind of magistrate under a governor, duke or kind of the German States. A colony of French Huguenots, encouraged by King William of England, came to Va., and in 1707 they moved from there to Trent river, N. C., with Rybourg, their pastor, and settled.

The colony of German palatines was from Heidelberg and vicinity of the Rhine. These people had suffered greatly from religious persecution and other troubles. They were finally driven into exile by their cruel and oppressive rulers, and receiving sympathy from Queen Anne, 6000 of them fled to England. Christopher DeGraffenreidt, a Swiss, and Lewis Mitchell wished to secure lands and make adventures in the British colonies. The lords proprietors of Carolina agreed with these men that 10,000 acres be laid off for them, in one body between the Neuse and Cape Fear, they paying 20 shillings for every hundred acres and six-pence the yearly quit-rent. The surveyor general was also instructed to lay off 100,000 acres to be reserved for them for twelve years. One of them was to receive a title when he would pay the usual price for 5000 acres, and DeGraffenreidt making the purchase was created a baron. The company having thus obtained lands now wished tenants and the German Palatines applied and were accepted. Commissioners had been appointed by the Queen to collect and receive money for the use of the Palatines, and to provide them with settlements; and with these commissioners DeGraffenreidt and Mitchell covenanted that they would transport to North Carolina 650 Palatines and lay off for each family 250 acres, to be held for five years without cost, and after that at the annual rent of two-pence per acre. The Palatines were to be supplied twelve months with necessary provisions, and to be furnished gratis with tools and implements. These people had each received 20 shillings of charitable collections in England, and this money placed in charge of DeGraffenreidt and Mitchell to be returned on their arrival in Carolina.

In December 1709 they arrived at the confluence of the Neuse and Trent rivers and erected temporary shelters, calling the place Newbern, from Berne in Switzerland where DeGraffenreidt was born, and in whose service Mitchell had formerly been employed. The Palatines had reason to complain of their trustees; and DeGraffenreidt, in whose name the lands were taken up, returned to England without giving them a title to their settlements. Being in need of money, he mortgaged the lands to Thomas Pollock for 800 pounds sterling, and they passed to the heirs of that gentleman. In the meantime the colonists flourished, and some years afterwards on petition to the King, they were indemnified by a grant of 10,000 acres free of quit-rents for 10 years.

Much of the ground below here possesses much historic interest. If the old legends and incidents of Eastern North Carolina were properly woven into romance, song and history, so as to amuse, interest and instruct the people, we would find our history read, sought after and applauded. There is ample material for a master pen — fully as much as Simms of South Carolina has used for his

5. War on the North Carolina Home Front

successful labors, and much more than Washington Irving built a world-wide fame on. I will relate some further items of historic interest relative to the early inhabitants of this immediate section:

The Tuscaroras were the most numerous, powerful and warlike tribe in Eastern Carolina, and in 1708 it is said they could muster 1,200 fighting men. Their towns were principally on the Neuse, Contentneay and Tar rivers; and as DeGraffenreidt had laid off some of their land without treaty or compensation, their jealousy was aroused. In September 1711 the Surveyor-General of North Carolina, John Lawson, and DeGraffenreidt took a small boat at Newbern and undertook to ascend the Neuse and explore the country. On the evening of the first day, they stopped at an Indian town near the river, and intended to lodge for the night; but being received in an unfriendly manner they concluded to return to the boat. They were seized by a party of well-armed savages and compelled to travel through the night to a distant village of the Tuscaroras. Here before a numerous council of the chief men of the various towns of the tribe, they were solemnly arraigned. Lawson especially was complained against as the man who with compass and chain had marked off and sold their land. After a discussion of two days the death of the prisoners was decreed. A large fire was kindled, a ring was drawn around the victims and strewn with flowers. On the morning appointed for the execution, a new council was held; around the white men sat the Chiefs in two rows, and behind them were three hundred of the Indians engaged in festive dancing. DeGraffenreidt saved his life by a claim of rank, by pledging his people to neutrality, and on promising to occupy no land without the consent of the tribe. Lawson was put to death. DeGraffenreidt was allowed to escape after a captivity of five weeks. On his return he found his settlements in a state of desolation. On the 22d of Sept small bands of Tuscaroras and Carees, acting in concert, approached the scattered cabins along the Roanoke and Pamlico sound. As night came on, the war whoop summoned the murderous savages from their places of concealment to the universal slaughter. At Bath, the Huguenot refugees and the planters in their neighborhood were struck down by the aid of the glare of their own burning cabins, and with a lighted pine-knot in one hand and a tomahawk in the other the infuriated savages pursued the terrified citizens like game through the forest.

For three days and nights they scoured the country and did not desist from slaughter till exhausted by fatigue. One hundred and thirty persons fell by the tomahawk on the 22d, and for many years, by act of Assembly, the anniversary of the massacre of 1711 was solemnized as a day of fasting and prayer. The Legislature of the southern portion of the colony, now South Carolina, rendered prompt assistance. The feuds, divisions and want of harmony in the Northern colony made it necessary to ask for help from their neighbors.

Col. Barnwell of South Carolina (the two Carolinas were not separated till 1729 though they acted under different authorities and charters) marched into North Carolina with a party of whites and a number of Cherokee, Creek and Catawba Warriors. In several battles he killed many of the Carees, Bear River and Mattamuskeet Indians, and took 200 women and children prisoners. In the upper part of Craven precinct or county near the Neuse, the Indians entrenched themselves in a rude fort. Col. Barnwell with his own force and some troops from North Carolina besieged the fort, but made a treaty with them and ended the siege. The Indians, unwisely were allowed to escape, renewed hostilities on defenceless citizens. Large reinforcements of Indians and whites again arrived from South Carolina, and the enemy were driven to their fort near Neuse river, Naharuke — in what is now Craven county, and 800 prisoners taken on 23d March, 1723. The spirit of the Indians was completely broken by this disaster and suing for peace, it was granted on humiliating terms. King Blount with a remnant of the Tuscaroras, remained faithful allies of the whites, often warring and harassing other hostile tribes. The greater part however, of this warlike nation, unwilling to submit, and unable to resist, migrated to the vicinity of Oneida Lake in New York and were welcomed by their kindred, the Iroquois, and became the sixth nation of that Confederacy, where a few descendants of those Indians still remain.

LONG GRABS.

[June 4, 1863]

KINSTON, May 28.

Messrs. Editors: — There has not been much of general interest for a correspondent — ye veritable "Long Grabs" for instance — to note down this way. It is getting "mighty dry" now, — even "new dip" has almost ceased to bubble in the fountain. A shower of rain is daily expected, however, but that will depend very much on the weather.

Some cases of small pox are reported among the troops about here. The health of the army otherwise is very good. We have here now Ransom's and Cook's Brigades and Colquitt's Georgia Brigade, Moore's, Cumming's Bunting's, Starr's, Cameron's, Branch's and perhaps other batteries. The first three are from Wilmington, the fourth from Fayetteville, the last from Petersburg. Pettigrew's Brigade left here some time ago, and Daniel's left recently, both for Virginia. There are other Brigades and troops in the Eastern part of the State, and all our troops in this department are constantly changing and moving. Gen. Hill's Headquarters are now at Goldsboro,' though he is here frequently. Gen. Ransom is in command of this post now and has been unwell for a few days. Col. Clark of the 24th commands the Brigade as senior Col. in Ransom's absence or when he commands the post. Maj. Haskell of S. C. has been chief of artillery in this Department for several months, but I learn is now assigned to duty elsewhere, and Major Branch, of Branch's Virginia Battery, has been promoted to Chief of Artillery.

Gen. Jones, the yankee officer in Newbern who commands the enemy's expeditions up this way, is said to be a lawyer in Philadelphia. He was Col. of the 58th Penn. reg't, said to be a splendid regiment. He is certainly a brave, daring officer, and has a guide of the same character, by the name of Wiggs Tilman, a native of this county and once a member of Capt. Foy's Co. in Nethercutt's Battalion. He accompanies Jones and pilots the yankees in their raids through the country. His father lives west of this place and his wife now lives some miles south of here on the river road and within our lines. Tilman is represented as a shrewd reckless character and would do as good service for one side as the other, and it is said, he has made application once or twice to get back in our army since he left his old company. Gen. Jones has also for servant and guide a negro

5. War on the North Carolina Home Front

named Caesar, the property of Mr. Lane, who lived near Core Creek till the enemy occupied that section. The boy has been runaway a good deal and had usually hired his own time and worked from place to place through the country. He is very intelligent and altogether a bad, daring, desperate character. I believe he was captured once, but by some means escaped. There is another negro by the name of Bill, belonging to Dr. Cobb, who has a plantation on Southwest Creek just below here, of similar character, who serves as guide for the 3d N. Y. Cavalry. Of yankee troops that are and have been at Newbern are the 27th, 32d, 44th and 45th Mass. Reg'ts., 58th Pa. and 3d N. Y. Cavalry. Some artillery companies returned North a short time ago, their time having expired. Gen. Palmer, of N. Y. I think, is said to be in immediate command of the Post at Newbern. Gen. Wild is to be there soon to organize a negro Brigade. Every facility is to be afforded him by all concerned.

I think it is very desirable to retain the same Brigade (or more) here permanently, that they might get more thoroughly acquainted with the country and citizens. Heretofore the troops have changed here so much that none of them possessed sufficient knowledge of the country to foil and entrap that evil and bold raider, Jones, while he and his forces have been here since the fall of Newbern I believe.

I learn that all of the 56th Reg't have come in but 148, who are no doubt prisoners. I suppose this includes Starr's men also.

Writing love letters for the negro cooks to their sable "dulcineas" is a common amusement with the young man and officers in the army. Every letter is sure to be answered, and a most extravagant, classic, lengthy and superlatively exquisite love correspondence is kept up. The "agony" is piled on with all the approved flirtations. And after the most excruciating wooing and coquetry and "plot" enough for a dozen first class novels, "his own lubly angelic Dinah fros herself into his buzum and begs forgiveness." But the poor darkeys do not invent all this mischief themselves, and although often intending amusement, yet sometimes cupid's darts's are really meant and felt. A "nice young Lieut." writes an eloquent love epistle for a negro boy to some curly haired damsel. Her young mistress, of "sweet seventeen" and just out of school, poetry, albums and flowers, reads the letter for her and writes a rainbow sunset reply which the "young Lieut." reads again for Cuffee. Oh! isn't that pleasant!—and then the excitement and curiosity to find out,—"Oh who is it? Who is it?" Exit omnes.

Now that writing paper is scarce and expensive, I would suggest to the friends of the soldiers at home to send to their relatives and friends in the army the blank leaves at the beginning and end of books. There are nearly half a dozen blank leaves in every book about the house that will do very well to write on with a pencil, and in many cases will do for pen and ink. The soldier has to pay from $2 to $4 a quire for inferior paper, and sometimes it cannot be had at all.

Truly,
Long Grabs.

[June 1, 1863]

Raleigh, June 1.

Messrs. Editors: Once more doth "Long Grabs" enjoy ye cool waters and ye pleasant shades of ye City of Oaks. He looketh out from ye window into ye back yard and admireth ye Irish potatoe patch, ye beans and ye "greens" while he eateth a cold biscuit ot two. (Ye "Long Grabs" knoweth all ye hotel keepers and servants, and he goeth to ye pantry and ye cupboard, between meals, like one of ye family.)

The other day as I left Kinston a Minister got on the train with an arm load of tracts to distribute to the passengers on the principle of "preaching the gospel to every creature." He has been at this a long time and knows his business well. He eyed every one closely to see what tract would apply in the case. Coming up to me he scrutinized me very closely a moment, and looking through his bundle he picked out a tract of 4 pages headed, "Don't Swear," and enjoined me to read it carefully. I did so and I must say it is one of the ablest and most appropriate publications for the times that I have seen. It is written by the Rev. Mr. Jeter of Richmond, Va.

Various plans have been proposed for stopping the war, but a friend has given me his ideas on the subject which are more practicable than any yet made public. It is proposed that all who want to fight, both North and South, equip themselves and organize as they see fit and go out to Kansas and the territories beyond, and there let the Yankees form line of battle north of the line 36 0 36,' and the Confederates form a similar line south of it. This all done, let them fight and keep fighting to their hearts' content, both governments to furnish rations and pay expenses. Meanwhile let all, North and South, who prefer to stay at home and attend to their business, do so. Then after that much be agreed upon, let a strip of land be laid off between the two governments, of two or three miles in width, and left entirely unoccupied. Then let it be the law of both countries that all office seekers and men found kicking up a mess in politics, be sent to this half-way territory to cut up their antics among themselves. A strong guard from both sides should be posted all round, and no one should be allowed to get out till he took the "oath" to behave himself. I hope the committee of Foreign Affairs and also the one on Propositions and Grievances will consider this at the next meeting of Congress.

LONG GRABS.

[June 11, 1863]

In the next letter, Long Grabs describes Kittrell's Springs, which is located in Vance County and was the site of North Carolina's first summer resort. During the Civil War it was used as a hospital. Only a cemetery where 54 Confederate soldiers were buried between 1864 and 1865 remains to mark the site where wealthy people came during the spring and summer to play, enjoy the weather, and drink the curative water of the mineral springs.

KITTRELL'S SPRINGS, N. C., June 5.

Messrs. Editors: Nominative. Kittrell's; Gonitive, Kittrell's Springs; Dative, Kettle's Springs; Accusative, Warm Springs; Vocative wanting; Ablative, Tempest in a Tea-pot.

About a year ago I dated a letter from here to you, and the prospect for a big crowd now is not so good as then. There are now only 15 or 20 boarders, but the season has hardly opened. This has been quite a noted place for 3 or 4 years, but the Spring has been a place of resort 25 years. It is in Granville county, a half mile west of Kittrell's Depot, on Raleigh and Gaston Rail Road, Great crowds of fashionable society of Warren, Halifax, Edgecombe, Franklin and the Roanoke section, flock here during the last summer months. Dancing, gaming, flirting, riding, sporting and increased velocity generally are the usual occupations.

This is perhaps the most fashionable watering place in North Carolina, though the scenery is repulsive compared with our superb mountain regions, and the water is not as cool and invigorating as the Red Springs water in Robeson county. The buildings are light, rough wooden structures, consisting of one large three-story gothic building with ball-room, dining-room, parlors, &c., and several rows of whitewashed cabins. The ten-pin-alley is in the "suburbs," also a little church or temperance hall or something of the kind. The "sutler's" quarters, where are kept some liquids and other things, are more conspicuous. There is a little old mill, with a little muddy pond, just above the spring, and you cross the race below on a little old rickety bridge, just rickety and shakey enough to frighten a timid lady to death. The water is chalybeate, and on close analysis I find chemical properties as follows: Iodide of potassium 12 3–7 percent; corrosive sublimate .663 per cent; sulphuric acid gas 18 per cent; nitric acid 120 per cent; bi-carbonate of soda, 85 per cent; tincture of iron .002; syllabub 20 per cent; prussic acid 500 per cent; and galvanic magnetism 40 per cent. This unprecedented combination of chemicals cannot fail to have a wonderful effect on all debilitating diseases.

These old fields and sterile hills are enduring "land marks' of a former population that has sought better fortunes in other climes. Where once the golden harvests loaded the air with sweet odor, the weeping willow with its down-cast branches, now mourns the long absence of the sturdy yeomen of olden time.

The argumentative old gentleman is already here, as is also the successful businessman — now retired. The military hero, warrior and critic is here too, and he has already discussed the merits of Lee, Johnston, Bragg and Beauregard, and marked out their future duties. Oh! It is a pity that he is not at the very head of affairs, that things might be immediately wound up.

Granville has more negroes than any other county in the State, and considerable enterprise and prosperity are displayed in portions of the county. Wheat, tobacco, and all kinds of produce are the main staples. There are a great many Virginians in Granville and the people have more intercourse with South-eastern Va. than with their own State. There is more energy and equality in classes than in the adjoining counties.

LONG GRABS.

[June 11, 1863]

Chapter 6

Return to Virginia
June 9, 1863 – July 1, 1863

The 35th Regiment North Carolina Troops, commanded by then Colonel Matt W. Ransom, had been stationed at Kinston during General Hill's moves on New Bern and Little Washington. It took no part in the action, but was involved in the action at Gum Swamp below Kinston that drove the Union troops back toward New Bern. The 35th was then ordered back to Virginia in the area of Petersburg.

Sometime during this period Ransom had induced McSween with certain promises to join his regiment. McSween will reveal this information and a great deal more in letters he wrote to Governor Vance after the 35th's return to Virginia. These letters of 1863–1864 are unpublished and are in the State Archives of North Carolina in Raleigh. I did not discover them until finding hints of Long Grabs' identity in a letter that the editor of the *Fayetteville Observer* received but did not publish, preferring for some reason to print a summary on September 8, 1864. In another unpublished letter, written on October 31, 1864, from Hospital No. 24 in Richmond and still signing as Long Grabs, he stated he was wounded again in a charge with the 26th North Carolina.

In the following letter, McSween mentions a man named Vallandingham — "he arrived yesterday morning and went South this morning."

The man was Clement Vallandingham, a member of the U. S. House of Representatives from Ohio's 3rd District, serving from 1858 to 1863. After his defeat at Fredericksburg, General Burnside had been assigned charge of the Department of Ohio. In April 1863, he had issued General Order No. 38, which made it illegal for anyone in the department to criticize the North or express sympathy and support for the South. One punishment was deportation to the Confederacy. Vallandingham, being vocal in his Southern support, was arrested, tried by a military tribunal, and ordered sent to a Federal prison. President Lincoln commuted the sentence, and Vallandingham was sent through the Confederate lines.[1]

6. Return to Virginia

Petersburg, Va., June 9.

Messrs. Editors. This has become a large and rapidly growing place before the war, and there is now a considerable business done here. I see a less number of Jews and foreigners than formerly. It is probable that "a mice was being smelt" in reference to military duty as protection papers are getting below par. Time was when "our people" sold at their ease in well filled aristocratic stores, and the Jews had auctions and peddled. Now Jews deal from large full stores and "our people" have auctions and "notions."

Cooke's Brigade has gone to Richmond.

Vallandingham arrived here yesterday morning, and went South this morning. I learn he was not permitted to go to Richmond. I did not get a close view of him. There is a general desire to see him though no demonstration.

It now seems that Smith has been elected governor of Va., by some 2,000 majority. The State probably did not poll two-thirds the usual vote. Mr. Smith has been Governor and member of Congress before, and is now a Brig. Gen. in Lee's army. He lived in Fauquier, and it will be remembered that he acted a conspicuous part in one of the very first engagements with the enemy. He is a man of talent, great energy, daring, perseverance and popularity, characteristics always appreciated in Virginia. He is wholly a self-made man, having been once a stage driver, and afterwards an extensive stage contractor. He once got a great deal of extra pay for carrying the mail on some of his lines, since which he has been known as 'Extra Billy.' There was no material difference, politically, among the candidates here this time.

I applied yesterday to a broker to get some specie, and he required only seven and a half Confederate dollars for one in gold, whereupon I left him to his own reflections and his certain doom after death. I also went to a fashionable tailor to get some work done, but he will no doubt meet with the same fate as the other. He would charge $20 for a piece of work that I afterwards agreed with a seamstress to have done at $8 — the very same seamstress too that he would have hired to work, I learn. I found butter at $3 25 per lb. that had been bought out of carts at $2, mostly barter. Oh! ye nation of cormorants, ye generation of vipers, how can you escape. But thus it hath been, and will be again, and there is nothing new under the sun.

I have noticed that people of every community have sent necessary articles to their own immediate friends in the army, often in great abundance. But what must the brave boys from New Orleans, Nashville and Fredericksburg do, who have no one to send them anything? If they have sisters and relatives they are hardly able to take care of themselves, much less to help the sick and naked in the army. These men whose homes have been desolated and whose families are exiled, get nothing but $11 a month, with their scanty rations and a supply of clothing. I hope our generous, liberal and sympathetic people will think of these things and while working for those of their own household they may give aid to the unfortunate who would not stoop to beg although dire necessity urges them to.

The recent indications of conflict of authority in North Carolina present some important considerations. It has always appeared to me that Judge Pearson's decision in reference to men between 18 and 35 who got substitutes, is correct. I expressed this view in a letter nearly a year ago. The real meaning of the Act of Congress is thought to be rather indefinite, but the whole matter of substitutes is left almost entirely to the War Department, and of course the Department in its discretion will not make issue with the chief tribunals of a State. Our government is based on States' Rights, and the safest principle we can adopt perhaps is, that when a State in the capacity of a State or through her regularly constituted authorities comes in conflict with the general government the latter must yield. If the general government does not assimilate itself to the States, it must coerce them so as to conform to it, — the principle we are now fighting against.

It would have been better for our army if no substitutes had been allowed, but it is the act of Congress we should blame and not those who availed themselves of its benefits. Congress, I think, did not mean to call again into service those whom it had once called and who had responded strictly in accordance with its own provisions. No demand existed for men except between 18 and 35, nor was any assurance given that any others ever would be called. The law implied that the furnishing of a substitute was equivalent of going into service once, and why must some go twice before others only a year or two older go once? In justice to all, the substitute arrangement, since it has been adopted at all, should be carried out in good faith, and Congress should exhaust the original material before returning to the exempts. Although this may have been an unwise act, yet the government should carry it out in good faith. Let Congress call out all the men it may think suitable for service — say up to 50 years of age — and then if there is still need for men, they must be procured from classes before exempted. From present appearances I think the war will continue long enough and hard enough to require the service of the entire fighting population. Getting a substitute is like getting an office — only intended for few, and should not excite any more dissatisfaction than many other advantages of the few over the many. I know some poor men of large and helpless families who after much trouble borrowed enough money to hire a substitute, even mortgaging their little property, and a few weeks afterward found that they had to go into service themselves. There are many poor men too who got two and three thousand dollars to go as substitutes when they would soon be liable to service anyhow. I don't know that the poor man is worsted by the substitute law, properly construed.

There is a time in the affairs of men when we should take a somber second thought, when the wire edge is worn off and when we should stop and blow and start on again at our work with more skill and economy. This time has now arrived in the Southern Confederacy. We have not whipped the yanks before breakfast, nor have ten killed a thousand, nor one put ten thousand to flight. We must economize our men as well as our means. We must work for effect, and skillfully, too, every man at his calling. Every part of the body politic is now more strikingly necessary to the health, harmony and efficiency of the whole. The duty of the soldier is to be at his post and obey order. Every good citizen should yield a ready compliance with the great requirements of the government, and he should stand ready to serve the interest of his country in whatever capacity his services can be most available, whether that service be raising produce, manufacturing necessaries, or undergoing the harder duties of war. There can be but little wisdom now in carrying on things pell mell and without system as was somewhat the case a year ago. Then volunteers were called for and it was proper that the measures of the Government be sustained. But now the government has indicated those required for military service and also those required for other duties. It then becomes every good citizen and honorable man to stick at his post and perform his part to the best of his ability, till his specified duties call him elsewhere. It is plain this is now the proper rule for all to observe, notwithstanding a Major General recently said in N. C., that he "would believe no man on oath under 40 out of the army," and that a certain deserter "deserved being shot almost as much as an exempt." But the great duty of a man in the army is to be at his post and obey orders. He is required only to obey lawful and proper orders. A soldier or officer cannot be punished for not executing an unlawful order. The determining such an order is a delicate question, however, and unless its legality clearly appears, the issue had better not be made. It is certainly improper and often disastrous for a man in the army to assume duties not pertaining to his position. If he is a Quartermaster he has no business in battle unless ordered. Indeed I think it nothing in a man's favor to go into a fight at all if it is not strictly his duty. Time was when it was proper to rush of their own accord to battle, but now, my opinion is that all should keep out of battle who can do so honorably, but when plain duty calls all should go and stay manfully to the last.

A few nights ago I attended church and received many happy associations. It was a delightful night and with the same sweet sacred music and familiar service felt myself once more under those holy and inspiring influences so often witnessed along with sisters, brothers and friends. The soldier should go to church when opportunity offers. He should go at night. He will there find a greater combination of all that is calculated to elevate the morals, to inspire the heart, and to purify the nature of man, than at any other place of devotional exercises. He sees around him once more family groups, and all the emblems of christian duty. The scene reminds him more forcibly of his own vows and obligations. It recalls to his mind the best and holiest efforts of his life. He is in the presence of Deity and everything addresses itself to his conscience.

Truly,
LONG GRABS.

[June 15, 1863]

CAMP NEAR PETERSBURG, June 14, 1863.

Messrs Editors:—This is a delightful section of country and has not suffered materially from the war. The people are liberal, refined and accommodating, and treat the soldier more kindly than is usual where so many troops have been quartered. The country around Petersburg and for some distance south and east resembles the classic shades and forests and the rich smooth farms of the Old Dominion east of Richmond. One is impressed with the entire absence of that dazzling, superficial display so common in newer countries and along our railroads—too often an index of a delusive prosperity. For solid, real success in agriculture, advantages of superior society, health and all the principal objects a man lives and labors for, I have seen no section that surpasses this. These old, age-colored dwellings and carelessly shaped fields possess a charm, a hallowed modesty that certainly "lends enchantment to the view." This land is undulating, gravelly and about half cleared. The fences are such as the ladies usually paint in beautiful scenery, viz: two or three old posts almost ready to fall down, with two or three old planks of different length and width tacked across them. Wide level roads enclosed by ditches and tall thick hedges intersect the country, each known by a particular name for a century. The residences are seldom near the public road, and long avenues skirted with cedar and elms lead from the big gate at the roadside to the "old homestead." Clear, cool springs gush from among the roots of the large oaks on the hill-side. In every valley the road crosses a little brook or creek where the water glides gently over the clean, pebbly bottom a short distance and then falls over a precipice into the cavern below. You inhale the sweet scent of clover fields that extend far in the distance. You hear the suppressed hum of the bumble-bee as he steals the sweets from the clover blossoms; the butterfly flits through the perfumed atmosphere; the clang of the distant bell brings to view the grazing herds that are literally "wading in clover;" and the greasy mouthed little "contrabands" glisten in the sun-shine as they wallow over the grass about their cabins. Suddenly the scene is varied by the rapid approach of a fine rockaway whirling over the smooth turnpike and drawn by a pair of splendid horses. It is a party of young ladies taking an evening ride. You get on a stump by the road that you may see and be seen. The carriage is richly lined and decorated within; and the top opens from the middle and has been let almost down before and behind. The ladies are young and beautiful, and are adorned with all that skill and taste in dress can suggest, and resemble a bunch of rich flowers in an ornamental vase. As the vehicle flies by you throw up your cap, bow, salute, slap your hands, and jump up, (forgetting where you are standing) and then come down kerwhallop, right into the aforementioned ditch of water. Whereupon the ladies very rudely laugh out, and hollow and scream and roll from one side of the rockaway to the other. (if any body says this was L. G. he may consider himself challenged.) Exeunt omnews.

Recently I saw a notice that there would be a grand fancy ball in Richmond, the proceeds of which would go to the fund for raising a monument to Stonewall Jackson. This is certainly in very bad taste, if not disgusting. No such means are necessary or appropriate to induce the Southern people to show their affection for the lamented hero. The pure out-gushing admiration and affection of a devoted and liberal people is sufficient to guarantee voluntary offerings enough for a half dozen monuments. When all monuments have crumbled into oblivion the memory of Jackson will live like that of Caesar, of Bonaparte, and of Washington. Yet at the Capital of the Confederacy, while the sod is not yet dry on the hero's grave, while the whole nation is in mourning for the death of our great chieftain, a call is made for a grand fancy dance to raise money for his monument! Must the holy shrine of the nation's affection be thus invaded with impunity? Will we not rebuke such an insult upon our feelings, such a slander to his memory and his pure life? Are there any so devoid of patriotism and self-respect who will on reflection encourage such an enterprise? A recent article in the Richmond Examiner presents considerations very appropriate in this connection. Balls and parties are proper and desirable in their place; indeed there is a "time to laugh, a time to cry, a time to dance;" but this is no time to trifle with a nation's grief, nor mock the dispensations of Providence.

A very unwise and injurious order was recently put in place at Weldon. All boxes, barrels, trunks, &c., against which [undecipherable] contained, were stopped, examined, and if "contraband," immediately confiscated. An acquaintance of mine from Marlboro' District had two or three boxes of provisions for relatives and friends in the 8th S. C. Reg't. They were opened and searched, and to wait for them he would miss connection. He was compelled to go on immediately and requested an officer to have them fastened up and sent on, but the boxes have not been heard from since. One man had a trunk full of buttons and combs packed closely, which he had bought at auction sale in Charleston. The key had been sent on with another lot of goods. A hatchet was brought and the trunk hacked and knocked open. Each package had to be torn open and being placed back hurriedly and loosely the trunk would not hold the articles. Private trunks of passengers were sometimes opened in the same way. All packages of the Express Company were examined rigidly also. There being no accommodation for storage, many boxes and barrels of valuables had to remain exposed to weather and thieves till entirely wasted. I learn the War Department as soon as informed of the matter revoked or modified the order. I suppose the officer in charge did what he could to ascertain the character of the goods with as little delay and injury to the owner as possible, but his duties were difficult. You can form no correct idea of what a box, barrel or bale contains now till you open it, as merchants have to use whatever they can get whether box, bag or cask. I have seen shoes shipped in a barrel, butter in a box, and candles in a bale with a frame around it.

There has long been a desire to have some way by which to get full, early and reliable intelligence from the army through the Press for the benefit of those at home as well as for the mutual advantage of those in different portions of the army. I have expressed my opinions to you before I believe, and further experience and observation has only tended to confirm it. Without hesitation I repeat that the only proper and sure way for the Press to get early, impartial, full and reliable news from the army is through regular, competent and reliable correspondents not in military service. Many have said that the best plan is to have some one selected in each Regiment to send all news of interest to papers at home for publication — the Adjutant for instance, or some other officer, to be prepared under the direction of the Colonel or commanding officer. Such would be a sort of official duty which the Army regulations neither authorize or allow. Official reports are to be made through the proper superior officer or the Department, where the time and manner of publication is alone determined. A simple list of killed and wounded may be sent by any one, but is now generally sent under direction of the commanding officer of the Reg't or Company for publication as soon as any communication is allowed from the army. But a simple statement of killed and wounded after battle is not all that is desired. It does not satisfy the general desire of all at home to know all about those in the army or as much as is not inconsistent with the public interest. The soldier in the army although he cannot get papers often would like to see in those he gets some detailed account of his friends and relatives in others portions of the army. Some military commanders will not allow one in their command to publish any matter relative to the army if the slightest criticism or speculation is indulged. Can open, independent truth be had under such censorship? The man in the army is not allowed to condemn although he may praise as much as he pleases. He could well discuss or applaud what he did himself, for "self-praise is half slander." There are also in nearly every Regiment little jealousies and animosities existing between certain cliques and persons, for weak human nature shows itself the same under all circumstances. Sometimes this feeling has culminated to bitter and deadly hate, and is it not reasonable to suppose that a Col. would underrate some Lieutenant towards whom such feelings were entertained, and overrate another who was a favorite? Any one who has never been in the army cannot imagine the extent to which bad faith and injustice has been practiced towards a great portion of the army by others having temporary advantage over them. It is impossible for those men to receive justice in all respects at the hands of such officers, while others who are least deserving may get all the credit. The great majority of officers in our army have nobly done their duty, and given in all cases praise or censure where it was due; but there are many regularly commissioned officers in the Confederate army who have acted like dogs and made themselves contemptible — who have deceived and ruined many a useful and worthy man, and protected many a scoundrel. In addition, an Adjutant or any one or two officers have not really the time and opportunity to attend to incidental matter of this kind. Now it is not the amount of work done in the army that requires such attentiveness — indeed there is much idle time — but it is the fact that every one must be ready for any kind of work at a moment's notice. He must be at his post — some order may come — the regiment may move — a court-martial in session may want some important witness immediately — there may be inspection — or a detail — or extra guard, picket or work — in fact, almost anything at any time and he must be ready for it. If he writes anything he must do so on hearsay; but how can he rely on that as every body else should be at his own post too. Matters pertaining to one Reg't might be collected, however, in this way at some inconvenience, but the difficulties before alluded to would still be in the way. In battles one man, or a dozen men, at their post on one part of the field can see but very little of the whole action. General officers who observe different portions of the battle very nearly at the same time, of course get a more thorough knowledge of it. There is great inconvenience experienced too by men in the army in the delay they are necessarily subjected to in receiving and getting off letters. The post office is often 10 or 20 miles away, and even if it is near, the soldier cannot get to it but must depend on the tedious and uncertain mail arrangement of the army. Then he has few conveniences in camp, no table, no candle, perhaps not allowed to build a fire, and probably no writing material, and often tired, wet, sleepy and hungry. On the other hand an intelligent, energetic and judicious correspondent would be free from all or nearly all these difficulties. He is independent as well as reliable; he is in the interest of no Commander; he applauds or censures wherever and whenever in the exercise of a wise discretion and sound judgment it may be due; he can go and come when and

6. Return to Virginia

where he pleases; he can visit different regiments and commands and learn the news in each, and the conflicting opinions, and see more clearly the motives of all concerned; he can go all over the battle field during the action and participate and see for himself (and he should always do that when it would aid his own business or benefit the army or the cause;) and he could receive subscriptions for papers and have them directed through him and thus avoid somewhat the uncertainty and delay of the mails. Place a man of the right kind in that capacity with such duties before him and the desired object will be secured, but in no other way. The Press of the State for my section have it entirely in their power to do this, at small expense to each paper.

I have known some editors to speak very despairingly of newspaper correspondents — hired penny-a-liners, &c. It is true there are some very incompetent and trashy persons that are newspaper correspondents, and there are likewise many editors that are very trashy, useless characters. A correspondent does the same business that an editor does and is not so much "hired, paid, penny-a-liner" as the editor himself. It is honorable to work for one's living, but many of the best contributors to the Press never charge a cent for their labor; but the editor says at the beginning and end and middle of his paper, that he will not work for nothing (and every issue of his paper is, to many of his subscribers a renewal of the old dun in a more ingenious way.) Let us have no more of this tirade against all correspondents by editors. I admit that both occupations are hardly fit for a decent white man, but there is no sense in abusing each other when one is as deep in the mud as the other is in the mire. It is like the pot calling the kettle black. What think ye, knights of ye quill — ye Press gang. I'm pretty well, thank ye; how d'ye do yourself?

Truly yours,
Long Grabs.

P. S. Merely in illustration of some argument advanced above I will mention an interview I had with Gen. Lee when I first visited his army. I first saw his Adj't Gen'l Col. Chilton — a very gentlemanly man — and asked what conditions were allowed correspondents of the Press. He asked me a few general questions, and satisfying himself of my character and motives, he replied that they were allowed to exercise their own discretion entirely, that they might publish whatever they thought proper, but he hoped I would observe due caution and prudence as to the strength and position of the troops and any new movements I might learn. He said that the Commanding General was desirous that the people at home would know all they could about the condition of his men and do all they could for them. Gen. Lee afterwards told me himself the same in substance and wished to urge upon all the necessity of sustaining and filling up the army. He wanted me to see every thing, say what I pleased about it so as not to injure the service. This was Gen. Lee, but some others are not Gen. Lee by a long shot.
[June 18, 1863]

Richmond, VA., June 18.

Messrs. Editors:— As I landed from the cars once more in the Capital of the Confederacy, a number of voices greeted me with "How are you, Long Grabs?"

It is pleasant to be a great man and to be received with consideration in great cities. Who would have thought_____.

There is not half the crowd in Richmond now that was last Winter. The number of officers has wonderfully decreased. Good egg. The weather has been oppressively hot and dry; but the soft soothing showers this evening have revived the drooping vegetation and purified the heated dusty atmosphere. I found but one effective antidote to-day for the heat — the continued sucking of mint-juleps in a cool place with cravat off and collar unbuttoned. I went up to the Whig office and found the Whig man in the last stages of existence from the excessive heat. He had laid aside hat, boots, coat, pen, scissors and "every weight and the sin which," &c., and was stretched full length on an old sofa plying a huge fan as rapidly and as regularly as a boat does its paddle wheel.

I intended once or twice to give you a detailed account of the Richmond Press, but the difficulty of obtaining reliable and full information prevented. The Enquirer is said to have the largest circulation — perhaps twenty thousand. The Dispatch has a large circulation and at first of the war was read more down South than all the others. The Examiner has undoubtedly the most able and eloquent editorials, though the articles in the Whig are more elegant, chaste, orthodox and conservative. Some new publications have started here recently and more are under way.

I have seen the London Times up to the 5th inst., and several other English papers. There is scarcely any thing worthy of attention in any of them. There is but little said about our affairs and that is scattering extracts from Northern papers. The London Index is brought through pretty regularly. This paper, it will be remembered, is published by our own government and private contributions together. It is a well edited, eight page weekly, on beautiful paper, and devoted almost exclusively to the discussion of affairs in the South for the information of Europe. It also contains matters of local interest in London, proceedings of Parliament, and things of importance to the British Government. It is edited by Mr. Holtz, a Swiss and formerly connected with the Press in Mobile. The paper has at yet a limited circulation. The New York and Philadelphia papers reach Richmond as quick and as regularly as they did by mail before the war.

An excellent arrangement has been effected here for the soldier in the establishment of the North Carolina Depot and Soldiers' Home. Both are under the charge of Dr. O. F. Manson of Granville county, N. C., and a native of this city. Dr. Manson has immediate charge of Moore Hospital, and has a superintending control of all the North Carolina Hospitals in this city. He stands high as a physician, and is certainly one of the kindest and most accommodating and attentive Surgeons I have met with in the army. He devotes himself assiduously and sincerely to the welfare of North Carolina's soldiers and North Carolina's interests. He has gentlemanly and attentive assistants in charge of the Depot and Home. The soldier can get eating and lodging here free, and the commissioned officer and citizen can stay here at $2 a day with as good accommodation as is furnished at the hotels and boarding houses at $8 and $12 a day. Ladies going after a sick or wounded husband, father or brother, are not charged for stopping here. The State does more good for its troops in this way than if it were to vote them a hundred dollars bounty. The State has a plenty of supplies on hand, and if these places continue to be well and economically managed they should be kept up.

Not near so many are sent to the Hospitals as at an earlier period in the war. The men are more inured to the hardship and get on with less treatment as well as less clothing and rations. The Hospitals, where they have been long established, have sufficient supplies of clothes and bedding; indeed in some instances the old bedding and underclothing have been accumulated till they are in the way. The bedding that was once filthy has been cleaned and sunned and is now as serviceable as if entirely new. The vessels, buckets, seats and stationary furniture need but little replenishing.

Our crops are abundant and there need be no difficulty in obtaining a supply of provisions for the army — both man and beast; but we should begin to prepare to shoe and clothe our troops next winter. There was suffering last Winter before the needful supplies reached them. There need be no suffering from that cause next Winter, if our people begin in time and proceed right. The people should know by this time that it is unwise to wait for a call from some of the authorities before beginning to make arrangements. There will be a call to provide for the army, and when it is made the people should be ready to respond and not ready to begin work at that late date. If such articles prepared in advance be not called for or needed let them be kept on hand, for they are equal in value to that much money and may be of service at any time. Leather, cloth and arms are to us like gold in the bank — the basis of our circulation.

Ladies' goods are cheaper and plentier here now than for several months before. Gentlemen's ready made clothing and hats and shoes have gone up occasionally. There is now as strong a mania for dress among persons out of the army (and some in it too) as ever before. In fact the men who think dress the most important item to existence now fairly spread themselves. You can get plenty of fine clothes for money enough; and if you don't wear a fine coat the very plain presumption is that you are not able — the most disgraceful impression that could exist in the estimation of the dandy. So that the fashionable fop "lays the flattering unction to his soul" that his habits and fashions are at last beyond the reach of the vulgar and impoverished masses, and with improved aristocratic impulses he is transported in oblivious happiness to new realms — the El Dorado of his life-long ambitions.

There is to be heard at the street corners and elsewhere great constitutional arguments about the late call for the militia. The militia service is like the Universalist doctrine. If all other religions fail or are imperfect the Universalist faith comes in and saves the whole human race. So when volunteering, conscript, brigade guards, government service and citizenship, substitutes, have all played out, the militia comes in and sweeps stakes and many that are now making long arguments will be making long marches in a few weeks.

I stopped at a boarding house here where it is a rule that the boarders must all pay up after breakfast before anything can be bought and prepared for dinner. I paid and left. Will remember the landlord when I come again.

Our need for factories and manufacturing machinery is becoming greater. Every day we hear of a factory burnt, an engine smashed up &c., and every accident of the kind causes one engine less, one factory less in the Confederacy. We have as yet no means within ourselves of supplying these necessaries, and can not be able to do so fast enough when we do undertake to make them. We are likely to be brought to straits sooner from want of appliances, machinery and clothing than by scarcity of eatables, should the war last some years yet. But if the women and children and wounded can be taken care of, the boys in the army can put up with long shirts for clothing, and for arms they can use the pikes adopted by Gen. Martin at Camp Mangum. These pikes are long sharp spears (with the reap-hook attachment — Gen. Martin's invention) fastened in long wooden handles. The advantages of the reap-hook part is to cut the bridle reins of your enemy if he has any, and if not, after sticking the yankee you can make a "long grab" and bring him up to you and take his accoutrements and valuables without breaking ranks. The explanation given to this hook at Camp Mangum was different. At the first of the war it was supposed that every yankee would run and this hook was intended to prevent his retreat till you could stick him with the spear. It would be quite a novelty with the little boys of the 19th century to hear of their fathers, brothers and uncles charging a battery with Gen. Martin's Pikes in long shirts and sandals, a la Egyptians in the year B.C. 2848.

The people of Richmond still lend a kind ear to the tales of disaster. Their doors are still open to the exile and the unfortunate. They deserve the lasting gratitude of humanity for the unceasing attention and whole-souled liberality they have bestowed on their needy and suffering countrymen whom this war has brought to their doors. The Southern people hereafter will appreciate Virginia more highly as a State. It is difficult to conceive a more noble and sublime illustration of self-sacrifice for principle and true devotion to a cause than Virginia has presented in this Revolution. Well did she know her beautiful farms and happy homesteads would be one vast battle-field. She hesitated but did not falter. The time had arrived for her to decide her destiny and she paused but not long. Her people from the mountains to the sea responded in thunder tones: "The home of Washington and the Mother of States and of Statesmen must never be dishonored. Rather than sacrifice the principles of our fathers and the rights they bequeathed to us, to a vile despotism, let our rivers flow with blood, our families be banished from their burning homes and our land be covered with ruin and desolation." Well have they kept their word. The old Mother of States has bared her bosom to the brunt of battle and shielded us from the storm. One half of her best territory has been laid waste, and half of her best citizens have been made penniless and homeless, yet we hear not a murmur from any true Virginian. The old State has proved herself worthy of her ancient renown. The blood of Washington and "Light Horse Harry" is not extinct in the Old Dominion yet. She has given us men and means; munitions and machinery; bread for our soldiers and leaders for our armies. Her people have suffered much and suffered longest, yet none are truer nor cling with such firmness and tenacity to our cause and the gaining of our independence. A disloyal government has been established among an ignorant class in the Northwest by demagogues and traitors under the pressure of Lincoln's bayonets. But let our army once get control there and the people of the east and west of the State again mingle together and they will be one. And the noble women of Virginia — history's brightest page should be left to record their pure virtues and noble traits of character. The best friends of our noble old Old State are found among Virginians. The two States have much the same interests, sympathies and feelings.

Truly,
Long Grabs.

[June 29, 1863]

Petersburg, June 22.

Messrs. Editors: This is the longest day in the year and I must write you one of the longest letters you ever saw. I know the type-setters sighed long and heavy when they saw this large document. But then you know the habits of "Long Grabs" are very peculiar.

Petersburg and vicinity have been much improved by the recent rains. Crops of all kinds are now vigorous and flourishing. Crowds of exchanged prisoners pass through here every few days. My curiosity for seeing and talking with a parcel of lying yankees has long since been gratified. Col. Ould (Old) conducts the exchange on our part. He has been an eminent lawyer of Washington, and once was a Bureau officer in one of the Departments there. Colonel Ludlow is the Federal officer and I believe they are on very good terms and exchange papers regularly as well as prisoners. Whether they "smile" or exchange "cobblers" and "juleps" I am not informed.

Petersburg, like Augusta ('Gusty away down in 'Jorjy,) prides itself on its negro churches and the moral and religious treatment of ye Africans. There are a great many free people of color here and they have houses, horses, cows and shops of their own. These people out-dress anybody I ever saw except their colored brethren of 'Gusty. It makes Virginia darkies very mad to call them "niggers." You must call them "cullud pussons." Yesterday I witnessed a grand negro funeral procession. There was a long train of carriages (the same used as whites) containing de family and relations ob de deceased. The committee ob arrangement were busily engaged in their official capacity. The black horses, black carriages, black coffin, and black niggers presented a somber appearance of concentrated and combined blackness.

Col. Solomon Williams who was killed in the late cavalry fight on the Rappahannock, was one of North Carolina's best and most gallant officers. He was a native of Warren County, and graduated with distinction at West Point. I saw a letter recently from Gen. Stuart speaking in the highest terms of Col. Williams. He had been appointed to the command of his old regiment — the 12th N. C., but Stuart prevailed on him to remain in his cavalry, telling him that he could not spare him and would have him promoted as soon as possible. He conducted himself with great bravery and coolness in that hard fought battle and fell near the close of the action. He was young — under 30 — and had been married only two or three weeks. He commanded the 19th Reg't N. C. T., known as the 2d N. C. Cavalry, or Spruill's old Cavalry.

[Here follows a *resume* of the movements and battles around Vicksburg, which we are obliged to postpone.—Editors *Observer*]

It is almost impossible for those unfamiliar with the fact, to realize or conceive the vast connection and common interests between the Northwest and the

Southwest by means of the Mississippi river. The river was the outlet and the inlet, the high-way and the by-way for both sections. Great rivers are always great foundations on which to build the whole frame work of a nation's greatness. The Mississippi from one end to the other was one great market of barter or trade. The cotton planter never thought of raising a grain of corn or a pound of meat when he could have them landed at his door cheaper than he could produce them at home. Hundreds and hundreds of steamboats passed up constantly loaded with foreign goods, sugars, molasses, fruits, fine goods and the more difficult manufactures, and returned with bacon, corn, flour, cattle, shoes, clothing, metals, furs, ice, liquors, farming utensils, furniture and all plantation supplies.

Thousands of flat boats floated down from the Northwest as regularly as the current itself. Many of these flat boats came loaded with cabbage, poultry, butter, eggs, whiskey, brandy, honey, cigars, cheese, clocks, jewelry, notions, and so on, floating down from one plantation landing to another. The negro trade was valuable and also that from boat hands and government employees along the river. If you wished a mess of potatoes, a glass of ice cream, fresh butter, some good old brandy, a pound of wool, a writing desk, a lead pencil, or a pair of trace chains, all you had to do was to get to the river bank and make a signal for a flat boat. If you wanted a mule, a wagon, a load of lumber or bricks, or a lot of furniture, corn, pork or fish, or a steam mill, just leave your order with some landing agent and it would be procured when the next boat came along.

You could leave cotton which they would barter for a market price, or the money, or give a draft to your factor in New Orleans, or get the articles on credit. Very often the flat boats carried black-smith shops along and they would hitch up at a landing and do all the black-smith work for that neighborhood and then move down to another place. The loss of this communication must have been and must still be a serious inconvenience to the Southwest and almost a total stoppage of business to the Northwest. The politicians in each section are much the same, and understand each other well. Crafty, selfish, unreliable, superficial, regardless of the future and disposed to hobbies and demagoguism, they may yet make up some compromise or arrangement and cheat both North and South.

There is a practice in the army that has come to be an evil tending strongly to demoralization. I allude to the appointment of officers in companies and regiments by Colonels and other commanding officers. When there is a vacancy in a company the law allows other inferior officers to be promoted if they pass as competent before a properly organized examining board, and then the company is entitled to elect an officer or officers for the lowest vacancy. Notwithstanding the right secured to the company by law, the Col. or commanding officer sometimes appoints and forces a favorite on the men without election. I could mention some names and particulars, if necessary, among our own North Carolina Colonels, too. All this tends to destroy the confidence of the men, and they become dissatisfied and in most cases they forever dislike the officer thus put over them against their will. In a few cases these officers are better selections than the company could make, and the company becomes much attached to them, but this is seldom the case. Sometimes a Col. prevents a worthy officer from promotion just because he has some dislike or prejudice against him. A commissioned officer has great control and authority over the men he commands, and their life and destiny may be said to be in his hands. He has much discretion in discipline, can punish for what he esteems wrong, recommend their promotion or their disgrace, set on trial on their lives, and they have no redress but submission till freed from service or till they may accidentally get a hearing with some superior officer who will investigate their case. Is it not natural and proper then that honorable independent Southerners desire the privilege provided by law of selecting their immediate officers themselves?

North Carolina has contributed faithfully and freely her men and means to this war, but no section of the Confederacy has shown more liberality than the Cape Fear region. That gallant people rushed to arms at the first battle cry with more unanimity and determination than any other section of the State. The people have given and worked manfully for the army and for all others in needful circumstances, but they have not heralded it to the world. It is their daily occupation to supply their soldiers and to invent some new means of comfort and aid. The refugee, the exile, and the unfortunate find a warmer hand and a friendlier welcome among the Cape Fear people than is met with elsewhere. Contributions are sent to the suffering everywhere if called for, yet there is not as much wealth and much less extravagance than in many portions of the State. When our independence is won the whitest spot on North Carolina's bright page must be left for the people of the Cape Fear. I feel proud, though I hope not in vain, that the ashes of my parents and most of my kindred lie beneath the whispering pines of the Cape Fear region.

       Truly,
       LONG GRABS.

[July 2, 1863]

On June 27, 1863, McSween wrote to Governor Zebulon Vance, requesting permission to return to North Carolina to raise a company of men. He reveals for the first time that he has joined the 35th Regiment North Carolina Troops, led now by Colonel John G. Jones, who took over the regiment after the former commander; Matt W. Ransom was promoted to Brigadier General. McSween was placed in Company C.

       Richmond, Va.
       June 27th, 1863

Dear Sir:

I received a note from J. S. Thrasher Superintendent of the Press Association in reference to being appointed correspondent for the Press in some department or [other].

I am now a member of the 35th Regt. NCT and feel that I cannot accept this position.

I have applied to be detailed to go to North Carolina one month to raise a voluntary company of Militia under your recent call. I have not yet heard from the application though I feel certain Gen. Hill will disapprove it. Gen. R. [Robert] Ransom would not approve it though he said he would not mark it disapproved. He said you had no sort of authority over me and that you had plenty of Militia officers for your purpose, and that you had no right to call away persons from the regular army for such business, &c. &c. But altogether I have found Gen. R. Ransom gentlemanly and candid and much more reliable than his brother Gen. M. W. Ransom. I could probably be able to get a company or part of a company of Militia on such desirable conditions had I been favored with the opportunity in time. I prefer a new and independent command and although I may be in a good position here I would like to get some suitable place among the troops you design raising for state service soon — for instance Maj. of infantry — Capt. Quarter-Master or Adj. — or post commander.

P. S. — M. W. Ransom has been promoted to Brigadier of his brother's old Brigade and his brother has been made Maj. Gen. [Next sentence could not be read.] We are camped now a few miles east of Richmond.

I would expect a good position among the state troops you are to raise soon — unless advised otherwise and will then will make the best arrangement I can here. [Remainder of paragraph could not be read.]

There is another matter I would suggest to your consideration. I design collecting for publication sketches of North Carolina troops both for my own interest and that the honor and patriotism of the state may be vindicated as far as I am able. I am also connected with the Press and on this and other pretexts might have exempted myself from Military service, but as I had gone into the war among the very first I felt it my duty and interest to remain in service as long as my services might be valuable there or at least till I could have a long and full record to retire on. I might be useful as a reporter and correspondent of the Press Association and from further connection with North Carolina papers I might be able to do as much for the state and cause as in any other war and at the same time I might [undecipherable] a fight if disposed or engage temporarily in any other military duty. The President has the power to exempt persons when in his [judgment] the interest of the cause or of the country may render it proper. If you see proper you may recommend to President Davis upon the above ground, that I be exempted for those purposes — having been thus engaged before entering service recently. I had a substitute engaged that I could carry out my designs but learn Gen. Hill will in no way approve a substitute arrangement. We are temporarily out of his command now but it is difficult to get a substitute any where now.[2]

Very Respectfully,
M. J. McSween

Three days later, on June 30, 1863, McSween again writes Governor Vance of his desire to raise a company of men and of his relationship with General Matt Ransom.

Camp 35th Regt. NCT
Near Richmond, June 30

Dear Sir:

I have not yet heard from the application I made several days ago to go home and endeavor to raise a company of volunteer militia and feel now pretty certain that Gen. Hill will not approve it.

I wrote you a few days ago in reference to some matters and if it be impracticable to make any of the arrangements alluded to, I desire and prefer to get a good position among the militia when they are collected for organization. Perhaps my services in their organization and with them in the field can be more beneficial than in any way for the interests of the cause. I have been somewhat unfortunate in my relations with a few military authorities, and Gen. M. W. Ransom has not acted with that favor and good faith that he induced me to believe would be the case when I agreed to his solicitations to join his Regt. I want a place congenial with my interests and wishes, where I can have opportunity for distinction and for gaining the consideration of the citizens of my native state—a position of honor, danger, and advantage where I can do something and be somebody—where I must prove or disprove my merits.[3]

     Yours very respectfully,
     M. J. McSween

McSween wrote a second letter to Governor Vance on June 30, 1863. In this one he expressed his displeasure over the manner in which Captain Peter Mallett was handling soldiers who had come into service under the Conscription Act.

     Camp 35th Regt. N.C.T.
     Near Richmond
     June 30th, 1863

Dear Sir:

I see by a recent Raleigh paper that Col. Mallet has offered a lame apology for his course in sending so many conscripts to Regiments they were opposed to going to. He refers to a statement from the officer of the Bureau of Conscription that he was authorized to send men sometimes entirely to some commands whether their choice or not. Even this was violated by Mallett by allowing his friends or favorites to select their regiments.

The Bureau of Conscription was only established last fall long after some ten thousand conscripts had been collected and disposed of. In executing the first call of the conscript—from 18 to 35—I know Mallett assigned the men generally on his own responsibility and frequently sent them to large new regiments when some of the oldest and most decimated regiments had petitioned, made requisitions and had officers at the camps of instruction waiting for conscripts weeks & months.

At one time I had some 250 men from Wilkes Co. under my charge at Camp Holmes (in Sepr. last). These men nearly all wished to go to the 26th and 52nd Regts. A few scattered [?] ones had different preferences. Capt. McRae collected these men in Wilkes by mild measures and promises that they should be allowed to go to Regts of their choice. When they got to Camp Holmes, Mallett paid no attention to the entreaties of the men or Capt. McRae and sent me an order to prepare a certain number for the 26th and the balance for the 30th. I went to work on rolls, &c and the number for the 26th immediately volunteered. In half an hour or so he sent another order to allow some 100 to 26th and about 30 to the 52nd and the rest must go to the 30th Regt. The 30th Regt. is an eastern regt. entirely and not a man wanted to go to it, yet I had to send over 100 to it many of them with tears in their eyes and begging me to get them assigned some where else. They referred to several regiments they preferred to the 30th but Mallett would not yield to my intercession and threatened me with punishment — perhaps arrest — for my importunity. Some of these men deserted on their way with Lieut. Williams of the 30th. I visited the 30th last winter & found a great many of these men had deserted and nearly all were dissatisfied and demoralized. I feel certain that Mallett got no orders from any superior for these whimsical changes in assignment. These are facts & can be substantiated. I have always thought that the interests of North Carolinians & of the service require a rigid investigation of Mallett's official conduct.[4]

Truly Yours
M. J. McSween

CAMP NEAR RICHMOND, July 1.

Messrs. Editors: There is now a prospect for some fighting around Richmond. The enemy has been on the Peninsula for several days, apparently designing attack in force. We are encamped near the memorable ground of Seven Pines. To-day one year ago was fought the battle of Malvern Hill, some 12 miles southeast of here, and the bloodiest of the Seven Days' Fights. [See map, Chapter 2]. The country around here is low, swampy and springy, thinly settled with indifferent society; very few fine farms are to be seen. There is no chance of getting vegetables, poultry or milk. I called on a very talkative, fidgety old lady a day or two ago to see if I could get some buttermilk, fruit or vegetables. She was sweeping out the piazza with a very large broom, and I suppose anticipated my business as no doubt several hundred had called for the same things before me. At the very instant she heard "buttermilk" she straightened herself up and turning to me commenced in the most excited and rapid voice I ever hard as follows: "I haven't got nary cow, and she's gone dry anyhow, and besides we only get milk enough for our own use, and the soldiers have just taken and stamped down everything; they broke down my hen house and took every single chicken and all my ducks, and they burnt up the fence and pulled down the garden and stole the Irish potatoes and my peas and my raspberries and my cherries and they trod down the cabbage plants and I don't know what we are to do nor what will become of us, and they killed most all my hogs and broke into the smoke house and trod down the oats and stole our buggy lines and the axe and the water dipper and dropped the well bucket into the well and I don't know what upon earth we are to do, and they killed two of our sheep too and the quartermaster or the general or one of them he come and levied on our clover field and our wheat and wouldn't pay but half of what it is worth and they have taken every thing and we haven't got nothing, and they come all over the whole place night and day in great droves and I'm so uneasy and troubled so much about it till I'm near about run distracted and oh! mercy on me! There goes two of the gluttons now after one of my little chickens and I'm just broke down a running and a going constant to try to save what little I've got and I don't know what under heaven we are to do or how we are to live, and _____" and I had got out of hearing and left her. She had long before resumed her sweeping wrathfully and emphatically with her broom as she kept up a ceaseless clatter with her tongue. I suppose she has stopped by this time. I would defy any stage-actor to speak as rapidly and varied with as many emphatic gestures as she did. I will always shy around that place hereafter. Much of what she said was true and is a correct picture of the shameful conduct of many soldiers, although she exaggerated slightly.

Many graves of dead Yankees and Confederates have been found near here. Several of these have been opened and it is found that the bodies are not entirely decomposed. It was reported that some fellow had dug up a dead Yankee and got two dollars and a half in specie, whereupon many others began to hunt specie. The stench where the graves have been opened is said to be very offensive.

The troops here are now receiving new clothing and shoes, although they are already well clothed. The jackets issued now are of blue gray and resemble at a distance the Yankee uniform. Most of this clothing is of English material and is cheap for the times. The entire suit, including shoes, caps and underclothing is supplied at less than half the cost of the same articles from merchants and tailors.

The rations have also been increased and are now half pound of bacon, full rations of meal or flour, rice and peas, with some sugar. The health of the men is good. The weather has been wet and disagreeable.

One of the most gallant engagements of the war occurred at South Anna bridge on the Virginia Central Railroad, about 25 miles North of Richmond. Lt. Col. Hargrove, with Co. A, 44th Reg't N. C. T., fought most gallantly and desperately against two or three thousand of the enemy, and did not surrender until over half their number was killed or wounded. Lt. Col. T. L. Hargrove[5] is a lawyer of Granville County, was a member of the Convention in 1861, and raised a company for the 44th Reg't. He afterwards became Major and then Lt. Col. of that Reg't. There is not a more high-toned gentleman and gallant soldier in the army.

The Militia and citizens of Richmond have been organizing and drilling. I saw a company of little boys and others contained old men. Some of the companies were drilling a few evenings since when a shower came up and the whole concern, rank and file, hoisted umbrellas. The drill-master walked them around to the sound of "hep," avoiding mud holes and puddles.

Provost guards have become a nuisance. It is proper perhaps to have some such police regulations in cities or exposed places. The regular picket or guard of each army, post or department is sufficient for all purposes, or fully as much so as the Provost guard. It is an enormous expense to the Government to keep up so many Provost officers and troops, and the Provost guard does but little good anywhere. They embarrass honest people while shrewd men and scoundrels dodge them or ingratiate themselves into their good graces and carry on their devilment unawares. The Provost system keeps a great many able-bodied man out of the service. If such places must exist let wounded and disabled soldiers occupy them. The Provosts often gratify private malice and hate by arresting men they do not like or putting them to trouble. They don't stop crime nor aid the army nor expedite the enforcement of law or good order. There is a regiment or more doing Provost duty at different places in N. C. The office is a nice soft place for some favorite or officer who wishes to shun the hard duties of war to slide into, and there go through with the farce of having a couple of bayonets at his door while writing out formal passes upon papers either forged or genuine.

When he hears the whistle blow he lays away his pipe, puts on his red sash and sword and struts down to the depot, smells through the cars, asks several decent persons imprudent questions and carries a parcel of rowdies back to his room to get on a spree on "confiscated" whiskey. These are his duties. His business hours are from half past eleven to twelve, and any one who don't get a passport during that interval must lie over or be put in the "cage" among lice and filth. If the system effected any good, its inconveniences would be cheerfully submitted to. Down with the system! down with it, and send those sleek, fat, foppish mock soldiers where they can earn their mush. Here, here t-t-t-ake the pen! The yanks are coming and we must dash out to meet them! A battle!

> Truly,
> LONG GRABS.

[July 16, 1863]

On July 3, 1863, Governor Vance wrote to James A. Seddon, Secretary of War, seeking to get McSween a position as a war correspondent to report on the activities of the North Carolina troops. Basically, McSween has been doing this, except for times when something piques his interest, and as he has said, "he digresses" into other topics. Vance is responding to complaints that North Carolina's soldiers are not getting fair treatment in the Virginia papers for their contributions to the war efforts.

> Executive Department
> Raleigh, July 3d, 1863

Hon. James A. Seddon
Secretary of War
Dear Sir:

There has been much complaint among our people that the participation of our troops, has not been noticed, with that commendation to which they are supposed by us to be entitled. This has resulted in some measure from the fact, that there [are] no Army correspondents from this State. I am exceedingly anxious of removing this ground of complaint, and at the same time to provide that the deeds of daring and gallantry of our Soldiers shall be duly recorded. With this view I respectfully request that M. J. McSween connected with the 35th Regiment may be detailed to attend the Army of Genl Lee as an Army correspondent and that you will give him such permission as will effect this object, with such restrictions as the public service may demand.

Mr. McSween is a gentleman of intelligence, a graduate of our University and in such feeble health that he cannot render very active service in the field.[6]

> With sentiments of great respect
> Your obedient servant
> Z. B. Vance

CAMP NEAR RICHMOND, July 4.

Messrs. Editors: We have been encamped about six miles from Richmond on the Williamsburg road and about 7 or 8 miles from Bottom's Bridge, where that

6. Return to Virginia 181

road crosses the Chickahominy. [See Map Chapter 2 — Vicinity of Richmond and Petersburg.] Ransom's and Jenkin's Brigades crossed Chickahominy at this bridge Thursday evening and went 4 or 5 miles beyond with several pieces of artillery. We shelled the Yankees and they fell back rapidly to the Pamunkey and we occupied the place where they had been. The enemy's artillery did not fire more than four or five times at our troops. Jenkin's S. C. Brigade was in front and the 24th N. C. was the foremost of Ransom's Brigade and within better range of the enemy's artillery than Jenkin's Brigade. It was thought the enemy had a plenty strong force. They hardly remained long enough for our gunners to get the range, although they had formed line of battle. One man in the 24th Reg't was killed, ____ Tate,[7] from Person county, in Company H. There were two or three others slightly wounded. A shell exploded in a few feet of Col. Clarke, but he was not touched! The 24th is a splendid Regiment, has done gallant service and is "all right on the goose." Some few of the enemy were killed and 8 or 10 prisoners, some of them wounded, one mortally.

It was nearly sunset when we arrived in front of the Yankees and we returned in a few hours afterwards to this side of the Chickahominy, from where Ransom's Brigade returned to camp, and Cook's Brigade and other troops went to look after some Yank's who it was said had a hankering after Hanover Junction and sundry horses, chickens and preserves up that way. The North Carolina Troops about Richmond are Ransom's and Cook's Brigades, the 41st Reg't (Cavalry) and 44th Reg't, Pettigrew's Brigade. The rest are South Carolinians and Virginians — altogether a strong force — a forced that will use up Dix and Keyes if they give us the opportunity. This may be put down in the Almanacs as a "phact." I have been over the battle ground of Seven Pines and saw a good many yankee skulls and ribs and I also ate huckleberries from bushes that grew by the side of Yankee graves. By the way huckleberry gathering is a great thing now. The Chickahominy and other swamps have now large quantities of these delicious berries. The battle field of Seven Pines is among swampy bays, and slashes, with here and there a field or small farm. The name is from a pine tree with seven prongs or forks, and there has never been any cross road, post office or blacksmith shop.

I see recruiting to raise companies has again become the order of the day under the call for volunteer militia for six months. Better go it, boys. There will be another conscript or some other devilment by the end of that time that will take you in, and perhaps if the government has to pull you in, it may everlastingly hold on to you after it gets you in. And recollect it will never do for us to lag now. We must keep up the army and push on the war till the North will let us alone and allow us our rights. The North began this unnecessary, inhuman and ruinous conflict, and it will stop the very moment they agree to quit it. Speaking of recruiting, though, reminds me of some little incidents that occurred about the beginning of the war when we all did not have as much sense as we have now. In those days everybody that considered himself "somebody" had recruiting papers from the governor to raise a company, and many were raising battalions, legions, &c., several of which enterprises had been "razed" long ago. Well, "Long Grabs" he thought he would raise him a company. He got a trunk full of blankets, muster rolls, pay rolls, descriptive rolls, &c. &c., and et cetera, and goes accordingly to a big militia meeting or muster, at Elizabethtown, where he met up with Josh from Wilmington on the same business, only more so. Now at that particular time and place I knew nobody but Josh, and Josh he knew nobody but me, consequently we were very thick. We concluded to form the acquaintance of several important personages at once as the best means to succeed in our object. So we managed in two or three hours to get acquainted with all the "prominent men," who promised us their influence, wished us success and invited us to "call" on them if we ever passed through the country. We then brought out our documents and walked up to various individuals and asked them to volunteer. We dwelt on the glories of war — patriotism — the pleasures of camp — bounties — how they would be loaded down with clothing and rations and get their doctor's bill paid free gratis for nothing, &c. Imagine our surprise and disappointment when we found that while we had been forming the acquaintance of the "prominent men," a plain old citizen, formerly a postmaster, miller, deputy sheriff and justice of the peace in that county, had gone round and got all the volunteers — some 80 or 100 — for another company. I thought the thing was out then, but it was thought proper as a last resort to make some desperate war speeches and redeem the lost fortunes of the day. Lt. B. of Fayetteville was there and insisted on this plan. I and Josh put on our studying caps, began to think over, "victory or death," "'Tis sweet to die or one's country," "Open wide the gate of Janus," "Let slip the dogs of war," and such like patriotic phrases. Now Josh and I wanted a company apiece or just enough men to get a "pesish" in any other company, and there was no jealousy between us. There was a sort of a scramble for the goods box when the time came for speaking, and Lt. B. succeeded in mounting it first — I on one side and Josh on the other, ready to take the stump as soon as B. would be through. Lt. B. had been in the battle of Bethel and of course had seen a larger portion of the elephant than I and Josh (I had been at Fort Sumter but did not like to mention that, as a good many of the people were prejudiced against South Carolina.) B. made an eloquent and patriotic appeal and closed by saying (in substance) "Fellow citizens! I have already stood amid the carnage of battle and staked my life, my fortunes, and my sacred honor for our cause on the bloody fields of Bethel under the folds of that proud flag as it floats on the breeze of liberty that blows up from the sunny South like a breath of inspiration, (pointing to a Confederate flag on the top of the Court House) I do not say to you, "go!" but "come" with me and let us stand or fall together under that noble banner." On the strength of this he laid out blank rolls, pens and ink in abundance, but the hesitating sons of Mars declined to walk up and "swear in" and "sign" or make their cross-marks, but gradually retreated in the direction of sundry cider carts and whiskey wagons. Lt. B. remarked (sotte voce,) "If I had thought nobody would volunteer I wouldn't have made a speech" (!) I and Josh exchanged glances and concluded we would save our reputations and extra supply of eloquence also. Further speaking was postponed. I and Josh adopted the prevailing custom and took a drink but did not "get on a spree" as the song erroneously stated. We lingered yet a little while longer and witnessed many strange antics that were cut up promiscuously among the hereinbefore mentioned wagons, and we shook hands confidentially and parted — he for Wilmington and I for the

"Green Pond," "without the loss (or gain) of a man." "Thus ended the first lesson."

Truly,
Long Grabs.

P. S. N. B. The weather is very hot now. This is fourth of July — a big day among the ancients. The Yanks pretend to celebrate it same as ever and I suppose still do so up about Chambersburg and York and Carlisle.

L____g G____bs.

[July 16, 1863]

In the following letter, written July 15, 1863, to Governor Zebulon Vance, McSween writes of the possibility of being sent to General Lee's army as a reporter and of his continuing dissatisfaction with his treatment by General Matt W. Ransom. He explains why he joined the 35th Regiment.

Camp near Petersburgh
July 15th, 1863

Dear Sir:

After being informed that you had written the Secretary of War relative to my being sent to Lee's army as reporter or correspondent, I applied at the War Department a few days ago to ascertain if it had been acted on. I was informed that it [had] just been referred to Lee for his opinion and a final answer would be made as soon as he considered the application. He may probably disapprove it. From what you are pleased to say I am led to confidently expect a position from you in the Militia and if I receive it will endeavor to fill it properly. Gen. M. W. Ransom has acted toward me in such consummate bad faith that it would be unpleasant to remain in his Brigade in any [undecipherable] position.

Some four months ago some friends recommended me to him for Adjutant without my knowledge — I saw him soon after and having been informed of it I consulted him in reference to a position in his Regt. He said if he could not give me Adjt he would certainly give me a Lieutenancy or Captaincy and offered every inducement to me to go to his Regt and would write me more definitely soon. Meantime Mallett [Peter} wanted to know if I was in service and if not to report to him. I had written Ransom but got no reply and now telegraphed him and no reply. Rather than go to Mallett or resort to pretexts to exempt myself, I joined 56th Regt which was thought irregular and void and I had to go to Mallett. M. W. Ransom and he insisted on my coming to his Regt with same promises — I did so and he has since made no effort to get me a place in Regt or on his Staff— I could not properly pitch in electioneering with strangers and risk my standing in such [undecipherable] and the Regt has been constantly on the move and M. W. Ransom said this would be —[8]

[McSween wrote the remainder of his letter on both sides of the paper, and it bled through making it unreadable on the microfilm.]

On July 20, 1863, Ransom's Brigade was ordered to Weldon, North Carolina to protect the vital Weldon & Petersburg Railroad Bridge over the Roanoke River. Federal cavalrymen had been raiding in the area, but Ransom's troops, numbering 200, met and defeated the Union force of 5,000 at Boone's Mills, on June 28. Ironically the battle was fought on Ransom's plantation in Northampton County and within two miles of his home.[9]

Three days after McSween moved with Ransom's Brigade on the 20th, Governor Vance received Secretary Seddon's reply to his request to make McSween a war correspondent.

> Confederate States of America,
> War Department,
> Richmond, Va., July 23d, 1863
>
> His Excellency Z. B. Vance
> Governor of North Carolina
> Raleigh, N. C.
> Dear Sir:
>
> You were informed on the 7th inst. that your letter requesting the detail of M. J. McSween as an army correspondent to accompany Genl Lee, as it was alleged that N. C. Troops do not receive the meed of praise justly due them, was referred to Genl Lee for consideration, and your attention is now respectfully called to the annexed copy of his reply.
>
> Very Respectfully
> Your Obdt Servt
> James A. Seddon
> Secretary of War
> "Copy"
> Head Quarters Bunker Hill
> 18th July 1863
>
> I very much regret that an impression should prevail that injustice is done to any portion of this army. I know of no cause and have heard of none. If the official reports of the officers commanding the troops cannot be believed or relied on I know of no way of obtaining the truth. The plan proposed by Gov. Vance I think will work great evil and produce embarrassment to the service. I cannot recommend that it be adopted. It must then be extended to all the States and it can readily be seen what would be the result. If the officers commanding the troops do not tell the truth they should be removed.[10]
>
> Respectfully submitted
> (signed)R. L. Lee
> Genl

Two days before the fighting at Boone's Mill, Governor Vance had responded to Secretary Seddon's letter concerning McSween.

> State of North Carolina
> Executive Department
> Raleigh, July 26th, 1863

Hon. J. A. Seddon
Secy of War
Richmond Va.

Sir:

You note in reference to the permission asked by me to send M. J. McSween to the army of N. Va. as a newspaper correspondent, with Genl Lee's reply refusing the same has been received —

It seems strange that Genl Lee and yourself should so utterly misconstrue my meaning — I had no reference of course to the "official reports" of our army officers, as doing injustice to N. C. Troops. They are rarely furnished to the newspapers — never except by consent of the War Dept. — I simply desired to correct as far as possible, the daily neglect and frequent slanders of a portion of the Richmond press, which has its corps of reporters in every department of the Army — by sending a similar corps to report for the press of this State — But I know that without Genl Lee's permission, they could not move with the Army or have access to any sources of reliable information. The Richmond press allege as an excuse for not speaking of N. C. Troops, that there are no correspondents from this State to report &c., and this I was in part trying to remedy — I asked for the detail of McSween, not for the purpose of giving him an official character, but simply because he is an accomplished scholar and in such feeble health, that he will soon die or be discharged from service —

I only desired, Sir, in other words that newspaper correspondents from N. C, should be allowed to attend an Army, with the same protection, and the same access to information as I learn given to others. But as Genl Lee objects to it and has seen proper to think that I object to official reports, which have never yet been published, I beg leave to withdraw the request.

The troops from N. C. can afford to appeal to history: I am confident that they have but little to expect /from/ their associates. Just after the battle of Chancellorsville, notwithstanding N. C. troops furnished one half of all the killed and wounded, it was reliably reported throughout the State that Genl Lee had refused applications for furloughs, to our wounded soldiers, on the grounds that they would not return when recovered — If such an endorsement was in fact made officially it would of course be credited by the historian, and injustice be done to the very men, who won that victory. The Richmond Enquirer in recent article, on the authority of its special correspondent charges our defeat at Gettysburg upon the cowardice and incapacity of the N. C. troops composing Heth's division.

Such things are hard to bear, if true, and if untrue we are denied the right of having correspondents in the Army to correct them, and must wait for the publication of official reports, which may or may not be published —

How such things can contribute to the success of the cause I am unable to say.[11]

Very respectfully
Your obt. Servt
Z. B. Vance

This seemed to end the matter of McSween becoming an official war correspondent. He would still continue to send correspondence to the *Fayet-*

teville Observer about what was happening on the Virginia battleground till the end of the war. Meanwhile Ransom's Brigade moved to Garysburg, North Carolina, remaining there until the end of August. McSween appears to have been with troops in Goldsboro, as he writes his next letter to Governor Vance from that place and says that the rest of Regiment is in Weldon. He also complains to Vance about the poor treatment he is receiving from General Ransom and Colonel Jones and asks for a transfer.

Goldsboro, [North Carolina]
August 30th

Dear Sir:

Probably by this time you have matured your plans of organization of the militia forces of the State under the new law. I suppose you will give me an appointment —

If so, please do it immediately for my position here is intolerable. Col. Jones uses every opportunity to gratify a malignant hatred towards me — His vulgar despotic use of authority knows no limit nor propriety. If I possess anything of truth and character in your estimations these statements are sufficient without particulars at this time.

I cannot submit to such treatment much longer — No man of character can consent to serve under such circumstances. Yesterday upon his ordering me punished in a degrading way, the company to which I belong and numbers of men from other companies (in all I am told about two thirds of the Regt) fell in line and loaded their pieces, but were finally prevailed on to desist from violence. Had I given the slightest encouragement to this move or had the officers generally done so the result would certainly have been very serious. Jones sent orders to all the companies but mine, but especially to what he regarded "loyal" companies to be ready at a moment's notice. What sort of discipline is this you will ask? The Regt — officers and men except his own company and a few favorites — have never had respect or confidence for Jones and it is pretty [well] affirmed that he has now ruined himself with the Regt. Rest of Brigade at Weldon.

If the President would release me entirely as Press correspondent and him to [undecipherable] N. C. Troops or if he could be transferred (out of the Brigade preferable) it would be satisfactory. But if you can give me some suitable appointment immediately or soon it would better at present as well as a more certain and speedy relief.

It is time I should know what I can certainly rely upon though I have some idea of the difficulty and disappointment you have met with in your efforts to raise a State force.

I have been entirely unable to do any thing towards the completion of historical sketches of the troops. I have had to drill and march and fare like the others and have of course had no opportunity for such duties. If I had to submit to nothing but the common duties of the private soldier there would be no valid ground of conflict. But of course there is no necessity for my being drilled as a private soldier. My time in service at the very first of the war as a private and then my drilling a large number of the Regts of the State for a year or so would

6. Return to Virginia

be sufficient to let any man of sense and right principles know that I knew enough of filing, whirling, loading, hepping and that I could be as serviceable at something else. But where I am subjected to degrading punishment not authorized by laws of the Army and for no just cause I think it an outrage. Please reply immediately and excuse this. If convenient would prefer this answered without referred to any one as it is confidential[12]

Very Respectfully,
M. J. McSween

The 35th Regiment had moved several times since McSween wrote the letter above. It came back to Weldon on the Roanoke River for a while, then went south to Tarboro' in late October, before returning to Weldon in November and settling in to winter quarters. McSween will say more in a following letter about the incident in which members of his company came to his support. Meanwhile, Vance issued McSween a commission in the Home Guards in September 1863 — the commission was Adjutant of the 3rd Regiment Home Guards. This was what McSween was hoping for — an opportunity to get away from Ransom and Jones. However, Col. Jones had him arrested and placed in the guard house for reasons which McSween explains in the next letter.

Governor Vance, hearing that McSween has been arrested, revoked his commission in the Home Guards. McSween, on learning this, writes to Vance about it and asks for a chance to defend himself.

Weldon, [North Carolina]
Oct. 3rd, 1863

Dear Sir:

I have just received notice from the Adjt Genl's office that my commission has been recalled with a request to return it. This surprises me very much, and under the circumstances it is just now the most serious and profound disappointment I have ever met with. I have however never yet failed when relying on my own native energy of character and my own strong right arm. I think I have a spirit and a fortitude that cannot be crushed except by that Great Power that created them. I did not believe you would act on the representations of my enemies until you had heard both sides fully. I knew they could afford to do any thing to injure and ruin me, but it was only a few hours before I got this letter from the Adjt Genls office that I had any intimation of this movement against me. The Regts are camped cross the river and it is a day or two before we can communicate backward and forward. I learn a paper has been presented to you by Col. Jones in person gotten up by him and Gen. Ransom and signed by some officers in the 35th Regt — containing a most outrageous and scandalous account of me. I hope you will let me see this document that I may know who they are that would ruin me and what charges they try to sustain against me. I only ask you to reconsider the matter for enough [time] to give me the same or another commission again long enough to afford me opportunity to get into another

Regt or Brigade. Or renew the very same commission (or another) and after I and my friend can present you my side of the case to discharge or retain me unconditionally at your discretion. I think I deserve this much. I am not conscious of any crime or course of conduct that deserves any such treatment as I have received from Gen. Ransom and Col. Jones. I will endeavor to give you a correct and brief statement of all the essential circumstances of the case. In March last I found myself subject to conscription and not wishing to exempt myself if I could get in service advantageously — (I had been in service as private and officer from the Secession of S. C. to latter part of 1862.) Passing Goldsboro I met Col. Faison who told me Col. Ransom wanted an adjutant and if I would see him I would probably get it. I intended to join 56th Regt unless I got a position elsewhere. I saw Col. Ransom at once who was presiding on Court Martial in Wilmington. He said he had had communication with another young man about Adjutant and could not answer me definitely then but would at an early day. He then told me to come to the Regt when I entered service again and he would secure me a Lieutenancy if he could not give me Adjutancy. I agreed to this arrangement and went away on the campaign to Washington where I expected to act some volunteer part in the battle. In May afterwards I met with 35th Regt at Kinston and soon after was required to go in service under conscription. I had notice from Provost Marshall. Ransom had not rejoined the Regt and I got the Provost Marshall to wait some days for Ransom before reporting. I heard nothing from him and by advice of Capt. Lockhart I enlisted in [here McSween has crossed out the words "his company in"] a Regt. I joined Lockhart's Co. 56th Regt, Lt. Peebles commdg. Lockhart being on detached duty. Col. Faison had told me he thought it would be invalid, but that I ought to be familiar with conscription and that I might do the best I could. I did not understand him to prohibit my joining. Capt. Roberts of 56th administered to me the oath and witnessed my enlistment. Peebles proposed voluntarily that my name would merely remain on the rolls and I would not be required for duty till I would hear from Ransom or make some arrangement. I told Peebles too that Faison thought my volunteering would not be valid but it would make matters no worse in my opinion and I would risk it. Peebles said, "Well, we will hold you if we can, and if we can't, there will be no harm done"— or words of the same meaning. Peebles afterwards when it was decided that my volunteering at that time was not regular or strictly lawful and Peebles in defending his conduct said I had told him before volunteering that Col. Faison had freely consented to my joining the Regt. I did not understand Faison to prohibit or consent and did not tell Peebles that he had done either. Peebles afterwards became Adjt, of the 35th Regt instead of me and has been very industrious in operating against me in a small way. In a day or two I went to Camp Holmes and had myself assigned to 35th Regt and returned there in a day or two. When I joined 56th Regt, Peebles told me Ransom had promised him Adjutant, but that he had no confidence or reliance in Ransom. He was determined to get out of the 56th Regt for he could not get on with Col. Faison. Col. Faison had him arrested and court martialed for going home without leave. On my way to Raleigh however I met Ransom at Goldsboro. He told me there he had decided to give Adjutant to Peebles and that unless he (Ransom) was at the Regt he could do nothing for me. With

6. Return to Virginia 189

reference to others, I think I should properly belong to the 56th Regt as I had not been enrolled and the question whether I was exempt or not had never been tested as the Conscript Law provides before I volunteered. On returning to 35th Ransom did not assign me to company or duty — but told me to come or stay where I pleased but to be near the Regt then in case of any need for me I could be called on. He told me if I wished I might drill the conscripts or do writing or other business for the Regt. But the Regt moved about so much around Kinston, Gum Swamp, Contentnea Creek, Petersburg, Ft. Darling Drewry's Bluff, Seven Pines, Chickahominy, and back to Garysburg, Weldon, Rocky Mount and Goldsboro that it hardly staid a day in a place and there was little or no drilling or other camp duties. This was the case six or eight weeks after I joined the Regt. Ransom mentioned to me once or twice himself this time that he would look round and get me a place and insisted on my making effort to get a place too as soon as possible for time was wasting and my connections with the Regt was not regular and proper and I might be required to go on duty before long. I understood then pretty clearly (some three weeks after joining the Regt) that Ransom meant for me to get a position if I could. All this time we had been moving so much and doing such little camp duty (and for some time after too) that I had no opportunity for becoming favorably known in the Regt. There were some vacancies but I was a stranger in the Regt a perfect stranger in those companies and had been deceived by Ransom, disliked by Peebles, and Jones did not fancy me nor I him and he was somewhat jealous of my promotion as he wanted his brother (a sergeant) to get in and had several other needy friends and this was his first opportunity to favor them. Consequently the non-commissioned staff was filled from his company — in some instances with men who can hardly write their names and who have never distinguished themselves. What few friends I had in the Regt had been somewhat unfriendly to Jones. Col. Ransom had threatened to court martial Jones for pretending sickness and evading the battles of New Berne and Malvern Hill. Ransom wanted Maj. Kelly (formerly Captain of my company) to be promoted to Lt. Col. over Maj. Jones. He tried to insult Jones so he would resign and admit Kelly to Lt. Colonelcy direct but Jones would not take the insult. It is said public opinion forced Jones into the battles of Sharpsburg and Fredericksburg. There was some feeling between Jones and Kelly in these matters which their companies participated in. Kelly became Major and was killed at Fredericksburg — a noble gallant fellow. Lt. Col. Petway a club-mate and intimate friend of mine was killed at Malvern Hill. Three or four weeks after my connection with the Regt. Ransom was promoted and Jones became Col. I asked Ransom for place on his staff. He said he would give me clerkship and I told him to let me know when he wanted me. Jones did not interfere with the privileges Ransom had allowed me and the Regt moved about and matters went on thus for two weeks longer. I consulted with Ransom several times of my business and prospects but to no satisfaction. I felt certain there would be no chance for promotion by my own efforts for some time. Because I would be regarded as an office seeker — and outsider — and there being several candidates for all vacancies among the old veteran soldiers — I concluded any effort in that direction would injure me more than benefit. I felt stung too at the way Ransom had deceived although I would say nothing. Ransom approved my judgment about running for office under the circumstances. Jones was delusional, jealous and unfavorable and Peebles was an enemy. About this time I applied to you to give me appointment in six months or get me exempted that I might accept Col. Thrasher's appointment of reporter for Lee's army of Press Association and that I might fill my obligations of correspondent of the Press and proceed with my historical sketches of N. C. Troops. Adj. Gen. Fowle gave me permission to raise a company and I applied for detail which application went to that "bourne whence no document ever returns." I had asked before for detail as scout in eastern N. C. but failed. Soon after Ransom's promotion we went to [the] Chickahominy. One day I passed Ransom's headquarters just after he got fixed up. I asked Lt. Goodloe A. A. A. Gen. to tell the Genl. to order me to duty as clerk with him at once and was anxious to get located. I knew I could go to ranks ultimately but preferred not to do so while I was permitted to do otherwise and expected duties in different sphere. It required a robust constitution to stand the marches and weather the Regt went through then on foot — though I voluntarily accompanied them when expecting a battle — that I might have chance to distinguish myself and also to report news to the Press. Lt. Goodloe told me some days after that the Gen. could not employ me then. Soon after Brigade was ordered to Petersburg — 35th Regt was on picket a few miles off and I happened to be at the camp of one of the other Regts — 35th did not get to Richmond as soon as the Regt I was with. I wanted to send off dispatches about battle of Gettysburg. Private dispatches could not be sent till after 7 o'clock in the evening. Brigade Quartermaster said 35th might go on the train during the evening or not till morning. I wanted to stay in Richmond till after 7 o'clock or get to Petersburg before that time and Quartermaster told me I had better go on right then with 56th — about 2 o'clock — I did so.

On [arrival] at Petersburg I met Genl. Ransom. He reprimanded me severely and angrily [for being] away from my Regt — Threatened to place me under guard. I explained [this part of sentence is illegible] ... of which he seemed to get very mad and threatened to send [me] to the Guard House if I said [any] thing [else]. He then ordered me to report to the Regt on its arrival in the morning and go to the [undecipherable]. I did so and was entered on the [undecipherable] roll of Co. C, Capt. Blue.

I, from that time till now, have been subject to all their duties. I have obeyed all requirements of any Captain — and have attended all drills, parades and except a few days that I think I was physically unfit for such duty. The Capt allowed me all favors and privileges and could of his own accord and sometimes at my request. I messed and quartered with him and was not requested to attend roll calls, general and work details and though I had to go on drills when able here the Col. expressly ordered it. I was to be Company clerk, keep the accounts, and do the official writing of the Company. The Col and some of his staff and [others] have kept a continual [undecipherable] and annoyance to me and my Company officers about my duties and it causes me all possible trouble and inconvenience.

I [have expressed] my opinions pretty freely about these things as did my officers but of course I had to submit. I don't know that I was formally excused on the Doctor's book for one or either of the two times I went to the Doctor for treatment. I did not report myself to be excused and supposed that a doctor would judge a case on its merits any time in the day as well as if brought up by the Orderly Sergt. at sun-up. When Regt left Petersburg to come here before [the] Boone Mill skirmish I had been under treatment for piles. Every thing was ordered to the Depot about night. Before all the wagons got there all the sick, ambulance wagons, were ordered back to camp. As I was not well and supposing I was on sick list (had not been on duty for several days — there had been no regular duties till I came here) I returned to camp. Regt expected to do considerable marching which would cause a return of the disease. On two or three days I heard of skirmishing and probable battle about Weldon and I came immediately to Weldon with the mail for the Regt and on my arrival Capt. Lockhart as commander of force at Weldon ordered me on a scouting expedition to Hamilton. Enemy was landing at Williamston and I went down establishing a line of couriers and was to report all advances and movements of the enemy. But enemy retired before I got there. I was away some three days and on going to the Regt. was reprimanded for being absent and for having gone off scouting. Some time after this Regt. went to Goldsboro. After getting there I had violent dysentery and received treatment of the Doctor. Lt. Jones of my company got permission for himself and 10 men to go church half a mile off in town. I went with him. The Regt had not been drilling but I had not been fit for duty two days. After getting to town that night I felt too unwell to return with the others from church. The weather was wet and cool and I remained in town that night. Not feeling fit for duty next day I remained till night and went back to camp. Col. Jones paid no attention to my excuse and put me under guard — Friday night 28th August (and I have been under guard ever since) — Next day he ordered me to carry a log. I thought this extreme punishment for an excusable offense — and I hardly think an officer has the right to inflict corporal punishment without court martial. I refused for this reason. This is the only order I ever disobeyed that I know of. He then had me bucked and gagged for some two hours. My company and portions of other companies took their arms and threatened to release me violently. The Col. sent orders to the other companies to be ready for Co. C. The officers pacified things by the Col's promising to release me. He released me and tied me to a tree for some hours and then bucked and gagged me again a while and then sent me to the guard house in Goldsboro with orders to keep me in close confinement. So I [undecipherable] a grand rascal. I had 8 or 6 men [undecipherable] to [guard] me. He ordered them to "shoot me" or "run me through and through with bayonets" if I showed the least resistance. He ordered that [remainder of sentence unreadable]. He promised the Captain repeatedly he would have a court martial but he has refused all the time to allow any hearing or investigation. I have been in the guard house over five weeks and can have no trial or find out what are the charges. I have been treated outrageously, unjustly, and maliciously. Many friends in the Brigade besides my own Company are ready to establish these things. Consequently I seriously want you to comply with your promise to give me an opportunity or put me in a position beyond the [remainder of sentence unreadable]. After the Regt left Goldsboro and came here, Gen. Martin ordered me to my Regt. I was brought from there to the guard house.

I think Ransom has insulted the dignity of the state which has nurtured him and educated him and trespassed on our honor by degrading her seal and one of her officers in prison. The recall of my commission is dated Oct 2nd and Ransom should have respected me and my commission from the time of my acceptance till its expiration. I am unjustly and unfortunately in the power of my worst enemies. They will go all lengths to degrade and ruin me. I can refute any charge they can make if I have any trial. I have done no crime. I can establish as good character in the Brigade and in the State as any one concerned in the movement to injure me. I have sustained the cause and interests of my country in every way I could. My influence for good was just beginning to ripen into efficiency when an unnecessary and diabolical attempt is made from the basest motives to ruin me. This affair is notorious and will certainly result in serious injury to the cause if allowed to go thus. Such proceedings will ruin our army and defeat our noble cause. But "The mills of the gods grind slowly."

Excuse the length of this.[13]

Respectfully, I am
M. J. McSween

In the following letter, written October 6, 1863, to Governor Zebulon Vance, McSween denies that he ever encouraged mutiny in the 35th Regiment against General Matt Ransom.

Weldon, N. C.
Oct. 6, 1863

Dear Sir:

I feel it proper to renew attention to the recent difficulties of which I have written you already. Since then I have learned something more definite of the character of the representations made to you by Col. Jones of the 35th Regt. It seems that he and Ransom have endeavored to make it appear that I have instigated and encouraged mutiny in the Regt or company; that I always evaded duty and that my whole conduct and character was not that of a gentleman and soldier.

I pronounce every one of these charges a base and unmitigated falsehood — and I believe I can so prove it by every man in my company. As soon as I knew this was the nature of the charges I requested my Captain to get the testimony of the Company direct and send it to you immediately. It will no doubt reach you tomorrow. If competent evidence is all that is necessary I think this will be amply sufficient. I have been with the Regt only a short time and as already indicated, in such a way as not to have had opportunity of extending my acquaintance beyond the company to which I belong. I am not acquainted with half a dozen company officers and could not recognize a majority of the officers of the Regt. I am certain many of them would not know me on sight. I don't think I know more than two or three privates and noncommissioned officers in the Regt outside of the company nor never said a dozen words to any of them. I have always obeyed the orders of my company officers and have I believe the entire confidence and respect of every man in the company. I have carried my musket in the ranks, drilled and gone on marches in all kind of weather. I have gone with the Regt when battle was expected where too I was not required to go — and have disobeyed but one order of the Col.— that of carrying the log. The most prominent officers were absent from the Regt at the time this paper of Jones' was circulated and supposing there are a dozen or more names to it I am satisfied that half of them could not know me if they should accidentally meet me in Raleigh. Most of them too can be influenced and forced into measures by Jones and Ransom when in command of them. I am more surprised at Dr. O'Hagan (if he has signed the paper) as I have been more intimate with him and regarded him as a man of more ability and force of character than any officer in the Regt. He is an eccentric man of easily excited and bitter prejudices and a complete tyrant.

When Col. Jones ordered me to carry a log at Goldsboro (Aug 29th last) I was not aware of the feeling and action of my company until some hours afterwards as the affair took place some 200 yards from the Regt and I did not hear or see or have information of the company. I did not then or any other time make one gesture or motivation towards mutiny, but submitted to necessity and brute force. I was afterwards informed that when Jones had me bucked and gagged the natural outburst of sympathy for me and of in disputation against such an outrage was so great that my entire company and portions of other companies spontaneously fell in with their arms and threatened to release me by force — I was further informed that the officers succeeded in pacifying the men on Col. Jones' promise to release me at once — which he did not do but ordered the Regt out to drill in charge of the Lt. Col.

These are the facts of that affair. The Col. sent orders to the other Captains to be ready for Co. C and has not allowed me to be with the company since. It is entirely a malicious assumption and fiction for him to make this pretext of mutiny. I received my commission on Thursday forenoon Oct 1st and immediately took the oath and returned acceptance by mail. That evening I wrote request to Ransom to release me — An hour or two after, he and Nick Long Jr (Volunteer Aid) came to the Guard House and Ransom and I had the interview I spoke of before. In an hour more he went away. After all this Gen. Ransom and Col. Jones were seen in long conversation at Weldon till night. By midnight and before Col. Jones was getting the officers of the 35th Regt to his headquarters at camp to sign the document which he carried to you I suppose by 5 o'clock train Friday morning and succeeded in getting my commission recalled on that day Oct 2 — of which I received notice from Adjt Genl's office on Saturday evening — 3rd Oct. I have had no communication with Ransom or Jones since Thursday evening, as mentioned, but submitted to force and necessity and remained in confinement. My commission was certainly in force from the time I qualified and accepted on Thursday till your action on the matter on Friday and I should not have been kept in the Guard House [and] not treated by Ransom in such a manner. The great seal of the State whose bounty and charity raised him from obscurity and poverty — educated him and entrusted to his charge many of her gallant sons, he disregards and insults her mandates. I know of no greater attempt at injustice, tyranny and usurpation. Has the army no law except the will of the officer! Has the poor private no chance when officers are intent on his ruin! Col. Jones says that I learn that "I have sworn that I would rather die a thousand deaths than be a private soldier." This is simply a lie. Such a thought never entered my mind. Several officers in the Brigade sympathize with Jones and Ransom and count favor with Ransom and are really afraid to vary from his dictations. He must rule or ruin — he cares little which. He may manage things in his own Brigade as he pleases. He has the power and certainly will leave nothing undone to gain his point. He may succeed to all appearances in crushing truth and right and by mere force and malicious advantage triumph over bleeding innocence. If you can see the truth of my position and receive the testimony of those who alone are competent to know the facts can you not afford protection and justice to a private soldier devoted by every tie to our noble cause and a true native son of our gallant State? I am interested in this not more on personal grounds than for precedent and the principles involved in which my countrymen are as alike interested. Ransom and Jones know if I succeed in getting a proper hearing or released from them I can make known their conduct that they are irreparably injured while if they succeed they have much to gain and little to lose as concerns their positions or themselves. They look not to the ultimate effect on the cause. Ransom has generally shown want of confidence and even contempt for Jones until recently. He threatened to court martial Jones or prevent his promotion. Jones acted very cowardly in a skirmish or rather reconnaissance below Chickahominy in July last. The Regt knows this and has had but little respect or confidence in his fighting qualities since — and much the same before. On the appearance of two yankee cavalrymen (it was reported a yankee force was advancing) he told his men to "run," "Get out of the road" and "Into the woods" and went as hard as his horse could carry him away some distance to the rear. Skirmishers were ahead and had not given an intimation authorizing this movement. He and Adjt Peebles it is said acted very excitedly. He had a pretty large force — portions of several companies and was 3 or 4 miles from his base. It was not supposed that the enemy had in that vicinity more than a company or so of infantry and outpost of cavalry which was ascertained afterwards to be about correct. Any impartial members of the Regt will say the same that it will corroborate this statement in substance if not in letter. It is not necessary to specify several particulars where Jones was ignorant of the duties of his position — not many little partialities and under handed acts unbecoming a gentleman and soldier. Though such conduct is practiced by many officers Ransom has notoriously shirked duty. While other Colonels were compelled to march at the head of their Regiments and be subject to exacting requirements he managed to take his ease about himself and give but little attention to the drill and discipline of his Regt. I was credibly informed that he was relieved as presiding officer of the court martial in Wilmington and ordered to his Regt because he had gone home without leave. It has been his custom to get leave to go home on Saturday and return on Monday and it seems he went once without permission. He has promised many favors and places to men and then disregards them totally — and as you are probably well aware regarded by those that know him best as a slippery unreliable politician and not competent — firm — and comprehensive as a military man. He orders all private letters of the prisoner sent or received to be opened — and it is said detains those he dislikes. My letters have been opened in this way. He has the prisoners — me especially — to do police duty not only about quarters but all about Weldon — the depot — hotels — [undecipherable] and orders the guard if we do not work hard and regular to run us through with bayonets without a moment's hesitation. He issues orders to the commissary to give out just rations enough to keep us alive. We are kept in a tight, dark smoky hut not to go out except when absolutely necessary. This house is about 16 by 20 feet and 56 men have been crammed and quartered in here at once — and 20 or 25 generally since I have been here. When very crowded I learn a few have been allowed to lie outside on the ground. These are facts and can be proven. There is a good deal of sickness in the guard house and occasional cases of fainting. Some of the prisoners are handcuffed together by twos or threes and have been here many weeks. One prisoner was quite sick and sent for surgeon of the Post. The Adjt (through whom applications have to go) sent word back for him "to die and go to hell." F. Clabaugh is Adjt. Post — a Marylander — and fast reckless character. Another chief operative in the Provost office — detective [undecipherable] is Edward Roberts — another Marylander and of similar stripe. I ask of you a careful consideration of this and have an abiding confidence that on impartial review of the evidence and statements of my friends and myself you will reinstate me in the place you were kind enough to give me or relieve me from further outrage and injustice these base and unscrupulous men intend to inflict on me.

I have no wish to ruin these men or blight their characters. I simply want justice and want that returned to me which they have used falsehood and unfair means to remove. They may go their way: "they know not what they do." I admire what they have done for the cause, though I despise the principles and motives they have shown in this thing. They bear aloft the same banner that I uphold, but they should not make me a victim of their unprovoked vengeance and malice. I submit the case and — myself— to you — Direct through Capt. Blue Co. C 35th Regt.[14]

      Truly yours,
      M. J. McSween

The Rev. Andrew McMillan, who was a Presbyterian minister and who had prepared McSween for college, wrote to Governor Vance on his former pupil's behalf. It is unknown how he knew of McSween's plight; perhaps McSween had written him to speak on his behalf.

      La Grange Ga.
      Oct. 17th 1863

Hon. Z. B. Vance Governor of the State of N. C.

I write to you in behalf of M. J. McSween, Co. C, 35th Reg. N. C. T. Ransoms Brigade who I hear is under arrest and in danger of severe punishment. I will not undertake to say whether he deserves such treatment from his Superiors or not, but I deeply regret to hear that he has incurred their displeasure. Can you do anything to relieve him from his present unpleasant condition? Either appoint him to some position where he will have a fair opportunity of exhibiting his talents or at least have him transferred to some other Company in another division of the army. I know McSween well and I have always found him moral and upright in his deportment. I can speak freely of this for I was his teacher and prepared him for College; for six months of this time he remained in the same room with me and behaved himself so [undecipherable] in and out of school that I never had reason to reprove him. He was at that time a professing Christian and such was his diligence in study and punctuality in every duty required of him, that I regarded him as a pious youth that bid fair to make a man of extensive usefulness in the church. Since he went to our University I have seen very little of him. He is a poor orphan having lost both his parents when a child. He is aspiring and unfortunately for him he is sensitive, this may have had much to do with his present unhappy condition. I have been informed that our excellent Governor is what is termed a self-made-man, if this be so he knows something of the ordeal that a poor friendless boy has to pass through from the envies and jealousies of those who happen to have rich and influential parents and friends, and who, on this account think themselves entitled to position in the world. Neither can you be a stranger to the hatred such men bear toward any that may dare to contest for the object of their desires or how mercilessly they persecute them when they get them in their power. Whether this has had anything to do in placing my friend in his present condition or not you perhaps may be able to determine. But however this may be I do not hesitate to commend Mr. McSween to your favorable regard as a sober and upright young man, and I hope that after considering his case that if you can consistently with a sense of your own duty and responsibility that you will relieve. Since I am a stranger to you I will just add that I am a Presbyterian minister and write you in behalf of Mr. McSween because he was my pupil and in whose welfare I have become deeply interested.[15]

With the highest esteem and regard I am
Andrew McMillan

Giles Leitch also wrote to Governor Vance on behalf of McSween: Leitch was born in Robeson County around 1828, so there is the possibility he had some connection with the McSween family. He was an 1849 graduate of the University of North Carolina at Chapel Hill. During the Civil War he was a State Senator in the North Carolina General Assembly. He also served Robeson County as county registrar and as a county judge.

Lumberton, N. C. Oct 18th, 1863

Gov. Vance
Dear Sir:

I have recently learned that M. J. McSween of Richmond County is badly treated by some of the Officers of the 35th Regt N. C. T. and by representations made to you by Officers of that Regiment you were induced to revoke a Commission you had given to him as Adjutant of the 3rd Regiment of Home Guards. I am urged by the friends of McSween to intercede with you in his behalf. I know nothing of the facts of his case of my own knowledge nor do I know personally or otherwise the character of the Officers of that Regiment but I am informed that while McSween was a member of the Press Association or connected with the Press and thereby exempted from conscription he joined the 35th Regiment upon the express promise of Ransom the Col. of the [Regiment concerning the] appointment of Adjutancy of the Regt or of a Lieutenancy. While promise has not been fulfilled, upon Ransom's promotion one Jones became Colonel and who I am informed is a vain weak and incompetent Officer who having a dislike for McSween has improperly exercised his authority to disgrace McSween without any proper cause and to exclude him from the position expressly promised him by Ransom and that so deep is his prejudice that he even got a paper disparaging McSween signed by some of the Officers of that Regiment and bore it in person to you and otherwise to induce you to revoke McSween's Commission as Adjutant. I am further informed that M. J. McSween can establish as good character in the Regiment and in the State as any of those who have been traducing him. You doubtless know that he has been an Army correspondent of the Fayetteville Observer under the name Long Grabs and that generally his letters have been very interesting. He has shown himself to be evidently a man of mind and extensive information. He has I have been informed for some time busily engaged in collecting material for historical sketches of the war which will do justice to North Carolina which by the late action of his Officers he is unable any longer to do unless something is done for his relief.

Now if it be true that Col. Jones is a vindictive Officer who withholds promotion solemnly promised by his predecessor — or in order to have revenge of one he dislikes and avails himself of his position to put him under arrest without any just cause and not only will not promote him but prevent officiously his receiving promotion from any other source especially when the object of his revenge is a man of mind intelligence and extensive acquirements and as far as I know of unsullied character I think he ought to be thwarted in his purpose and McSween's Commission renewed or some arrangement made for him to vindicate himself which in a Regiment a private has not got as against his Colonel.[16]

Yours Truly,
Giles Leitch

While these appeals were coming in to Vance and McSween was still held in the Guard House, a General Court Martial had been convened at Weldon, North Carolina, to try him and a number of other Confederate soldiers on various charges. On October 27, 1863, Captain Evander McN. Blue[17], of Company C, 35th North Carolina Regiment, telegraphed Governor Vance at McSween's request.

Weldon, Oct. 27, 1863

His Excellency

M. J. McSween requests me to telegraph to you and learn if you can possibly attend as a witness in his case now progressing. He has other motives of importance for wishing to see you immediately.[18]

Your humble Servant
E. McN. Blue Capt. Co C 35th

Lt. Alexander Barrett also telegraphed Governor Vance the following on October 28.

We want you here as witness in case of McSween. Trial is progressing. The court is not constituted according to rules heretofore observed. Your presence here immediately is considered [undecipherable] to law and Justice [undecipherable].[19]

Alex. Barrett
Counsel for McSween

McSween's trial has begun in Weldon and he writes to Governor Vance about it.

Weldon, Oct. 28th/63

Gov. Vance
Dear Sir:

My trial has commenced and the past two days — Monday and Tuesday have been taken up in Col. Jones' testimony and cross-examination. I have reason to believe that a majority of the court are prejudiced against me. Maj. Taylor[20] and Capt. Blackwell[21] of the 35th Regt. on the Court were contrived against my earnest promotion. These men signed that scandalous and lying petition sent you by Col. Jones concerning me. This of course clearly shows their deadly malice and prejudice against me and having thus formed and expressed the opinion that I am guilty of the charges and much more I challenged them properly and respectfully — protested and implored against the injustice likely to ensue but with very little consideration the Court overruled my objections. Gen. Pickett I believe has the approved or confirmation of the proceedings of the Court. I have no idea how he will react. There is not positive proof thus far to sustain the 1st charge and specification. [The next sentence was unreadable.] The two other specifications of the 2nd charge are no violation of any article of war and I must believe are illegal. They both originated from and really refer to one and the same thing. The evidence in my defense on all the charges and specs will be very strong in my favor. I did however refuse to carry the log as laid down in the last or 3rd spec of 2nd charge — but did not refuse as there stated. All of my witnesses have not been got here — and will not be — one or two very essential witnesses will not probably be here. The prosecution will perhaps take up to-day and may-be tomorrow — I shall before my defense make affidavit for continuance. I want you here as a witness and also to see for yourself. I want you to have the court dissolved and have the matter referred to one of the regular Confederate Courts Martial — There is one for this Department Wm. B. Rodman presiding I believe and sits at Richmond — but I do not want to have to stay in Castle Thunder. I have received legal advice to the effect that it was not in your power to revoke my Commission after being accepted — This opinion obtained on the assumption that the Act of Legislature authorizing Home Guard does not delegate to you such authority — However this may be I am of opinion that my case presents one or two points by which I may be relieved by Habeas Corpus — I have just now no counsel. I am most shamefully and unlawfully treated by authorities here which you should have investigated at once.[22]

Truly,
M. J. McSween

Bettie Coleman, who lived in Weldon, North Carolina, near the 35th Regiment Guard House, was aware of the harsh treatment McSween was receiving and wrote to Governor Vance on his behalf.

6. Return to Virginia

Weldon, Oct 28th 1863
Gov. Vance

Most honored Sir:

At a time like this nothing is strange and I hope you will pardon the liberty I am taking of thus writing to you. It is a very important object and one on which the life of a fellow mortal depends. I presume you know something of Mr. M. J. McSween. His trial is now going on, and he is most unjustly being tried. More falsehoods are being told by his Col; None of his friends are allowed to speak to him, all of his letters are taken out of the Post Office, and read, and now he is not allowed scarcely any thing at all to eat — just enough to maintain life. The guard house is near my home, and I know how McSween is treated, and I appeal to your noble and generous heart to aid this poor fellow, who is no more guilty — nor who deserves such unheard of barbarous treatment than [undecipherable]. He has already been bucked and gagged, and now his malicious enemies will crush his very life out —, if no friendly aid comes to his rescue. A petition was sent to you asking to have his commission revoked. It was signed by men who do not know McSween. McSween has no hearing at all, all of his friends are below the rank of Gen'l, or Col, so of course their word will not be taken, and Gen'l Ransome and Col Jones are his most bitter enemies, and will not even allow privileges usually granted to prisoners, although he has protested and requested the removal of some of the court yet they still remain and every person who knows any thing of the case, say the court has no idea of trying him fairly.

I do not see how our "national" cause will ever prosper, when there is so much injustice being practiced by men who ought to set good examples.

Do excuse my long epistle, yet — do not fail to take some immediate steps in regard to poor McSween. I would like to have a line or two from you. I am entirely disinterested in the matter only I do not want to see a man suffer because his enemies have him in their power.[23]

Most Respectfully,
Bettie Coleman

On December 1, 1863, Alexander Barrett[24] of Company D, 35th Regiment wrote a letter to Governor Vance on McSween's behalf. The letter is unreadable; however, on the back of it Vance wrote the following: "I will hear any thing in his favor of course, but his fate does not depend on me. I have written to Gen. Pickett on his behalf.— ZBV."

While McSween was being held in the Guard House, Ransom's Brigade was moved to Kinston where it participated in an unsuccessful attempt to retake the city of New Bern, and later took part in attacks on the towns of Plymouth and Little Washington. The brigade along with other detachments were recalled in May and sent to Petersburg.

While Ransom and the Brigade were away, the results of the Court Martial were released.

HEAD QRS. DEPARTMENT NORTH CAROLINA,
January 22, 1864.

GENERAL ORDERS,
No. 4.

I. At a General Court Martial convened at Weldon, North Carolina, by virtue of Special Orders No. 7, Head Qrs. Dep't N. C., were arraigned and tried the following prisoners: The specifications being lengthy and minute, are omitted in this order.

12.—Private M. J. McSwain, Co. C, 35th Reg't N. C. T.
Charge 1st, - - Leaving his Regiment in face of the enemy without permission.
Charge 2d, - - Positive disobedience of orders
Finding.
Of the specification of the 1st charge, - Guilty.
Of the 1st charge, - - - - Guilty.
Sentence.
And the court do therefore sentence the said M. J. McSwain, private company C, 35th N. C. Regiment, to be confined at hard labor for six (6) months in the penitentiary.
Finding.
Of the 1st specification of 2d charge, - Guilty
Of the 2d specification of 2d charge, - Guilty
Of the 3d specification of 2d charge, - Guilty
Of the 2d charge, - - - - Guilty
Sentence.
And the court do therefore, sentence the said M. J. McSwain, private Co. C, 35th Reg't N. C. T., to carry a log weighing fifty pounds, in the presence of his Reg't on parade, and to be afterwards confined at hard labor in the penitentiary for six (6) months, exclusive of the time specified in the foregoing sentence.

13. Private J. A. Poteet, Co. B, 35th Reg't N. C. Troops
Charge, - - - - - - - Desertion.
Finding.
Of the specification, - - - - Guilty except as to the words until arrested.
Of the charge, - - - - - Guilty.

General Orders, No. 4 (1864). Report of a General Court Martial Convened at Weldon, N. C.. Author: Confederate States of America. Army Department of North Carolina, Signed Major General George E. Pickett, W. Stuart Symington, A. D. C. Published in Petersburg, Virginia. Used by permission of the David M. Rubenstein Rare Book & Manuscript Library, Duke University, Durham, North Carolina.

6. Return to Virginia

General Orders, No. 4 was a ten page document, listing all the individuals who were tried and convicted at Weldon by the court martial. A number were sentenced to be shot to death by firing squad for desertion. Others were branded on the hip with the letter "D" before starting their prison sentences, and others were sentenced to a period of time in prison. At the end of the document was the following: "In the cases of Privates M. J. McSween, Company C, 35th Regiment N. C. Troops [other persons receiving sentences were listed after McSween's name] their Brigade Commander will at once make the proper arrangements for having them received at the Penitentiary and send them there."[25]

On February 17, 1864, McSween wrote to Governor Vance informing him that he had been convicted by a military court.

Weldon, N. C.
Feb. 17th, 1864

Dear Sir:

After nearly six months of most inhuman imprisonment and about four months since my trial I have heard the sentence of the court. They find me guilty of every charge and specification. I told you long ago that this court was merely a pale reflex of Ransom and Co. Ransom controls them, picked them out and of course they did his work. I allude more particularly to five of the seven composing the court. They have sentenced me to carry a log before the Regt and to twelve months hard labor in the penitentiary. The law, the evidence of my enemies even — justice, and every consideration of policy and discipline forbid the infliction of such unreasonable, degrading and unnecessary punishment. This sentence must be regarded as most cruel, outrageous, and unmerited and the result purely of malice, prejudice and tyranny. My friends are vexed [undecipherable] indignation and bitter seeds are sown that must grow into trouble and injury to the service while my enemies gloat and chuckle over their triumphal success. I and my friends have tried to show you the malicious tyranny and unjust treatment I have received and will give you further and definite information that you may know fully the merits of the case. I want you to get me clear of this matter through the President or reinstate me fully in my position in the Home Guard. If you make an earnest appeal to the President with a plan and favorable statement of facts and circumstances I have no doubt but that he will order my release. What earthly good can it be to the service to try to degrade me by this court as Ransom and Jones would do. I repeat with more firm conviction and greater emphasis that it must result injuriously to the service. This is no time for gratifying malice and the mean brutal passions of man. In order that I may derive the benefit desired something practical, prompt and efficient must be done. I want this whole case brought before the War Department. I do not think a court martial has the right lawfully to make a man carry a log. I was carried before my Regt a few days ago and compelled on pain of death by order of the court to me [to perform] this part of the sentence. I think the proceedings of this court in my case can be invalidated. I think the members of the court can

be indicted. I want the approval or disapproval of the government in these matters. Please act at once. Write me care of Capt. Blue, 35th Regt.[26]
Gov. Vance

Truly,
M. J. McSween

Across one of the pages of the letter, Governor Vance scribbled "I have written the President." ZBV

On February 18, 1864, Alexander Barrett wrote one last letter to Governor Vance expressing his feelings on the treatment of McSween.

Near Weldon Feb 18th 1864

Gov Vance

I know you must be tired [illegible] with the many appeals which have been written in the case of private M. J. McSween co. C 35 N.C.T. but I hope you will do me the favor to hear me on this — I hope my last letter on the subject. I was informed some time since through your Aide, Col Barnes, that you had written to Gen Pickett in his behalf, but it seems your letter had no influence with the General, for the full sentence of the case has been approved viz to carry a log before his Regt on conscript Parade and twelve months hard labor in the penitentiary. He has already carried the log, and I presume will be forwarded to penitentiary as soon as proper arrangements can be made for the further execution of the sentence.

It is not my purpose to criticize the motives or action of the court such perhaps would be a violation of XXVI Art of Army Regulations, but I may state the fact that McSween has been confined between five and six months which of itself is a serious punishment, and although he may have acted imprudently, I think he is entitled to consideration.

Paragraph 879 of the Army Reg tells us that the President has the power to pardon. All with whom I have conversed on this subject concur in this opinion that through your mediation or influence the President would pardon him.

I presume you are well enough acquainted with the character of McSween and his case without particulars from me I have been in his company and counsell with him recently and am satisfied that if he has ever been intractable and manifested a spirit of insubordination he is now sufficiently subdued.[27]

Very Respectfully
Your obt servt
Alex Barrett
Co. D 49th N.C.T.

On March 10, 1864, D. B. McSween wired Governor Vance the following message over the Southern Telegraph Companies lines:

By telegraph from Columbus To Gov. Vance

Dear Sir: I understand that the sentence of the court martial in the case of M. J. McSween has been published. He is sentenced to twelve months imprisonment. Have any steps been taken to [undecipherable] his respite. Can any thing be done. Telegh back immedy My expense[28]

D. B. McSween

A few days later Capt. E. McN Blue wrote to Governor Vance.

> Camp 35th N. C. T.
> Williamston, N. C.
> March 14th, 1864

His Excellency Gov. Z. B. Vance
Dear Sir:

Allow me for a few moments to ask your attention to a subject which I have already brought to your notice. I am loth to bring this subject before you again feeling that your time and attention are engaged in laboring for the benefit of our bleeding country. But while you are using every exertion for the benefit of the nation I trust and believe you will not overlook the interest of one of your individual citizens. When I recollect your faithful adherence to the cause of truth and justice your zealous attention to the rights and liberties of your fellow citizens, I am emboldened to ask this favor. The case of which I wish to speak is that of M. J. McSween of my company. I will not speak of the circumstances of his arrest, trial, confinement and sentence as I presume you are acquainted with them already. He has been most maliciously, unjustly and cruelly treated from beginning to end. He has now been in the guard house nearly seven months under the strictest orders and has suffered much. What I wish to ask of you is this — Can you do anything for him?

He is as true to the cause as any man in North Carolina. He is a man of talent and moral worth. A large number of the citizens of our State desire his release. A petition to this effect with thousands of names could be obtained in the Cape Fear region and in the Southern part of the State where he is most generally known. His friends in that country have been speaking of the project. I do not know that it has been commissioned. I hope it will not be necessary. I hope you can and will do something for him. The good of the service, justice and humanity demand that he should be released.

I feel a deep interest in his case and trust I have said nothing to give offense.[29]

> Most [illegible] and Respectfully
> Your obt. Servt. E. McN Blue Capt
> Co. "E" 35th N. C. T.

P. S. If you think proper, I would be glad to hear from you, address me at Tarboro, N. C.

> E. McN. B.

On the bottom of the letter Governor Vance wrote "I have written an urgent letter to the President." ZBV

In May, McSween wrote the following to Vance:

> Weldon, N. C.
> May 3rd, 1864

Dear Sir:

Yours of the 29th [undecipherable] thru Col. Little has been received. It is strange the President has not replied. Probably the press of business on his hands has prevented. I think the present a very opportune time for my friends to operate. About 80 prisoners were sent away to day to Castle Thunder I suppose only leaving six here. Col. Hinton is in command here just now (Ransom away in eastern part of the State) and retained me here as special favor so that I might hear from the President through you in a few days. Perhaps I may be detained here a week or two. I would prefer almost anything to going to Castle Thunder. In the meantime I hope you will again remind the President of the matter and urge on him the importance and justice of relieving me at once. Capt. Blue and all the officers of my company Co. E 35th Regt and Lt. Alex. Barrett 49th Regt stand ready to furnish any information or testimony in support of what I have stated all the while about the case. I would be very glad if you would write to Gen. Beauregard of my case. His Headquarters are here and if he is absent it is only temporary. Instruct him not to rely for his points on Ransom and Jones my most bitter and malicious enemies but also to get the facts from my Captain and allow me some hearing. Beauregard is the right sort of a man I think. I can never knuckle to Ransom and Jones. I expect to beg no favors from them and do not wish my friends to do so for me. There seems to be no room in anything like a penitentiary. Why should I be kept in Castle Thunder indefinitely? Please act at once. If no redress can be had I want to know it and my purposes are fixed, so help me God! I am the same man I was before this hellish design was conceived. I defy the fiends. If I live, it will be long before my voice and influence will cease in N. C.[30]

Truly — M. J. McSween

That McSween's patience at his captivity is wearing thin is shown in this letter to Vance.

Weldon, N. C.
May 25th, 1864

Dear Sir:

I have as yet heard nothing from the President in relation to my case. Have you written to him again since the reopening of communications? I have been imprisoned now about nine months and for no cause. I defy anyone to say after thorough investigation that there exists sufficient cause or indeed any cause for this imprisonment. Myself and friends have again and again called your attention to this matter. We have given you fully the facts of the case. You listened to the base lying representatives of my enemies — men as corrupt and base as traitors and murderers. I have never yet been informed whether you have as yet made an earnest practical effort to secure me justice even. My patience is about exhausted. I have as much fortitude as any man. I can stand any thing that any one else can and with as little injury — and just as long. I can bear the entire sentence of the court with proud defiance with the malignity and treachery of enemies and pretended friends thrown in. It is certainly very unnecessary and unjust to impose so much cruel and unlawful punishment on me. I would ask I hope for the last time that some thing be done at once for my relief. I am bound to feel that my earnest and reasonable requests and efforts have been treated with stone indifference. Some of those who made the loudest promises on behalf of the private soldier now are the last to aid him. The multitude now begin to see plainly the hole where the hoe went through.

Please let me know of this case at once.[31]

> Truly yours,
> M. J. McSween
> Camp 35th Regt. N. C. T.

On July 18, 1864, the *Fayetteville Observer* carried the following:

> Fayetteville, N. C. July 16, 1864.

Messrs. E. J. Hale & Sons — Gentlemen: For the information of the friends of Mr. M. J. McSween, and for reasons personal to myself, I respectfully request a publication of the enclosed order. Mr. McSween was discharged from "Castle Thunder" on the 6th or 7th inst., and was immediately transferred to the 26th Regiment N. C. T. (Vance's old Reg't) and was appointed Sergeant-Major thereof.

> Very respect'y your ob't serv'y,
> THOS. C. FULLER.
> [COPY.]
> ADJUTANT AND INSPETOR GENERAL'S OFFICE,
> RICHMOND, June 27, 1864.

Extract: SPECIAL ORDERS, No. 149,

II. The sentence pronounced against Private M. J. McSween, Co. C, 35th N. C. Troops, in October 1863, by a General Court Martial convened by Maj. Gen. George E. Pickett, of which Col. Lee McAfee, of the 49th N. C. Inf'y was President, is remitted by order of the President.

The Court committed a serious error in refusing to sustain the objection of the accused to the Major and a Capt. of his Reg't, sitting as members of the Court when they had expressed opinions as to his guilt, and the finding of the Court is not in accordance with the facts of the case.

The harsh and unauthorized conduct of Col. J. G. Jones, commanding the Regiment, meets with the gravest disapprobation of the President and of the War Department. As a protection against future persecutions by his Commanding Officers, Private McSween will be transferred to any Regiment of the same arm of the service as he may elect to join.

This order will be read to his Regiment at the first Dress Parade after its receipt.

> SAM'L W. MELTON, Ass't Adj't Gen.

Private McSween through Lieut. Gen. Ewell.[32]

McSween could have chosen any Regiment to join, but I feel he went to the 26th because that was the Regiment Governor Vance had commanded in the early days of the war.

Ransom's Brigade was north of Richmond and on June 4 moved to south to Bottom's Bridge. (See map, Chapter 2.) McSween was at Weldon and would head north to join it. He was very angry over what he had had to deal with over the past nine months, and in this mood he lashed out at Vance in the following letter.

> Camp 35th Regt. N. C. T.
> Near Bottom's Bridge, Va.
> June 8th, 1864
>
> Dear Sir:
>
> Yours of the 27th was received just as I was leaving Weldon a few days ago for my Regt. I was released about the first of the month and returned to duty. The continuous marching and skirmishing we have been occupied with since my arrival at the Regt has not allowed me time to reply until now. I have thought a reply proper. I wrote a note hurriedly by the train to Mr. Battle an hour or two before I got your letter from the Post Office and should have not written him had yours been received first. I was surprised and mortified at the tone of your letter and the constructions you place on remarks of mine in a former letter. You charge me seriously with abuse, ingratitude &c. You are mistaken. You have certainly misconceived my meaning and motives. But I will now be more candid and explicit. You can easily imagine how long months of weary imprisonment wears out a man's patience and makes him unhappy. The thought that his life, his welfare and his character to some extent is at the mercy of his malignant enemies and that he — once a freeman — is almost helpless and crammed for nine long months into a miserable hole with deserters and buffaloes is enough to shock the feelings and break the spirit of most men. And when all hope of relief seems shut out and no constant, earnest, practical efforts made on his behalf by those likely to effect any thing any man will, under such circumstances and when all this is for nothing and simply malicious despotism, lose his temper and equanimity although his fortitude and real grit may never be subdued.
>
> I had put myself to considerable trouble and put my friends to much pains for a long time that you might be fully informed of this case — its glaring injustice — its cruelties — its illegality and all the facts and minutes of the matter. I was led to believe that you did not regard my efforts with due consideration. I believe so still and so do my friends. You did me a palpable and severe injustice by acting on the representative of Ransom, Jones and others before you heard my side at all and when you did hear my side you set aside my statements, the statements of Capt. Blue, his three Lieutenants and 75 or 80 as gallant men as any company can boast and also the statements of other friends and persons cognizant of the facts and still adhered to the showing and wishes of Brigadier General Ransom and Col. Jones and this notwithstanding the fact that Capt. Blue's whole company — the very persons above all others who should know the facts — informed you in writing over their own signatures that the representatives of Ransom, Jones, &c were utterly false. Now this you cannot deny. You were also duly informed of the injustice and prejudices of the court and the irregularity and illegality of their proceedings; also of my cruel and unjust treatment as a prisoner — how my letters were opened — how we were denied the rights even of brutes. But not so much of a scratch of a pen did I get. My complaints were disregarded. I had believed that if I would apply in earnest and on good reasons to

Gov. Z. B. Vance who had made such professions of devotion to the rights of the citizens and soldiers that my case would be strongly and manfully brought before the authorities for redress and should your effort there fail the full responsibilities of the issue would fall on the proper shoulders and the matter would be exposed and it would be [undecipherable] who it is that recognizes these and dangerous and [undecipherable] vicious practices. I and others then could confidently rely on the faithfulness and patriotism of our Governor and bear our ills more easily. The tenor of your letter also indicates that you take it as a matter of course and as fixed fact that I was properly and lawfully "convicted" of "nefarious crimes," when the truth is there was no crime committed — no fairness in the trial and the proceedings are not lawful and valid. Yet I have been so [shut] up in prison that I have been unable to avail myself of any of their points as defense or benefit. I have no means of knowing whether you wrote fully and earnestly to Gen. Pickett or whether you expressed yourself in those "glittering generalities" you usually do in reference to soldiers and which Gen. Pickett would be likely to construe as a modest bait for a vote and not intended for any serious consideration. But as to your communications to be — [undecipherable] common sense would teach me that if the Chief Executive of a state should make an earnest appeal to the President on a case involving the points and facts that mine do he would not be two or three months without a reply. Your communication however with the President as I see from Raleigh papers since your letters have been unsatisfactory especially on the Habeas Corpus and for all I know the President may not be disposed to answer your communication except as official duty and courtesy may demand. I most fully and heartily endorse your position on the Habeas Corpus and I regard his reply altogether unsatisfactory if not disrespectful. Now you imagine yourself in my place and I in yours and you will easily see how such views as I have indicated may be indulged by myself and friends. I feel that I have been trifled with — that my case was [undecipherable] up from expediency and policy — that I was a pretty clever fellow, but it would not pay to go to certain lengths and more might be gained by letting things pass &c — that I had [undecipherable] colored up my complaints — was not a practical, established, or matter-of-fact man — that with views imperfect and exaggerated — impractical and inexperienced I wished chiefly a sensation or notoriety [undecipherable]. If any such convictions exist they are entirely wrong though I may be unable to remove them. As to your charge of ingratitude I unhesitatingly deny it. If you charge me with ingratitude you charge what is not so. Am I or have I ever been under obligations [to] you? What have you done to benefit me or build me up as an individual? At the very time I needed a faithful friend you abandoned me to my worse enemies and it is believed you did this without authority of law — and this is what I get for supporting you in 1862!

I have uniformly admired your course as Governor of North Carolina in these trying times and have so expressed myself publically and privately but I [undecipherable] your bombastic Buncombe promises of "retrenchment and reform" and that the rights and interests of the people must be respected, &c and then your slow undecided wigglish course in carrying out those promises. I have never stooped to beg favors from you and never expect to. I am no stranger to misfortune — to disappointment — to opposition — to slander and malignant attempts to injure me and the recent efforts of unprincipled persons in this Regt. will be as unavailing as others. I feel proud of an independent unyielding Scottish nature — and that what I am I am by my own resources — without friends and without money — I hope however you can more justly and properly appreciate my motives and acts.[33]

> Truly Yours,
> M. J. McSween

McSween never forgave Jones or Ransom, even though Jones was killed gallantly leading his regiment in a near midnight charge against the Federal lines June 17, 1864, at Petersburg.

> Ransom's Brigade was ordered to charge and re-establish the line. The Thirty-fifth Regiment struck the heel of the salient, formed in the shape of a horseshoe and received the enemy's fire both from the front and flanks. Reaching the works a hand to hand combat took place, the men fighting with only the parapet of the rifle pits separating them.
> Its gallant commander, John G. Jones, was shot down early in the charge; rising he advanced a few feet, when he fell a second time. Calling for help, he was again going forward; when shot a third time he fell to rise no more.
> In the death of Colonel Jones the Regiment sustained a loss almost irreparable. He had been a student at Wake Forest College; was a Baptist preacher before he entered the army; was without any military training, awkward and unsoldierly in his carriage; but of unsullied character and indomitable courage. His military aptness was of slow growth, but developed as he gained experience until at his death he was recognized as one of the best soldiers of his rank in the army.[34]

On June 2, 1869, five years after Jones had been killed, McSween was in Goldsboro gathering news for *The Eagle*. He chanced to pass by a place where he and Jones had been in conflict, and even after the passage of time, he still could not speak kindly of his former commander.

> I glanced over towards the Sasser plantation where that base tyrant and cowardly sycophant John G. Jones of Person Co., tried to disgrace me in August 1863, and when the 35th Regt., rallied to release me and without my knowledge or consent. These things awaken recollections of oppressive despotism under the iron heel of unscrupulous military power. The mind recalls the treacherous eye of that polished rascal Ransom, the stupid perjury of Peebles, and the pompous airs and brief authority of certain gawky backwoodsmen. But all these things will be more appropriate elsewhere and at another time. The train is crowded and leaves in a few minutes.[35]

His bitterness toward Matthew Ransom was just as strong, as shown in this article penned from Rockingham County in November 1870.

Some feeling and interest has been shown among the Press and people as to the duty of the Conservative Party [Democrat] at this moment and as to the men we would call to represent us. I have thought proper to dispute the claims of certain aspirants and to oppose their election for certain reasons. For this plain expression of the EAGLE as a free and public journal, a few floating newspapers attack me, and call the remarks of the EAGLE in reference to Matt Ransom as scurrilous, weak, contemptible, mudsill epithets, &c.—

I have alluded to Ransom as a public man and have opposed his election to the U. S. Senate. My just contempt for the fellow in our private relations does not govern my public duty. I have just cause which is pretty well known, and heretofore explained in my paper long before this discussion for Senator, and hundreds of other Confederate soldiers have just cause for holding the name of Ransom in disgust and odium. Yet if I did not think him unfit and unworthy for each station, I would remain silent.—

Ransom and his immediate supporters gave us no visible aid in the last August election. He is an old changeable politician. He is an eastern man, and the West is entitled to Senator if they want it. The name of Ransom in the army is popular with staff officers and officials generally, but became to be feared and hated by the great mass of soldiers whose honest efforts upheld the cause.

These soldiers, plain conservative men who did not go into the war for politics like Ransom, are now the strength of our party.

Our whole people want new and more representative men. Elect old political flunkies and men whose public acts thousands of good men spurn and hate, and then we will see our grand conservative success wasted into a simple contest for office. Adopt such policy and we are beaten next election by ten or twenty thousand for the people will see no difference, where the difference is only in the name. For such reasons I cannot support Ransom and men of his stripe as our representative men.

I shall expose him and his public conduct when and how I please, regardless of adventurers from Virginia, or floating school-teachers, "dead heads," or advertising agents who part their hair in the middle and have no visible means of support. I defy the whole of them, as I defied Ransom's tyranny and bayonets in the army. It is intimated too that I deserved censure as a soldier. We have faults and for fear I may be charged with too much vanity or egotism, I will only say that I challenge a comparison of my record as a soldier in all respects with that of Ransom or any of his supporters. I have not expressed myself on the matter of Senator and others duties now before our party, in any dictating manner, nor recklessly, but deliberately and candidly. I have some right to a voice in our party affairs, and as to my influence, it is better known by this and adjoining counties, where conservatism was victorious, than by pipers whose existence seems to be unknown to the public.

McSween's animosity towards the two men remained till the day he died.

Chapter 7

Richmond and Petersburg: The Final Year
July 12, 1864 – February 22, 1865

Camp Near Petersburg, July 12, 1864.

Messrs. Editors:—Again doth ye veritable "Long Grabs" intrude his royal ugliness among ye "rebels." As opportunity may present I will endeavor to give you whatever of interest may transpire around me. I presume people do not expect me to write continually, and consequently I suppose no apology is necessary for my negligence for some months past. In fact, it is just exactly nobody's business where I have been or what I have been doing; but if the folks must know, I will tell them. I have been on "detached duty," mostly at "Fort Ransom." Details of this kind are seldom allowed, because very few of the applicants are found to be sufficiently competent and qualified for the duties. Should any arrogant "rebel" make a disparaging reflection about this special detail, he may consider himself challenged. Suffice it to say, that "Long Grabs" has turned up all right again, and in a heavy game that has just been played he has taken the "odd trick" with the ace of trumps, and "honors are easy"—it is written, "you had as well try to dam up the waters of the Nile with bulrushes as to stop "Long Grabs" in his course." Your attention will be called to other points of the text again.

There has been no fighting of consequence around here for the past several days. The sharpshooters and skirmishers of both armies keep up a pretty regular fire. There is constant danger in exposing yourself above the breastworks. The minies go whizzing by your head and hit up "spat against a tree, like a blind June bug, only more so." The yanks are about two miles from the Eastern limits of the town, and the breastworks of the two armies are from a quarter to a half mile apart. The enemy can shell all portions of the city with their long range cannon, though the city has not been damaged much yet by shell and shot and but few persons have been hurt. It is all humbug about a few days shelling being sufficient to knock a city all to pieces. Nearly all the citizens in the Eastern part of the town have moved farther back, and most of the population seem to have gone away to a safer place. Very little business is

7. Richmond and Petersburg: The Final Year

Loading a Mortar. "This illustration represents a 13-inch mortar, the largest in general practice, weight 17,000 pounds, exclusive of the carriage. The number of men required to work one of these guns is seven, for all of whom there is distinct and adequate occupation. Mortars are not used in hand-to-hand encounters, their value consisting in pitching shells into camps and towns, or shelling fortifications erected on elevations, against which cannons are of no avail."—Source: Frank Leslie, *Famous Leaders and Battle Scenes of the Civil War* (New York: Mrs. Frank Leslie, 1896) p. 177. Used by permission of the Florida Center for Instructional Technology, College of Education, University of South Florida.

going on. It is hard to get a loaf of bread and more difficult to get a mint julep.

The yankees use mortars in throwing shells at our troops. The mortar, you know, is a very short cannon, swinging on pivots, and can shot straight up or nearly so. The shells are thrown nearly perpendicular, and fall over by a gentle curve in the vicinity of our breastworks and camps. It is seldom that these shells do much damage, though they are pretty certain to burst after falling.

It is understood that in the 25th N. C. Reg't, that as soon as a shell falls in the entrenchments among the Reg't, the nearest man is to seize it quickly and throw it over the breastwork. This has been done in several instances by members of this Reg't and other Troops also. The danger of such experiments can be imagined when it is known that the shell explodes as it hits the ground or a few seconds after.

The drought and heat here have become almost intolerable—all vegetation is suffering and dying for want of rain. It is very hard now to get garden vegetables, berries, &c.—usually so plentiful in this country at this season. But there is one luxury that is abundant and cheap, and that is ice. The rations are not so plentiful just now as heretofore, though a soldier can live comfortably with them. A man gets a day one pound of corn meal, a third of a pound of bacon, some coffee, peas and rice. I think there is a good supply of forage on hand, though grazing is very inferior on account of the dry weather. Two or three good showers is all that is necessary for the clover fields to "turn over a new leaf" and enable our jaded teams and prancing chargers to be led "through the green pastures and beside the still waters."

Our losses in this summer's campaign are much smaller than many have supposed. We have lost more in prisoners than I had supposed. From 100 to 500 convalescent and slightly wounded soldiers return to their commands from the hospital at Richmond every day. There is but little very serious sickness in our army here now.

It is the universal opinion that Grant cannot in his present position drive us away from any portion of our breastworks. It is probable he will await reinforcements from the new levies before he attempts much more.

We have had no mail nor papers from N. C. in some time, as mail communication has been suspended. This is very annoying to the soldiers as it is their greatest pleasure among all their hardships to communicate with their friends and get North Carolina news. Freight trains come through with supplies, and it would be a great favor to the soldiers if some arrangement would be made at Raleigh or Weldon with some Railroad man or suitable person to forward letters and papers by any sufficient and reliable communication that might exist. It would be a great relief if this could be done once or twice a week when yankee raids interrupt our regular communication. Similar raids may be expected in future, and it is to be hoped that our friends at home will provide against our isolation again.

>Truly,
>Long Grabs.

[July 21, 1864]

>Camp Near Petersburg, July 14.

Messrs. Editors: The lines around Petersburg are quiet and things appear to be much the same. I have heard of a cavalry fight or skirmish towards our right in the neighborhood of the Weldon Rail Road, but am unable to give any particulars. It seems a well ascertained fact now that Grant has sent away some troops from here, and probably to Washington.

I suppose politics rages in North Carolina. There is not much feeling on the subject in the army; some quartermasters and others occupying the rear indulge in very earnest political discussions, but the great mass of the soldiers at the front express but little interest. They keep a sharper lookout for Grant.

I send you an account of casualties in some of the companies of Ransom's Brigade from your section, and will again send you similar information as to Kirkland's Brigade and other N. C. Troops. The present account refers to Co. C, Capt. Blue, from Moore, and Co. D, Capt. Petty, from Chatham, both of the 35th Reg't, since they came to Va. some two months ago.

Ransom's Brigade was in Hoke's division in Eastern Carolina and was called away from the gates of Newbern to Petersburg early in May, and from the 12th to the 20th of that month was engaged in several severe actions around Drewry's Bluff and on the South Side. About the 5th of June it moved across the James to the vicinity of Bottom's Bridge on the Chickahominy, where it remained a few days and returned to the vicinity of Chafin's and Drewry's Bluff, and then to the fortifications east of Petersburg, near the City Point & Norfolk Rail Roads, where it was engaged in heavy fighting on the 17th of June. Since then it has occupied nearly the same position, and has been exposed to occasional skirmishing. For sometime past the Brigade has been in Gen. Bushrod Johnson's division, recently the commander of a Tennessee Brigade. Ransom's Brigade has lost very heavily in killed, wounded and prisoners.

Company C, Thirty-Fifth N. C. Reg't.

Lt. N. R. Kelly, wounded in right leg, 18th May — amputated, died at Chimborazo Hospital, Richmond, June 3. Lt. Malcom Bay, wounded right leg same time and place — erysipelas, died same hospital about last of May. Both buried there. Sergt. John A. Patterson, killed instantly, same battle, minnie ball through breast. Also killed, same, John A. G. Johnson, minnie in head. Also killed Nathaniel Morris, shot in head. Duncan C. McDonald was killed the day before (12th May) on way to Drewry's Bluff; ball through right hip. In the action near Bermuda Hundred, May 20th, Archy Johnson shot through breast and arm, died at Winder Hospital last of May. Daniel Hale shot through knee, severe, now at Winder Hospital. George W. Sibbitt wounded severe in left shoulder, still in Winder Hospital. John C. Ferguson flesh wound in thigh; Henry C. Goings flesh wound in thigh; Daniel Cameron missing. Battle around Petersburg, June 17: Garrett Thompson killed by cannon ball in the morning. At night, in charge to retake the works formerly occupied by Wise's and other troops, Richard Roan was killed, minnie ball; Solomon N. Cole shot in breast, now at Fair Ground Hospital, Petersburg; Malcom A. McNeil badly wounded in knee, since died at Confederate Hospital, Petersburg. Noah R. Jackson slight wound in breast; W. H. H. Fry bad wound in hand; John W. McCaskill would slight in head. All three in hospital at Kittrell's. Corpl. Alex Cameron wounded in shoulder, at hospital, Petersburg; B. Stricklin, slight wound in foot on 17th June, now at Kittrell's; George A. Wadsworth wound in head about 21st June, died at Fair Ground hospital, Petersburg, about 6th July; Hugh Moore wounded in hand last of June, at hospital Richmond; Wm. Shields flesh wound in thigh, 7th July, now at hospital, Petersburg.

Captured and missing: in fight of night of 17th June, Capt. E. McN. Blue, Lt. W. T. Jones, Ord'ly Sergt. D. A. Blue, Sergts. Neill Hannon and John W. Black, Corpls. Hugh M. McDonald and Archd Ray, privates Angus Ferguson, Danl. P. McDonald, John McDonald, John McArthur, N. A. Patterson, John Smith, James Stewart, Gilbert Thompson and Rufus Wallace. Jacob Goodman wounded in side and missing. Some think Lt. Jones was unhurt, others think differently. Capt. Blue, Lt. Avent of Co. D, and Capt. Dixon of Co. H, were heard from at City Point and all well. I must put off further details at present.

Truly,
Long Grabs.

[July 21, 1864]

Long Grabs describes a troop movement to Chaffin's Bluff, which is across the James River from Drury's Bluff, called Fort Darling on the map. Both were strong fortifications built to resist Union gunboats attempting to come up the river to bombard Richmond. (See map, Chapter 2.)

BELOW CHAFFIN'S BLUFF, VA., July 30th, 1864.

Messrs. Editors: Three days ago we moved from our position south of Petersburg to this place, to correspond with a move the enemy had made across the James. It was a very hot fatiguing march and many of our men broke down. About the next hardest thing to fighting is long weary marching. When the brigade starts there is much diversion and merriment. Every person met, especially if he be a negro or a mule, is addressed in a very undignified manner along the whole line. Sometimes a man tries to be sharp and return wit for wit. In such cases he soon finds that "there is no use in talkin." He becomes the butt of all the old saws, calls, and conundrums in the memory of the whole brigade, and new ones too, and the more recent literature of this kind is a decided improvement on the old. All imaginable speculations are indulged as to the objects of the move, and at every turn on the road some old soldier calls attention of his comrade to something that he saw when the Reg't passed there last year. They both recognize the very same old place and strike out together for the spring by a "near out." Presently they come by the same kind old lady's house where they used to get such nice dinners and fruit and milk — all gratis. Oh, how their mouths water and how they smile to each other as they lift the well known latch on the gate and walk round to the kitchen — the place a soldier visits first. But they are doomed to bitter disappointment of heart (or rather of stomach,) and their air castles are suddenly upturned when the old lady informs them very pointedly that she has nothing to spare on any terms, and says in effect, "Depart from me ye workers in iniquity." Even the old lady who was so pious and hospitable is now cold, selfish and crabbed. The blighting breath of war has blown over her quiet and plentiful home. The soldiers — the everlasting soldiers — have camped all over her premises, pulled down her fences, killed her stock and eaten her chickens and vegetables, and her feelings towards them are not exactly so affectionate as formerly. Then she welcomed a reg't or brigade as her defenders; now she looks on them as murderers of her little chicks and the destroyers of everything she possesses. Then she saluted them with smiles and waving of handkerchiefs, as they came, but now the doors are shut and the house looks sullen, scarcely a chicken or other "varmint" shows his head, and argus eyes are watching the garden and orchard. Times have changed, you know, and we have all changed with them. Indeed it is generally true that hospitality has "played out" where the army has been. But still the soldiers have been consistent and fair — that is, they have acted on the principle of "give and take." At the first of the war they enjoyed what was given them and now they enjoy what they take (!) — and there is no material difference in result — philosophically.

But I was speaking of the incidents of the march. As the column moves along, the further it gets the less it talks and laughs. Finally everything becomes silent except the irregular tottering step of the scattered ranks and an occasional cough produced by the stifling dust. You go on and as you believe for miles and miles (but really not so far as you might suppose,) at one time through an open cornfield, again through woods and again through swamp and mud, and still it is on with the same tiresome effort and weary jerk of the body. You get stiff and insensible; you seem to move mechanically because those before and behind are moving — the string of automatons is pulled unconsciously along. You feel like you are in a dream. You say to yourself, "Now I will stop and rest when I get to that tree yonder;" but when you get there all the others are moving on and your conscience or some other mysterious agent moves you on too. Again you select some place ahead where you "will certainly stop awhile even if you be shot for it." But again courage fails and you find yourself "pegging away." Thus you continue along the exhausting march, your mind in vaults, your thoughts in a stupor, and your body "in a sweat." After an eternity of time you stop, congratulating yourself on "holding out faithful unto the end" but alas! delusive hope! Your troubles break out in a new place, and you are double quicked into a fight or sent away to the front on picket without rations. Thus passeth away the "pomp and circumstance of war."

We are stationed here near New Market which is a landing on the James river about 4 miles below Drewry's Bluff. This place was formerly a market or fair ground where people from the surrounding country collected to buy and sell various articles at certain times. Swinney's Tavern is close by. The distance from here to Richmond is stated to be 10 miles. There is a pretty heavy force of enemy in our front on this side. The enemy's lines embrace Malvern Hill I think, which is 3 or 4 miles from here. The enemy's pickets are in sight of ours and there is a good deal of firing occasionally. There has been considerably shelling at times and several of our men have been wounded. I think it is probable that Grant intends attacking Richmond now by divisions — or in other words by feints distant from those where the real attack is designed.

The country has remained desolated since McClellan's campaign. A farm here and there has been partially cultivated. I saw to-day two gunboats and one ironclad from the top of a hill. You could distinguish them very plainly with a field glass and also the stars and stripes that floated from the flag staffs. The election passed off quietly among the troops here. Vance gets about ten to Holden's one.*

Truly,
LONG GRABS.

[August 11, 1864]

*[Our correspondent here gives the vote in several Reg'ts and Companies, but as the telegraph anticipated him we omit that.— Editors, *Fayetteville Observer*]

CAMP NEAR PETERSBURG, Aug. 4, 1864.

Messrs. Editors: We remained but 3 or 4 days over the James when we were marched back to our former position on the right of the lines around Petersburg. Since then we have moved farther to the left and nearer the Appomattox. The Troops usually relieve each other on the line at certain times. The men in our brigade have not been paid off very recently but will be soon I learn. We get coffee and tobacco regularly and I heard a soldier say if old Jeff would order a few pies and things to be issued by the Government we would be all right and independent of sutlers and cake women. I think it would be a very wise and beneficial thing for the Government to make occasional purchases of vegetables for the army. Vegetables are an absolute necessity for the soldier. He must have them, else, weakness, debility and disease follow. At present he must buy them at exorbitant prices with his own money. At corresponding government prices $1000 would buy enough vegetables — cabbage, Irish potatoes, green peas, tomatoes, cucumbers, fruit, corn, &c — for any one brigade for one mess, and that amount would be sufficient ordinarily for two or three brigades a day.

One dollar a day to the man at government rates would supply enough of all kinds of vegetables for a day's use. I cannot conceive of any better way in which the government could occasionally lay out a few thousand dollars — say once a month. To prevent waste, theft, cheater, &c., let one Brigade at a time be supplied from the market gardens and farms of the surrounding country. The Brigade commissary could take charge of the supplies after the tithe man collects them and issue them at once as other commissary stores. A small portion of the vegetable crop would thus be gathered at a time while all the rest would be growing. I hardly think this would work injury to the citizens dependent on the market for vegetables, but would rather lower the prices. For the soldiers are the chief consumers of marketable vegetables, and the more they are furnished by the Government the less they will purchase in market, and the market supply would then be more abundant for the citizens. If it be said that there would not be an adequate supply of vegetables for the markets if the Government would impress heavily, it may be answered, that since the government has been furnishing tobacco to the army, the price of the article has fallen, as is believed partly on account of the quantity issued to the soldiers. The army is the great source of consumption now — supply the wants of the army and you almost supply the wants of the country. The government has thought proper to impress the permanent agricultural interest of the country on its own terms in addition to the tithe tax. The regular producing farmer pays one-tenth of his grain and meat to the government and is still liable to have the rest impressed and taken at Government prices; but the huckster, the milkman, the fruit grower and the owner of large and productive market gardens, with all their enormous profits, pay nothing! They lay out comparatively nothing in labor or capital, but their [undecipherable] of receipts in cash is counted by the hundred and the thousand. The weak emaciated soldier from the hospital buys from the marketman about as much vegetables as he can eat at one or two meals for $10, the real cost of which to the grower was not 50 cents. Why should not the marketman and dairy-man contribute a tithe of their immense profits to the army as well as the others? It would be better policy to do this for the hospitals than to send extravagant agents to market with a pocket full of government money to compete in the extortionate prices and for the benefit — not of the patients very often — but for the delicate stomachs of the clerks, ward masters, &c. But from the latest unofficial reports the using of hospital supplies by proxy appears to be a decided improvement on the old fogy plans formerly adopted. Especially has it been found beneficial to the patients' health for the Surgeons to consume the liquors sent as Medical stores than for the patients themselves to use them. Nearly all the best hospitals in the Confederacy are examples of this timely change. The moral effect is great too in this confining intemperance to narrower limits.

7. Richmond and Petersburg: The Final Year

The tobacco furnished the army is generally of inferior quality and there is certainly a great cheat somewhere.

You have been pretty fully informed about the attack on our lines last Saturday and the springing of a mine by the enemy. They no doubt intended it to be a grand surprise and success, but with the explosion of the mine their hopes and plans exploded also. The mine blew up some 75 yards of our line containing four pieces of artillery with their complement of men and about three infantry companies of the 22d S. C. Reg't. Our loss in killed, wounded and missing is put down at 1000. The yankees were massed in front of the mine in readiness to charge through at the instant the mine exploded. And when the chief explosion took place they dashed in several companies deep. It is said some portions of the mine did not explode till the yankees were on it and they were carried into it also. Most of the enemy's troops were negroes and but few of them returned to tell their tale of disaster. Our forces rallied promptly and by fierce stubborn charges cleared the gap and slaughtered and captured almost the whole force that had come inside — some 4000. The slaughter of the enemy in retreating and advancing to the break was terrific, owing to our cross fire.

The 25th N. C. Reg't and a portion of the 49th were engaged in this fight and suffered as heavily as any other troops from the fighting. The 25th was more fully engaged and acted very efficiently and gallantly. Lt. Col. Fleming of the 49th was killed. He was a young man, brave sociable and highly respected and came into the war as Captain of Company A, 49th Reg't, from McDowell county. He had been a private in the first Regiment under D. H. Hill as Colonel. Col. Fleming's father had a difficulty with Hon. W. W. Avery and was killed in Morganton Court House by that gentleman, as will be remembered. Capt. Harris[1] of the 49th, from Iredell, was also killed.

Every thing is very quiet and there is not much shelling. There is usually pretty sharp picket firing at night. Furloughs continue to be given — one to a hundred men I believe. We have no late reliable news from Early. It is thought Grant had been reinforced recently, but Early's success on the upper Potomac will interfere with his plans. More mining is expected here. Lee and Grant may be said to be operating like to schoolboys in the game of "tag," "hide and seek," where each tries to catch the other and not get caught himself. One boy runs around one corner and the other around another and they run clap together — then one hides in the corner and waits till the other runs round and just as he thinks of overtaking the other he is himself caught where he least expected it. Sometimes in this game too each both gets in a good place and then they watch each other through the crack and halloo out "bo beep!" Now Lee acts the part of the wise boy. He hides in the corner and presently Grant comes full tilt, wanting nothing but a glimpse of his antagonist and then an open race — when all at once Lee naps him in the rear — Grant slips away in an instant across the James and halloos out "bo beep" when Lee answers back from Chaffin's Bluff, "I see you through the crack." Grant then slips back and tries to break in by force, which is contrary to the rules of the game, whereupon Lee beats him and cripples him severely, and now probably Grant's parents will stop him from that school. We think Lee and the other generals to be great men, but they only carry out the same principles and rules laid down by little school-boys. Would that it were an innocent game, this cruel, everlasting war! The slaughter of our countrymen can never be pastime. But we must not pine away in despair because misfortunes thicken over us. Be cheerful and hopeful — be funny — say and do all manner of funny things [or try at least] — be virtuous — put your trust in Providence, and above all be honest and steal not.

Truly,
LONG GRABS.

[August 18, 1864]

The following was written by the editors of the *Fayetteville Observer:*

FROM "LONG GRABS." — We have a letter from our correspondent. He was wounded in the battle of Reams,' a ball entering between the eyes and passing out just below the left ear — a wound which he thinks "not serious," though it knocked him down, stunned, and bled profusely. It occurred in 30 or 40 yards of the breastworks which he was charging with his Reg't, the 26th. He is with Dr. Manson, doing well, and with whom, he says, patients fare well.

He informs us that James M. Lilly[2] of Montgomery county, a noble young man, of fine ability, a member of Ruffin's cavalry, was killed on the 21st ult.

Gen. Kirkland, of his Brigade, has not commanded since his wound on the 3d June, and is now assigned to command Martin's late Brigade — Col. McRae of New Hanover, of the 15th Reg't, commanding Kirkland's late Brigade. He is a brave man and good officer. He was Engineer on the W. C. & R. railroad, and went into the service as Captain of a company from Union county.

Our correspondent promises, as soon as able to write, some descriptive letters of the last month's campaign and the fights of the 21st and 25th.[3]

[September 8, 1864]

HOSPITAL , NO. 24, RICHMOND, Oct. 31.

Messrs. Editors: — For fear it may be thought that "Long Grabs" hath "gone up the spout" anyhow, I do issue this my Proclamation warning all persons the absurdity of such an opinion and of gross criminality of indulging such notions farther. In the latter part of August I went with a parcel of other rebels to drive the yanks away from the Weldon Railroad. The yankees manifested some indignation at our conduct and one of them immediately fired his gun at me, inflicting a severe wound in the face and head, whereupon they became greatly alarmed and ran away in confusion. I was unable I may say to write much for some weeks afterwards. However, in the meantime, by sundry operations known to the soldier, I got a furlough and went home. While my rebellious comrades were lying in the trenches and running to and fro watching the sly yank and living on their sour corn bread and third of a pound of "Nassau," I was luxuriating on the fat of the land and wearing "biled" shirts at home. One day I even walked out under an umbrella. The umbrella is a species of garment worn above the head and stretched and spread out somewhat like a tent to protect against the weather. It was used by the ancients and several are still to be seen in a remarkable state of preservation. From my appearance while about home you would suppose that I was really one of the "seventeen stout able-bodied men" who in years past were in the habit of "taking sugar in their'n." Indeed I think I would have got married if my furlough had just been a little longer — a soldier can have no certainty of marrying unless he has a long furlough. My time ran out and I returned to my command a few days before the fight last week Southwest of Petersburg. In the battle there last Thursday evening, while charging the enemy in company with that notorious band of rebels called the "Pee Dee Wild Cats," [Company K, 26th Regiment] and many others, I was wounded again in that same big head. A yankee minie ball raked along over the bone on the top of the head, leaving a sore scar. It came with considerable shock and glanced out of its direct course. We were fighting the same portion of the yankee army that opposed us at the Railroad, and it may have been the same fellow who made the former wound. The wound is not severe and I am doubtful whether it will be sufficient to give me a furlough. So I am at a Hospital again for treatment. I left our army masters of the situation, in good spirits and considerably recruited in numbers. Now that my hand is in I will write you soon, often and fully.

Truly yours,
Long Grabs.

[November 10, 1864]

Richmond, Nov. 3.

Messrs. Editors: — The present campaign has been the most severe for the Army of Northern Virginia has ever experienced. It began on the 5th of May at the Wilderness, and there and also at Spotsylvania and Cold Harbor Grant hurled his legions against our veterans with the impetuosity of despair, resulting only in the slaughter of his troops. The direct advance of the invader has been so effectively barred that he was compelled to adopt that series of flank movements to the left which has characterized the whole campaign. Consequently Grant has slid around to our right continually, with a base of water navigation all the while until he has moved from the Rappahannock to South of Petersburg, with a line of battle now 30 miles long. Had he moved up the James at first, it seems he might have occupied this line in six days instead of six months. In that case he would not have found our defences as formidable as now, and his army would not have experienced such immense loss and fatigue as has been inflicted upon it. So that Gen. Grant's invasion against Richmond was badly planned and has not been successfully or skillfully executed. It therefore bears evident marks of failure; and after all manner of movements and feints and positive promises, reinforcements are still demanded.

Soon after his appearance in front of Petersburg, the enemy occupied a portion of the Weldon Railroad, but was immediately driven away by our forces under Gen. Mahone. This Road, running straight South from Petersburg, was continually exposed to the left flank of the enemy, for it would be impracticable for us to extend our right along the whole length of the Road — over 60 miles — in order to head off any sudden flank movement of the enemy in that direction. Our troops occupied the Road in force only a few miles out from Petersburg and from there the defence of the Road was entrusted to an ordinary cavalry picket line. One dark night the enemy suddenly collected a force of 30,000 or more

and moved on the Weldon Road beyond the end of our fortifications and driving away our small picket force. Such a movement could be made at any time, and our only alternative was to dislodge them from the Road immediately after their taking it. On Thursday evening 18th August, the enemy occupied the Weldon Road in heavy force. Probably our authorities did not know the force of the enemy, as only some two Brigades were sent to drive them away on Friday. The attack failed, and on Saturday a larger force was sent against them, but the enemy was found strongly fortified and reinforced, and our troops were still unable to dislodge them. On Sunday the 21st Aug. a more extensive demonstration was made, resulting in a considerable engagement, in which our Division or the most of it participated. The enemy was driven back from all his outer lines, but he was found too strongly entrenched on the Railroad, with an immense number of cannon, to justify a sacrifice of life on our part necessary to take the works. So it was deemed proper to make no further attack on the enemy at that point, and he has held the road there ever since. On the 24th of August a part of our army, including two Brigades of our Division, moved by a circuitous route around the left flank of the enemy and came to the Railroad near Reams's Station, in rear of the place where we attacked the enemy on the previous Sunday. Here on the 25th August, we found the enemy's infantry and artillery in line of battle behind ordinary breastworks immediately on the Railroad. A short and brilliant battle ensued, and we took all of the works attacked and a large number of prisoners, completely routing the enemy. We have I believe held the Railroad from this point Southward ever since, and the enemy holds only some 3 or 4 miles of the road between Reams's Station and Petersburg.

About the last of September and 1st Oct. the enemy again extended his left in heavy force with a view to flank our right and get possession of the Southside Railroad, which runs out West from Petersburg. This movement was frustrated and the enemy driven back with heavy loss, though by it he advanced his line over a mile nearer the South Side Road, for we did not drive him entirely back to his line near the Weldon Road.

On the 26th of Oct. the enemy again massed his troops in heavy force on our right, and early on the morning of the 27th, surprised and broke across our line of dismounted cavalry to the right of our extreme infantry line, and about seven miles southwest of Petersburg. They moved forward towards the south side road, in a force of some 30,000, commanded by Grant in person, our small cavalry force fighting and retreating slowly. A large force of our infantry, including our Division, were rapidly thrown around to meet the advancing column of yankees, and late in the afternoon came in collision with them at several points. There followed pretty heavy and continued fighting, and there was every indication of

Opposite: "Battle of Ream's Station — the attempt of the enemy to regain the Weldon Railroad on the evening of August 25th, 1864. The enemy having been repulsed, the Federal skirmishers followed, advancing to the position they had formerly held, and capturing a number of prisoners. Shortly after the enemy again advanced, and were again driven back with heavy loss; and their third assault, made about four o'clock P.M., was attended with a like satisfactory result. In the first three charges the enemy used no artillery, but about five o'clock P.M. they opened a heavy, concentrated fire from a number of batteries, pouring a storm of shell and other missiles over the entire amphitheatre included within the Federal lines. After about twenty minutes of this artillery fire the enemy again made their appearance in front of General Miles's division, their assault being directed mainly against his centre. Emerging from the woods, they advanced in two lines of battle. The Federal artillery and musketry greeted them, as before, with a rapid fire, but without checking their progress. On they came, with bayonets fixed and without firing a shot. They approached the Federal lines, gained the outside of their entrenchments, and at some points a hand-to-hand conflict ensued over the top of the breastworks, the Federals beating back the Confederates with their bayonets as they attempted to climb over. But soon it was found that the Federal line was broken near the centre, and the gap once made rapidly grew wider, until nearly the entire line was swept back, leaving the Federal breastworks and artillery in the hands of the enemy. General Miles, with great coolness, set to work to rally the men, and in a short time succeeded in forming a line with its right resting against the breastworks. At the same time General Hancock ordered the Second Division to be faced about, and cheering and urging the men forward, led them in person in a charge at double-quick. This charge, which was made under a heavy fire, was gallantly executed, and in conjunction with the line rallied by General Miles instantly checked the enemy and regained the entrenchments for some distance further toward the left. After the enemy had been checked in the centre and along that portion of the line against which they had chiefly directed their attack the greatest, part of the Second Division returned to their own entrenchments. By this time it was dark and the fighting ended. Our sketch shows the repulse of the last Confederate assault."— Frank Leslie, 1896. Source: Frank Leslie, *Famous Leaders and Battle Scenes of the Civil War* (New York: Mrs. Frank Leslie, 1896) p. 426. Used by permission of the Florida Center for Instructional Technology, College of Education, University of South Florida.

a general engagement in an open field fight. The enemy in his own grand flank movement found himself flanked and surprised. Even some of his stragglers, who ran as they thought to the rear to escape danger at the front, found themselves at once prisoners in our hands. Our troops were pressing and flanking the enemy, while the rapid and deafening roar of cannon and the brief rattle of musketry would every now and then force you to believe the grand ball had opened.

Thus went the game on the military chess board till darkness and rain put an end to the scene. Then the weary and hungry soldier with some gloomy thoughts of the morrow laid himself on the wet leaves to rest. These are the times that try the soul of a soldier. But the veterans of this Army, with their noble leader, are equal to all emergencies. They deserve all the consideration and aid their generous friends at home can bestow on them. The enemy retreated in haste under cover of night back to his former position, leaving hundreds of his dead and wounded and arms and clothing strewed all over the ground. So after a decided Confederate victory things have relapsed into their former state of quiet and monotony.

Of the battles of the 21st and 25th August I deem it unnecessary at this time to speak at length. Our brigade (McRae's — formerly Pettigrew's and then Kirkland's) was exposed to a very terrific shelling on the 21st while advancing with the other troops in front of the enemy's strong works on the Weldon Road. Gen. Mahone had moved his command to the right in order to flank the enemy's left, but failed, and our action in front being dependent on his, we could not well do anything. On the 25th McRae's, Cooke's and Lane's brigades, all North Carolinians, and the only infantry on the field, made a successful charge on the enemy's works near Reams's Station, captured the works and routed a force of the enemy more than double their own in numbers. Here we fought Hancock's corps, the brag fighters of the yankee army. Our loss was not heavy. Gen. Lee gives due credit to our troops for their valor and success on this occasion, so it is not necessary for anybody else to say much. When Gen. Lee cannot have time or opportunity to give full honor to N. C. Troops, "Long Grabs" will endeavor to do them justice. So that either Gen. Lee or "Long Grabs" one will always try to give them their merited fame. (Bully for me!)

I was not present at the battles of 30th Sept. and 1st Oct., and do not know much of what occurred. McRae's Brigade captured several hundred prisoners, and the 44th and 52d Reg'ts made a gallant charge and suffered heavy loss. The other Regiments, I believe, were in a different position and not ordered in the charge. I have been informed that on the 1st Oct., while the Brigade was advancing under heavy fire, Gen. McRae ordered the men to go slower, but they paid no attention. He then told them to half, but on they went at a double quick, charging the enemy with a yell. He had to let them go and keep up as best he could. I have had no opportunity to learn the action of either N. C. Troops, but will use every effort at all times to get all facts and information of interest.

These battles occurred along the Squirrel Level road, and the enemy succeeded in planting his line a mile or more nearer the South Side Railroad. We had thrown our breastworks in advance of those we now occupy, and had about completed them. One or more forts or elevated positions for artillery were made on the space occupied by each Brigade, and for convenience these positions were named after the Generals of the Brigades. Fort Archer was on the right, then Fort McRae, &c. There seemed to be no necessity of a strong infantry force so far to the right, and these Brigades were moved further forward towards our left, and a few cavalry pickets were left to hold the new line of works. As soon as this was done the yankees came forward in heavy force and drove the pickets away from the breastworks, taking the line with Forts McRae and Archer and advancing considerable distance beyond. McRae's, Archer's and other commands immediately moved round and drove the enemy back, re-taking Fort McRae and all their former line except Fort Archer and what is on the right of it, which the enemy has held ever since. So it is not true, as reported in the papers that the enemy successfully resisted our attacks on Fort McRae. The enemy successfully held Fort Archer, but our pickets still hold Fort McRae and we have erected a new line of breastworks.

It was still to the right of the places just mentioned that the enemy advanced on the 27th Oct. and surprised and broke across the line held by Butler's Brigade of Cavalry, capturing the camp and also the camp of Dearing's and Young's Brigades, and advanced to the Plank Road that runs from Petersburg south west to Boydton. Here near Rowanty Creek our forces attacked the enemy, resulting in his hurried retreat that night back to his former position. In this engagement McRae's, Mahone's and another Brigade, all under Gen. Mahone, made a flank movement, passing to the left and rear of the yankee force that was on the Plank road. To get in this position we had to pass through a vacancy or gap between the force on the Plank road and the rest of their army to our left while there was fighting immediately on each side of us. The thick woods protected us till we got in position and very soon we charged forward on the Plank road from the rear, surprising and driving the enemy — the object being to confuse them, divide their force and capture the right wing or part next to our lines. We succeeded in confusing the enemy and causing him to fall back.

The enemy had two and perhaps three entire corps on the Plank Road and our flanking force was certainly inefficient for the purpose, and the necessary reinforcements could not be brought up before night. Mahone's Brigade formed on our left (I know nothing of the other Brigade) and we charged forward, driving the enemy and capturing prisoners and cannon, until we reached an open field close to the Plank road. Here at the edge of the wood, most or all of Mahone's Brigade halted, from what cause I know not, while our Brigade charged on to the Road, and finding themselves right among an immense yankee force and entirely unsupported, were compelled to fall back with a loss of four or five hundred prisoners, though not very many killed or wounded. This was a gallant charge — the Brigade went forward with a noble dash and unity through as hot a fire as thousands of excited yankees could make. I am unable at present to give lists of casualties. Gen. McRae displayed his well established coolness and bravery. He has become quite popular and his whole command has full confidence in him.

Truly,
Long Grabs.

[November 17, 1864]

RICHMOND, Nov. 7th.

Messrs. Editors: It gladdens the heart of the soldier to see that efforts are being made to supply him with [undecipherable] and necessaries from home. It is to be regretted some sufficient and systematic arrangement has not [undecipherable] rule to convey packages and boxes to the soldier in the field from their friends at home. I hope that hereafter the army will be amply and promptly accommodated in this matter. [The remainder of this first paragraph was too faded for the microfilming process to copy legibly.]

Then send along supplies to the soldier. It will give cheerfulness to the army as well as relieve actual necessity. It will help to satisfy the soldier with his condition and arouse his feelings of patriotism. And in your generous contributions don't overlook the friendless and the homeless. The poor penniless boy in the ranks who has no place he can call home, and the more aged son of poverty who to defend his cause and yours has left a helpless family dependent on the cold charity of the world deserves as much as any others, and they would appropriately expect it from the community where they had lived. Let it not be then that the poor and unfortunate must stand by in want while others fare sumptuously. When you supply your own loved ones with choice viands send also a few potatoes or a bag of meat to the unfortunate but faithful soldier who has neither a home to go to nor friend to provide for him. From notice in the newspapers it will be seen that boxes, packages, &c., will be sent to the army by certain reliable agents in Fayetteville, Wilmington, Raleigh and elsewhere at Government expense entirely. Should any person wish to go with things himself, I presume these agents would procure the necessary papers for him.

Way-side Hospitals are now established at most stopping places along the Railroads. There is one at Greensboro, established by the State authorities, that is well conducted and is certainly a pleasant and welcome resort for all North Carolinians. It is under charge of Dr. J. L. Neagle of Gaston Co., a kind and attentive man. The domestic management is directed by Mr. Thos. A. Long of Chatham, a most efficient and agreeable man for such a position. The building is too small and it is intended to get a larger one as soon as possible. Dr. Neagle had charge of the State Way-side Hospital at Wilmington for a while and was in the army previously, and Mr. Long was formerly Lieutenant in the 44th N. C. Reg't. Here a soldier is not questioned and looked at as though he was on trial before some self important Provost Marshal, but can simply show his furlough or other evidence of what he is, and he is then welcomed to the best they can afford in such an easy and sincere manner as to make him feel at home and enjoy real old North Carolina hospitality. This place is between the Danville and Central Road where they come together, some 200 yards from each, and about a quarter of a mile east of the depot. The Confederate way side is near the depot in front or south of it.

Richmond still seems full of people and business. A man can buy anything he wants here with money enough, and prices are not so high for most articles as might be expected. I think groceries and clothing can be bought here on better terms than any where else in the Confederacy.

Everything is quiet along the front, but more fighting is expected before the armies go into winter quarters. Gen. Early has recently issued orders prescribing the most rigid discipline for his army. I have never seen a good state of discipline arrived at all of a sudden. It must be effected gradually. There is discipline without tyranny, but oftener tyranny without discipline.

Truly,
Long Grabs.

[November 17, 1864]

Richmond, Va., Nov. 10, 1864.

Messrs. Editors: The people of Cumberland in forming an organization looking to the education of orphans whose fathers died in the army, have undertaken a noble work. But few counties have taken such steps. The only practical and efficient way to accomplish the object in view is to act by communities and counties. A State organization with all necessary funds and officers could not effect as much nor do it as thoroughly as more local bodies. It could establish an institution of a higher grade for the advancement of such as wished to enter it and could be provided for there, and its executive officers could manage the school well. But "let there be light"— the masses must be reached and education must be brought home to the people. Colleges and seminaries greatly benefit a class but are of very little direct advantage to the entire population. Like the great pillars of a house, colleges and universities are the great columns on which rest the structure of education and learning. But of what use would be those majestic pillars were the hundreds of props, posts and joints of the building removed? Then we would behold either a great ruin or a huge mass without shape or harmony and so inverted and bulky as to admit of no repair except from a new foundation. Just so with out primal schools and family education. Drop or neglect them and the learning and civilization of the age will eventually degrade into superstition and barbarism with no living memento of former greatness. Or else, the ambitious, the avaricious and depraved will seize the falling emblems and poison the fountains of learning with their own base sophistry and corrupt customs and thus establish mentally and physically a blighting despotism. So did a corrupt Roman papacy in centuries past usurp alike the halls of learning and temples of religion, and a few priests assumed all the powers of a nation, to which the nation yielded faithfully as it was taught to do. Then also followed the horrid Inquisition as a philanthropic means of reform for the rest of mankind.

The only sure foundation then for education is a universal system of primal schools. Let the counties establish these just as they would county roads or bridges and at the most available places. The county should pay the tuition of such scholars — children of deceased soldiers — as have not, or cannot well spare, the means themselves, and if the orphan needs money to pay his board let that be furnished too. Thus the county becomes the guardian for the orphan — and might also require a consideration or remuneration from the orphan to the effect that he or she should for a while teach other orphans in the county free of charge. They might even go further and require them to refund the expense of their education with an annual percent of their wages for some years. If they would repay ten or twenty dollars a year for several years from their wages it would amount to a large sum. It is no injury but generally an advantage for a young man or woman to commence life slightly in debt. People often think that scholars in school who are paid for by the public are ridiculed by other scholars. This is a mistake. It is not at school that the distinction of poverty and wealth is carried out, but at home under the direct teaching of the children's own mothers. If a poor boy in school (or a poor man) happens to be a dunce or a thief he is regarded a worse dunce or thief just because he is poor. And the opposite is equally true. If he is talented, popular, &c., he attracts more favorable attention on account of his poverty. If a boy or girl at school be even a poor orphan and possess the proper elements of ability and traits of character, he or she will always at school, and very often elsewhere, gain the affection of companions and take a high stand in any circle. If the parents of poor children want to do away with those great distinctions between rich and poor children, in my opinion they effect more by sending them to the same school and associating them together as much as possible, then by keeping them secluded, and especially if the teacher has been a poor orphan.

But no matter what a burden poverty may be on the minds of some people, the child of the man who fell in defence of his country will never be derided or frowned on by the Southern people, young or old. The children of deserters and criminals may possibly be more unfortunate, but they will receive generous sympathy and aid if merited. For one I am opposed to throwing young orphans from all sections together in charity schools. It may do for cities, but not elsewhere. They are there habituated to strange associations, and have no way of cultivating filial affections. They soon recognize their condition — poverty is their lot — and they feel they must remain a class of isolated inferiors. Some hideous, long faced, blue nosed yankee school mistress is the only familiar source from which they can derive ideas of human greatness and nobleness, and she is also their model of accomplishments and character. In such a prison they are generally trained till in maturity of years they are thrown out on the path of life. Here they are apt to be utterly paralyzed about what to do and how, and very probably fall back into those retrograding habits which so often prove a fatal and unknown ruin. Let the orphan stay among his friends and childish associations, and there let him grow up in the way he should go, with equal opportunities and on an equal footing with the rest of the world.

The general Government and the State government, even after their present arduous duties are done, will have enough of their own pecuniary affairs to attend to for years. There seems then no feasible plan but the one indicated, and it should be at once adopted with economy and vigor. The demoralization and corruption resulting from this vast war are already alarming. We must keep the great lever of society in motion, else the physical may soon predominate over the moral elements of our being.

Truly,
Long Grabs.

[November 21, 1864]

While recovering from his wounds, McSween had a chance to think about his stinging letter to Vance. He also had a chance to see the documentation of his case. Now convinced that Vance *had* acted in his behalf, he sends an apology.

Hospital 24 — Richmond
Nov. 21st, 1864

Gov. Z. B. Vance,
Dear Sir:

It affords me pleasure to correct a misunderstanding between us in reference to your actions on the case between Col. Jones and myself. I have made efforts to procure a copy of the proceedings in the case and also all endorsement and correspondence relating to it but failed to obtain the information. I had been unable to apply in person either by disability by wound or close confinement to duty with the company. So no opportunity has been presented for access to these papers till now while I am here in hospital and sufficiently recovered to attend to the matter in person. I have just examined the record of the case, endorsements on it &c and am now convinced that my complaint as to your motive and earnestness in your effort with the President in my behalf is groundless. I find that your letters to the President were strongly in my favor and also presented many facts and merits of the case not so plainly visible in the regular proceedings. This no doubt aided materially in securing the sympathy of the authorities here in my favor and in arousing their indignation against my opponents or persecutors.

Under a misapprehension I addressed you in a harsh and indignant manner at which you might justly feel offended though not so insulted as you seemed to indicate. With patience exhausted and a spirit though never to be subdued yet smarting the more under a burden of insults and indignities and feeling that I had been trifled with — my cause abandoned — the efforts of my friends — justice — truth — all ignored and my enemies adhered to and their favor courted perhaps for their more available influence afterwards &c &c — all combined to put me in the proper frame of mind to say almost any thing to any body and in any form. I was wrong — hasty, and displayed imprudence and disrespect and I sincerely regret that there was any cause for offense to one whose manly energies [undecipherable] devoted to the welfare of his countrymen and the propriety of the cause. As a duty then — a matter of justice as well as generosity — I would ask your pardon for the offence stated; or, if it be insult, then I retract it.[4]

Truly and Respectfully Yours,
M. J. McSween

RICHMOND, Dec. 1st, 1864.

Messrs. Editors: Autumn, the sabbath of the year, has closed, and the "seer yellow leaf" now flutters in the chilly breeze of winter. The mellow Indian summer has passed into a thing of memory — an emblem of olden peace times.

I regret to see manifestations of party feelings and disagreements in our Legislature. I believe, as I have often said heretofore, that the promotion of more parties among us in times like the present destroys patriotism and counteracts our efforts toward independence. The times demand forbearance and the abandonment of former prejudices. All must make sacrifices for our common interest and common safety; and selfish or partisan interests should not force us from the plain path of duty nor weaken the great cause on which our existence depends. There are complaints and abuses; "rights of men and rights of things;" and "public wrongs and private wrongs," and much else that is oppressive, unprotected, and uncorrected; but we should promptly heal these defects or patriotically endure them. The paramount duty of every citizen, politically, it seems to me, is to remain true and devoted to his country under all circumstances. The patriot will not try to produce strife and ruin in his own home and native land because things are not done as he wishes.

This great war has its glories, its majesty, its grand deeds of patriotism, and its heroes and martyrs, but it has its private wrongs and griefs; its cruelties and tyrannies; and its unknown deeds of villainy and malice. The page of the historian will shine in dazzling brilliancy with our victories, our sacrifices and our struggles; but must fade into deep blackness of the horrible story of private injustice and outrage, of numberless betrayals, bereavements, and oppressions; and of "man's inhumanity to man." Many a ray of merit has been extinguished, many a noble soul crushed to misery and many a fond hope blighted by base and cruel means. The soldiers have borne more of the hardships of this war than any of our people, and they are generally the most hopeful and determined on our success. Many soldiers however give way in discouragement, or more often under injustice and cruelty, and desert their comrades. Many good men have fallen victims to this rash fatality. Desertion cannot possibly improve the soldier's situation, let the cause be what it may. Although his superior in rank may treat him as a brute and even torture him into agony, I cannot see wherein desertion would be a remedy; it would most certainly make the matter worse. His enemies would then have good opportunity to wreak their malice and revenge on him, and he would forfeit much of respect and sympathy from friends. The deserter must live in concealment and dread. He cannot eat at his own table nor sit in domestic quiet around his own fireside. He cannot rise with the sun like an honest freeman and follow his plow in broad daylight as he once did, but must lie in some hidden recess in gloomy thought and stupid fear. He consumes the food of his troubled wife and suffering children and can afford them no assistance in return. He comes generally to ruin and disgrace — and perhaps dies in infamy, leaving a lasting odium on his innocent family. Two or three leading men in the South or in North Carolina did not put us into this war. We went into it willingly ourselves. If we did not originate or recommend the secession of the Southern States and the forming of the Confederacy, we consented to it. We refused to act in the matter at first, but when Lincoln declared war almost every man in the State at once determined to resist coercion of sovereign [undecipherable] volunteering or aiding in some way. We were all in for the thing then, and we can't deny it. Suppose we all had continued our refusal to act in the matter and kept out of it, what would the two or three "leading men" do to us about it?

As this war went on, however, the difficulties and hardships of the thing got more severe and we found we had more than we bargained for. Then many began to complain and try to disown their connection with it in any way. But we are in it now and must come out successfully or submit to ruin. In such a crisis, soldiers, there is no plainer duty then to perform the duty your own native State has assigned to you. To that State you owe what political rights and protection you have enjoyed, and she now expects you to defend her. By a solemn act of her own, through a large majority of your countrymen, she has placed on you these responsibilities. That good old State has never been untrue to you. She has nourished you and provided for you, and it is your highest duty to remain devotedly attached to the land of your homes and firesides. Then, be our fate what it may, stand by your colors, boys, and be forever true to the honor and interests of the Old North State. Officers and superiors may sometimes treat you basely and rascally, but your country does not. Many are the petty grievances and disappointments inflicted on you in this way, but this is human nature. You can work and worry till you get these pests removed and give their places to more worthy men. There is always a lawful way to correct wrongs and redress injuries, and be assured that the best and largest portion of mankind will sustain you in pursuing this course. Then plant yourselves firmly on sound principles and remain forever true to your country in all respects, though you may not be true to scoundrels in office.

Truly,
Long Grabs.

[December 22, 1864]

Camp McRae's Brigade.
Near Petersburg, Va., Feb'y 22, 1865.

Messrs. Editors:— Perhaps I may have been regarded as negligent and indifferent as your correspondent for not appearing your columns for several weeks past. Through the irregularity of the mails a month or more ago some of my letters to you were lost and for some time past my duties have been so heavy that I had not time to write to you as I wished. We have been pretty closely confined to one locality and there have been but few opportunities to get news of items of interest. The day time here is almost entirely devoted to army duties by those who have most to do, and the scarcity of candles and other means of light prevents writing or study at night. So that after dark we have to crowd into our little huts and play the game of "sockum" and sing corn-shucking songs till bed time.

We have been on the line in front of the enemy several miles southwest of Petersburg during the winter. The weather has often been extremely severe, but the troops have all enjoyed much of comfort and very good health. Our rations are enough to live on, but were it not for supplies from home many a North Carolina soldier would suffer. The greatest injustice or deficiency the soldier has experienced this winter was short rations, and above all things this should be remedied if possible. Soldiers here from North Carolina and most of Virginia and South Carolina are generally able to get supplies from home, but these from other States have not been thus favored. People at home, if they have to spare, cannot send too much eatables to the army. But this is a great time for robbery and swindling and great care must be exercised or boxes and packages will be lost or stolen. Good barrels are better, safer and more convenient for conveying supplies than large boxes. It is always better to send provisions raw — just simply meal, flour, bacon, beef, potatoes, turnips, peas. The army has ample opportunity for cooking, and the provisions can be saved so much longer raw than cooked.

The army has suffered much inconvenience from not being paid regularly and promptly. The private soldier at the front should be paid of the first and best, and it is a disgraceful shame that such injustice should be allowed.

We have been under marching orders here pretty often and on the 5th inst. were in a fight some two miles farther to the right. The enemy with very heavy force — thought to be 50,000 — moved towards our right, and extended his line farther along, parallel to our line, and a half mile or more nearer to our line than his former line was. Our position is still the same — that is, our line of works and the enemy's line of works is now near where our outside pickets were before. Our Brigade did not suffer much in the engagement of the 5th, and we were not in the actions of the 6th and 7th, but there was some severe fighting some of the time by other troops. The enemy was repulsed with considerable loss in his main attempts, and except this there was nothing decisive or important in the whole affair. Serg't D. A. McIntosh, Co. I, 26th N. C. Reg't, from Taylorsville, Alexander Co., was killed Feb'y 5th. He was an excellent young man and much esteemed. Private A. Robinson of the same company, from Caldwell Co. was also killed. But few if any others were killed in the brigade; several were wounded — only a few badly. Notwithstanding the general demoralizing influence over the country, I will be more punctual hereafter.

Truly,
LONG GRABS.

[March 9, 1865]

Chapter 8

Fayetteville, North Carolina: Reconstruction Years

Long Grabs wrote his last letter from Petersburg on February 22, 1865, and the *Fayetteville Observer* published it on March 9, 1865. Exactly one month later on April 9, General Lee surrendered the approximately 25,000 men remaining in the Army of Northern Virginia to General Grant. The 26th Regiment North Carolina Troops surrendered 137 soldiers. I did not find Murdoch John McSween's name on the list of those receiving paroles at Appomattox.

After the war McSween returned to Richmond County, North Carolina, and studied law once more. On June 16, 1866, the following article was published in the *Old North State*, Salisbury, North Carolina:

Supreme Court.

The following gentlemen were licensed to practice law in the County Courts of this State, on Monday last, after due examination. We are happy to state, that while this is the largest class which has been before the Court at any one time, it is the opinion of the Court that it is the best average class and better sustained their examination, than any previous one. We wish them a bright future.[1]

The article contained a listing of over fifty lawyers, and among them was one Murdoch J. McSween of Richmond County.

The Civil War brought destruction to many small farms in North Carolina, and farmers were slow to recover during the period of Reconstruction. Richmond County was no exception. The state of Maryland had sent a shipment of corn and bacon for distribution to the poor of the South. Editor McSween would later write in October 1868 of a trial taking place in Richmond County, charging that the person distributing corn and bacon did not do it fairly.[2] In May he is still practicing law, and in a letter to the *New York Times*, the substance of which was published on May 27, 1868, McSween wrote to Mayor Hoffman seeking assistance for these men and their families.

General City News.

Distress in North Carolina — Mayor Hoffman yesterday received from Mr. M. J. McSween, of Rockingham, Richmond County, North Carolina, a letter begging him to make some effort to obtain relief for the small farmers, white and black, in that section of the country, who, the writer of the letter says, will soon be in a starving condition. Their crops, wheat and rye, cannot be harvested before the 1st of July, and in the meantime their stock of provisions will be completely exhausted. From two to five hundred bushels of corn would, if sent immediately, be of great assistance in eking out their scanty stock of grain. The laborers are said to be better off than the small farmers, as they can obtain plenty of work on the railroads and need no assistance. Mayor Hoffman will gladly receive at his office any contributions handed in for the relief of the people of Rockingham.[3]

John Thompson Hoffman (1828–1888) was mayor of New York City from 1866 to 1868 and was twice elected governor of the state. No information was found on the response to McSween's plea for assistance or why McSween chose to write to him for assistance.

In 1868, McSween began publishing a newspaper, *The Eagle*, in Fayetteville, North Carolina, and two fellow newspapers took notice of it. The *Wilmington Daily Journal* wrote on August 21, 1868: "We welcome to our sanctum *The Eagle*, published in Fayetteville. Its editorial columns are under charge of our friend, M. J. McSween, who has acquired a reputation in this State as the correspondent of the glorious *Fayetteville Observer*, under the nom de plume of LONG GRABS. The Eagle enters at once with spirit and ability into canvass, and we look to it for efficient aid. It has our best wishes for success."[4]

On September 4, 1868, the *Watchman* and *Old North State*, of Salisbury, North Carolina, followed with its own laudatory comments:

NEW PAPER.

We have received the first two numbers of *The Eagle*, a new paper just started at Fayetteville, N. C., by M. J. McSween & Co., M. J. McSween Editor. It is handsome well printed and [undecipherable] and an ardent supporter of Seymour and Blair. Mr. McSween [was well] known during the war as "Long Grabs," of the *Fayetteville Observer*. Success to the enterprise.[5]

In the August 18, 1868, edition of *The Eagle*, McSween discussed the principles and intentions under which his newspaper would operate.

In assuming editorial control of the EAGLE, duty as well as custom, requires that I make known the principles and intentions of the paper. The wisdom and success of the enterprise is with the future. I am aware of the very difficult and responsible duties of an editor, and of my incompetency to discharge those duties properly. This place is not of my own seeking. [I] yield to the earnest and repeated solicitations of friends [undecipherable] my humble abilities, in defence

8. Fayetteville, North Carolina: Reconstruction Years   233

of Liberty, of Peace, and of Law. I prefer a quiet life and the quiet pursuit of my professional business. But in this day of revolution, danger and ruin, every man should remain at his post of duty, wherever that post may be and there do with his might whatsoever his hands find to do. I shall therefore support, with all the power that in me lies, the noble principles of the great Democratic Party, as announced in the Platform adopted by the National Convention in July last. I shall also advocate the election of that able statesman, Horatio Seymour, and gallant soldier, Frank P. Blair, to the chief executive offices of the nation. I shall endeavor to trace out and expose the corruption, illegality and despotism of our State and national governments.

I shall not hesitate also to give the biography of that filthy creature, the scalawag, and his mate, the carpet-bagger, a species of vermin that inhabit the "body politic" in time of severe "national disease." I shall devote myself particularly to the interests of North Carolina and to the welfare and prosperity of all her honest, industrious, and good people, white and black. And both before and after the election, I shall try to make the EAGLE a safe, reliable, instructive and amusing newspaper to all. I ask in advance, the forbearance and sympathy of an indulgent public. I am young in years, young in the wily ways of the world, and young in all that knowledge so necessary to conduct a literary and political paper. I ask the aid of this liberal community and of my friends throughout the country to sustain me in this undertaking, and I will endeavor to meet their expectations and hopes. I wish to avoid profane abuse and spread-eagle displays and will follow reason, sense and duty; but in imitation of the American emblem, I build my eyrie on that high, firm rock of the Constitution, where the sun of Peace shines in all splendor under the broad canopy of Liberty.—M. J. McSween.[6]

On August 12, 1869, McSween published an editorial in which he looked back over his first year as an editor.

Of course our business is small compared with that of the large city papers. We have practiced close economy and fair management to do what we have done. We have not been able to have all the labor and assistance necessary. The editor of this paper has to engage in the drudgery of office work, proof-reading, localizing, collecting bills, reporting, bookkeeping, business correspondence, &c., all at once, in addition to reading, thinking, writing and selecting. We have no time to loaf on the streets, and but little chance to form acquaintances in town, or drum up custom. We are also prevented from the delightful enjoyment of ladies' society, and can seldom be with that charming, lovely, angelic creature whom we adore.

We came here a year ago at a week's notice and without preparation to undertake a work entirely new, most laborious and responsible. We knew nothing of printing, and had never struck a lick of editorial work in our life. Almost before we had crossed Mallett's bridge in the edge of town, our future "devil" was dunning us for "copy." We had hardly put on a clean shirt before we were called on to read "proof." We had left our law practice right in the middle, and letters and messages continued to flood on us about administrators, bankruptcy, dower, the remnants of imaginary estates, defunct New York claims, &c., and still the cry was "more copy," new subscribers, and special contracts about nondescript advertising.

But we have paid our way through, although we spent a few hundred dollars that might have been saved, had we known more of the newspaper business. Capitalists, both of the fickle and fogy kind, put in their enormous share of stock, in the original purchase, and they have not darkened our door with their money or their hideous faces, from that day to this. So financially, we have had to "root hog or die." When we came here a year ago, it was of course uncertain we would be with the EAGLE more than a year. We had thought we might run the paper awhile, gain a world-wide reputation, marry rich, and then return to our numerous and highly elated constituency at Rockingham, to go to the Legislature a few times, and finally be elected to Congress.

But though our success has not been so great, nor so showy, it has been substantial, and very satisfactory, and in many respects most cheering. The EAGLE has become a power in the land, and we are happy to believe that good has resulted from our labors. We are proud to know that our bold, fearless course for the right against the wrong, is appreciated by the public, and that we strike a chord of sympathy in the bosoms of thousands of true Carolinians, although our homes and hearts are subjugated. Our lot is with our noble, but unfortunate people. Their sorrows are our sorrows, their happiness our happiness. In childhood and youth we shared their destiny. We shared with them the glories, the dangers, the wounds, the cruelties of near five years of war. We have also shared with them the troubles, the degradation, the poverty, the despotism, and the pain of near five years military reconstruction and mongrel government.

While there is prospect to build up old Fayetteville or to make North Carolina flourish, we shall stay and work night and day for such results. If after all reasonable effort, these objects cannot be secured, then in self-defence, THE EAGLE will take his flight in sadness and sorrow, to some brighter and better country. There is now most encouraging hope both for our town and the good old state. We shall stay to cherish and realize these bright hopes. We shall claw harder and fly higher. We shall say what we please, and do what we honestly believe to be right. We have established a paper in one year among the poor sand hills, away from telegraphs and rail roads, that is nearly equal in circulation and influence, to the best papers in the state, and far ahead of many that are better situated and supported. We do ask and expect, an increased patronage from our business community, and we hope to merit a continuance of that liberal support which a generous public has so freely bestowed heretofore. We have fought for Conservatism [Democrats] against Radicalism [Republicans], liberality against proscription, for liberty and truth against force and fraud. We shall do so still.[7]

In the following years McSween would travel in the state, visiting Richmond County often, and traveling to Georgia, South Carolina, and as far west as Tennessee. He would gather information about how each state was doing under Reconstruction, and as always would be seeking new subscribers, selling advertising, and collecting bills.

In Tennessee he married Mary Katherine McSween — no relation. She was born in 1843 and was a daughter of William McSween. The ceremony took place in Hamblen County, Tennessee, in 1873, and the couple returned to Fayetteville, North Carolina, that same year. Sorrow touched their lives the following year with the birth and death within a few days of a daughter. They would later have a son, William Daniel McSween, born in June 1875.

On December 7, 1874, McSween wrote an editorial in which he expressed a desire not to have to travel so much. Part of it is excerpted here.

> The readers of *The Eagle* need not think that I love to be away from home so much. I am compelled to travel over the country to collect part of what is due me for the paper. For near seven years these bills have been accumulating all over the counties of this section. Especially for the whole past year of panic and business distress, we, like all others, have kept up a large credit business, and have waited long and hopingly with most of our patrons to pay their dues. The amount of these dues is surprisingly large, enough to provide every necessary and to enable us to gratify a long-felt ambition of establishing two useful newspapers, one in Fayetteville and the other in Raleigh.[8]

McSween would never achieve this ambition.

In April 1875, under the heading "To the Old Subscribers of *The Eagle*," he published a decision he had made. Part is excerpted here. "We have moved our paper from Fayetteville to Charlotte where we expect to publish Daily and Weekly. We decided on this removal about the 1st of January last, and closed business at Fayetteville. We had hoped to collect up accounts and settle up affairs of the office enough to buy a new outfit, get located in Charlotte, enlarge our paper and be issuing *The Eagle Daily* and *Weekly* by middle or last of February."

He tried to collect on what was due him but could not get enough for this purpose. He was unsuccessful in trying to sell the old material; no purchaser was available. He packed everything up and shipped it to Charlotte. However, the North Carolina Railroad was changing gauges, so he did not get into an office nor receive the material till early April.

This he attributed to

> the failure of our patrons to pay us what they have been owing us so long. Out of eight ot ten thousand dollars due us, three thousand would have been enough to put *The Eagle, Daily* and *Weekly*, in complete new outfit. The times are hard, but a large number of our patrons could have given us better treatment than this.
>
> We shall drop off several hundred of our old subscribers, but do so in no unkindness, and will be glad to serve them again when they pay up.
>
> In leaving Rockfish, Barbecue, and Drowning Creek we do not propose to forget old friends, the McNeils, McLeods, McLeans, McGaskills, [a long list of Macs is included here]. Mecklenburg is an old Scorch-Irish country and the Mack's here are second cousins to the rest of us.

We will visit our old section of country occasionally. We hope and earnestly ask that each old friend and subscriber of *The Eagle* will go to work for its success, and whenever opportunity offers to get new subscribers and send us business, news and information of any kind. We expect to keep up regular reports of markets and local news from Fayetteville, Wilmington, and Raleigh, and to supply latest telegraph news and market reports from abroad, to improve in all respects, and maintain the same old honored principles.[9]

Although his editorial seemed hopeful and optimistic, *The Eagle* ceased publication in 1875.

Long Grabs and his family returned to Tennessee.

Murdock John McSween died January 5, 1880, in Newport, Cocke County, Tennessee. His widow died in 1921. Their son also died in Newport in 1945. His son (Murdock's grandson), Donald Murdock McSween, was born in 1915 and died in 1979.

Chapter Notes

Introduction

1. Editorial published in the *Fayetteville Observer* (Fayetteville, NC), April 16, 1863.
2. Article published in the *Fayetteville Observer* (Fayetteville, NC), January 15, 1863.
3. Jacob Nathaniel Raymer, *Confederate Correspondent: The Civil War Reports of Jacob Nathaniel Raymer, 4th North Carolina*, ed. E. B. Munson (Jefferson, NC: McFarland, 2009).
4. Letter published in the *Fayetteville Observer* (Fayetteville, NC), March 16, 1863.
5. Letter published in the *Fayetteville Observer* (Fayetteville, NC), February 9, 1863.
6. Letter published in the *Fayetteville Observer* (Fayetteville, NC), March 16, 1863.
7. Letter published in the *Fayetteville Observer* (Fayetteville, NC), June 22, 1863.
8. Letter published in the *Fayetteville Observer* (Fayetteville, NC), June 29, 1863.
9. Letter published in the *Fayetteville Observer* (Fayetteville, NC), November 10, 1862.
10. Letter published in the *Fayetteville Observer* (Fayetteville, NC), January 8, 1863.
11. Letter published in the *Fayetteville Observer* (Fayetteville, NC), April 18, 1863.
12. Letter published in the *Fayetteville Observer* (Fayetteville, NC), July 21, 1864.
13. Editorial published in the *Fayetteville Observer* (Fayetteville, NC), September 8, 1864.
14. Louis A. Manarin and Weymouth T. Jordan, Jr., comps., *North Carolina Troops, 1861–1865: A Roster* (Raleigh, NC, Division of Archives and History, Department of Cultural Resources, 1966–), Vol. 7, p. 465.
15. Article reprinted in the *Carolina Watchman* (Salisbury, NC), January 28, 1880.
16. Andrew McMillan to Gov. Zebulon B. Vance, October 17, 1863, Governors' Papers, State Archives, Office of Archives and History, Raleigh, NC.
17. Letter published in *The Eagle* (Fayetteville, NC), June 5, 1869.
18. University of North Carolina at Chapel Hill, *Alumni History of the University of North Carolina, 1795–1924*, 2nd ed. (Durham, NC: Christian & King Printing Company, 1924), p. 404.
19. Howard P. Nash, Edward H. Virgin, and William Collin Levere, *The Sixth General Catalogue of Sigma Alpha Epsilon* (Evanston, IL: Sigma Alpha Epsilon, 1904), p. 269.
20. Stephen B. Weeks, ed., *Register of Members of the Philanthropic Society, Instituted in the University of North Carolina, August 1st, 1795*, 4th ed. (Raleigh, NC: Edwards, Broughton & Co., Power Printers and Binders, 1887), p. 44.
21. Murdock J. McSween to Thomas Ruffin, September 27, 1858, *The Papers of Thomas Ruffin*, J. G. De Roulhac Hamilton, ed. Publication of the North Carolina Historical Commission (Raleigh, NC: Edwards & Broughton Printing Company, State Printers, 1918), pp. 610–611.
22. Letter published in the *Fayetteville Observer* (Fayetteville, NC), May 2, 1863.
23. Kemp P. Battle, *History of the University of North Carolina from Its Beginning to the Death of President Swain, 1789–1868* (Raleigh, NC: Edwards & Broughton Printing Company, 1907), p. 815.
24. Letter published in the *Charleston Courier Tri-Weekly* (Charleston, SC), March 8, 1860.

25. Manarin and Jordan, *A Roster,* Vol. 10, p. 48. (Hereafter referred to as *A Roster.*) Oliver Hart Dockery was a planter in Richmond County prior to his enlistment in the 38th Regiment NCT. He was elected Captain of Company E in October 1861 and in January 1862, elected Lieutenant Colonel of the Regiment.

26. *A Roster,* Vol. 10, p. 48. Duncan G. McRae was a lawyer in Richmond County prior to enlisting in the 38th Regiment NCT. He began his military career as a Corporal and rose through the ranks to Captain. He was killed at Chancellorsville, May 3, 1863.

27. *A Roster,* Vol. 9, p. 358. Matthew W. Ransom became Colonel of the 35th in 1862. Wounded at Malvern Hill, he was appointed Brigadier-General in 1863.

28. *A Roster,* Vol. 9, p. 358. John G. Jones began his military career as Captain of Company E. He was promoted to Colonel of the regiment upon Ransom's promotion to Brigadier-General. He was killed in action at Petersburg, Virginia, in June 1864.

Chapter 1

1. Eighth Census of the United States, 1860, Population (Washington: GPO, 1864), pp. 348–363.

2. "State of North Carolina — A Proclamation," published in the weekly *Raleigh Register* (Raleigh, NC), February 6, 1861.

3. *Raleigh Register* (Raleigh, NC), March 13, 1861.

4. "What Should North Carolina Do Now?," *Raleigh Register*(Raleigh, NC), April 17, 1861.

5. "Proclamation of Abraham Lincoln," published in the *Raleigh Register* (Raleigh, NC), April 17, 1861.

6. United States War Department, The War of the Rebellion: A Compilation of the Official Records of the Union and Confederate Armies (hereafter referred to as O.R.), Ser. 3, Vol. 1, pp. 68–69.

7. O.R., Ser. 3, Vol. 1, p. 72.

8. "A Proclamation by John W. Ellis, Governor of North Carolina," *The Daily Register* (Raleigh, NC), April 20, 1861.

9. Barrett, John G., *The Civil War in North Carolina* (Chapel Hill: The University of North Carolina Press, 1963).

10. "Governor Ellis's Message to the General Assembly of North Carolina," *Fayetteville Observer* (Fayetteville, NC), May 6, 1861.

11. Notice published in the *Daily Register* (Raleigh, NC), April 27, 1861.

12. *A Roster,* Vol. 9, p. 251. In April 1862, Richard H. Riddick was appointed Colonel of the 34th Regiment, North Carolina Troops. During the fight at Gaines' Mill, Virginia, on June 27, 1862, he was wounded but later returned to duty. On September 1, 1862, while leading the 34th at the Battle of Ox Hill, Virginia, he was mortally wounded and died September 7, 1862.

13. Orders published in *The Weekly Raleigh Register* (Raleigh, NC), May 1, 1861.

14. Samuel A. Ashe, ed., *Biographical History of North Carolina from Colonial Times to the Present* (Greensboro, NC: Charles L. Van Noppen, Publisher, 1905–1917), Vol. 7, p. 142. Daniel Harvey Hill (1821–1889) was one of North Carolina's best combat commanders, but a tendency to be critical of his associates, especially General Braxton Bragg, "led to his removal from command and his enforced inactivity."

15. "Governor Ellis's Message to the General Assembly of North Carolina," *Fayetteville Observer* (Fayetteville, NC), May 6, 1861.

Chapter 2

1. OR, IV, Ser. 1, 574.

2. OR, IV, Ser. 1, 575.

3. *A Roster,* Vol. 10, p. 54. Dempsey R. McInnis was a planter in Richmond County prior to his enlistment. He was mustered in as First Sergeant and served with the 38th North Carolina Regiment until his death from disease at Camp Gregg, Virginia, in May 1863.

4. Letter published in the *Fayetteville Observer* (Fayetteville, NC), December 30, 1861.

5. News item published in the *Fayetteville Observer* (Fayetteville, NC), February 3, 1862.

6. *A Roster,* Vol. 10, p. 48. Duncan G. McRae was a lawyer in Richmond County when he enlisted in 1861 in the 38th North Carolina Regiment. He began his military career as a Corporal and came up through the ranks to captain a company. He was killed May 3, 1863, at the Battle of Chancellorsville, Virginia. He is described in the records as "a good officer" who was "noted for bravery."

7. Notice published in the *Fayetteville Observer* (Fayetteville, NC), May 12, 1862.
8. Notice published in the *Fayetteville Observer* (Fayetteville, NC), July 7, 1862.
9. Editorial statement published in the *Fayetteville Observer* (Fayetteville, NC), July, 24, 1862.
10. News item published in the *Fayetteville Observer* (Fayetteville, NC), July 21, 1862.
11. Barrett, *The Civil War in North Carolina,* Chapter 2.
12. Sequestration Act information published in the *Fayetteville Observer* (Fayetteville, NC), September 9, 1861.
13. *A Roster,* Vol. 5, p. 6. Collett Leventhorpe, previously Colonel of the 34th North Carolina Regiment, assumed command of the 11th North Carolina Regiment in March 1862. At the Battle of Gettysburg he sustained wounds in his left arm and was captured. He was held a prisoner at several camps and was later paroled at Camp Lookout, Maryland, in March 1864. He never sufficiently recovered from his wounds for further service and resigned on April 27, 1864.
14. *A Roster,* Vol. 5, p. 1.
15. *A Roster,* Vol. 12, p. 149. Marshall D. Craton, formerly Lieutenant Colonel of the 35th North Carolina Regiment, was appointed Colonel of the 50th North Carolina Regiment in April 1862. Ill health forced him to resign his commission on December 1, 1862.
16. *A Roster,* Vol. 3, p. 543 (3rd); Vol. 5, p. 264 (13th); Vol. 12, p. 276 (51st). John Lucas Cantwell, formerly Captain of Company D, 13th Battalion North Carolina Infantry, was appointed Colonel of the 51st North Carolina Regiment in April 1862, but resigned in October of the same year for personal reasons. Returning to the service in November 1863, he was appointed Captain of Company F, 3rd North Carolina Regiment. Captured at the Battle of Spotsylvania Court House, Virginia, he moved through various prisoner of war camps until he was released at Fort Delaware, Delaware, on May 26, 1865.
17. *A Roster,* Vol. 12, p. 415. James Keith Marshall was killed at the Battle of Gettysburg, July 3, 1863.
18. *A Roster,* Vol. 12, p. 415. Wounded in both legs, Marcus A. Parks was captured during the Battle of Gettysburg, July 3, 1863, and held a prisoner of war until exchanged March 22, 1865.
19. *A Roster,* Col. 12, p. 415. John Q. Richardson was shot and killed instantly at the Battle of Gettysburg, July 3, 1863.
20. Letter published in the *Fayetteville Observer* (Fayetteville Observer), May 5, 1862.
21. *A Roster,* Vol. 13, pp. 118–119. William F. Martin commanded the 7th Regiment North Carolina Volunteers in its first organization. He and his regiment were captured at Fort Hatteras on North Carolina's Outer Banks on August 29, 1861. Martin was held a prisoner of war at forts in New York and Boston harbors. Later exchanged, he returned to North Carolina. The 7th was renumbered the 17th North Carolina Regiment with Martin as its Colonel again.
22. *A Roster,* Vol. 13, p. 64. James Johnston Iredell, born in 1828, served as Major of the 53rd North Carolina Regiment. He was killed at the Battle of Spotsylvania Court House, Virginia, May 10, 1864.
23. *A Roster,* Vol. 13, p. 247. John Wimbish was appointed Colonel of the 54th North Carolina Regiment in May 1862. He was about 50 years old at the time. He later resigned in September of the same year for business reasons.
24. *A Roster,* Vol. 5, p. 393 (14th), Vol. 12, p. 7 (45th). Junius Daniel was a West Point graduate and United States Army officer. He was appointed Colonel of the 14th North Carolina Regiment in June 1861 and elected Colonel of the 45th North Carolina Regiment in April 1862. He was promoted to Brigadier-General in September 1862 and was mortally wounded while leading his brigade in action at the Battle of Spotsylvania Court House in May 1864.
25. *A Roster,* Vol. 10, p. 293. Thomas S. Kenan was Captain of Company A and Lieutenant Colonel of the 43rd North Carolina Regiment before being promoted to the Colonelcy in April 1862. He was wounded at Gettysburg on the third day of the battle and taken prisoner. He spent the remainder of the war in prisoner of war camps.
26. *A Roster,* Vol. 10, p. 293. William Gaston Lewis assumed command of the 43rd Regiment after Col. Kenan was wounded and captured. Lewis was promoted to Brigadier-General on May 31, 1864.
27. Samuel A. Ashe, ed., *Biographical His-*

tory of North Carolina from Colonial Times to the Present (Greensboro, NC: Charles L. Van Noppen, Publisher, 1905–1917), Vol. 2, pp. 250–258.

28. *A Roster,* Vol. 13, p. 64. William Allison Owens was later wounded May 12, 1864, at Spotsylvania Court House, Virginia. He returned to duty in July 1864. Owens was severely wounded in the fight at Snicker's Ferry on the Shenandoah River in Virginia on July 18, 1864, and died the next day.

29. *A Roster,* Vol. 13, p. 64. James Turner Morehead, Jr., was Captain of Company C in the 45th North Carolina Regiment before his appointment as Lieutenant Colonel of the 43rd. He was wounded on the first day of the Battle of Gettysburg and returned to duty in the fall. Upon the death of Colonel Owens, he was promoted to the Colonelcy of the regiment. He was wounded on September 22, 1864, in the fight at Fisher's Hill near Winchester, Virginia. Captured at Fort Stedman, Virginia, March 25, 1865, he was held a prisoner of war and released in June 1865.

30. *A Roster,* Vol. 13, p. 64. James Johnston Iredell, Major of the 53rd North Carolina Regiment, killed at the Battle of Spotsylvania Court House, Virginia, May 10, 1864.

31. *A Roster,* Vol. 13, p. 47. Alexander Pope McDaniel was a physician in Guilford County before enlisting at the age of 42. He resigned in September 1862 due to chronic illness.

32. *A Roster,* Vol. 13, p. 78. Joseph Harvey White was a South Carolinian and a graduate of Davidson College. He was wounded at Gettysburg and killed at the Battle of Spotsylvania Court House, Virginia, May 12, 1864.

33. *A Roster,* Vol. 13, p. 89. John S. Leach resigned his commission in March 1863 due to illness.

34. *A Roster,* Vol. 13, p. 99. David Scott, Jr., was a Private in the 1st Regiment North Carolina Infantry, the "Bethel" Regiment. Elected company Captain in April 1862, Scott contracted a disease that impaired his vision, and he resigned in April 1863.

35. *A Roster,* Vol. 13, p. 109. James Currie Norman resigned his commission in December 1862 due to illness.

36. *A Roster,* Vol. 13, 119. George M. G. Albright, a farmer, enlisted at age 34. On the first day's fight at Gettysburg, his right leg was shattered, requiring its amputation. He was captured and taken to a hospital in Frederick, Maryland, where he died July 16, 1863.

37. *A Roster,* Vol. 13, p. 131. George W. Clark was a physician prior to his enlistment. No reason was given for his resignation in May 1862.

38. *A Roster,* Vol. 13, p. 138. Spotswood Bassett Taylor was ill on a number of occasions during his term of service and resigned in November 1863 because of it.

39. *A Roster,* Vol. 13, 149. Eber A. Jerome enlisted at age 39. He resigned his commission in June 1862.

40. *A Roster,* Vol. 13, p. 161. William J. Miller was a farmer prior to enlisting at age 24. He was killed on the first day of the Battle of Gettysburg.

41. *A Roster,* Vol. 12, p. 20. William Adlai Eliason had previously served with the 7th North Carolina Regiment. He was appointed Lieutenant Colonel of the 49th Regiment in April 1862 and served until June 1862, when he resigned because of ill health.

42. *A Roster,* Vol. 5, p. 6. Before becoming Major of the 11th Regiment "Bethel," William Joseph Martin was Captain of Company G in the 28th North Carolina Regiment. In May 1862, he was promoted to Lieutenant Colonel. In the fight at Bristoe Station, Virginia, October 14, 1863, he sustained arm and head wounds. Promoted to Colonel of the regiment in April 1864, he was wounded at Jones' Farm, Virginia, in September 1864. He returned to duty and was with Lee's Army at the surrender at Appomattox Court House, Virginia, April 9, 1865.

43. Samuel A. Ashe, ed., *Biographical History of North Carolina from Colonial Times to the Present* (Greensboro, NC: Charles L. Van Noppen, Publisher, 1905–1917), Vol. 1, 384–391.

44. *A Roster,* Vol. 11, p. 134. Edward Dudley Hall was Major of the 7th North Carolina Regiment before his promotion to the Colonelcy of the 46th Regiment. Having been elected Sheriff of New Hanover County, North Carolina, Hall resigned his commission in December 1863.

45. *A Roster,* Vol. 11, p. 368. Robert Clinton Hill served in the Artillery Corps and as Assistant Adjutant General on the staffs of General Toombs and Branch. He was ap-

pointed Colonel of the 48th Regiment in April 1862. Hill became ill in 1863 and died at his Iredell County home in December of that year.

46. *A Roster,* Vol. 12, p. 26. Stephen Dotson Ramseur was a Major in the 10th North Carolina Regiment (1st Regiment North Carolina Artillery) before becoming Colonel of the 49th Regiment. He was wounded at the battle of Malvern Hill, Virginia, July 1, 1862. Promoted to Brigadier-General in November 1862, he led his brigade in the battles of Chancellorsville, Gettysburg, the Wilderness, Spotsylvania Court House, and Cold Harbor. He was later promoted to Major-General with the command of a division. Ramseur learned he was the father of a daughter the day before he was mortally wounded at the Battle of Cedar Creek, Virginia, on October 19, 1864. He died October 20 at General Sheridan's headquarters in Winchester, Virginia, as his old friend George Armstrong Custer sat at his bedside.

47. *A Roster,* Vol. 10, p. 109. David Coleman was a lawyer before enlisting at the age of 37. He rose through the ranks to the Colonelcy of the 39th Regiment. He was wounded in the fighting at Murfreesboro, Tennessee, in December 1862. Displaying great courage and leadership, Coleman led a charge during the Battle of Chickamauga, Georgia, that captured ten enemy cannon. He survived the war.

48. Article published in the *Weekly Standard* (Raleigh, NC), May 7, 1862.

49. Samuel A. Ashe, ed., *Biographical History of North Carolina from Colonial Times to the Present* (Greensboro, NC: Charles L. Van Noppen, Publisher, 1905–1917), Vol. 6, pp. 289–295.

50. *A Roster,* Vol. 10, p. 396. George Badger Singeltary was killed at the Battle of Trantner's Creek, June 5, 1862.

51. *A Roster,* Vol. 11, p. 224. Sion Hart Rogers was Captain of Company E, 14th North Carolina Regiment (4th Regiment North Carolina Volunteers) and was appointed Lieutenant Colonel of the 47th Regiment in April 1862. He was promoted to full Colonel in January 1865.

52. *A Roster,* Vol. 13, p. 430. John Kerr Connally was wounded in the hip and left arm on the fight day's fight at Gettysburg. His arm was amputated and he was later taken prisoner. After passing through a number of Federal prison camps, he was exchanged in March 1864.

53. *A Roster,* Vol. 13, p. 430. Abner Sydenham Calloway resigned his commission in January 1863.

54. *A Roster,* Vol. 13, p. 430. James S. Whitehead served as Captain of Company E prior to his promotion to Major. He died in Wilson, North Carolina, on August 7, 1862. Cause of death was not given.

55. *A Roster,* Vol. 13, p. 433. William J. Bullock was a physician in Wilson County, North Carolina, prior to his enlistment. He resigned in February 1863.

56. *A Roster,* Vol. 13, p. 430. Abner Sydenham Calloway resigned his commission in January 1863.

57. *A Roster,* Vol. 13, p. 453. Dixon Falls was a farmer in Cleveland County prior to his enlistment. He resigned his commission in November 1862. No reason was given.

58. *A Roster,* Vol. 13, p. 464. Silas Dixon Randall was a farmer in Cleveland County prior to his enlistment. He sustained facial wounds on the first day of the Battle of Gettysburg and was taken prisoner. He was incarcerated at Johnson's Island, which was located off the coast of Lake Erie, from July 20, 1863, to March 14, 1865, when he was paroled.

59. *A Roster,* Vol. 13, p. 430. James S. Whitehead served as Captain of Company E prior to his promotion to Major. He died in Wilson, North Carolina, on August 7, 1862. Cause of death was not given.

60. *A Roster,* Vol. 13, p. 485. Peter M. Mull was a Private in Company K, 1st Regiment North Carolina Infantry, the "Bethel." He was appointed Captain in April 1862. During the fighting at Washington, North Carolina, in September 1862, he was wounded in the head and left lung. Mull would spend the remainder of the war reporting back for duty, then being hospitalized. He survived the war.

61. *A Roster,* Vol. 13, p. 497. Jesse P. Williams enlisted as a Private in Company E of the 20th North Carolina Regiment. He was appointed Captain in April 1862, but resigned in March 1863.

62. *A Roster,* Vol. 13, pp. 505–506. Vandever Teague was 1st Sergeant of Company G, 37th North Carolina Regiment prior to his appointment as Captain in April 1862. He later resigned his commission.

63. *A Roster,* Vol. 13, p. 514. Wilson Hugh Williams was a farmer in Franklin County prior to his enlistment. He was appointed Captain in April 1862. He was wounded during the fighting at Washington, North Carolina, in September 1862. He was captured during the Battle of Gettysburg. He was held in a number of Federal prison camps and was released at Fort Delaware, Delaware, on June 12, 1865.

64. *A Roster,* Vol. 13, p. 523. Maurice Thompson Smith served as 2nd Lieutenant of 2nd Company D, 12th North Carolina Regiment. He was appointed Captain in May 1862. In March 1863 he was appointed Lieutenant Colonel of the regiment. Smith was killed at the Battle of Gettysburg.

65. Stewart, Bruce H., Jr., *Land Battles of the Civil War, Eastern Theatre* (Jefferson, NC: McFarland, 2002), pp. 20–29.

66. Stewart, *Land Battles of the Civil War, Eastern Theatre,* pp. 40–41.

67. Stewart, *Land Battles of the Civil War, Eastern Theatre,* p. 40.

68. *A Roster,* Vol. 4, p. 42. Charles L. Johnson was wounded in the fighting in Maryland in September 1862. After recovering, he rejoined the regiment before May 1863. At the Battle of Gettysburg he was wounded and captured again. He spent the remainder of the war in the prison camp at Fort Delaware, Delaware, and was released from there in June 1865.

69. *A Roster,* Vol. 4, p. 86. John B. Bowles (correct spelling), after being wounded, was absent until July 1864. He was then retired to the Invalid Corps and served as a hospital guard in Richmond. When the Federal Army took the city in April 1865, he was captured.

70. *A Roster,* Vol. 7, p. 168. Anderson Green returned to duty after being wounded at the Battle of Seven Pines. He was again wounded during the Battle of Gettysburg. He returned to duty before May 1864 and served till the end of the war.

71. *A Roster,* Vol. 7, p. 66. Ambrose F. Scarborough enlisted as a Private and rose to the rank of Captain. Near Seven Pines he was "struck by a shot from a sharpshooter's rifle at a distance of nine hundred yards and instantly killed."

72. *A Roster,* Vol. 7, p. 167. Frank Wall Dumas enlisted as a Private in September 1861. He was killed at the Battle of Seven Pines, May 31, 1862.

73. *A Roster,* Vol. 7, p. 143. Before his promotion to Major, Edmund J. Christian was Captain of Company C of the 23rd North Carolina Regiment. Wounded at Seven Pines, he died July 3, 1862. "He received two wounds either of which would have justified his retirement. But he pluckily went forward at the head of his men till stricken down with [a] third and mortal wound."

74. *A Roster,* Vol. 7, p. 165. John R. Nicholson, 1st Lieutenant of Company C., 23rd North Carolina Regiment, was wounded in the face at Seven Pines. The Official Records indicate Nicholson died in March 1863, about a year after Long Grabs' report.

75. No information found on John Holmes.

76. *A Roster,* Vol. 7, p. 162. Jacob Reynolds, a Private in Company B, 23rd North Carolina Regiment, was killed at the Battle of Seven Pines. He "received three wounds before he stopped moving forward."

77. No information found for Andrew Hyles.

78. *A Roster,* Vol. 7, p. 155. Sidney A. Shuford had been 3rd Lieutenant before his promotion to Captain of Company B in May 1862. Barely three weeks later, he was killed at the Battle of Seven Pines.

79. *A Roster,* Vol. 7, p. 177. John W. Covington joined Company D, 23rd North Carolina Regiment as a Private in May 1861 and a year later was promoted to Sergeant. Wounded at the Battle of Seven Pines, he returned to duty a month later and was wounded again at Gaines' Mill, Virginia, or Malvern Hill. He was accounted for until December 1864.

80. *A Roster,* Vol. 7, p. 145, p. 184. John Calvin Ussery was not killed, but captured, in the Battle of Seven Pines. He was held prisoner at Fort Delaware, Delaware, and later exchanged. He returned to the 23rd North Carolina Regiment in November 1862, and was appointed Sergeant Major in January 1864. He was wounded in the hip at the Battle of Spotsylvania Court House in May 1864.

81. *A Roster,* Vol. 7, p. 180. At the Battle of Seven Pines, William A. McKethan was "struck by a grape shot in the forehead and instantly killed."

82. *A Roster,* Vol. 7, p. 176. Parks Chappell

was captured at the Battle of Seven Pines, later exchanged, and returned to duty. He was captured again at the Battle of Gettysburg, confined at David's Island, New York Harbor, and exchanged later in 1863. He was wounded in the right arm and captured for a third time at the Battle of Winchester, Virginia, September 19, 1864. His arm was amputated and he was imprisoned at Point Lookout, Maryland. Parks was exchanged in February 1865.

83. *A Roster,* Vol. 7, p. 180. Thomas Benson Ledbetter of Company D was wounded at the Battle of Seven Pines. He later was returned to duty and was accounted for through December 1864.

84. *A Roster,* Vol. 7, p. 181. Edmund C. Moorman, wounded at Seven Pines, was reported absent wounded through April 1864. He was accounted for through December 1864.

85. *A Roster,* Vol. 7, p. 184. Stephen W. Webb was a clerk in Richmond County prior to enlisting. He was wounded in the left thigh at the Battle of Seven Pines and returned to duty prior to July 1, 1862. He was wounded again in the thigh at Malvern Hill, Virginia. He was present and accounted for until December 1864.

86. *A Roster,* Vol. 7, p. 181. Angus R. Morrison was wounded at the Battle of Seven Pines and returned to duty in September 1862. He was severely wounded and captured at the Battle of Winchester, Virginia, September 19, 1864. He was held in several Federal hospitals, confined at Point Lookout, Maryland, and exchanged in March 1865.

87. *A Roster,* Vol. 7, pp. 182-183. Michael Scott was a native of Ireland and was a bricklayer in Richmond County, North Carolina, before enlisting. He was captured at Chester Gap, Virginia, in July 1863. Confined at Point Lookout, Maryland, he later took the Oath of Allegiance and joined the U. S. Army in February 1864. He later escaped and made his way back to Confederate territory where he rejoined his old company. He was wounded near New Market, Virginia, in September 1864.

88. *A Roster,* Vol. 6, p. 412. Robert M. DeVane, Captain of Company K, 18th North Carolina Regiment, entered the service as a 2nd Lieutenant and rose through the ranks to the Captaincy. Ill health forced him to resign in October 1862.

89. *A Roster,* Vol. 6, p. 423. Sampson B. Tolar was wounded at Hanover Court House, Virginia, May 27, 1862. He received a medical discharge later that year.

90. *A Roster,* Vol. 6, p. 412. Thomas J. Wooten entered the service as a Private and rose to the Captaincy of Company K, 18th North Carolina Regiment. He was wounded at the Battle of Chancellorsville, Virginia, in May 1863. Later promoted to Major of the regiment, he commanded the regimental sharpshooters during the Petersburg, Virginia, campaign.

91. *A Roster,* Vol. 6, p. 421. Timothy Fletcher Pridgen was not killed but captured at Hanover Court House, Virginia, May 27, 1862. He was later exchanged and wounded in the fighting at Ox Hill, Maryland, in September 1862. He was again wounded in the arm at the Battle of Chancellorsville, Virginia, in May 1863. He returned to duty and was wounded in the thigh and captured at Gravel Hill, Virginia, in July 1864. He was held in several federal hospitals until released in November 1865.

92. *A Roster,* Vol. 6, p. 423. William H. Sykes was 24 years old when he enlisted as a Private. He was captured at the Battle of Hanover Court House, Virginia, May 27, 1862, and exchanged in August of the same year. He was wounded during the Battle of Chancellorsville, May 1863 and was back with his regiment at the beginning of 1864. He sustained wounds in the right arm at the Battle of the Wilderness, Virginia, May 5, 1864, and was back with his regiment by the end of the summer. He later deserted to the Federal forces on February 18, 1865.

93. *A Roster,* Vol. 6, p. 419. John M. McKethan was a farmer in Bladen County and was 20 years old at the time of enlistment. He was killed during the fighting at Hanover Court House, Virginia, May 27, 1862.

94. Alex Andrews. No information found.

95. *A Roster,* Vol. 6, p. 419. William J. Maultsby was a farmer in Bladen County and was 21 when he enlisted. He was captured during the fighting at Hanover Court House, Virginia, May 27, 1862, and exchanged in August 1862. He was wounded in the leg near Fussell's Mill, Virginia, in August 1864. He returned to duty and was captured near Petersburg, Virginia, on April 2, 1865, one week before General Lee surrendered at Appomattox.

96. *A Roster,* Vol. 6, p. 425. James A. Cromartie enlisted at the age of 20. He was wounded in the right side and captured at the Battle of Hanover Court House, Virginia, May 27, 1862. He spent time in several Federal hospitals and was exchanged in September 1862. He returned to duty and was paroled at Appomattox Court House, Virginia, April 9, 1865.

97. *A Roster,* Vol. 6, p. 422. Martin V. B. Sutton was a Bladen County farmer and enlisted at age 21. Captured at Hanover Court House, Virginia, May 27, 1862, he was exchanged in August 1862. He was wounded at the Battle of Chancellorsville, Virginia, May 1863. He returned to his regiment and was present and accounted through February 1865.

98. No information found for this particular Captain Sykes.

99. *A Roster,* Vol. 6, p. 344; Vol. 12, p. 332. William Stokes Norment, Captain of Company D, 18th North Carolina Regiment, was not reelected when the regiments reorganized in April 1862. He later served as Captain of Company F, North Carolina Regiment, beginning in August 1862. Norment was wounded in the leg at Fort Harrison, Virginia, September 30, 1864.

100. *A Roster,* Vol. 6, p. 370. Duncan M. Gibson was a farmer in Richmond County and was 18 when he enlisted. He was wounded and captured at Hanover Court House, Virginia, May 27, 1862, and died of his wounds at Yorktown, Virginia, June 10, 1862.

101. *A Roster,* Vol. 6, p. 371. Alexander F. Jones was a Richmond County farmer and enlisted at age 19. He was wounded in the legs and captured at Hanover Court House, Virginia, May 27, 1862, and exchanged in September 1862. He was captured again at the Battle of the Wilderness, Virginia, May 1864. He was sent to Point Lookout, Maryland, and then to a prison camp in Elmira, New York. He died there March 29, 1865, about two weeks before the surrender at Appomattox.

102. *A Roster,* Vol. 6, p. 369. Andrew Jackson Clark was a Richmond County teacher. He was killed at Hanover Court House, Virginia, May 27, 1862.

103. *A Roster,* Vol. 6, p. 372. Alexander B. McLauchlin enlisted at age 20 in 1861 and was killed at the Battle of Hanover Court House, Virginia, May 27, 1862.

104. *A Roster,* Vol. 6, p. 371. Murdoch McDuffie was a Richmond County farmer and enlisted at age 41. He was captured at the Battle of Hanover Court House, Virginia, May 27, 1862. McDuffie was exchanged and discharged from further service in August 1862 because he was over age.

105. *A Roster,* Vol. 6, pp. 373–374. Archibald L. McRae was a Richmond County farmer before he enlisted at age 37. At Hanover Court House, Virginia, May 27, 1862, he was wounded and captured. He was exchanged in September 1862 and later discharged from service because he was over age.

106. *A Roster,* Vol. 6, p. 375. Hugh L. Patterson was wounded at the Battle of Hanover Court House, Virginia, May 27, 1862. He was accounted for through February 1865.

107. *A Roster,* Vol. 6, p. 376. Amos W. Roper enlisted as a Private at age 22. He was wounded at Hanover Court House, Virginia, May 27, 1862 and later captured at the Battle of the Wilderness, Virginia, in May 1864. Imprisoned at Point Lookout, Maryland, he died there August 4, 1864.

108. *A Roster,* Vol. 6, p. 368. William Buchanan, Jr., enlisted as a Private and rose to the rank of Sergeant. He was wounded at Hanover Court House, Virginia, May 27, 1862. Buchanan was captured at Spotsylvania Court House, Virginia, in May 1864. He was held a prisoner of war at Point Lookout, Maryland, and later transferred to the prison camp at Elmira, New York. He was exchanged in February 1865.

109. *A Roster,* Vol. 6, p. 372. Daniel McKinnon was a Richmond County farmer and enlisted at age 21 as a Private, later rising to the rank of Sergeant. He was captured at the Battle of Hanover Court House, Virginia, May 27, 1862 and exchanged in August 1862. He was captured during the Battle of Chancellorsville, May 1863 and exchanged a week later. McKinnon was wounded at Gravel Hill, Virginia, July 28, 1864.

110. *A Roster,* Vol. 4, p. 344; Vol. 14, p. 97. James A. Craige, Captain of Company G, 6th North Carolina Regiment, was elected Major of the 57th North Carolina Regiment in July 1862. He was wounded in the knee at Winchester, Virginia, on July 20 1864. He received his parole in Salisbury, North Carolina, on May 3, 1865.

111. *A Roster,* Vol. 4, p. 345. John P. M.

Barringer, a Rowan County farmer, was killed at the Battle of Seven Pines, Virginia, May 31, 1862.

112. No information found for Rufus Owens.

113. *A Roster,* Vol. 4, p. 348. Andrew Gullet was a Davie County farmer prior to his enlistment in May 1861. He was taken prisoner at the Battle of South Mountain, Maryland, September 14, 1862, and exchanged in November of the same year. He was wounded in three places at the Battle of Gettysburg and later captured. He was confined at Point Lookout, Maryland, from September 1863 until he was exchanged in January 1865.

114. *A Roster,* Vol. 4, p. 352. William Henry Porter was a Davidson County farmer prior to enlisting in May 1861. He was wounded at the Battle of Seven Pines, captured, and died in a hospital about two weeks later.

115. *A Roster,* Vol. 4, p. 294. William Johnson Freeland was Captain of Company C, 6th Regiment North Carolina Troops. He was wounded and captured at the Battle of Seven Pines, and died June 21, 1862, at Fortress Monroe, Virginia.

116. *A Roster,* Vol. 6, p. 300. William Jones Laycock was 23 when he enlisted as a Private in Company C, 6th North Carolina Regiment. He was wounded at the Battle of Seven Pines on May 31, 1862, and again at the Battle of Chancellorsville in May 1863. He was reported missing in action at Rappahannock Station, Virginia, in November 1863.

117. *A Roster,* Vol. 6, p. 84. James G. Cockram was wounded at the Battle of Seven Pines. He recovered and was promoted to the Regimental Band in 1863. He was paroled at Appomattox Court House, Virginia, April 9, 1865.

118. *A Roster,* Vol. 6, p. 90. William P. Reese was mustered into Company I at age 18 as a Musician (Drummer). He was wounded at the Battle of Seven Pines, May 31, 1862. He returned to duty in the fall of 1863 and was transferred to the Regimental Band in the winter of 1864.

119. *A Roster,* Vol. 6, p. 86. Mallory L. Henly was wounded in the arm at the Battle of Seven Pines. He was later elected 2nd Lieutenant of Company G, 35th Regiment North Carolina Troops. He was wounded in the foot in 1864 and later promoted to Captain in the same year.

120. *A Roster,* Vol. 6, p. 29. William J. Edney was 1st Lieutenant of Company C, 16th Regiment, North Carolina Troops. He was wounded at the Battle of Seven Pines and in December of the same year, he was captured at the Battle of Fredericksburg, Virginia. He was paroled and returned to his company.

121. *A Roster,* Vol. 6, p Louis A. Ward enlisted as a Private in Company I, 16th North Carolina Regiment in May 1861. He was appointed 2nd Lieutenant in late April 1862, just before he was wounded at the Battle of Seven Pines.

122. *A Roster,* Vol. 6, p. 87. Joseph P. Johnson was a Henderson County farmer before his enlistment at age 24. He was wounded at the Battle of Seven Pines. Johnson returned to duty and was wounded again at Shepherdstown, Virginia, on September 20, 1862, right after the Battle of Sharpsburg.

123. No information found for J. L. Hitcher.

124. *A Roster,* Vol. 4, p. 83. Thomas F. Whitlock was 24 when he enlisted in Company G of the 4th North Carolina Regiment, in July 1861. He died June 16, 1862, from wounds received during the Battle of Seven Pines.

125. *A Roster,* Vol. 4, pp. 77–78. James Cook was an eighteen-year-old Davie County farmer when he enlisted in March 1862 in Company G, 4th North Carolina Regiment. He was killed just two months later at the Battle of Seven Pines.

126. *A Roster,* Vol. 4, p. 76. John J. Barlow enlisted at the age of 38 in Company G, 4th North Carolina Regiment. He was killed at the Battle of Seven Pines.

127. *A Roster,* Vol. 4, p. 34. 1st Lieutenant Joseph C. White enlisted at age 23 and was killed at the Battle of Seven Pines.

128. *A Roster,* Vol. 4, pp. 9, 13. Absalom Knox Simonton enlisted at age 26 and was appointed Captain of Company A, 4th North Carolina Regiment. He was promoted to Major on May 1, 1862, and was killed thirty days later at the Battle of Seven Pines.

129. *A Roster,* Vol. 4, p. 56. Edward Q. Redding enlisted at age 19 and was 2nd Lieutenant of Company E, 4th North Carolina Regiment. He was severely wounded at the Battle of Seven Pines and later died.

130. *A Roster*, Vol. 4, p. 21. Earnest A. Morrison had enlisted in Company A, 4th North Carolina Regiment, as a substitute and was killed at the Battle of Seven Pines.

131. *A Roster*, Vol. 7, pp. 217–218. James E. Hill enlisted in Company H, 23rd North Carolina Regiment as a Private in June 1861 and was elected 2nd Lieutenant in May 1862. Wounded at the Battle of Seven Pines, Hill resigned his commission in October 1862.

132. *A Roster*, Vol.7, p. 217. William P. Hill was mustered into Company H, 23rd North Carolina Regiment as a Sergeant in June 1861 and appointed Captain of the company in December of the same year. He was severely wounded at the Battle of Seven Pines and died in June 1862.

133. *A Roster*, Vol. 7, p. 224. James A. Calhoun Robinson enlisted as a Private in Company H, 23rd North Carolina Regiment in June 1861 at the age of 18. Wounded at the Battle of Seven Pines, Robinson died a few days later.

134. *A Roster*, Vol. 7, p. 195. Jacob H. Miller, Captain of Company F, 23rd Regiment North Carolina Troops, was wounded at the Battle of Seven Pines and died in the hospital at Richmond, Virginia, June 2, 1862.

135. *A Roster*, Vol. 13, 604. Franklin N. Roberts had served as a Private in the 36th North Carolina Regiment before his appointment as Captain of Company B, 56th North Carolina Regiment. He was killed near Petersburg, Virginia, in June 1864.

136. *A Roster*, Vol. 13, pp. 592, 671. Thomas C. Halyburton was a physician in Alexander County, North Carolina, prior to enlisting at age 29. He was appointed Captain of Company H, 56th North Carolina Regiment in June 1862 and in the fall of that year was appointed Assistant Commissary of Subsistence. He resigned because of illness that winter.

137. *A Roster*, Vol. 13, p. 638. Jarvis B. Lutterloh was a Private in Company H, 1st Regiment North Carolina Infantry before his appointment as 1st Lieutenant of Company E, 56th North Carolina Regiment. He was mortally wounded at the Battle of First Gum Swamp near Kinston, North Carolina, on April 28, 1863, and died in that city the next day.

138. *A Roster*, Vol. 13, p. 638. William S. Moody was a Northampton County farmer prior to his enlistment. He was appointed 3rd Lieutenant of Company E, 56th North Carolina Regiment in April 1862 and resigned his commission in January 1863 because of business problems.

139. *A Roster*, Vol. 13, 592, 647 Henry Franklin Schenck was a merchant before enlisting at age 26. He was appointed Captain of Company 7, 56th North Carolina Regiment in April 1862 and was promoted to Major in July 1862. Illness forced his resignation in August 1863.

140. *A Roster*, Vol. 13, p. 648. Valentine Jackson Palmer was a physician prior to enlisting at age 33. He was appointed 1st Lieutenant of Company F, 56th North Carolina Regiment in May 1862. He was struck in the leg during the fighting at Plymouth, North Carolina, on April 20, 1864, and was absent wounded through August of that year. He returned to duty and was captured at Five Forks, Virginia, on April 1, 1865. Confined at Johnson's Island, Ohio, he was released from there in June 1865.

141. *A Roster*, Vol. 13, p. 648. 2nd Lieutenant John Richard Williams of Company F, 56th North Carolina Regiment, was a Cleveland County farmer prior to enlisting at age 28. He was killed at Ware Bottom Church, Virginia, in May 1864.

142. *A Roster*, Vol. 13, p. 648. Alfred R. Grigg was a Cleveland County farmer before enlisting in Company F, 56th North Carolina Regiment as 3rd Lieutenant. He was wounded at Drewry's Bluff, Virginia, in May 1864, and promoted to 2nd Lieutenant in the same month. He was again wounded at the Battle of the Crater, Petersburg, Virginia, in 1864. Grigg was captured at Fort Stedman in March 1865 and held a prisoner of war until released in June 1865.

143. *A Roster*, Vol. 13, pp. 592, 595. Granville Gratiott Luke was Captain of 1st Company H, 32nd North Carolina Regiment before his appointment as Captain of Company A, 56th North Carolina Regiment. Elected Lieutenant Colonel of the 56th, Luke was wounded at Drewry's Bluff, Virginia, in May 1864. He was captured at Dinwiddie Court House, Virginia, in April 1865 and held a prisoner of war until released in July 1865.

144. *A Roster*, Vol. 13, p. 626. Robert Davidson Graham was elected 2nd Lieuten-

ant of Company D, 56th North Carolina Regiment in May 1862 and rose to the Captaincy in September 1863. He was wounded at Fort Stedman, Virginia, in March 1865 and captured while in a Petersburg hospital.

145. *A Roster,* Vol. 13, 9. 659. 1st Lieutenant Otis P. Wills of Company G, 56th North Carolina Regiment was a Henderson County farmer prior to his enlistment. He was promoted to Captain in May 1864. Slightly wounded at Globe Tavern, Virginia, in August 1864, he survived the war.

146. *A Roster,* Vol. 13, pp. 592, 625–626. John Washington Graham was a 2nd Lieutenant of Company G, 27th North Carolina Regiment and was appointed Captain of Company D, 56th North Carolina Regiment in March 1862. He was appointed Major of the regiment on September 1, 1863. Near Petersburg, Virginia, he was wounded in the arm in June 1864. He returned to duty and was later shot through both legs at Fort Stedman, Virginia, in May 1865. He survived the war.

147. *A Roster,* Vol. 13, pp. 658–659. Henry E. Lane was 53 when he enlisted in Company E, 56th North Carolina Regiment. He was appointed Captain in April 1862. He had a checkered career. He was reported under arrest twice in 1863, but no reason was given. He was later furloughed home as sick, but came back. He resigned in May 1864 after giving a number of reasons.

148. *A Roster,* Vol. 13, pp. 637–638. Joseph Gray Lockhart was a Northampton County farmer prior to being appointed Captain of Company E, 56th North Carolina Regiment in April 1862. From May to December 1863, he was Provost-Marshal at Weldon, North Carolina. He resigned in September 1864 because of ill health.

149. *A Roster,* Vol. 13, pp. 592, 638. George B. Barnes was a Northampton County lawyer prior to his appointment as 2nd Lieutenant of Company E, 56th North Carolina Regiment in April 1862. Barnes served as Assistant Quartermaster of the Regiment with the rank of Captain in August 1862 and held the same position in Brigadier-General Matt Ransom's Brigade in 1864.

150. *A Roster,* Vol. 13, p. 659. Benjamin D. Lane rose from the rank of Sergeant in the 16th North Carolina Regiment to 1st Lieutenant of Company G, 56th North Carolina Regiment. He was in the surrender at Appomattox Court House, Virginia.

151. *A Roster,* 13, p. 616. John B. Lyon was appointed 2nd Lieutenant of Company C, 56th North Carolina Regiment in May 1862. He was reported killed in 1864.

152. *A Roster,* Vol. 13, p. 595. Thomas P. Savells (correct spelling) began his military career as a Private in the 32nd North Carolina Regiment. Appointed a 3rd Lieutenant of Company A, 56th North Carolina Regiment, he rose to the Captaincy in June 1864. He was wounded that same month at Petersburg, Virginia. Savells surrendered at Appomattox Court House, Virginia.

153. Article published in *The Eagle* (Fayetteville, NC), October 22, 1868.

Chapter 3

1. J. G. De Roulhac Hamilton, *"North Carolina Courts and the Confederacy"* (Raleigh, NC: The North Carolina Historical Review, October 1927) Volume 4, Number 4, p. 366.

2. Article published in the *North Carolina Standard* (Raleigh, NC), April 23, 1862.

3. O.R., Ser. 4, Vol. 1:1091–92.

4. Letter published in the *Fayetteville Observer* (Fayetteville, NC), May 8, 1862.

5. Albert Burton Moore, *Conscription and Conflict in the Confederacy* (New York: MacMillan, 1924), p. 114.

6. O.R., Ser. 4, Vol. 1: 1097.

7. Walter C. Hilderman, III, *They Went Into the Fight Cheering!* (Boone, NC: Parkway Publishers, 2005), pp. 24–27.

8. *A Roster,* Vol. 13, p. 592. Paul Fletcher Faison had been Major of the 14th Regiment before becoming Colonel of the 56th Regiment North Carolina Troops. He survived the war and was surrendered at Appomattox Court House, Virginia, April 9, 1865.

9. *A Roster,* Vol. 13, pp. 592, 595. Granville Gratiott Luke was Captain of 1st Company H, 32nd North Carolina Regiment before his appointment as Captain of Company A, 56th North Carolina Regiment. Elected Lieutenant Colonel of the 56th, Luke was wounded at Drewry's Bluff, Virginia, in May 1864. He was captured at Dinwiddie Court House, Virginia, in April 1865 and held a prisoner of war until released in July 1865.

10. *A Roster,* Vol. 13, 604. Franklin N. Roberts had served as a Private in the 36th North Carolina Regiment before his appointment as Captain of Company B, 56th North Carolina Regiment. He was killed near Petersburg, Virginia, in June 1864.

11. *A Roster,* Vol. 13, pp. 615–616. Alexander P. White was a Captain in Company E, 17th Regiment North Carolina Troops before being appointed Captain of Company C in the 56th. He was captured at Five Forks, Virginia, eight days before Lee surrendered and held prisoner on Johnson's Island, Ohio. He was released in June.

12. *A Roster,* Vol. 13, pp. 592, 625–626. John Washington Graham was a 2nd Lieutenant of Company G, 27th North Carolina Regiment and was appointed Captain of Company D, 56th North Carolina Regiment in March 1862. He was appointed Major of the regiment on September 1, 1863. Near Petersburg, Virginia, he was wounded in the arm in June 1864. He returned to duty and was later shot through both legs at Fort Stedman, Virginia, in May 1865. He survived the war.

13. *A Roster,* Vol. 13, pp. 637–638. Joseph Gray Lockhart was a Northampton County farmer prior to being appointed Captain of Company E, 56th North Carolina Regiment in April 1862. From May to December 1863, he was Provost-Marshal at Weldon, North Carolina. He resigned in September 1864 because of ill health.

14. *A Roster,* Vol. 13, 592, 647 Henry Franklin Schenck was a merchant before enlisting at age 26. He was appointed Captain of Company 7, 56th North Carolina Regiment in April 1862 and was promoted to Major in July 1862. Illness forced his resignation in August 1863.

15. *A Roster,* Vol. 13, pp. 658–659. Henry E. Lane, Captain, Company G, 56th Regiment, had a checkered career. He was arrested several times, was sick, and finally resigned in 1864 at the age of 56 because he needed to take care of his aging wife.

16. *A Roster,* Vol. 13, pp. 592, 671. Thomas C. Halyburton was a physician in Alexander County, North Carolina, prior to enlisting at age 29. He was appointed Captain of Company H, 56th North Carolina Regiment in June 1862 and in the fall of that year was appointed Assistant Commissary of Subsistence. He resigned because of illness that winter.

17. *A Roster,* Vol. 13, 682. Lawson Harrill was a Captain in the 16th Regiment before he was transferred to Company I, 56th Regiment. He was captured at Fort Stedman, Virginia, in March 1865. Held a prisoner at Fort Delaware, Delaware, he was released in June.

18. *A Roster,* Vol. 13, p. 693. Francis R. Alexander was a private in the 1st Regiment (6 months) 1861. He became Captain of Company K, 56th Regiment, in July 1862. He was severely wounded at Petersburg, Virginia, June 17, 1864, and died two days later.

19. Hilderman, *They Went into the Fight Cheering!* pp. 34–35.

20. Stewart, *Land Battles of the Civil War,* pp. 55–57.

21. *A Roster,* Vol. 14, p. 97. Archibald Campbell Godwin was appointed Colonel of the 57th Regiment in 1862. He was wounded at the Battle of Chancellorsville in May 1863, and captured at Rappahannock Station, Virginia, in the fall of 1863. Held prisoner in three different places, he was released in April 1864, and shortly thereafter, promoted to Brigadier-General.

22. *A Roster,* Vol. 14, p. 97. Hamilton Chamberlain Jones, Jr., was Captain of Company K, 5th Regiment, before he was appointed Lieutenant Colonel of the 57th Regiment in July 1862. He was captured at Rappahannock Station, Virginia, in the fall of 1863. Held prisoner in three different places, he was exchanged in February 1865. He returned to duty and was wounded in the arm at Fort Stedman, Virginia, in March 1865.

23. *A Roster,* Vol. 14, p. 97. James Alexander Craige was Captain of Company G, 6th Regiment, before being appointed Major in the 57th Regiment in July 1862. He was wounded in the fighting at Winchester, Virginia, in July 1864. He survived the war and was paroled at Salisbury, North Carolina, in May 1865.

24. *A Roster,* Vol. 8, p. 521. Henry M. Shaw was appointed Colonel of the 8th Regiment in 1861. He and his command were captured during the Burnside assault on Roanoke Island in February 1862. He was exchanged, and in February 1864, in the fighting at Batcheler's Creek, near New Bern, North Carolina, he was killed.

25. Obituary published in the *Fayetteville Observer* (Fayetteville, NC), September 29, 1862.

26. Obituary published in the *Fayetteville Observer* (Fayetteville, NC), September 22, 1862.

27. *A Roster,* Vol. 1, p. 444. Robert Walker Anderson was 1st Sergeant of 2nd Company G, 40th Regiment (3rd Regiment NC Artillery). He was later transferred to the staff of his brother, General George B. Anderson, with the rank of 1st Lieutenant.

28. *A Roster,* Vol. 6, p. 368. Lawrence Stewart was 1st Lieutenant in Company F, 18th Regiment. He was killed September 1, 1862, at Ox Hill, Virginia.

29. *A Roster,* Vol. 4, p. 521. William J. Price, appointed Lieutenant Colonel of the 8th Regiment in May 1861, was captured at Roanoke Island in February 1862. Exchanged in the summer, he resigned in October 1862 because of his age — he was 58.

30. *A Roster,* Vol. 4, p. 521. George Williamson, Major of the 8th Regiment, was captured at Roanoke Island. Exchanged in the summer of 1862 and soon promoted to Lieutenant Colonel, he was forced to resign in 1863 due to asthma.

31. *A Roster,* Vol. 4, p. 523. James W. Hinton, Captain of Company A, 8th Regiment, was captured at Roanoke Island. Released in the summer, he was promoted to Major of the regiment.

32. *A Roster,* Vol. 4, p. 533. James M. Whitson, Captain of Company B, 8th Regiment, was captured at Roanoke Island and held prisoner at Fort Columbus, New York Harbor. Released in October, he was promoted to Major in April 1863.

33. *A Roster,* Vol. 4, p. 542. Henry McRae, Captain of Company C, 8th Regiment, was captured at Roanoke Island and released the following August. He was promoted to Major in February 1863.

34. *A Roster,* Vol. 4, p. 551. Andrew J. Rogers, Captain of Company D, 8th Regiment, was captured at Roanoke Island and released the following August. Wounded at Morris Island, Charleston Harbor, South Carolina, in July 1863, he rejoined his company in the fall. He was promoted to Major of the regiment in June 1864.

35. *A Roster,* Vol. 4, p. 561. John Reed Murchison, Captain of Company E, 8th Regiment, was captured at Roanoke Island and released in August. He was promoted to Major in October 1863.

36. *A Roster,* Vol. 4, p. 572. Charles Johnston Jones, Captain of Company F, 8th Regiment, resigned in October 1862 due to heart disease.

37. *A Roster,* Vol. 4, p. 581. Edward C. Yellowly, Captain of Company G, 8th Regiment, was captured at Roanoke Island and released in August. He was promoted to Major in July 1863.

38. *A Roster,* Vol. 4, p. 591. Rufus A. Barrier, Captain of Company H, 8th Regiment, was captured at Roanoke Island and released in August. He was promoted to Major in February 1864.

39. *A Roster,* Vol. 4, p. 603. Gaston D. Cobb, Captain of Company I, 8th Regiment, was captured at Roanoke Island and released in August. During the fighting at Morris Island, Charleston Harbor, South Carolina, August–September 1863, he sustained wounds in both eyes and was forced to resign the following December.

40. *A Roster,* Vol. 4, p. 614. Pinkney A. Kennerly, Captain of Company K, 8th Regiment, was captured at Roanoke and released in August 1862. He survived the war and was paroled at Salisbury, North Carolina, in June 1865.

41. *A Roster,* Vol. 8, p. 429. John V. Jordan, Colonel of the 31st Regiment, was captured at Roanoke Island and paroled two weeks later. He was in a Richmond hospital in May 1864 for gunshot wounds and resigned in October.

42. *A Roster,* Vol. 8, p. 429. Edward R. Liles, Lieutenant Colonel of the 31st Regiment, had formerly been Captain of Company B. He was captured at Roanoke Island and later exchanged. He resigned his commission in April 1863.

43. *A Roster,* Vol. 8, p. 429. Jesse Johnston Yeates, Major of the 31st Regiment, was captured at Roanoke Island and later released. He resigned for health reasons in November 1862.

44. *A Roster,* Vol. 8, p. 431. Condary Godwin resigned as Captain of Company A, 31st Regiment, in October 1862.

45. *A Roster,* Vol. 8, p. 438. Charles B. Lindsey, at that time a Lieutenant in Company B, 31st Regiment, was captured at

Roanoke Island and later released. He was promoted to Captain in October 1862, and resigned in April 1863.

46. *A Roster,* Vol. 8, p. 447. William J. Long, a Sergeant in Company C, 31st Regiment, was captured at Roanoke Island, later released, and promoted to Captain of the company in September 1862.

47. *A Roster,* Vol. 8, p. 454. Ruffin L. Bryan served as Lieutenant and Captain of Company D, 31st Regiment.

48. *A Roster,* Vol. 8, p. 464. Julius F. Allison, 1st Sergeant of Company E, 31st Regiment, was captured at Roanoke Island, later released, and appointed Captain in September 1862. He was in the hospital in Richmond with a gunshot wound in June 1864, and released to rejoin his company. He survived the war and was paroled in Greensboro, North Carolina, in May 1865.

49. *A Roster,* Vol. 8, p. 471. Charles W. Knight, Captain of Company F, 31st Regiment, was captured at Roanoke Island and later released. He was promoted to Lieutenant Colonel in June 1863. He survived the war and was paroled in April 1865.

50. *A Roster,* Vol. 8, p. 480. Isaac Pipkin was a Lieutenant in Company G, 31st Regiment, when he was captured at Roanoke Island. He was promoted to Captain in September 1862, and resigned in January 1865.

51. *A Roster,* Vol. 8, p. 488. James E. Todd, Corporal in Company H, 31st Regiment, was captured at Roanoke Island, released the same month, and promoted to Captain in September 1862. Hepatitis caused him to resign in December 1863.

52. *A Roster,* Vol. 8, p. 497. John A. D. McKay, Captain of Company I, 31st Regiment, was captured at Roanoke Island and later released. He was wounded at White Hall, North Carolina, in December 1862. He was appointed Major of the Regiment in June 1863, and resigned in July 1864.

53. *A Roster,* Vol. 8, p. 505. Joseph Whitty, Captain of Company K, 31st Regiment, was captured at Roanoke Island and later released, and returned to duty.

Chapter 4

1. David Maurer, "Set in Stone" *The University of Virginia Magazine* (Spring 2008).
2. Stewart, *Land Battles,* pp. 55–57.

3. Mark Grimsley, *The Hard Hand of War: Union Military Policy Toward Southern Civilians* (Cambridge: Cambridge University Press, 1995), pp. 85–95.

4. Murdoch John McSween to Governor Zebulon B. Vance, November 17, 1862. *Papers of Zebulon B. Vance,* Volume 1, 1843–1862 (Raleigh: State Department of Archives and History, 1963), pp. 368–371. Used by permission Publications, State Archives and History.

5. Alfred Grant, *The American Civil War and the British Press* (Jefferson, NC: McFarland, 2000), pp. 122–123. Francis Charles Lawley (1825–1901) was an English correspondent sent by *The Times of London* to cover the Civil War.

6. William B. Styple, Ed., *Writing and Fighting the Confederate War: The Letters of Peter Wellington Alexander* (Kearney, NJ: Belle Grove Publishing, 2002). Peter Wellington Alexander (1825–1886) was the most outstanding journalist attached to the Army of Northern Virginia. Using the byline of "P. W. A.," he wrote over 800 letters to the *Savannah Republican* about the war.

7. Louis A. Brown, *The Salisbury Prison: A Case Study of Confederate Military Prisons, 1861–1864,* Rev. and enl. (Wilmington, NC: Broadfoot Publishing, 1992). The Salisbury Prison, located in Rowan County, was North Carolina's only prisoner of war camp for Union soldiers. It opened in December 1861, and by May 1862, there were 1,400 soldiers held there in fairly good conditions. However, as the war intensified, 10,000 were incarcerated by October 1864, in a prison built for 2,500. This caused overcrowding, unsanitary conditions, and lack of enough food to maintain the health of the prisoners, resulting in the deaths of 4,000 soldiers by the end of the war.

8. Letter published in the *Fayetteville Observer* (Fayetteville, NC), January 12, 1863.

9. Article published in the *Sentinel* (Raleigh, NC), March 15, 1871.

10. Charles Alphonso Smith, Ed., *Library of Southern Literature* (Atlanta, GA: The Martin and Hoyt Company, 1907, 1910), pp. 6293–6296. While it might appear from McSween's wording that Cousin Sally Dillard was a relative, it was far from so. Actually, "Cousin Sally Dillard — A Legal Sketch in the Old North State" was a humorous piece writ-

ten by Hamilton C. Jones. He was a state representative from Rowan County, North Carolina, solicitor of his district and also served as reporter of the North Carolina Supreme Court. He is the author of a number of humorous skits, including "Jones's Fight" and "A Quarter Race in Kentucky," but by far his most popular skit was "Cousin Sally Dillard."

11. Buffalos were North Carolina civilians or soldiers who supported the Union side in the Civil War, much like the Tories in the state supported the British Crown during the Revolutionary War. Confederate soldiers, "buffalos," who went over to the other side could, if caught in Yankee uniforms, suffer severe penalties, as did the twenty-two soldiers who were caught, tried, and hanged at Kinston, North Carolina, in 1864. Gerald A. Patterson, *Justice or Atrocity: General George E. Pickett and the Kinston, N. C. Hangings* (Gettysburg, PA: Thomas Publications, 1998).

Chapter 5

1. Barrett, *The Civil War in North Carolina*. General John Gray Foster (1823–1874) commanded the Department of North Carolina from 1862 to 1863. He led several raids into North Carolina, especially against the important railroad bridge at Goldsboro and opposed General D. H. Hill's movements against New Bern and Little Washington.

2. Barrett, *North Carolina as a Battleground State*, p. 44.

3. Barrett, *The Civil War in North Carolina*, pp. 133–134.

4. Barrett, *The Civil War in North Carolina*. General Nathan George Evans (1824–1868) was a brigade commander who was sent to Eastern North Carolina after participating in the Battle of Sharpsburg, Maryland, to oppose a Federal raid against Kinston and the Goldsboro railroad bridge.

5. Murdoch John McSween to Governor Zebulon B. Vance, March 12, 1863. Courtesy of the North Carolina Office of Archives and History, Raleigh, North Carolina.

6. Article published in the *Fayetteville Observer* (Fayetteville, NC), May 18, 1863.

7. Barrett, *Civil War in North Carolina*, p. 149.

8. Letter published in the *Fayetteville Observer* (Fayetteville, NC), March 26, 1863.

9. Samuel A. Ashe, ed., *Biographical History of North Carolina from Colonial Times to the Present* (Greensboro, NC: Charles L. Van Noppen, Publisher, 1905–1917), Volume 6, pp. 288–295. Edmund Burke Haywood (1825–1894) was appointed surgeon by Governor Ellis and sent to tour medical hospitals on Morris Island. When he returned, he organized North Carolina's first medical hospital in May 1861. In July following he was appointed president of the board to examine applicants for the position of surgeon in the state troops. During the fighting around Richmond, he was on duty at Seabrook Hospital. In 1862 he became medical director for the Department of North Carolina. In 1865, as Sherman's Army was approaching Raleigh, he was in charge of the Pettigrew Hospital. He remained at his post, refusing to leave and ministering to the wounded soldiers. He would stay beyond the surrender until the last soldier was discharged on July 4, 1865. Then he returned to his medical career.

10. Letter published in the *Fayetteville Observer* (Fayetteville, North Carolina), April 16, 1863.

11. William S. Powell, ed., *Dictionary of North Carolina Biography* (Chapel Hill: The University of North Carolina Press, 1979–1996), Volume 5, p. 439. Edward Stanly (1810–1872) was a native of New Bern, North Carolina, and a supporter of the Union. He was appointed by President Lincoln to be the military governor of North Carolina.

12. Letter published in the *Fayetteville Observer* (Fayetteville, NC), April 16, 1863.

13. O.R., Series 1, Vol. 18, Chapter 30, p. 215.

14. Letter published in the *Fayetteville Observer* (Fayetteville, NC), April 30, 1863.

15. Letter published in the *Fayetteville Observer* (Fayetteville, NC), May 11, 1863.

16. Letter published in the *Fayetteville Observer* (Fayetteville, NC), April 27, 1863.

17. O.R., Series 1, Vol. 18, Chapter 30, p. 215.

18. *A Roster*, Vol. 13, p. 643. Neill T. McNeill, Company E, 56th Regiment, was killed at the Battle of First Gum Swamp.

19. *A Roster*, Vol. 13, p. 646. Washington M. Vickers, Company E, 56th Regiment, was killed at the Battle of First Gum Swamp.

20. *A Roster*, Vol. 13, p. 643. Malcolm D. McNeill, Company E, 56th Regiment, was

wounded in the foot at the Battle of First Gum Swamp and permanently disabled. He survived the war.

21. *A Roster,* Vol. 13, p. 644. J. B. Parrish, Company E, 56th Regiment, was wounded in the hip at the Battle of First Gum Swamp.

22. *A Roster,* Vol. 13, p. 639. William Thomas Brewer, Company E, 56th Regiment, was wounded in the right arm at the Battle of First Gum Swamp, resulting in the amputation of the limb. He survived the war.

23. *A Roster,* Vol. 13, pp. 682–683. Phillip Harrison Gross, Company I, 56th Regiment, was a Private in the 16th Regiment, before being transferred to the 56th. He rose to the rank of 2nd Lieutenant and was surrendered at Appomattox.

24. Article printed in *The Eagle* (Fayetteville, NC), June 24, 1869.

25. *A Roster,* Vol. 7, p. 355. Col. Henry Middleton Rutledge commanded the 25th Regiment and was wounded at Malvern Hill, Virginia. He survived the war and was paroled at Appomattox Court House.

26. *A Roster,* Vol. 1, p. 199. John Whitmore, 1st Lieutenant, 2nd Company B. 36th Regiment (2nd Regiment NC Artillery) was a native of Pennsylvania. He was captured at Gum Swamp in May 1863 and held prisoner at Fort Delaware. After taking the oath of allegiance, he was allowed to return to his family.

27. *A Roster,* Vol. 1, p. 206. Sergeant Bond E. Sedberry, 2nd Company B. 36th Regiment (2nd Regiment NC Artillery), was captured at Gum Swamp in May 1863, and held prisoner at Fort Monroe, Virginia. He was paroled at the end of May and returned to duty.

28. *A Roster,* Vol. 1, p. 201. John H. Dobbin, Corporal, 2nd Company B. 36th Regiment (2nd Regiment NC Artillery), was captured at Gum Swamp, May 1863, and held prisoner at Fort Monroe, Virginia. He was exchanged at the end of May and returned to duty.

29. *A Roster,* Vol. 1, p. 200. John W. Carroll, Private, 2nd Company B. 36th Regiment (2nd Regiment NC Artillery), was captured at Gum Swamp, May 1863, and held prisoner at Fort Monroe, Virginia. He was exchanged at the end of May and returned to duty.

30. *A Roster,* Vol. 1, p. 200. Thomas J. Campbell, Private, 2nd Company B. 36th Regiment (2nd Regiment NC Artillery), was captured at Gum Swamp, May 1863, and held prisoner at Fort Monroe, Virginia. He was exchanged at the end of May and returned to duty.

31. *A Roster,* Vol. 1, p. 201. William L. Duke, Private, 2nd Company B. 36th Regiment (2nd Regiment NC Artillery), was captured at Gum Swamp, May 1863, and held prisoner at Fort Monroe, Virginia. He was exchanged at the end of May and returned to duty.

32. *A Roster,* Vol. 1, p. 200. Henry Clonninger, Private, 2nd Company B. 36th Regiment (2nd Regiment NC Artillery), was captured at Gum Swamp, May 1863, and held prisoner at Fort Monroe, Virginia. He was exchanged at the end of May and returned to duty.

33. *A Roster,* Vol. 1, p. 207. Starling Waller, Private, 2nd Company B. 36th Regiment (2nd Regiment NC Artillery), was captured at Gum Swamp, May 1863, and held prisoner at Fort Monroe, Virginia. He was exchanged at the end of May and returned to duty.

34. *A Roster,* Vol. 1, p. 200. John A. Brown, Private, 2nd Company B. 36th Regiment (2nd Regiment NC Artillery), was captured at Gum Swamp, May 1863, and held prisoner at Fort Monroe, Virginia. He was exchanged at the end of May and returned to duty.

35. *A Roster,* Vol. 1, p. 205. Bernard Plummer, Private, 2nd Company B. 36th Regiment (2nd Regiment NC Artillery), was captured at Gum Swamp, May 1863, and held prisoner at Fort Monroe, Virginia. He was exchanged at the end of May and returned to duty.

36. *A Roster,* Vol. 1, p. 199. Robert B. Braswell, Private, 2nd Company B. 36th Regiment (2nd Regiment NC Artillery), was captured at Gum Swamp, May 1863, and held prisoner at Fort Monroe, Virginia. He was exchanged at the end of May and returned to duty.

37. *A Roster,* Vol. 1, p. 204. John A. McLean, Private, 2nd Company B. 36th Regiment (2nd Regiment NC Artillery), was captured at Gum Swamp, May 1863, and held prisoner at Fort Monroe, Virginia. He was exchanged at the end of May and returned to duty.

38. *A Roster,* Vol. 1, p. 202–203. Irving Jones, Private, 2nd Company B. 36th Regiment (2nd Regiment NC Artillery), was captured at Gum Swamp, May 1863, and held prisoner at Fort Monroe, Virginia. He was

exchanged at the end of May and returned to duty. In September 1863, he transferred to Company I, 51st Regiment.

Chapter 6

1. J. G. Nicolay and John Hay, "Abraham Lincoln: A History of Vallandingham," *The Century* Volume 38, Number 1 (May 1889), pp. 127–137.
2. Murdoch John McSween to Governor Zebulon B. Vance, June 27, 1863. Courtesy of the North Carolina Office of Archives and History, Raleigh, North Carolina.
3. Murdoch John McSween to Governor Zebulon B. Vance, June 30, 1863. Courtesy of the North Carolina Office of Archives and History, Raleigh, North Carolina.
4. Murdoch John McSween to Governor Zebulon B. Vance, June 30, 1863. Courtesy of the North Carolina Office of Archives and History, Raleigh, North Carolina.
5. *A Roster,* Vol. 10, p. 396. Tazewell L. Hargrove was Lieutenant Colonel of the 44th Regiment. After his capture at the South Anna Bridge, he was held prisoner at five different camps and finally released from Fort Delaware in June 1864.
6. Governor Zebulon B. Vance to James A. Seddon, July 3, 1863. *Papers of Zebulon B. Vance,* Volume 2, 1863, Joe Mobley, ed. (Raleigh: State Department of Archives and History, 1995), p. 205. Used by permission Publications, State Archives and History.
7. *A Roster,* Vol. 7, p. 329. John G. Tate, Company H, 24th Regiment, was killed around July 2, 1863.
8. Murdoch John McSween to Governor Zebulon B. Vance, July 15, 1863. Courtesy of the North Carolina Office of Archives and History, Raleigh, North Carolina.
9. Barrett, *The Civil War in North Carolina,* pp. 168–169.
10. James A. Seddon to Governor Zebulon B. Vance, July 23, 1863. *Papers of Zebulon B. Vance,* Volume 2, 1863, Joe Mobley, ed. (Raleigh: State Department of Archives and History, 1995), pp. 219–220. Used by permission Publications, State Archives and History.
11. Governor Zebulon B. Vance to James A. Seddon, July 26, 1863. *Papers of Zebulon B. Vance,* Volume 2, 1863, Joe Mobley, ed. (Raleigh: State Department of Archives and History, 1995), pp. 225–226. Used by permission Publications, State Archives and History.
12. Murdoch John McSween to Governor Zebulon B. Vance, August 30, 1863. Courtesy of the North Carolina Office of Archives and History, Raleigh, North Carolina.
13. Murdoch John McSween to Governor Zebulon B. Vance, October 3, 1863. Courtesy of the North Carolina Office of Archives and History, Raleigh, North Carolina.
14. Murdoch John McSween to Governor Zebulon B. Vance, October 6, 1863. Courtesy of the North Carolina Office of Archives and History, Raleigh, North Carolina.
15. The Rev. Andrew McMillan to Governor Zebulon B. Vance, October 17, 1863. Courtesy of the North Carolina Office of Archives and History, Raleigh, North Carolina.
16. Giles Leitch to Governor Zebulon B. Vance, October 18, 1863. Courtesy of the North Carolina Office of Archives and History, Raleigh, North Carolina.
17. *A Roster,* Vol. 9, p. 379. Evander McN. Blue was Captain of Company C, 35th Regiment. He was wounded at the Battle of Sharpsburg in 1862 and later returned to duty. His record in the Roster indicates he was captured near Petersburg, Virginia, June 17, 1864, and held in prison camps in Delaware, South Carolina, and Georgia, and not released until June 1865. However, he telegraphs Vance for McSween in October 1863, and later sends Vance a letter dated March 14, 1864, from Williamston, telling Vance he can contact him at Tarboro, North Carolina.
18. Captain Evander McN. Blue to Governor Zebulon B. Vance, October 27, 1863. Courtesy of the North Carolina Office of Archives and History, Raleigh, North Carolina.
19. Alexander Barrett to Governor Zebulon B. Vance, October 28, 1863. Courtesy of the North Carolina Office of Archives and History, Raleigh, North Carolina.
20. *A Roster,* Vol. 9, p. 358. Samuel Bruton Taylor was Captain of Company A, 35th Regiment, before his promotion to Major in June 1863. A year later he was promoted to Lieutenant Colonel. In the fighting near Five Forks, Virginia, in April 1865, he was wounded in the leg and arm and later captured. He survived the war.
21. *A Roster,* Vol. 9, p. 370. Thomas J.

Blackwell was Captain of Company B, 35th Regiment. He was killed near Petersburg, Virginia, in June 1864.

22. Murdoch John McSween to Governor Zebulon B. Vance, October 28, 1863. Courtesy of the North Carolina Office of Archives and History, Raleigh, North Carolina.

23. Bettie Coleman to Governor Zebulon B. Vance, October 28, 1863. Courtesy of the North Carolina Office of Archives and History, Raleigh, North Carolina.

24. Alexander Barrett to Governor Zebulon B. Vance, December 1, 1863. Courtesy of the North Carolina Office of Archives and History, Raleigh, North Carolina.

25. General Orders, No. 4 (1864). Report of a General Court Martial Convened at Weldon, NC. Author: Confederate States of America. Army Department of North Carolina, Signed Major General George E. Pickett, W. Stuart Symington, A. D. C. Published in Petersburg, Virginia.

26. Murdoch John McSween to Governor Zebulon B. Vance, February 17, 1864. Courtesy of the North Carolina Office of Archives and History, Raleigh, North Carolina.

27. Alexander Barrett to Governor Zebulon B. Vance, February 18, 1864. Courtesy of the North Carolina Office of Archives and History, Raleigh, North Carolina.

28. D. B. McSween to Governor Zebulon B. Vance, March 10, 1864. Courtesy of the North Carolina Office of Archives and History, Raleigh, North Carolina.

29. Captain Evander McN. Blue to Governor Zebulon B. Vance, March 14, 1864. Courtesy of the North Carolina Office of Archives and History, Raleigh, North Carolina.

30. Murdoch John McSween to Governor Zebulon B. Vance, May 3, 1864. Courtesy of the North Carolina Office of Archives and History, Raleigh, North Carolina.

31. Murdoch John McSween to Governor Zebulon B. Vance, May 25, 1864. Courtesy of the North Carolina Office of Archives and History, Raleigh, North Carolina.

32. Article published in the *Fayetteville Observer* (Fayetteville, NC), July 18, 1864.

33. Murdoch John McSween to Governor Zebulon B. Vance, June 8, 1864. Courtesy of the North Carolina Office of Archives and History, Raleigh, North Carolina.

34. Walter Clark, ed., *Histories of the Several Regiments and Battalions from North Carolina in the Great War, 1861-'65, Written by Members of the Respective Command* (Goldsboro, NC: Nash Brothers Book and Job Printers for the State of North Carolina, 1901). Reprint Wendell, NC: Broadfoot's Bookmark, 1982.

35. Article published in *The Eagle* (Fayetteville, NC), June 10, 1869.

36. Article published in *The Eagle* (Fayetteville, NC), November 17, 1870.

Chapter 7

1. *A Roster*, Vol. 12, p. 72. Edwin Victor Harris, Captain of Company E, 49th Regiment, fought at the Battle of the Crater, July 30, 1864. He was struck in the neck and killed by a minie ball.

2. *A Roster*, Vol. 2, p. 76. James M. Lilly was a member of Company H, 9th Regiment North Carolina Troops (1st Regiment, North Carolina Cavalry). He was killed in action August 21, 1864, in the fighting below Petersburg on the Petersburg & Weldon Railroad.

3. Article published in the *Fayetteville Observer* (Fayetteville, NC), September 8, 1864.

4. Murdoch John McSween to Governor Zebulon B. Vance, November 21, 1864. Courtesy of the North Carolina Office of Archives and History, Raleigh, North Carolina.

Chapter 8

1. Article published in *The Old North State* (Salisbury, NC), June 16, 1866.

2. Article published in *The Eagle* (Fayetteville, NC), October 15, 1868.

3. Article published in the *New York Times*, May 27, 1868.

4. Article published in the *Wilmington Daily Journal* (Wilmington, NC), August 21, 1868.

5. Article published in the *Watchman and Old North State* (Salisbury, NC), September 4, 1868.

6. Article published in *The Eagle* (Fayetteville, NC), August 18, 1868.

7. Article published in *The Eagle* (Fayetteville, NC), August 12, 1869.

8. Editorial published in *The Eagle* (Fayetteville, NC), December 12, 1874.

9. Editorial published in *The Eagle* (Fayetteville, NC), April 29, 1875.

Bibliography

Andrews, E. Benjamin. *History of the United States from the Earliest Discovery of America to the Present Day, Volume III.* New York: Charles Scribner's Sons, 1895.

Ashe, Samuel A., ed. *Biographical History of North Carolina from Colonial Times to the Present.* Greensboro, NC: Charles L. Van Noppen, Publisher, 1905–1917.

Barrett, John G. *The Civil War in North Carolina.* Chapel Hill: University of North Carolina Press, 1963.

___. *North Carolina as a Civil War Battleground, 1861–1865.* Raleigh, NC: Division of Archives and History, North Carolina Department of Cultural Resources, 1987.

Battle, Kemp P. *History of the University of North Carolina from Its Beginning to the Death of President Swain, 1789–1868.* Raleigh, NC: Edwards & Broughton Printing Company, 1907.

Beckett, Ian F. W. *The War Correspondents: The American Civil War.* London: Sutton Publishing, 1997.

Brown, Louis A. *The Salisbury Prison: A Case Study of Confederate Military Prisons, 1861–1864, Rev. and enl.* Wilmington, NC: Broadfoot Publishing, 1992.

Campbell, R. Thomas. *Storm Over Carolina: The Confederate Navy's Struggle for Eastern North Carolina.* Nashville, TN: Cumberland House Publishing, 2005.

Carbone, John S. *The Civil War in Coastal North Carolina.* Raleigh, NC: Division of Archives and History, North Carolina Department of Cultural Resources, 2001.

The Confederate Veteran. Vol. 21, May 1913. Nashville, TN.: S. A. Cunningham.

Dees-Killette, Amelia. "The Union Occupation of Coastal North Carolina." Master's thesis, North Carolina State University, 1991.

Douglas, William W. *Relief of Washington, North Carolina by the Fifth Rhode Island Volunteers.* Providence, RI: Rhode Island Soldiers and Sailors Historical Society, 1886.

Dowd, Clement. *The Life of Zebulon B. Vance.* Charlotte, NC: Observer Printing and Publishing House, 1897.

Elmore, Ashby Dunn. "Military and Naval Operations in the Region of the Albemarle Sound." Master's thesis, East Carolina University, 1971.

Gammons, John Gray. *The Third Massachusetts Regiment Volunteer Militia in the War of the Rebellion, 1861–1863.* Providence, RI: Snow & Farnham Co., 1906.

Grant, Alfred. *The American Civil War and the British Press.* Jefferson, NC: McFarland, 2000.

Grimsley, Mark. *The Hard Hand of War: Union Military Policy Toward Southern Civilians.* Cambridge: Cambridge University Press, 1995.

Hamilton, J. G. De Roulhac. *History of North Carolina, Volume III, North Carolina Since 1860.* Chicago and New York: Lewis Publishing Company, 1919.

___. "North Carolina Courts and the Confederacy." *The North Carolina Historical Review*, October 1927.

___, ed. *The Papers of Thomas Ruffin.* Publication of the North Carolina Historical Commission. Raleigh, NC: Edwards & Broughton Printing Company, State Printers, 1918.

Harris, William C. *North Carolina and the Coming of the Civil War.* Raleigh, NC: Division of Archives and History, North Carolina Department of Cultural Resources, 1988.

Hilderman, Walter C., III. *They Went Into the Fight Cheering!* Boone, NC: Parkway Publishers, 2005.

Humphreys, Jim. "The Federal Army in Eastern North Carolina." Master's thesis, North Carolina State University, 1989.

Lee, Henry S. *A Civil War Diary, January 1, 1863 – May 31, 1864.* Edited by John Dixon Davis. Black Mountain, NC: Craggy Mountain Press, 1997.

Leslie, Frank. *Famous Leaders and Battle Scenes of the Civil War.* New York: Mrs. Frank Leslie, 1896.

Mallison, Fred M. *The Civil War on the Outer Banks: A History of the Late Rebellion Along the Coast of North Carolina from Carteret to Currituck, and Comments on Prewar Conditions and an Account of Postwar Recovery.* Jefferson, NC: McFarland, 2005.

Manarin, Louis A., and Jordan, Weymouth T., Jr., comps. *North Carolina Troops, 1861–1865: A Roster.* Raleigh, NC: Division of Archives and History, Department of Cultural Resources, 1966–.

Marcinko, Tom. "Federal Operations at Hatteras Inlet, North Carolina 1861." Master's thesis, East Carolina University, 2000.

Marlow, Clayton Charles. *Matt Ransom, Confederate General from North Carolina.* Jefferson, NC: McFarland, 1996.

Maurer, David. "Set in Stone." *The University of Virginia Magazine* (Charlottesville, VA), Spring 2008.

Moore, Albert Burton. *Conscription and Conflict in the Confederacy.* New York: MacMillan, 1924.

Nash, Howard P., Edward H. Virgin, and William Collin Levere. *The Sixth General Catalogue of Sigma Alpha Epsilon.* Evanston, IL: Sigma Alpha Epsilon, 1904.

Nicolay, J. G., and John Hay. "Abraham Lincoln: A History of Vallandingham." *The Century.* New York: Century Co., 1889.

Papers of Zebulon B. Vance, Volume 1, 1843–1862. Edited by Frontis W. Johnston. Raleigh, NC: State Department of Archives and History, 1963.

Papers of Zebulon B. Vance, Volume 2, 1863. Edited by Joe Mobley. Raleigh, NC: State Department of Archives and History, 1995.

Papers of Zebulon B. Vance, 1863–1864. Unpublished. Raleigh, NC: State Department of Archives and History.

Patterson, Gerald A. *Justice or Atrocity: General George E. Pickett and the Kinston, N. C. Hangings.* Gettysburg, PA: Thomas Publications, 1998.

Powell, William S. ed. *Dictionary of North Carolina Biography.* Chapel Hill: University of North Carolina Press, 1979–1996.

Raymer, Jacob Nathaniel. *Confederate Correspondent: The Civil War Reports of Jacob Nathaniel Raymer, 4th North Carolina.* Edited by E. B. Munson. Jefferson, NC: McFarland, 2008.

Roe, Alfred Seelye. *The Fifth Regiment Massachusetts Volunteer Infantry in Three Tours of Duty 1861, 1862–'63, 1864.* Boston, MA: Fifth Regiment Veteran Association, 1911.

Shea, John Gilmary. *The Story of a Great Nation.* New York: Gay Brothers & Company, 1886.

Smith, Charles Alphonso, ed. *Library of Southern Literature, Volume 14.* Atlanta, GS: Martin and Hoyt Company, 1907, 1910.

Stewart, Bruce H., Jr. *Land Battles of the Civil War, Eastern Theatre.* Jefferson, NC: McFarland, 2002.

Styple, William B., ed. *Writing and Fighting the Confederate War: The Letters of Peter Wellington Alexander.* Kearney, NJ: Belle Grove, 2002.

University of North Carolina at Chapel Hill. *Alumni History of the University of North Carolina, 1795–1924,* 2nd ed. Durham, NC: Christian & King Printing Company, 1924.

The War of the Rebellion; A Compilation of the Official Records of the Union and Confederate Armies, prepared under the direction of the Secretary of War, by Bvt. Lieut. Col. Robert N. Scott, Third U. S. Artillery and pursuant to an act of Congress approved June 16, 1880. Washington: Government Printing Office, 1880.

Weeks, Stephen B. *Register of Members of the Philanthropic Society, Instituted in the University of North Carolina, August 1st, 1795, 4th ed.* Raleigh, NC: Edwards, Broughton & Co., Power Printers and Binders, 1887.

Wilson, Marcius. *History of the United States*. New York: Ivison, Blakeman, Taylor, and Co., 1872.

Newspapers

Carolina Watchman, Salisbury, NC
Charleston Courier Tri-Weekly, Charleston, SC
The Eagle, Fayetteville, NC
Fayetteville Observer, Fayetteville, NC
New York Times
North Carolina Standard, Raleigh, NC
Old North State, Salisbury, NC
Raleigh Register, Raleigh, NC
Sentinel, Raleigh, NC
Watchman and Old North State, Salisbury, NC
Wilmington Daily Journal, Wilmington, NC

Collections

Nathan R. Frazier Papers. Manuscript Collection (#390), Special Collections Department, J. Y. Joyner Library, East Carolina University, Greenville, NC. Letters describing Camp Magnum 1862; troop movements and skirmishes at Goldsboro, May/December 1862, January 1863; Kinston, February, April, May 1863; and the Battle of Washington, April 1863.

Matthew Ransom Letter, recounting the Battle of Second Gum Swamp (22 May), Kinston, 5/25/1862; photocopy of letter; transcript of letter. Manuscript Collection (#834), Special Collections Department, J. Y. Joyner Library, East Carolina University, Greenville, NC.

Index

Albright, George M.G. 33
Alexander, Francis R. 52
Allison, Julius F. 59
Anderson, Robert Walker 56
Andrews, Alex 41
Appomattox 5

Ballard Hotel 7
Banks, Nathaniel P. 37
Barlow, John J. 41
Barnes, George B. 45
Barrett, Alexander 199, 202, 204
Barrier, Rufus A. 58
Barringer, John 41
Barrington's Ferry 115
Battle, William 131
Battle of the Crater 217
Bay, Malcom 213
Beaufort 29
Bennett Place 5
Bethel Church, VA, Battle of 24
Bill 159
Black, John W. 213
Blackwell, Thomas J. 198
Blind Tom (Thomas Wiggins) 35–36
Blue, D.A. 213
Blue, Evander McN. 203, 204, 213
Bobcock, Thomas S. 101
Boone's Mill, Battle of 184
Bowles, John B. 40
Boyden, N., Jr. 87
Branch, Lawrence O'Brien 55–56
Braswell, Robert B. 155
Braxton, Nathan 47
Brewer, William T. 147
Brown, John A. 155
Bryan, Ruffin L. 59
Buchanan, William, Jr. 41
buffalos 103, 150
Bullock, William J. 36
Burgwyn, H.K., Jr. 24
Burnside, Ambrose 25, 29, 110, 112
burying grounds — University of Virginia 65
Butler, Benjamin 24

Caesar 159
Calloway, Abner Sydenham 36
Cameron, Alex 213
Cameron, Daniel 213
Cameron, Simon 19, 20
Camp Hill 51, 53–54
Camp Holmes 51
Camp Mangum 7, 15, 24, 26, 30–31; hospital buildings 114; reviews 46–48; sickness 34–35
Camp of Instruction (Raleigh) 23
Campbell, Thomas J. 155
Cantwell, John Lucas 31
Cape Fear Region 8, 12
Carroll, John W. 155
Castle Thunder (Prison) 64, 80, 198, 204, 205
Casualties — 35 NCT, Company C 213
Caswell, Richard 120–121
Chappell, Parks 40
Charlottesville 9, 65–67
Christian, Edmund J. 40
church services 165
civilians: treatment 68, 86, 139, 141, 150, 178; Washington 137
Clark, Andrew 41
Clark, George W. 33
Clark, Henry Toole 24, 50
Clark, William 27
Clingman, Thomas 34
Cloninger, Henry 155
Cobb, Gaston D. 58
Cockerman, James G. 41
Cole, Solomon N. 213
Coleman, Bettie 198–199
Confederate Hospital — Raleigh Fair Grounds 114
Connally, John Kerr 36, 41
conscript law 116–117
Conscription Act 50–51
conscription camps 51
conscripts 53, 57
Cook, James 41
Cooke, J.R. 87

260 Index

Cooke, Philip St. George 87
Cooper, Samuel 105
correspondents 6–7, 167–169
Covington, C.C. 94
Covington, John W. 40
Covington, William C. 94
Craige, James A. 41
Cromartie, James A. 41
Crowder, W.J.W. 62
Culpeper Court House 9, 10
Cumberland County 8
Currie, Malcom 27

Daniel, Junius 32, 115
Daves, Graham 21
Davis, Jefferson 9, 101, 105, 106–109, 117
Davis, Samuel 106
Deep Gully 115, 119, 123
DeGraffenreidt, Baron 157
desertion 121, 228
DeVane, Robert M. 40, 41
Dix, Dorothea Lynde 58
Dobbin, John H. 154, 155
Dockery, Miss M.E. 26
Dockery, Oliver H. 15, 28
Dover Road 118, 147
Drewry's Bluff 39
Duke, William L. 155
Dumas, Frank 40

The Eagle (newspaper) 16
Edney, William J. 41
education 225–226
18th Regiment NCT 39, 56
8th Regiment NCT 55
11th Regiment NCT 30, 34
Eliason, William Adlai 33
Ellis, Gov. John W. 17–18, 20–21, 23–24, 50
Evans, Nathan George 111

Faison, Paul F. 52
Falls, Dixon 36
Ferguson, Angus 213
Ferguson, John C. 213
50th Regiment NCT 34
55th Regiment NCT 36, 41
54th Regiment NCT 41, 150
52nd Regiment NCT 31, 34, 45
57th Regiment NCT 54, 117
56th Regiment NCT 52, 147, 154
53rd Regiment NCT 32, 33, 121
First Regiment N.C. Volunteers 24
Fisher, Charles F. 129
Fisher, Edward C. 58
Fleming, John A. 217
Foote, Henry S. 101, 117
Forestville Mills 55
Forestville Paper Mill 84
Fort Anderson: attack 115, 123–124
Fort Macon 29
Fort Sumter 18

40th Regiment NCT 34
forts 24
48th Regiment NCT 30, 33
45th Regiment NCT 30, 34
41st Regiment NCT 34
44th Regiment NCT 30, 34, 36, 179
49th Regiment NCT 33
47th Regiment NCT 30, 34, 36
46th Regiment NCT 30, 34
43rd Regiment NCT 30, 32, 34, 45, 119
Foster, John G. 110; raid 111–112; running blockade 145; Washington siege 136
4th Regiment NCT 39
Fredericksburg 88–90; bombardment 79, 81–83
Freeland, William Johnson 41
Frémont, John C. 37
Fry, W.H.H. 213
Fulford, Gideon 47
Fuller, Thomas C. 205

Gatlin, Richard C. 25
General Order No. 4 200–201
Gibson, Duncan 41
Godwin, Archibald Cameron 54
Godwin, Condary 59
Goings, Henry C. 213
Goldsboro bridge 112
Goodman, Jacob 213
Gordon, A. 47
Graham, John Washington 45, 52
Graham, Robert Davidson 45
Green, Anderson 40
Grigg, Alfred R. 45
Gross, Philip Harrison 147
Gulick, William B. 16, 42
Gum Swamp 147–149, 153–155
gunboats 134

Hale, Daniel 213
Hall, Edward Dudley 33
Halyburton, Thomas C. 42, 52
Hannon, Neill 213
Hargrove, Tazewell L. 179
Harrill, Lawson 52
Haywood, E. Burke 114
Henly, Mallory L. 41
Hill, A.P. 71, 100
Hill, D.H. 21, 23, 24, 88, 113, 136
Hill, James E. 41
Hill, William P. 41
Hill's Point 133
Hinton, James W. 58
Hinton, Lawrence 84
Hitcher, J.L. 41
Hoffman, John Thomas 232
Hoke, Robert F. 88
Holden, W.W. 49–50
Holmes, John 40
Holmes, Theophilus Hunter 51
Hookerton 145

hospitals: Charlottesville 65
Howell, Verina 106
Hunter, R.M. 102
Hyles, Andrew 40

inlets: Outer Banks 128–129
Iredell, James Johnston 32, 33

Jackson, Noah R. 213
Jackson, Stonewall 37, 113
Jerome, Eber A. 33
Johnson, Archy 213
Johnson, Charles L. 40
Johnson, John A.G. 213
Johnson, Joseph P. 41
Jones, Alex 41
Jones, Charles Johnson 58
Jones, Irving 155
Jones, John G. 16, 175, 188, 189, 192, 193, 194, 205; death 208
Jones, W.T. 213
Jordon, John V. 58

Kelly, L.R. 213
Kenan, Thomas S. 32, 45
Kennerly, Pickney A. 58
Kinston 10; early settlers 156
Kinston bridge 111
Kittrell Springs 160–161
Knight, Charles W. 59

Lane, Benjamin D. 45
Lane, Henry E. 45, 52
Lawley, Francis Charles 79–80
Lawson, John 157
Laycock, William Jones 41
Leach, John S. 33
Ledbetter, Thomas B. 40
Lee, Robert E. 9, 16, 73, 184, 185
Left Guide 31–32
Leitch, Giles 196–197
Letcher, John 105
Leventhorpe, Collett 30, 34
Levy, U.K. 67
Lewis, Gaston 32
Liles, Edward R. 58
Lilly, James A. 218
Lincoln, Abraham 17, 18–19
Lindsay, Charles B. 59
Lockhart, Joseph Gray 45, 52, 147
Long, Nick, Jr. 193
Long, Thomas A. 224
Long, William J. 59
Long Grabs 5, 15
Longstreet, James 113
Lower Trent Road 118
Luke, Granville Gratiott 45, 52
Lunatic Asylum — Raleigh 58
Lutterloh, Jarvis B. 45, 147, 149, 151–152
Lyon, John B. 45

Mallett, Peter 51, 177–178
Mangum, William Preston 24
Manson, O.F. 170
Marshall, James Keith 31
Martin, J.G. 46–48
Martin, William F. 32
Martin, William Joseph 33
Maultsby, William J. 41
McAfee, Lee 205
McArthur, John 213
McCaskill, John W. 213
McDaniel, Alexander Pope 33
McDonald, Daniel P. 213
McDonald, Duncan C. 213
McDonald, Hugh M. 213
McDonald, John 213
McDuffie, Murdock 41
McInnis, D.R. 26
McIntosh, D.A. 230
McKay, Alex 26
McKay, John A.D. 59
McKethan, John M. 41
McKethan, William A. 40
McKinnon, Daniel 41
McLaughlin, Alexander B. 41
McLean, John A. 155
McLeod, Duncan J. 150
McMillan, Andrew 195–196
McNair, John F. 130
McNeil, Malcom 147
McNeil, Malcom A. 213
McNeill, Neil T. 147
McRae, Archibald L. 41
McRae, D.G. 27
McRae, Duncan G. 15
McRae, Henry 58
McRae, James Cameron 52
McSween, D.B. 202
McSween, Donald Murdock 235
McSween, Mary Catherine 234
McSween, Murdoch John 12, 15–16, 26; admitted to the Bar 231; anger with Vance 206–208; apologizes to Vance 227; bucked and gagged 191, 199; commission in Home Guards 187; commission revoked 187; court martial begins 198; court martial decision 200–201; denies mutiny charge 192; dies 236; disagreement with Matt Ransom 183; disagreement with Peter Mallett 177–178; dispute with Gurlick 42–45; guard house 190, 191, 193, 199; imprisoned 201; Matt Ransom, bitterness toward 209; publishes *The Eagle* newspaper 232–236; recruiting troops — Elizabethtown 181–182; released 205; request to recruit 175–176; second wounding 219; Wilmington adventure 130; wounded at Reams' Station 218; writing project 112–113
McSween, William 235
McSween, William Daniel 235
Melton, Samuel M. 205

262 Index

Miles, William Porcher 101, 117
Miller, Henry Watkins 55–56
Miller, Jacob H. 41
Miller, William J. 33
Misenheimer, Enoch 47
Mitchell, Elisha 34
Monticello 67
Moody, William S. 45
Moore, Hugh 213
Moore, S.P. 106
Moore County 8
Moorman, Edmund C. 40
Mordecai, G.W. 84
Morehead, James T. 33
Morehead, James T., Jr. 33
Morehead, John Motley 32–33
Morehead City 12
Morris, Nathaniel 213
Morrison, Angus 40
Morrison, Earnest A. 41
mortars 211
Mull, Peter M. 36
Murchison, John Reed 58
Myers, A.C. 105

Neagle, J.L. 224
needy soldiers 163
Nethercutt, J.H. 123
Neuse River 111, 118–119
Neuse River Manufacturing Company 55
Neuse River Road 118
New Bern 29, 113; attack on 115, 119; refugees 153; treatment of civilians 150
Nicholson, John R. 40
Norman, James C. 33
Norment, William Stokes 41
North Carolina Depot and Soldiers' Home 170
Northrop, L.B. 106

Owens, Rufus R. 41
Owens, William A. 33

Palmer, Valentine Jackson 45
Parks, Marcus A. 31, 45
Parrish, J.B. 147
Patterson, Hugh S. 41
Patterson, John A. 213
Patterson, N.A. 213
Pee Dee Wildcats 11
Petersburg: description 165–166
Pettigrew, James Johnston 115, 123–124
Philanthropic Society 12
pickets 88
Pickett, George E. 205
Pipkin, Isaac 59
plan for stopping the war 160
Plummer, Bernard 155
pontoons 125
Pool, W.R. 84
Porter, William Henry 41

prayers 42
Price, Mary 83
Price, William J. 58
Pridgen, Timothy Fletcher 41
prisons: Richmond 64
provost guards 179–180

Quakers 146–147

Randall, Silas Dixon 36
Randolph, George W. 50, 51
Ransom, Matt W. 16, 175, 188, 189, 194
Ray, Arch'd. 213
Reams' Station 11; Battle of 219–221
recruiting 10–11
Redding, Edward Q. 41
Reese, William P. 41
religious publications 160
renumbering regiments 30
Reynolds, Jacob 40
Richardson, John Q. 31, 45
Richmond 7, 9; description 76; gambling 76–77; ladies 78–79
Riddick, R.H. 21
rivers: North Carolina, Eastern 132
Roan, Richard 213
Roanoke Island 25
Roberts, Franklin N. 42, 52
Robertson, B.H. 115
Robeson County 12
Robinson, A. 230
Robinson, James A. Calhoun 41
Rockfish 8
Rodman, William B. 133
Rodman's farm 133
Rogers, Andrew J. 58
Rogers, Sion Hart 36
Roper, Amos 41
Ruffin, Thomas 12, 13

Savells, Thomas P. 45
Scarborough, Ambrose 40
Schenck, Henry Franklin 45, 52
Scott, David, Jr. 33
Scott, Michael 40
secession convention (North Carolina) 17–18
Sedberry, Bond E. 155
Seddon, James A. 180, 184, 185
Sequestration Act 33–34, 67
Seven Pines, Battle of 39
17th Regiment NCT 32
Shaw, H.M. 58
Shields, James 37
Shields, William 213
Shuford, Sidney A. 40
Sibbitt, George W. 213
Siege of Washington 133–134, 135
Simonton, Absalom Knox 41
Singeltary, George Badger 36, 123
6th Regiment NCT 39
small pox 79, 114

Index 263

Smith, John 213
Smith, Maurice Thompson 36
snow-balling 91–93
soldiers, condition 68, 70–71, 75–76
South Anna Bridge 179
Southern Tract Society 62
Starr's Battery 154, 155
Stewart, James 213
Stewart, Lawrence 56
Stricklin, B. 213
Stringham, Silas H. 24
Stuart, J.E.B. 9, 87, 100
substitutes 164
Sutton, Martin V.B. 41
Swift Creek 119, 137
Swift Creek Village 124
Sykes, William H. 41

Tarboro 10, 131
Tate, John G. 181
Taylor, Samuel Bruton 198
Taylor, Spotswood Bassett 33
Teague, Vandever 36
theaters, Richmond 99
38th Regiment NCT 15, 28
35th Regiment NCT 16, 175, 187
31st Regiment NCT 55
39th Regiment NCT 34
37th Regiment NCT 39
Thompson, D.B. 121
Thompson, Garrett 213
Thompson, Gilbert 213
Thrasher, J.S. 175, 190
Tilman, Wiggs 158
Todd, James E. 59
Toler, Sampson B. 40
Trent River 118–119
Tuscarora War 157–158
12th Regiment NCT 39
28th Regiment NCT 39
25th Regiment NCT 154
21st Regiment NCT 88
22nd Regiment NCT 39
27th Regiment NCT 87
26th Regiment NCT 11, 15, 64, 115, 205
23rd Regiment NCT 39

University of North Carolina 12
University of Virginia 9, 65–67
Upper Trent Road 118
Ussery, John C. 40

Vallandingham, Clement 162–163
Vance, Zebulon Baird 12, 16, 31, 46, 47, 64, 112, 180, 183, 185
Vickers, Washington M. 147
Virginia Legislature 100–102

Wadsworth, George A. 213
Wake Forest 5, 9
Wake Forest Manual Labor School 84–85
Wallace, Rufus 213
Waller, Starling 155
Ward, Louis A. 41
Washington 10, 113; Confederate raid, 1862 110–111; failure of siege 144; retreat 142, 144
Watson, H.B. 41
way-side hospitals 224
Webb, Stephen 40
White, Alexander P. 52
White, Joseph C. 41
White, Joseph Harvey 33
Whitehall 112
Whitehead, James F. 36
Whitlock, Thomas F. 41
Whitmore, John 155
Whitson, James W. 58
Whitty, Joseph 59
Wilkes, John 27
Williams, Jesse P. 36
Williams, John Richard 45
Williams, Solomon 173
Williams, Wilson Hugh 36
Williamson, George 58
Wills, Otis P. 45
Wilmington 10; description 127–128; fortifications 128
Wilson, Louis D. 131
Wimbish, John 32, 41
Wooten, Thomas J. 41
writing paper 159

Yeates, Jesse Johnston 58
Yellowly, Edward C. 58

www.ingramcontent.com/pod-product-compliance
Ingram Content Group UK Ltd.
Pitfield, Milton Keynes, MK11 3LW, UK
UKHW041932140426
5217IPUK00014B/438